Oracle® Solaris 10 System Virtualization Essentials

Oracle® Solaris 10 System Virtualization Essentials

Jeff Victor, Jeff Savit, Gary Combs,
Simon Hayler, Bob Netherton

PRENTICE
HALL

Upper Saddle River, NJ • Boston • Indianapolis • San Francisco
New York • Toronto • Montreal • London • Munich • Paris • Madrid
Capetown • Sydney • Tokyo • Singapore • Mexico City

The publisher offers excellent discounts on this book when ordered in quantity for bulk purchases or special sales, which may include electronic versions and/or custom covers and content particular to your business, training goals, marketing focus, and branding interests. For more information, please contact:

U.S. Corporate and Government Sales
(800) 382-3419
corpsales@pearsontechgroup.com

For sales outside the United States, please contact:

International Sales
international@pearsoned.com

Visit us on the Web: informit.com/ph

Library of Congress Cataloging-in-Publication Data
Oracle Solaris 10 system virtualization essentials / Jeff Victor ... [et al.].
    p. cm.
Includes index.
ISBN 0-13-708188-X (pbk. : alk. paper)
1. Virtual computer systems. 2. Solaris (Computer file) I. Victor, Jeff.
QA76.9.V5O73 2010
005.4'3--dc22

                                    2010025500

ISBN-13: 978-0-13-708188-2
ISBN-10:   0-13-708188-X
Text printed in the United States on recycled paper at RR Donnelley in Crawfordsville, Indiana.
First printing, August 2010

Contents

Foreword

I'm no longer sure when I first became hooked. Was it when I overheard a casual conversation about running a "test" copy of MVS in parallel with the real copy of MVS on a new 390 mainframe? Or by the idea of Zarniwoop researching the *Hitchhiker's Guide to the Galaxy* in an electronically synthesized copy of the entire universe he kept in his office? Whatever the cause, I'm still addicted to virtual machine technology.

Fooling a whole stack of software to run correctly on a software simulation of the platform it was designed to run on has been a recurring interest in my career. Poring through the history of VM/370 as an graduate student, absorbing James Gosling's audacious idea of the Java VM, spending a few weeks building an experimental machine emulator to run SPARC applications on Solaris for PowerPC, the "aha!" moment when we realized how useful it would be if we arranged that a set of processes could behave as a little OS within an OS (the idea that became Solaris Zones), the first bring-up of OpenSolaris running as a paravirtualized guest on Xen—those are just a few of the highlights for me.

This book began as a project within Sun in mid-2009 during Oracle's acquisition of the company, so it both explores aspects of Sun's virtualization technology portfolio, and—now that the acquisition is complete—peers a little into 2010. Sun's unique position as a systems company allowed it to deliver a full set of integrated virtualization technologies. These solutions span the different trade-offs between maximizing utilization for efficiency and maximizing isolation for availability, while enabling the system to be managed at a large scale and up and down the layers of the systems architecture. Because that systems perspective informs everything we do, we have a wealth of solutions to match the diverse needs of modern enterprise architectures. Many of these tools are interoperable, enabling solutions that are otherwise impossible or impractical. Oracle's acquisition of Sun provides two further benefits to that portfolio: a secure future for these technologies and the exciting potential for integration with Oracle VM, Oracle Enterprise Manager, and the wealth of Oracle applications.

Here are some examples from the Sun portfolio. ZFS is a key storage virtualization technology at the core of the future of the Solaris operating system as well as the appliance products we build from Solaris technology today. Solaris networking virtualization technologies allow cutting-edge network hardware to be exploited and managed efficiently while providing a natural virtual network interface abstraction. For server virtualization, Solaris Zones (also known as Solaris Containers) have turned out to be very popular and very successful—a natural fit for the needs of many customers. The Logical Domains hypervisor is an extremely efficient design, and enables customers to get the most out of the tremendous throughput capability of SPARC CMT platforms. Our work with the Xen community enables a high-performance Solaris x64 guest for Oracle VM. For client virtualization, look no further than VirtualBox—for the laptop and desktop, both as a developer utility, and as a virtual appliance developer tool for the cloud. And it's not just a client technology: VirtualBox is the server component of Sun's virtual desktop infrastructure product, and VirtualBox continues to grow more server-class features with every release. As well as infrastructure virtualization platforms, we have created infrastructure management software—Ops Center -- intended to reduce the complexity that comes with using the new capabilities in large-scale deployments.

Let's remember that virtual machines of one form or another have been around for a long time. Yet virtualization is such a fundamental idea that it remains associated with many developing fields. In the past decade, the runaway success of hypervisor-based virtualization on x64 platforms has largely been driven by the operational savings achieved by consolidating Microsoft Windows guests. But now this layer of the system architecture is just part of the way infrastructure is done, a new raft of capabilities can be built on top of it.

Recently we've seen the emergence of the Infrastructure as a Service (IaaS) style of cloud computing. Enabled by the combination of ever-increasing Internet connectivity and bandwidth, coupled with Moore's law providing more and more computational power per dollar, users of an IaaS service send their entire software stacks to remote data centers. Virtualization decouples the software from the hardware to enable those data centers to be operated almost as a utility. This approach promises to revolutionize the fundamental economics across the IT industry. The capital expense currently spent on under-utilized equipment can be shifted to pay-as-you-go operating expenses, both within large enterprises and between service providers and their customers.

This new layer of the systems architecture brings new opportunities and new problems to solve: security, observability, performance, networking, utilization, power management, migration, scheduling, manageability, and so on. While both industry and the academic research community are busily responding to many of those challenges, there is still much to be done. The fundamentals remain important, and will continue to differentiate the various virtualization solutions in the marketplace.

And so I'm confident that there's yet more innovation to come.

This book is a deep exploration of virtualization products and technologies provided by or for Solaris, written by experienced practitioners in the art of delivering real solutions to data center problems. The book provides a holistic view of virtualization, encompassing all of the different models used in the industry. That itself is rare: No other organization has as complete a view of the entire range of system virtualization possibilities. A comprehensive background chapter leads neophytes into virtualization. Experienced data center architects will appreciate the individual chapters explaining the technologies and how you can use them to solve real problems—a critical resource in a rapidly changing world. I hope you find it as fascinating as I do!

Tim Marsland
Vice President and Fellow, Sun Microsystems, Inc.
Menlo Park
February 18, 2010

Preface

Computer virtualization has become its own sub-industry, with predictions that virtualization software and services revenues will exceed $10 billion annually in 2011. Although numerous corporations use some form of computer virtualization, today that usage may be limited to only a small portion of their computers. As the number of virtualization options increases, however, the types of computers that can take advantage of the virtualization and the benefits provided by virtualization will increase.

Oracle® Solaris 10 System Virtualization Essentials is part of a new series of books on Oracle Solaris system administration. It presents the multiple technologies that the Oracle Solaris operating system uses to virtualize and consolidate computing resources, from hardware partitioning to virtual machines and hypervisors to operating system virtualization.

The intent of *Oracle Solaris 10 System Virtualization Essentials* is to discuss computer virtualization in general and to focus on those system virtualization technologies provided by, or that provide support to, the Oracle Solaris or OpenSolaris operating systems.

Oracle Solaris 10 supports a rich collection of virtualization technologies:

- Dynamic Domains
- Oracle VM Server for SPARC (previously called Sun Logical Domains)
- Oracle VM Server for x86

- Oracle VM VirtualBox (previously called VirtualBox)
- Oracle Solaris Containers (also called Zones)

Virtualization offers a tremendous opportunity to add computing workloads while controlling operational costs and adding computing flexibility. For the system administrator, this new knowledge area requires skills with new technologies like hypervisors, which create virtual machines on a single hardware machine, and containers (also known as zones), which create virtual operating systems running on a single operating system.

Oracle Solaris 10 System Virtualization Essentials describes the factors that affect your choice of technologies and explains how to

- Use Dynamic Domains to maximize workload isolation on Sun SPARC systems
- Use Oracle VM Server for SPARC to deploy different Oracle Solaris 10 and OpenSolaris environments on SPARC CMT (chip multithreading) systems
- Use Oracle VM Server for x86 or xVM hypervisor to deploy a server with heterogeneous operating systems
- Use Oracle VM VirtualBox to develop and test software in heterogeneous environments
- Use Oracle Solaris Containers to maximize efficiency and scalability of workloads
- Use Oracle Solaris Containers to migrate Solaris 8 and Solaris 9 workloads to new hardware systems
- Mix virtualization technologies so as to maximize workload density

Oracle Solaris 10 System Virtualization Essentials contains nine chapters. Chapter 1 discusses system virtualization in general terms. This material includes the needs of consolidation, the value and benefits of virtualization, and a description of the most common types of computer virtualization. Along the way, Chapter 1 also describes many of the concepts, features, and methods shared by many implementations of system virtualization. The concepts introduced in Chapter 1 are included in all of the other chapters.

Chapters 2 through 6 describe Oracle's computer virtualization technologies that are directly related to the Oracle Solaris OS, including their relationship with the topics introduced in Chapter 1. Chapter 7 discusses the factors that should be considered when choosing a virtualization technology or combination of technologies. That chapter also details a process of analysis that can be used to choose a ·rtualization technology or combination of technologies. Chapter 8 walks you ·gh several examples of those technologies, and Chapter 9 completes the picture by describing virtualization management software. Finally, the Appendix offers a narrated tour of the history of virtualization.

Because this book focuses on system virtualization technologies, technologies and methods that do not virtualize a computer system are not discussed. These include storage virtualization and application virtualization.

Books in the Oracle Solaris System Administration Series

The *Oracle Solaris System Administration Series* includes the following books:

Solaris 10 System Administration Essentials

Solaris 10 System Administration Essentials covers all of the breakthrough features of the Oracle Solaris 10 operating system in one place. It does so in a straightforward way that makes an enterprise-level operating system accessible to system administrators at all levels.

Solaris 10 System Administration Essentials provides a comprehensive overview, along with hands-on examples, of both the key features that have made Oracle Solaris the leading UNIX operating system and the significant new features of Solaris 10 that put it far ahead of its competitors. Features covered include zones, the ZFS file system, Fault Management Architecture, Service Management Facility, and DTrace (the dynamic tracing tool for troubleshooting OS and application problems on production systems in real time).

Solaris 10 Security Essentials

Solaris 10 Security Essentials covers all of the security features and technologies in Oracle Solaris 10 that make it the OS of choice for IT environments that require optimal security.

Solaris 10 Security Essentials explains the strengths of Solaris security, including its scalability and adaptability, in a simple, straightforward way. It describes how security features in Oracle Solaris can protect a single-user system with login authentication as well as how those features can protect Internet and intranet configurations.

Solaris 10 ZFS Essentials

Solaris 10 ZFS Essentials describes the dramatic advances in data management introduced by ZFS. ZFS provides an innovative approach to data integrity, near zero administration, and a welcome integration of file system and volume management capabilities.

Solaris 10 ZFS Essentials explains how to set up, configure, administer, and manage ZFS file systems, including how to install and boot ZFS as a root file system. It covers managing pools, configuring ZFS snapshots, and sharing ZFS home directories. It also illustrates a lab setup in a virtual machine that can be created on a laptop for a complete experimental environment.

Intended Audience

The books in the *Oracle Solaris System Administration Series* can benefit anyone who wants to learn more about Oracle Solaris 10. They are written to be particularly accessible to system administrators who are new to Solaris—people who are perhaps already serving as administrators of Linux, Windows, or other UNIX systems.

If you are not presently a practicing system administrator but want to become one, this series, starting with *Solaris 10 System Administration Essentials*, provides an excellent introduction to this field. In fact, most of the examples used in the books are suited to or can be adapted to small learning environments such as a home system. Thus, even before you venture into corporate system administration or deploy Oracle Solaris 10 in your existing IT installation, these books will help you experiment in a small test environment.

Oracle Solaris 10 System Virtualization Essentials is especially valuable to several specific audiences. A primary group is generalists who desire knowledge of the entire system virtualization space. The only assumed knowledge is general UNIX or Linux administrative experience. Another group is data center staff who need an understanding of virtualization and use of such technologies in real-world situations.

- **Data center architects** will benefit from the broad coverage of virtualization models and technologies, enabling them to optimize system and network architectures that employ virtualization. The extensive coverage of resource controls can lead to better stability and more consistent performance of workloads in virtualized systems.

- **Computer science students** with UNIX or Linux experience will gain a holistic understanding of the history and current state of the system virtualization industry. The breadth of virtualization models discussed provides a framework for further discovery, and the real-world examples prepare students for data center careers.

- **Technical support staff** who troubleshoot virtualized systems will gain an introduction to system virtualization and interactions between virtualized systems. This background can shorten the time to diagnose problems, and enable personnel to readily distinguish between problems related to virtualization and ones that are independent of virtualization.

How to Use This Book

Readers who wish to learn about one specific Oracle Solaris virtualization technology should read Chapter 1 and the appropriate sections of Chapters 2 through 6, 8, and 9. If you would like to understand all of the virtualization technologies that use Oracle Solaris as a core component and determine how to choose among them, read all of the chapters in this book. If you already understand virtualization but want to learn about virtualization using Oracle Solaris or OpenSolaris, you should skim through Chapter 1 to understand the context of the rest of the book as well as the definitions of terms used throughout the book. If you are implementing virtualization technologies on many systems, you should read Chapter 9 to understand the unique problems that must be addressed as part of this work and to identify software that can significantly reduce the complexity of large virtualization farms.

Note

Oracle Corporation acquired Sun Microsystems, Inc., early in 2010, when this book was nearing completion. Although this book mostly uses the new product names, occasional reference is made to previous names. The following table provides a guide to the old and new product names.

Sun Product Name	Oracle Product Name
Solaris	Oracle Solaris
Solaris Containers, Containers, or zones	Oracle Solaris Containers, Containers, or zones
Logical Domains	Oracle VM Server for SPARC
Oracle VM	Oracle VM Server for x86
VirtualBox	Oracle VM VirtualBox

OpenSolaris

In June 2005, Sun Microsystems introduced OpenSolaris, a fully functional release of the Solaris operating system built from open-source software. Although the books in this series focus on Oracle Solaris 10, they often incorporate aspects of OpenSolaris. Since that time, the evolution of this OS has accelerated even beyond its normally rapid pace. The authors of this series have often found it interesting to introduce features or nuances that are new in OpenSolaris. At the same, many of the enhancements introduced into OpenSolaris are finding their way into Oracle Solaris. So whether you are learning Oracle Solaris 10 or already have your eye on OpenSolaris, the books in this series are for you.

Acknowledgments

A book of this scope could not have been written without the combined expertise of numerous people. The authors were supported by the following people during the writing of this book.

This book would not have been possible without the executive leadership of Hal Stern, Bill Nesheim, Jeff Jackson, and James Hollingshead. Our managers Matt Delcambre, Dawit Bereket, Michael Connolly, and Candido Formariz also provided significant support. Project managers and coordinators Jim Siwila and Susan Miller kept us on course for many months and taught us more than a few things about publishing. Dan Roberts and Jerri-Ann Meyer provided Solaris Engineering and Marketing coordination. Last but certainly not least, we'd like to recognize Jim Remmell, who provided significant "blocking and tackling" behind the scenes, and David Lindt, who joined us late in the game and "pushed us over the goal line" with tireless effort. The authors are grateful for their support.

The authors would like to thank the following for contributing content to this book: Robert Chur, Scott Dickson, Bart Muijzer, Doug Schwabauer, Nilesh Shirbhate, and Venu Mannem. Hallway and dinner conversations and a few too many late-night e-mail exchanges with Scott and with Linda Kateley, Isaac Rozenfeld, and Steffen Weiberle were invaluable shared learning experiences.

A small army of people reviewed this book, including technical reviewers Bob Bownes, Glenn Brunette, Alex Chartre, Gary Cutbill, Scott Dickson, Harry Foxwell, Brian Glynn, Dan Hain, Andy Hall, Duncan Hardie, Achim Hassenmüller, Jerry Jelinek, Martin Mayhead, Bart Muijzer, Enda O'Connor, Gary Pennington,

Chad Prucha, Jason Schroeder, Eric Sharakan, Terry Smith, Alex Sobolev, Tony Tomarchio, Huay-Yong Wang, Terry Whatley, Steffen Weiberle, Maran Wilson, and Steve Wilson. The authors are indebted to them for their countless suggestions and corrections. Our editor, Janice Gelb, and our graphic designer, Jeff Ramsey, were also brought in late in the project and we appreciate their improvements to the quality of the book.

Jeff Victor would like to thank his wife Cara and their daughter Kathryn for their patience and support during this endeavor. Jeff also extends additional appreciation to Scott Dickson for jumping in at the last minute, learning the intricacies of Oracle VM installation in record time, and immediately providing a thorough section on its use . . . in between flights to various destinations.

Jeff Savit thanks his wife Vicky for her support during this effort. He also thanks the reviewers for their corrections and comments.

Simon Hayler would like to thank his wife Hayley for her patience while he was working on this book.

Bob Netherton would like to thank his wife Pamela and their daughter Rebecca for all of their patience and support while he was working on this book.

About the Authors

This book is made possible by the hard work and expertise of the following contributing authors.

Jeff Victor is the principal author of *Oracle® Solaris 10 System Virtualization Essentials* and a principal sales consultant at Oracle Corporation. Prior to joining Oracle, Jeff was a principal field technologist for Sun Microsystems. He is an OpenSolaris Zones Community Leader, the creator of the `zonestat` open-source program, and a regular author, contributor, and speaker at corporate and industry events. His blog can be found at `http://blogs.sun.com/JeffV`. Jeff received a bachelor of science degree in computer science from Rensselaer Polytechnic Institute. In his spare time, he builds and launches high-power rockets. Jeff lives in New York with his wife and daughter.

Jeff Savit has more than 25 years of experience in operating systems, virtualization, and performance on multiple platforms, and is a principal sales consultant at Oracle Corporation specializing in these areas. He was previously a principal field technologist at Sun Microsystems with a similar focus. Before joining Sun, Jeff was a vice president at Merrill Lynch, where he had roles in development, systems management, market data, and web applications. He also managed a department responsible for the firm's virtual machine systems, wrote market data portions of Merrill Lynch's Internet trading applications, and created one of the Internet's first stock quote websites. Jeff is the author of the Sun Blueprint *Energy Efficiency*

Strategies: Sun Server Virtualization Technology, and the virtualization chapter of the *Datacenter Reference Guide* Blueprint. Jeff has written or coauthored several books, including *Enterprise Java, VM and CMS: Performance and Fine-Tuning*, and *VM/CMS Concepts and Facilities*, and his work has been published in *SIGPLAN Notices*, a journal of the Association of Computing Machinery. He has a master's degree in computer science from Cornell University.

Gary Combs is a SPARC specialist at Oracle Corporation. He specializes in midrange and high-end SPARC servers, which include the popular M-Series. Gary also covers virtualization technologies that are implemented on these platforms: Dynamic Domains, Logical Domains, and Oracle Solaris Containers. Prior to joining Oracle, Gary was with Sun Microsystems. He has more than 15 years of direct sales support experience as a systems engineer. For the last 10 years, Gary has held marketing positions in product management, product definition, and technical marketing.

Simon Hayler is a principal sales consultant for Oracle Corporation. Previously, Simon was a principal field technologist for Sun Microsystems. Simon has a telecommunications engineering background, encompassing the design, configuration, and implementation of multitiered information systems. His role at Sun over the past 12 years has included pre- and post-sales consulting, architectural design and implementation for both high-end commercial and high-performance computing, and, more recently, specialization in virtualization solutions.

Bob Netherton is a principal sales consultant at Oracle Corporation specializing in Oracle Solaris, virtualization, open-source software, and Linux interoperability. Prior to joining Oracle, Bob was a principal field technologist for Sun Microsystems, and was one of the architects and content developers of the Solaris Boot Camp and Deep Dive seminar series. In addition, he has developed several best practices guides for Solaris as well as an advanced Solaris training curriculum. Bob is also involved in several OpenSolaris users groups in the American Midwest and Southwest. Bob received a bachelor of science degree in applied mathematics from the University of Missouri, and he is a regular blogger on Solaris, virtualization, and open-source technologies.

1

Introduction to Virtualization

Virtualization is a "hot" technology. This chapter provides an introduction to the basic virtualization concepts and issues. It begins by defining virtualization and examining the motivations for using it. It then turns to system virtualization models.

1.1 Definitions and Motivations

Technology is developed in response to a need. Virtualization technologies were invented to address gaps in the functionality of existing computer systems. Let's take a look at the meaning of computer virtualization and the various needs that it fulfills.

1.1.1 What Is Virtualization?

System virtualization is technology that creates "virtual environments" that allow multiple applications to run on one computer as if each has its own private computer. Virtualization is achieved by creating a virtual computer or virtual operating system that behaves like a real one, but isn't. Workload isolation is the primary goal of system virtualization.

Three virtualization models are commonly used. First, the ability to provide multiple isolated execution environments in one operating system (OS) instance is called *operating system virtualization* (OSV). In this model, each environment contains what appears to be a private copy of the operating system in a *container* (a similar technology calls them *jails*). This approach is different than the second model, in which multiple operating system instances run on one set of hardware resources. The latter model takes advantage of *virtual machines* (VMs), which may run the same or different operating systems. Virtual machines are provided by hardware and/or software called a *hypervisor*, which creates the illusion of a private machine for each "guest" OS instance. In the third model, hardware partitioning ensures the electrical segregation of computer hardware resources—CPUs, RAM, and I/O components—so as to create multiple independent computers within one computer. Each isolated grouping of hardware is called a *partition* or *domain*.

Through the course of the book, we will describe different forms of computer virtualization in detail. The phrase "virtual environment" (VE) will be used to refer to any of these types of virtualization.

1.1.2 Why Virtualize?

The original and most common reason to virtualize is to facilitate server consolidation, although several other important purposes exist as well. Today's data center managers face a series of extreme challenges: They must continue to add to compute workloads while minimizing operational costs, which include the electricity to power and cool computing systems. In data centers that are already full, this requirement necessitates squeezing existing workloads into unused compute capacity on existing systems and increasing the workload density of new systems.

New servers are better able to handle this task than older ones. For example, you can move workloads on older Sun Fire V880 systems running Solaris 8 to Sun SPARC Enterprise T5240 computers running Oracle Solaris 10 with minimal effort. Because of the performance characteristics of the two types of systems, for most workloads six V880s can be replaced by one T5240.

Replacing 100 V880 computers with 17 T5240s would achieve the following improvements:

- Aggregate throughput performance would not change significantly for most workloads.
- Reduced space: 100 V880s use 50 data center racks, whereas 17 T5240s can fit in a single data center rack.
- Approximately 660,000 BTUs of heat generation would be removed from the data center.

- Approximately $200,000 would be saved in electricity costs per year (ignoring the cost of cooling).
- Acquisition costs for the new hardware would be balanced by the savings in operating costs achieved in the first year after its purchase.

How can you achieve such savings?

Workload consolidation is the process of implementing several computer workloads on one computer. It is not the same as the concept exemplified by installing multiple programs on a desktop computer, where you are actively using only one program at a time. Instead, a server with consolidated workloads will have multiple programs actively using the same CPU(s) at the same time.

Most computers that are running only one workload are under-utilized: There are more hardware resources than the workload needs. The result is inefficient use of an organization's financial resources. Which costs more: five computers to run five workloads, or one of those computers if it can run all five workloads? Of course, it is impossible to purchase exactly the right amount of computer. For example, it is not possible to purchase a computer with one half of a CPU for a workload that needs only one half of the compute power of a single CPU.

Figure 1.1 shows the amount of CPU capacity used by two workloads, each residing on its own system. Approximately 70% of the investment in the first system's CPU is wasted, and 60% of the second system's CPU goes unused. In this arrangement, the cost of a CPU—not to mention other components like the frame and power supplies—is wasted.

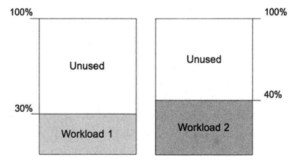

Figure 1.1 Two Under-utilized Systems

It is possible—and often desirable—to run another workload on that same system instead of purchasing a second computer for the second workload. Figure 1.2

shows the CPU consumption of the same two workloads after consolidation onto one system. The amount of wasted investment has decreased by an entire CPU.[1]

Of course, these examples use average values, and real-world computers do not run well at 100% CPU utilization. You must also avoid being overly aggressive when consolidating workloads.

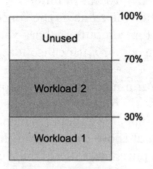

Figure 1.2 A Consolidated System

In the early days of the computer industry, all computers were so expensive that a corporation might be able to own only one. Given the precious nature of this resource, it was important for an organization to make the most of a computer by keeping it as busy as possible doing useful work.

At first, computers could run only one program at a time. This arrangement was unwieldy when a group of users sought to use the same computer, creating a need for a multiuser operating system. Software engineers designed such operating systems with features that prevented one program from affecting another program in a harmful way and prevented one user from causing harm to the other users' programs and data. Other features were designed to prevent one program from consuming more system resources—CPU cycles, physical memory (RAM), or network bandwidth—than it should.

Later, computer manufacturers developed inexpensive microcomputers, which were easier to afford than relatively expensive minicomputers. Unfortunately, these microcomputers and their early operating systems were not well suited to run multiple production applications. This led to a common practice of running one application per computer.

More recently, progress in computer performance has led to a desirable problem: too much compute capacity. Many servers in data centers run at an average

---

1.   The OS will spend some compute cycles managing resource usage of the two workloads and reducing the impact that one workload has on the other. This mediation increases CPU utilization, thereby reducing available CPU capacity, but we will ignore this effect for now.

CPU utilization near 10%. Many people would like to use most of the rest of this capacity, which can be achieved by consolidating workloads.

1.1.3 Why Is Virtualization so Important for Consolidating Workloads?

Operating systems designed for use by multiple users (e.g., most UNIX derivatives) have a long history of running multiple applications simultaneously. These operating systems include sophisticated features that isolate running programs, preventing them from interfering with one another and attempting to provide each program with its fair share of system resources. Even these systems have limitations, however. For example, the application might assume that only one instance of that application will be running on the system, and it might acquire exclusive access to a singular, non-shareable system resource, such as a lock file with a fixed name. The first instance of such an application locks the file to ensure that it is the only application modifying data files. A second instance of that application would then attempt to lock that same file, but the attempt would inevitably fail. Put simply, multiple instances of that application cannot coexist unless they can be isolated from each other.

Even if multiple workloads can coexist, other obstacles to consolidation may be present. Corporate security or regulatory rules might dictate that one group of users must not be able to know anything about programs being run by a different group of users. Either a software barrier is needed to prevent undesired observation and interaction, or those two user groups must be restricted to the use of different systems. The different user groups might also have application requirements for different OS patch levels, or operate with different system availability and maintenance windows. In general, however, UNIX-like operating systems are good platforms for consolidation because they provide user separation and resource management capabilities and scale well on large platforms.

Some other operating systems—particularly those that were originally designed to be single-user systems—cannot be used as a base for consolidated workloads as easily. Their architecture can make coexistence of similar workloads impossible and coexistence of different workloads difficult. Modifying a single-user OS so that it can run multiple workloads concurrently can be much more difficult than designing this capability into the system at the beginning. The use of these platforms as single-application servers led to the industry mindset of one application per server, even on systems that can effectively run multiple applications simultaneously.

Another solution is needed: the ability—or apparent ability—to run multiple copies of the operating system concurrently with one workload in each OS, as shown in Figure 1.3. To the hardware, this arrangement does not differ dramatically from previous ones: The two workloads have become slightly more complex, but they are still two workloads.

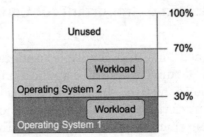

Figure 1.3 Multiple Operating System Instances on One Computer

To achieve the consolidation of multiple workloads onto one computer, software or firmware barriers between the workloads might be used, or entire copies of operating systems might be running on the system. The barriers separate "virtual environments," which behave like independent computers to various degrees, depending on the virtualization technology. Once virtualization is accomplished, several benefits can be achieved, which fall into two categories:

- Cost reductions
  - Reduced aggregate acquisition costs of computers
  - Reduced aggregate support costs of computer hardware
  - Reduced data center space for computers
  - Reduced need for electricity to power computers and cooling systems
  - In some cases, reduced support costs for operating systems
  - In some cases, reduced license and support costs for application software
- Nonfinancial benefits
  - Increased architectural flexibility
  - Increased business agility due to improved workload mobility

Of course, nothing in life is free: There is a price to pay for these benefits. Some of the drawbacks of consolidation and virtualization are summarized here:

- Perceived increase in complexity: One physical computer will have multiple VEs; this is balanced by having fewer computers.

- Changes to asset tracking and run books (e.g., rebooting a physical computer requires rebooting all of its VEs)
- More care needed when assigning workloads to computers: The computer and the virtualization technology represent a single point of failure for almost all technologies.
- Potential for increased or new costs:
  - A computer using virtualization may be larger than a single-workload system and, therefore, more expensive.
  - The level of support needed for a computer using virtualization will often cost more than the level of support for the least important of the workloads being consolidated; if most of the workloads were running on unsupported systems, support costs might actually increase.
  - Data center architects and system administrators will need training on the virtualization technologies to be used.

1.1.4 Other Reasons for Virtualization

After years of virtualizing solely to isolate consolidated workloads, people realized that some of the benefits of virtualization can be useful and are worth the effort, even if only one workload is present on a system.

One benefit is the business agility gained from simple VE mobility. The ability to move a workload (called *migration*) enables businesses to respond more quickly to changing business needs. For example, you can move a VE to a larger system during a day, instead of planning the acquisition of a new, larger system and the reimplementation of the workload on that system. The VE provides a convenient "basket" of jobs that can be moved from one system to another. Virtual machines are particularly effective at providing this benefit.

Some tools even enable regular migrations to respond to periodic fluctuations in demand. For example, a batch processing workload might have minimal processing needs during the day but perform significant work at night. It could be migrated to a small system with other light loads in the early morning and migrated to a large system in the early evening.

Because VEs are convenient, manageable objects, other business needs can also be addressed with virtualization. A snapshot (a complete copy of a VE) can be made before the VE boots, or after its workload is quiesced. If the VE becomes damaged while it runs, whether accidentally or maliciously, the workload can be quickly restored. The data in the damaged copy can then be methodically inspected, both for valid transactions that should be rerun against the workload and as part of a thorough security analysis. Many file systems and storage systems include the ability to copy a storage object very quickly, reducing the effects of this operation on the service being provided.

Another advantage of VEs, even in a nonconsolidated configuration, is realized more fully by some virtualization technologies than by others—namely, security. Some types of VEs can be hardened to prevent users of the VE (even privileged ones) from making changes to the system. Operating system virtualization provides the most opportunities for novel security enhancements.

Virtualization can also help prepare the organization to handle future workloads. If the needs of future workloads are not known, it may be easier to meet those needs if they can be met on a per-VE basis. For example, hypervisors can host different types of operating systems. The next workload might use software that is available on only one operating system, which is a different OS than the one used by the first workload.

In summary, consolidation is used to reduce the costs of acquisition and operation, and virtualization is needed to isolate one workload from another workload so that each can operate as if it is the only workload running on the computer. Further, virtualization can be used in some cases for the unique advantages it brings, even on unconsolidated systems.

1.1.5 Common Concepts

Many of the capabilities of VEs can be put into context and further investigated with common use cases.

All consolidated systems require resource management features to prevent one VE from overwhelming a finite resource and thereby preventing other VEs from using it. This possibility is discussed in the use case "General Workload Consolidation" (discussed later in this chapter).

All consolidated systems need firm security boundaries between VEs to prevent one VE from interacting with another in an unintended fashion. This scenario is discussed in the use case "Configurable Security Characteristics."

Virtualization creates the sense—and sometimes the reality—that there is something extra between the VE and the hardware. In some virtualization technologies, the extra layer creates performance overhead, reducing workload performance. This overhead also reduces scalability—the ability to run many workloads on the system. However, the separation provided by this layer can also be very beneficial, as it provides a more well-defined boundary between workload and hardware. This arrangement makes it easier to move a VE from one computer to another than it is to move an OS instance from one computer to another. This situation is discussed in the use case "Simplify Workload Mobility."

Learning to manage virtualized environments requires modifying your thinking and changing some practices. Some tasks that were difficult or impossible become easier. Other tasks that were simple become more complicated. The lack of a one-to-one relationship between workload and physical computer presents a new challenge for many people. Also, a new opportunity—moving a workload from one computer to another while the workload is active—offers its own challenges, including keeping track of the workloads that you are trying to manage.

Fortunately, you can choose from a set of tools that aim to simplify the task of virtualization management. These tools perform hardware discovery, OS provisioning, workload provisioning, configuration management, resource management, performance monitoring and tuning, security configuration and compliance reporting, network configuration, and updating of OS and application software. This topic is discussed in the use case "Flexible, Rapid Provisioning" and in Chapter 9, "Virtualization Management."

1.1.6 Use Cases for Virtualization

This section describes some of the uses for system virtualization:

- General workload consolidation: resource management and availability
- Asynchronous workloads: balancing resource utilization throughout the day
- Software development: consolidation of similar environments
- Test and staging: consolidation of similar environments
- Simplifying workload mobility
- Maintaining a legacy OS on new hardware
- Flexible, rapid provisioning
- Relieving scalability constraints of a given OS via multiple instances
- Fine-grained operating system modifications
- Configurable security characteristics

1.1.6.1 General Workload Consolidation

The most common use of virtualization is the consolidation of multiple, often unrelated, workloads from multiple computers into one computer. This approach avoids potential problems caused by mixing applications in the same VE. Once it has been determined that it is safe to run a particular application in a specific implementation of virtualization, there should be no need to verify a particular instance of that application or a particular combination of application instances for correct functionality.

Although the applications function correctly, their performance characteristics will probably change when they are running in a consolidated environment. A variety of factors may cause this change:

- Shared I/O channels are typical in most virtualization implementations, and will reduce available bandwidth to networks and persistent storage.
- Disks may be shared, increasing read and write transaction latency.
- If there are more workloads than CPUs, workloads may wait longer before getting a time slice on a CPU, thereby increasing response time.
- If multiple workloads share a set of physical CPUs and there are more workloads than CPUs, there is a greater chance of a process being assigned to a different CPU than the previous time slice, negating the benefits of a CPU's caches.

In addition to the potential for decreased performance, workload performance is less consistent in a consolidated environment unless resource controls are used. During one day, two workloads might have their daily peaks in CPU utilization at different times, and response times may be similar to those observed on unconsolidated systems. The next day, the peaks for those two workloads might coincide, leading to competition for physical resources such as CPUs and RAM. Response times for each workload may then suffer.

In other words, aggregate CPU usage of one workload should not change because of consolidation, but the deviation from average response time may increase. However, a complete understanding of the performance demands of the workloads should allow you to minimize the deviation because you will be able to place VEs on different systems to minimize this kind of performance deviation.

Resource partitioning technologies, including some virtual machine implementations, dedicate hardware resources to each resource partition. This practice provides insulation for each partition from the CPU consumption of other domains. You can use this feature to improve performance consistency.

Besides the effects of workload consolidation, virtualization can cause changes in workload performance. Many virtualization technologies require use of the system CPUs to perform virtualization activities. The result is performance overhead: CPU cycles that are not performing work directly related to the applications. The amount of overhead depends on several factors, including the following:

- The method of virtualization (e.g., partitioning, virtual machines, or operating system virtualization):
    - A partitioned system does not run virtualization software and has no overhead.

- A hypervisor runs on the system CPUs and causes overhead, but this is generally limited to I/O activities if the CPU has virtualization-assist features.
- Paravirtualization can significantly decrease performance overhead caused by a hypervisor.
- Operating system virtualization results in more processes in the one OS instance. This can be challenging for some operating systems, but the overhead directly associated with virtualization activities is negligible.
- Mix of computing activity versus I/O activity:
  - Computing activity does not increase overhead because the process runs directly on the CPU.
  - Memory-intensive applications can increase overhead unless the CPU has features to minimize this possibility.
  - For hypervisors, I/O activity must be controlled to prevent one VE from accessing information owned by another VE: This activity increases overhead.
- Hardware features may simplify some virtualization tasks, reducing overhead.

The combination of unpredictable patterns of effective performance and the potential for denial-of-service attacks makes resource management an essential component of any virtualization solution. Resource controls ensure that the consolidated systems can meet their service level objectives and be protected from resource starvation. Six resource categories are commonly managed:

- CPU capacity: Controls are used to ensure that each VE gets enough CPU time to provide appropriate responsiveness and to prevent denial-of-service attacks, either from compromised VEs on the same system or from traditional network attacks.
- Amount of RAM used: Controls should be used to ensure that each VE has enough RAM to perform well.
- Amount of virtual memory or swap space used: Unless each VE has its own private swap device or partition, this type of control can be used to ensure that each VE has enough swap space to work correctly and to prevent denial-of-service attacks.
- Network bandwidth consumed: Controls can be used to provide an appropriate quality of service for each workload and to prevent denial-of-service attacks.

- Persistent storage bandwidth consumed: Some technologies offer the ability to limit storage bandwidth consumed by one VE
- Use of kernel data structures: Examples include shared memory identifiers, including structures of finite size and ones that use another finite resource such as RAM.

Types of Resource Controls   Several methods of control exist. Some divide a resource into chunks and assign each chunk to one workload. Resources with a finite size, such as RAM or CPUs, can be divided using that method. However, this approach wastes a portion of the resource because the portion that is currently assigned to one VE is not in use but could be used by another VE. Some implementations of this method reduce the amount of waste by dynamically resizing the reserved resource based on resource usage.

Another method is a software-regulated limit, also called a *resource cap*. The controlling mechanism—hypervisor or operating system—prevents VEs from using more than a specified amount. Unused portions of the resource can be used by other VEs.

A third method to apportion CPU cycles—and the least wasteful of the three methods—is the fair share scheduler (FSS). If there is sufficient capacity for every VE to get the amount of CPU cycles it wants, each VE can use that amount. Conversely, if there is contention for the resource, instead of enforcing a maximum amount of consumption, this method guarantees availability of a minimum portion of a resource. An FSS allocates the resource in portions controlled by the administrator, a strategy akin to that underlying the concept of a service level agreement (SLA) that corporate customers require.

Allocation of network bandwidth is similar to allocation of CPU cycles. If you are patient, you can always get more of a resource: a time slice for CPUs, a time slot for network access. For this type of resource, it may not make sense to reserve a quantity, but it does make sense to cap the rate at which one VE consumes the resource over a brief sampling period.[2]

The following resource controls are available in virtualization implementations. They can be used to manage the resource categories listed earlier.

- CPU partitioning is the ability to assign a particular CPU or set of CPUs to a VE. It reserves all of the compute power of a set of CPUs, but any unused CPU cycles cannot be used by another VE and are wasted unless the reservation can be changed dynamically and automatically. However, this method

---

2. There are exceptions—for example, very-low-latency applications such as video and financial transactions that require reserved bandwidth to function correctly.

provides predictable performance and avoids performance overhead. A work-load assigned to a set of CPUs will always have access to its assigned CPUs, and will never be required to wait until another VE completes its time slice. A resource manager can reduce wasted capacity by reassigning idle CPUs. The amount of waste will be determined by two factors: (1) reconfiguration latency—the time it takes to shift a CPU from one partition to another and (2) resource granularity—the unconsumed partition of, at most, a single CPU. This model of CPU control is shown in Figure 1.4.

Figure 1.4 CPU Partitioning

- A software scheduler such as FSS may allow the administrator to enforce minimum response times either directly or via VE prioritization. Early im-plementations included software schedulers for VM/XA on mainframes and BSD UNIX on VAX 11/780s in the 1980s. This approach is often the best general-purpose solution. It is very flexible, in that the minimum amount of processing power assigned to each VE can be changed while the VE is run-ning. Moreover, a software scheduler does not force workloads to wait while unused CPU cycles are wasted.

System administrators can use an FSS to enforce the assignment of a particular minimum portion of compute capacity to a specific workload. A quantity of shares—a unitless value—is assigned to each workload, as depicted in Figure 1.5. The scheduler sums the shares assigned to all of the current workloads, and divides each workload's share quantity by the sum to obtain the intended minimum portion.

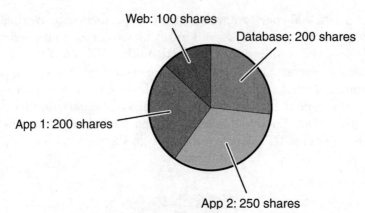

Figure 1.5 Using FSS to Ensure Minimum CPU Portions

- Insufficient memory can cause more significant performance problems than insufficient CPU capacity. If a workload needs 10% more CPU time than it is currently getting, it will run 10% more slowly than expected. By comparison, if a program needs 10% more RAM than it is currently getting, it will cause excessive paging. Such paging to the swap disk can decrease workload performance by an order of magnitude or more.

  Excessive memory use by one VE may starve other VEs of memory. If multiple VEs begin paging, the detrimental effects on performance can be further exacerbated by various factors:
- A shared I/O channel can be a bottleneck.
  - If VEs share swap space, fragmentation of the swap space can cause excessive head-seeking within the swap area.
  - If each VE has a separate swap area but all of these areas are present on one disk drive, the drive head will continuously seek between the two swap areas.

  If paging cannot be avoided, swap areas should be spread across multiple drives or, if possible, placed on low-latency devices such as solid-state drives (SSDs). However, it is usually difficult to justify the extra cost of those devices. Instead, you should try to avoid paging by configuring sufficient RAM for each VE.

  Memory controls can be used to prevent one VE from using up so much RAM that another VE does not have sufficient memory. The appropriate use of memory controls should be a general practice for consolidated systems. Inappropriate use of memory controls can cause poor performance if applications are granted use of less RAM than the "working set" they need to operate efficiently. Memory controls should be used carefully and with knowledge of actual RAM requirements.

Per-VE memory partitioning (RAM reservation or swap reservation) is available for some virtualization implementations. This control provides each VE with immediate access to all of its memory, but any reserved-but-unused memory is wasted because no other VE can use it. Also, modifying the reservation after the VE is running is not possible in some implementations.

Recently, virtual machine implementations have begun to include methods that enable the hypervisor to reduce a guest's RAM consumption when the system is under memory pressure. This feature causes the VE to begin paging, but allows the guest to decide which memory pages it should page out to the swap device.

- A per-VE limit, also called a *memory cap*, is more flexible and less wasteful than a memory partition or reservation. The virtualization software tracks the amount of memory in use by each VE. When a VE reaches its cap, infrequently used pages of memory are copied to swap space for later access, using the normal demand paging virtual memory system. There is a potential drawback, however: As with dedicated memory partitions, overly aggressive memory caps can cause unnecessary paging and decrease workload performance.

- Other controls have been implemented on miscellaneous resources offered by the hypervisor or OS. One such resource is locked memory. Some operating systems offer applications the ability to lock data regions into memory so that they cannot be paged out. This practice is widely used by database software, which works best when it can lock a database's index into memory. As a consequence, frequently used data is found in memory, not on relatively slow disk drives. If the database is the only workload on the system, it can choose an appropriate portion of memory to lock down, based on its needs. There is no need to be concerned about unintended consequences.

   On a consolidated system, the database software must still be able to lock down that same amount of memory. At the same time, it must be prevented from locking down so much more RAM than it needs that other workloads suffer from insufficient memory.

   Well-behaved applications will not cause problems with locked memory, but an upper bound should be set on most VEs.

- Per-VE limits on network bandwidth usage can be used to ensure that every VE gets access to a reasonable portion of this resource.

- Per-VE network bandwidth reservations can be used to ensure that a particular workload always has the bandwidth it needs, even if that means wasting some bandwidth.

Need for Availability With one workload per system, a hardware failure in a computer can affect only that workload and, potentially, workloads on other systems on which it depends. Consolidating multiple unrelated workloads onto one system requires different planning, because a hardware failure can then bring down multiple services. High-availability (HA) solutions are justified by the greater total value of workloads in the computer.

Fortunately, VEs can be configured as nodes in HA clusters using products such as Oracle Solaris Cluster or Veritas Cluster Server. If you want to minimize just downtime due to application failure or OS failure, the primary and secondary VEs can be configured on one computer.

More commonly, the two nodes are configured on different computers to minimize downtime due to hardware failure. Multiple HA pairs can be configured in the same cluster. Often, primary nodes are spread around the computers in the cluster to balance the load under normal operating conditions, as shown in Figure 1.6. This configuration requires sufficient resources on each node to run both workloads simultaneously if one computer has failed, albeit perhaps with degraded performance.

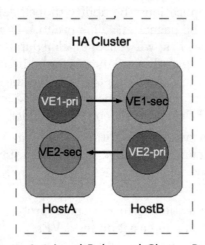

Figure 1.6 Load-Balanced Cluster Pairs

A slight twist on the HA concept uses several computers or VEs to simultaneously provide the same service to its consumers. With this model, the failure of any one computer or VE does not cause a service outage. The remaining entities continue providing the service, but the load-balancing mechanism no longer sends transactions to the failed unit.

Because no service outage occurs, this model is often preferred to the simpler failover model. Nevertheless, it can be used only with certain types of applications and customized applications. Applications that provide a read-only service, such as DNS lookups, scale well with this model. In contrast, applications that modify data, such as databases, must be modified to synchronize the modification activities across the cluster nodes.

Oracle Solaris Cluster implements this model via its Scalable Services functionality for web server software and some other applications. Oracle also provides this capability for a database service with the Oracle RAC product.

Figure 1.7 shows two VEs in each of two computers that are part of a scalable cluster. Each computer has two VEs providing the same service. This model is often used when the application does not scale well. After a failure, only one fourth of the processing power of the cluster is lost.

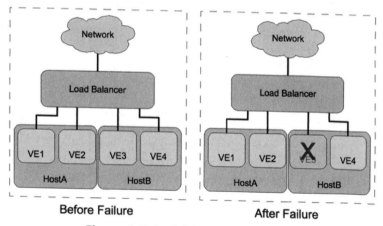

Figure 1.7 Scalable Services Cluster

Summary   In summary, consolidated systems provide clear benefits, but they also require a return to some of the mainframe practices of the past, including more assertive efforts to manage the resources and availability of the system. Using

VEs as cluster nodes improves isolation between workloads, making it easier to run more applications in the cluster.

1.1.6.2 Asynchronous Workloads

Many workloads are active for a certain period of time each workday but otherwise use few system resources. For example, employees of a small business may all work in one time zone, and their online transaction processing (OLTP) environment might have few transactions running at night. Conversely, a batch job may run for 6 hours each night. Although the business may use two separate systems for these workloads, the average utilization for each system will be less than 40%.

You can combine those two workloads on one system in several ways. For example, you can take advantage of their schedules by running both workloads on the same system, hoping that there will not be any adverse interactions between them. Alternatively, you can prevent adverse interactions by isolating the workloads with virtualization. If the two workloads need roughly equivalent resources to provide the desired response time and completion time, the graph of utilization versus time might look like Figure 1.8.

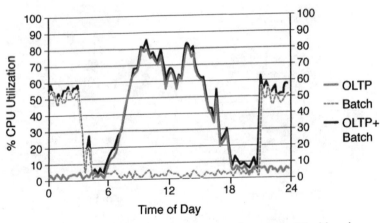

Figure 1.8 CPU Utilization of Asynchronous Workloads

1.1.6.3 Software Development and Other Bursty Workloads

A software developer typically generates intense system activity during short periods of time when compiling software, followed by periods of little activity. This uneven workload results in computers that are under-utilized most of the time, wasting most of the investment in those systems.

If a programmer's computer is compiling only 5% of the time, 20 programmers could share one computer if they took turns compiling. Of course, that is not an ideal situation, and would likely reduce productivity while each programmer waited for a turn to compile his or her programs. Several optimizations can be made to that model, but these problems must still be solved:

- Programmers must not be able to harm another programmer's activities.
- Some programmers will need specific versions of the operating system and its components, including development tools and test environments.
- Software development that modifies the operating system must be tested on a non-shared operating system.

In other words, the activities of each programmer must be isolated from the activities of the others. Each programmer needs an instance of an operating system for each target operating system. In many cases, each programmer needs an operating system instance for code development as well. However, for many types of programming, multiple developers can share an operating system instance.

Consolidation allows multiple programmers to use the same hardware resources. Virtualization provides the necessary isolation if application separation is needed.

Although this use case has been described as "software development," the concepts apply equally well to any large set of workloads that are characterized by frequent bursts of activity and have loose response time requirements.

1.1.6.4 Testing and Staging

Many test environments are configured for a specific testing purpose but are under-utilized because testing is not performed every day. It may not make sense to reinstall an operating system and configure it each time a different test is to be run, leading to a proliferation of test servers—which is a waste of capital investment.

Most functional testing can be performed in a virtualized environment without affecting the outcome of the tests. This allows consolidation of many testing environments, with one test per VE. A VE runs only while its test is being performed. Normally, only one of the VEs is running.

Other factors must be considered as well. In particular, this model is best applied to functional testing rather than performance or scalability tests. For example, one test might require exclusive access to all of the storage bandwidth of the system's I/O bus to produce meaningful results. It may not be possible to provide sufficient isolation, so tests must be scheduled at different times. Fortunately, most virtualization technologies allow VEs to be turned off individually, leaving just the one test environment running. Many teams can share one system, achieving a small number of test systems with little unscheduled time.

Performance testing in virtualized environments is appropriate only if the workload will be deployed in a VE. Similar resource controls should be applied to the test and production environments.

Another advantage of testing with VEs is the ability to take a snapshot (a point-in-time image) of a VE and save it to disk. This snapshot can be copied, and the copy may then be used to ensure that each successive iteration starts from exactly the same state, with the same system configuration and test data.

1.1.6.5 Simplifying Workload Mobility

Systems should originally be configured with sufficient excess resource capacity to accommodate expected growth in workload needs. Workloads occasionally outgrow the physical capacity of the system. If the computer was purchased with empty slots (e.g., for CPU or memory), additional resources can be added to the system to expand it and accommodate this growth.

Figure 1.9 shows a system at three points in time. In the first instance, the system is partially filled with a type of component, such as CPUs; the workload uses only a portion of the available resource. In the middle snapshot, the workload has grown to the point where it is consuming almost all of the physical resource. However, the system was purchased without a full complement of that resource. After filling the available physical slots, as shown in the last snapshot, the workload can grow even further without suffering performance problems.

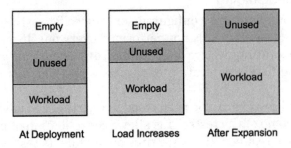

Figure 1.9 Accommodating a Growing Workload with Additional Resources

At some point, however, further system enhancements are neither possible nor desirable. Although in some cases the workload can be broken down into multiple components and run on multiple small systems, this solution is rarely appropriate. Instead, the workload must be moved to a new, larger system. Without virtualization, that process can be time-consuming and involve many manual, error-prone steps. The new system may need to be certified for proper installation and operation—another significant investment.

Virtualization provides useful separation between the VE and the hardware. This containment simplifies the process of extracting a VE from the original system and moving it to a new system. This operation, which is often called *migration*, is depicted in Figure 1.10.

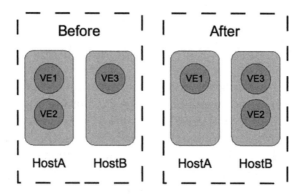

Figure 1.10 Migrating a VE

Three types of migration are possible, each of which is characterized by the amount of time during which the workload is not providing service, and by the amount of workload state that is lost during the migration.

"Cold" migration is simply the orderly halting of the original environment and its workload, the transfer of files from the old system to new storage or reconfiguration of shared storage, followed by start-up on the new computer. If shared storage is used to house the environment, this process is straightforward and does not require a lengthy service outage. If the application should retain its state, however, it might be necessary to save that state to persistent storage and reload the information when the VE restarts.

"Warm" migration and "live" migration do not require halting and rebooting the VE. Unlike cold migration, processes are not shut down during use of these methods, so they maintain the state of their current activities. Warm migration, shown in Figure 1.11, implies a noticeable service outage, usually on the order of tens of seconds. During that period, the system effectively pauses the VE in its original system, creates a new VE in the destination system, and copies a memory image of the related processes to the target system. The processes then continue their execution on the target system and the memory image for those processes on the original system is destroyed.

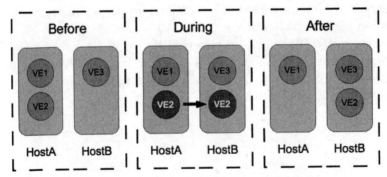

Figure 1.11 Migrating a VE: Warm Migration

Figure 1.12 shows live migration, which differs from warm migration in terms of the length of service outage. This outage is short enough that users do not notice it. Further, applications running on other systems are not affected by the outage. Unlike warm migration, which briefly pauses the VE while its memory pages are copied to the destination, live migration methods copy the VE while it is running. After the memory pages have been copied, the VE is paused and a final set of data is transferred. Control of the VE then passes to the target system. This transfer of control usually takes less than one second.

Both warm migration and live migration require the use of shared storage for the OS, applications, data, and swap space.

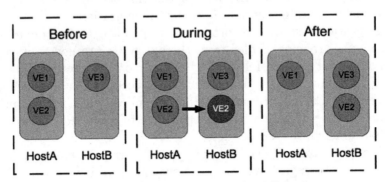

Figure 1.12 Migrating a VE: Live Migration

Another form of mobility is the conversion from a physical environment to a virtual environment, and from one virtualization technology to another. When discussing these activities, we use the letters "P" and "V" as a shorthand notation for "physical" and "virtual," respectively. For instance, moving an existing OS instance from a physical computer to a virtual machine provided by a hypervisor is called *P2V*. All four permutations are possible, and are shown at a high level in Table 1.1.

Table 1.1 Virtualization Conversions

	P	V
P	P2P Move a system (Tools predate virtualization)	P2V Virtualize a system, sometimes as part of consolidation
V	V2P Un-virtualize Uncommon, rarely used	V2V Migrate a VE to another system, or convert to an- other VE technology via a standard image format

1.1.6.6 Maintaining a Legacy Operating System on New Hardware

Thousands of older computers are running operating systems that are a version or more behind the current version. The difficulty of upgrading these computers to use new hardware or a new version of the OS varies. In some cases, software tools can be used to upgrade the operating system while the application is still running. Others systems are simply impossible to upgrade. Many systems fall between those two extremes.

For many of those systems, the best choice is rehosting the application on new hardware with new operating system features while still maintaining the application and its configuration. Achieving this "best of both worlds" solution requires a low-level layer of software—for example, a new version of an operating system that can pretend to be an old version. The new version would provide a virtual instance of an old version. This can be accomplished with a layer of software that translates old system calls into new ones. The result is the ability to maintain an older application environment while also benefiting from a new OS and new hardware.

1.1.6.7 Flexible, Rapid Provisioning

The computer industry has developed many solutions to address the challenge of deploying an operating system on a computer. These software solutions rely on the use of low-level tools embedded in the hardware of the target system. Because they are simple tools, their flexibility is limited, and the provisioning software must take on almost all of the burden of OS deployment. For example, hardware features do not usually include a simple command to install an OS image from a repository to local disk and boot from it. Also, because provisioning systems rely on hardware from different manufacturers, many methods must be maintained in an up-to-date state.

Virtualization can provide a rich set of tools as a foundation on which virtual environments are deployed. Its use simplifies the software that deploys virtual environments. An industry standard, VMDK, has been developed for an x86 operating system image, enabling the deployment of an image created with one vendor's hypervisor onto that of another vendor simply by copying the image.

Those two technological advancements enable the storage of preconfigured operating system images that can be copied easily to create a new VE and accessed via a shared storage framework such as SAN or NAS.

Because of the small disk footprint of OS virtualization environments (discussed in detail later in this chapter), provisioning from a preconfigured master image may take less than one second. This speed allows people to think of system provisioning and updating in a whole new light.

Figure 1.13 depicts a VE provisioning system. In this diagram, the provisioning system owns the master images for the various applications used by the data center, with one image per application. Each image has been tailored for the use of that particular application, including remote file system mount points for the application, an appropriate level of security hardening, user accounts and other factors. When a new instance of a particular application is needed, a management tool is used to perform the following tasks:

1. Clone the image.

2. Fine-tune the image—for example, with a link to the data to be used.

3. Complete the process of making the image ready for use, including steps necessary for use on a particular server.

4. Detach the image from the provisioning system and boot it on the deployment server.

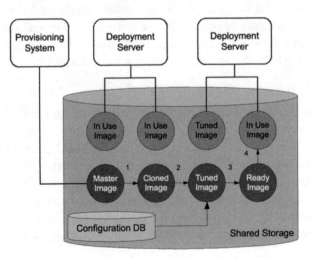

Figure 1.13 Provisioning System for VEs

1.1.6.8 Relieving Scalability Constraints

When you purchase a computer, especially a server, you must determine the maximum resource capacity that will be needed over the life of the system, including the quantity of CPUs, the amount of RAM, and other resources. If the workload grows to consume the maximum quantity of a particular resource, you must purchase a larger system and move the workload to it. Without virtualization, this type of upgrade typically means installing the operating system and applications on the new computer, which is a time-consuming and error-prone process.

With virtualization, fewer larger systems can be deployed, reducing the complexity of managing many systems. When a workload outgrows its system, an existing system with sufficient unused capacity can usually be found. Using the various tools available to migrate a VE from one system to another, this process can be as simple as clicking and dragging an icon in a management application. Figure 1.14 shows a migration to a larger system, where the application will rarely be constrained by the quantity of resources in the computer.

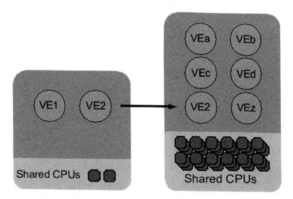

Figure 1.14 Providing More Room for a VE

1.1.6.9 Fine-Grained Operating System Modification

A challenge of consolidated but non-virtualized workloads is the decreased flexibility of the system. One workload may need a particular version of an operating system or a specific set of tuning parameters for the operating system. One application may be tested and supported only with a specific set of operating system components installed. Without virtualization, it is sometimes difficult to meet the needs of every workload on a consolidated system.

System virtualization technologies virtualize an instance of an operating system or of a computer. In each case, one VE can be tailored to meet the needs of its workload, while another VE is customized to meet the needs of another workload.

1.1.6.10 Configurable Security Characteristics

Single-user systems have security needs, such as firewall features to keep out intruders. Multiuser systems have all of these needs plus some unique ones of their own—for example, mechanisms to protect one user from another. Systems with VEs also have their own specific security considerations.

Some virtualization technologies offer the ability to modify the security environment of VEs. Configurable security enables you to selectively harden different aspects of a VE by allowing a VE to perform only those actions needed for its workload. An example is immutable service containers, which are described in Chapter 6, "Oracle Solaris Containers."

Any software component has the potential to create a security weakness, and virtualization software is no different. Virtualization software must be subject to the same stringent security analysis as other infrastructure software. For more on this topic, see the book *Solaris Security Essentials*.

If the hypervisor can limit inter-VE interaction to that already possible between separate computers, the hypervisor cannot be used as a covert channel and has not reduced security compared to separate systems.

1.2 System Virtualization Models

Many different models for system virtualization have been developed. They share many traits, but differences between them abound. Some virtualization features are appropriate for some models, others are not.

Each model can be described in terms of two characteristics: flexibility and isolation. Those two characteristics have an inverse relationship: Typically, the more isolation between VEs, the less flexibility in resource allocation. Conversely, flexibility requires sharing, which reduces isolation. You can then create a spectrum of resource flexibility versus workload isolation and place any particular virtualization model or implementation on that continuum, as shown in Figure 1.15.

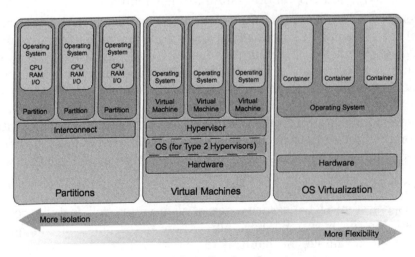

Figure 1.15 Virtualization Spectrum

As described in detail later in this chapter, hardware partitions offer the most isolation but the least flexibility. This arrangement is appropriate for business-critical workloads where service availability is the most important factor. Each partition has complete control over its hardware. At the other end of the spectrum, operating system virtualization (OSV) offers the most flexible configurations but the least isolation between the VEs, which are often called *containers*. Containers also provide the best scalability and have demonstrated the highest virtualization density. OSV is also discussed later in this chapter.

Between those two extremes, the virtual machines model creates the illusion that many computers are present, using one computer and a layer of firmware and software. That layer is the hypervisor, which provides multiplexed access from each operating system instance to the shared hardware. It also provides the ability to install, start, and stop each of those instances. Note that two types of VM implementations are possible: A Type 1 hypervisor runs directly on the hardware, while a Type 2 hypervisor runs on an operating system. Both types of hypervisors are discussed later in more detail.

Some of these virtualization models can be combined in one system, as shown in Figure 1.16. For example, one virtual machine can run an OS that also supports OSV. You can use layered virtualization to benefit from the strengths of each type. This strategy does, however, add complexity, which is most noticeable when troubleshooting problems.

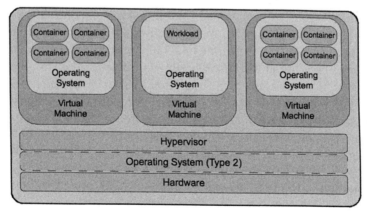

Figure 1.16 Multilayered Virtualization

The next few sections of this chapter describe each of the three virtualization categories shown in Figure 1.15: hardware partitions, virtual machines, and operating system virtualization. The descriptions are generic, discussing factors common to related solutions in the industry. Implementations specific to the Oracle Solaris ecosystem are described in Chapters 2 through 6.

Each of the descriptions in this chapter mentions that model's traits and strengths. A detailed analysis of their relative strengths and weaknesses is provided in Chapter 7, "Choosing a Virtualization Technology."

1.2.1 Hardware Partitioning

The epitome of isolation within the same computer comprises complete separation of compute resources—software and hardware—while still achieving some level of savings or flexibility compared to separate systems. In the ideal case, an electrically isolated environment (a partition) is an independent system resource that runs its own copy of an operating system. The OS runs directly on the hardware, just as in a completely non-virtualized environment. Any single failure, whether in hardware or software, in a component of one VE cannot affect another VE in the same physical computer. Hard partitions are used, for example, to consolidate servers from different company departments where isolation and technical support chargebacks are required.

In some implementations, the only shared component is the system cabinet, although such an approach yields little cost savings. This is especially true if the resources in different partitions cannot be merged into larger VEs. Other implementations share interconnects, clock control, and, in some cases, multiple hard partitions on a single system board. On a practical level, the minimum components held in common would consist of the system cabinet, redundant power supplies and power bus and, to promote flexible configurations and minimally qualify as virtualization, a shared but redundant backplane or interconnect. The label "virtualization" can be applied to these systems because the CPUs, memory, and I/O components can be reconfigured on the fly to any partition while still maintaining fault isolation. This limited set of common components provides the best failure isolation possible without using separate computers.

Because of the characteristics of hard partitioning, some people do not consider partitioning to qualify as virtualization. Because of the role that hardware partitioning plays in consolidating and isolating workload environments, we will include this model in our discussions.

The next few sections discuss some of the relevant factors of hardware isolation.

1.2.1.1 Failure Isolation

Limiting the set of components that are common to two different partitions increases the failure isolation of those environments. With this approach, a failure of any hardware component in one partition will not affect another partition in the same system. Any component that can be shared, such as the backplane, must also be partitionable so that a failure there affects only the one partition using that component. This isolation scheme is shown in Figure 1.17.

Figure 1.17 Failure Isolation of Hardware Partitions

1.2.1.2 Operating System

Separate hardware requires a distinct copy of an operating system for each partition. This arrangement reinforces the separation of the partitions and maintains the benefits, and effort, of per-partition OS maintenance, such as OS installation and patching. To maximize partition independence, a failure in one OS instance must be prevented from affecting another partition.

Also, specialized software (such as HA clustering) that links two partitions must prevent one failure from affecting both partitions. Some implementations in the industry achieve this level of independence more effectively than others.

1.2.1.3 Flexibility and Granularity of Resource Configuration

Most hard-partitioning systems allow the partitions to be different sizes. A partition can usually be resized. With some types, this operation requires stopping all software, including the operating system, that was using the resources being reconfigured.

Changing the sizes of two partitions can be viewed as moving the barrier between them, as depicted in Figure 1.18 on the next page.

Most of these systems are large-scale systems (more than eight CPU sockets per system) and contain multiple CPU sockets on each circuit board. If such a system is configured with multiple partitions per CPU board, a hardware failure on that CPU board can cause multiple partitions to fail. CPU failures affect only the partition that was using that CPU. For that reason, where failure isolation is the most important consideration, only one partition should be configured per CPU board. In contrast, if partition density is the most important consideration, multiple partitions per CPU board will be an important feature.

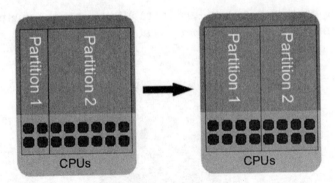

Figure 1.18 Dynamic Reallocation of Hardware Resources

1.2.1.4 Scalability

Two related types of scalability exist in the context of system virtualization: guest scalability and per-VE performance scalability. Guest scalability is the number of VEs that can run on the system without significantly interfering with one another. Hard partitions are limited by the number of CPUs or CPU boards in the system, but can also be limited by other hardware factors. For some of these systems, only 2 partitions can be configured for each system. For others, as many as 24 partitions can reside in the system.

Because these systems are generally intended to perform well with dozens of CPUs in a single system image, they usually run large workloads on a small number of partitions. Their value derives from their combination of resource flexibility, failure isolation, and per-VE performance scalability.

Because hard partitioning does not require an extra layer of software, there should be no performance overhead inherent in this type of virtualization. Applications will run with the same performance as in a nonpartitioned system with the same hardware.

1.2.1.5 Partition Management

Hardware isolation requires specialized hardware. This requirement usually includes components that aid in the management of the partitions, including the configuration of hardware resources into those partitions. These components may also assist in the installation, basic management, and health monitoring of the OS instances running on the partitions. Specialized ASICs control data paths and enforce partition isolation.

1.2.1.6 Relative Strengths of Hardware Partitions

Hardware partitions offer the best isolation in the virtualization spectrum. Whenever isolation is the most important factor, hardware partitions should be considered.

Partitions are the only virtualization method that achieves native performance and zero performance variability. Whether the workload is run in an eight-CPU partition or an eight-CPU nonpartitioned system, the performance will be exactly the same.

Partitions offer other advantages over other virtualization methods. Most notably, few changes to data center processes are required: Operating systems are installed and maintained in the same fashion as on non-virtualized systems.

1.2.1.7 Industry Examples

Several products offer excellent hardware isolation. This section provides a representative list of examples.

The first server to use SPARC processors and Solaris to implement hard partitioning was the Cray CS6400, in 1993. Sun Microsystems included Dynamic Domains on the Enterprise 10000 in 1997 and also in the Sun Fire family—the midrange 4800, 4900, 6800, and 6900, and the large-scale F12K, F15K, E20K, and E25K systems. Dynamic Domains are also available in the follow-on M4000, M5000, M8000, and M9000 systems. Their implementation in the most recent generation is described in Chapter 2, "Hard Partitioning: Dynamic Domains."

On the CS6400, E10000, and the following generation (4800-25K) of systems, this implementation provides complete electrical isolation between Dynamic Domains. There is no single point of failure in a domain that would affect all of the domains. However, a hardware failure of a component in the shared backplane can affect multiple domains. Starting in 1993, Dynamic Domains could be reconfigured without rebooting them.

Hewlett-Packard's (HP's) nPars feature was first made available on some members of the PA-RISC–based HP 9000 series. It is also a feature of some of HP's Integrity systems. In 2007, HP added the ability to reconfigure these partitions without rebooting them.

Amdahl's Multiple Domain Facility (MDF) and subsequently IBM's mainframe Logical Partitions (LPARs) are among the earliest implementations of hardware-based partitioning, available since the 1980s. MDF and LPARs use specialized hardware and firmware to create separate execution contexts with assigned CPUs, RAM, and I/O channels. A domain or partition may have dedicated physical CPUs or logical CPUs that are implemented on a physical CPU shared with other domains and shared according to a priority weighting factor. Physical RAM is assigned to one partition at a time, and can be added or removed from a partition without rebooting it.

1.2.2 Virtual Machines

The first type of virtualization, and one of the most popular, is virtual machines. This model provides the illusion that many independent computers are present in the system, each running a copy of an OS. Each of these VEs is called a *virtual machine*. Software or firmware, or a combination of both, manages the OS instances and provides multiplexed access to the hardware. This supporting layer, which acts as the hypervisor, gives this model its flexibility but adds a certain amount of performance overhead while it performs its tasks.

Failure isolation of hypervisors varies with implementation. Each shared resource is a single point of failure, including the hypervisor itself.

Most hypervisors provide virtual machines that mimic the physical hardware. A few of them emulate a completely different hardware architecture. Some of these are used to develop new hardware, simulating the hardware in software or testing software that will run on the hardware. Others are used to run software compiled for a CPU architecture that is not available or is not economical to continue operating.

1.2.2.1 Type 1 Hypervisors

A Type 1 hypervisor comprises software or firmware that runs directly on the computer's hardware. It typically has components found in a complete operating system, including device drivers. Some implementations offer the ability to assign a set or quantity of physical CPUs or CPU cores to a specific VE. Other implementations use a scheduler to give each operating system instance a time slice on the CPU(s). Some versions offer both. Each VE appears to be its own computer, and each appears to have complete access to the hardware resources assigned to it, including I/O devices. Although hypervisors also provide shared access to I/O devices, this capability inflicts a larger performance penalty.

These hypervisors implement a small feature set designed exclusively for hosting virtual machines. When the system starts, the hypervisor is placed into the main system RAM or specific area of reserved memory; in some architectures, additional elements reside in firmware, hardware, and BIOS. The hypervisor may make use of or require specialized hardware-assist technology to decrease hypervisor overhead and increase performance and reliability.

A Type 1 hypervisor is a small specialized environment designed specifically for the task of hosting virtual machines. This model has several advantages over Type 2 hypervisors—namely, simplicity of design, a smaller attack surface, and less code to analyze for security validation. The primary disadvantages of Type 1 hypervisors are that they require more coding and they do not allow a base operating system to run any applications with native performance. Also, they cannot freely leverage services provided by a host OS. Even mundane features such as a management interface or file system may need to be built "from scratch" for the hypervisor. Adding these features increases the complexity of the hypervisor, making it more like an OS.

Type 1 hypervisors generally use one VE as a management environment. The administrator interacts with that VE via the system console or via the network. That VE contains tools to create and otherwise manage the hypervisor and the other VEs, usually called *guests*. Some Type 1 systems also allow for one or more specialized VEs that virtualize I/O devices for the other VEs. Figure 1.19 shows the overall structure of a Type 1 hypervisor implementation, including a virtual management environment (VME) and a virtual I/O (VIO) VE.

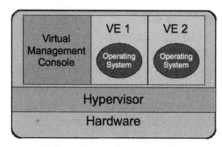

Figure 1.19 Virtual Machines and a Hypervisor

Hypervisors that offer VIO guests typically provide an alternative to their use: direct, exclusive access to I/O devices for some VEs. Direct access offers better I/O performance but limits the number of VEs that can run on the system. If the system has only four network connectors, for example, then only four VEs can have direct network access.

1.2.2.2 Industry Examples

IBM developed the first hypervisors (and coined the term) for its mainframes in the 1960s.[3] VM/370 was a popular hypervisor for IBM mainframes starting in 1972. Its descendant on current mainframes is z/VM, which supports virtual machines running IBM operating systems such as z/OS and z/VM (nested virtual machine environments are possible), and open operating systems including several distributions of Linux and an experimental port of OpenSolaris.

VMware Inc.'s VMware ESX is a Type 1 hypervisor for x86 systems. It supports common operating systems such as Microsoft Windows, Oracle Solaris, and some releases of Linux distributions such as CentOS, Debian, Red Hat Enterprise Linux, Novell SUSE Linux, and Ubuntu. Its VMC is called the *service console*.

---

3. The Appendix contains a detailed narrative of the history of virtualization.

Oracle VM Server for x86, xVM Hypervisor and Citrix Xenserver are commercial implementations of the open-source Xen hypervisor for x86 systems. Xen supports a variety of guest operating systems, but differs in architecture from VMware ESX: Xen uses specialized guest domains for parts of the virtualization infrastructure. A specially privileged "dom0" guest, running OpenSolaris, Linux, or BSD, provides a management control point and typically provides virtual I/O to other guests.

The Oracle VM Server for SPARC (previously called Sun Logical Domains) feature, which is discussed in detail later, is a SPARC hypervisor on chip multithreading (CMT) servers used to support guest systems running Solaris. The VMC is called the *control domain*. Virtual devices are implemented by the control domain or one or more specialized VEs called *service domains* and *I/O domains*. Service domains or I/O domains can be grouped into HA pairs to improve availability of I/O devices. System administrators can also assign devices directly to VEs.

IBM's PowerVM Hypervisor is a combination of firmware and software that creates and manages LPARs (logical partitions) on Power5 and Power6 CPU cores. These systems also support a virtualization technology called Micro-Partitioning that can run multiple OS instances on a CPU core.

Partitions may run AIX or Linux operating systems. PowerVM offers VIO partitions and direct device assignment.

1.2.2.3 Type 2 Hypervisors

Type 2 hypervisors run within a conventional operating system environment, enabling virtualization within an OS. The computer's OS (e.g., Oracle Solaris, Linux distributions, Microsoft Windows) boots first and manages access to physical resources such as CPUs, memory, and I/O devices. The Type 2 hypervisor operates as an application on that OS. Like the Type 1 hypervisor, the Type 2 hypervisor may make use of or require hardware-assist technology to decrease overhead attributable to the hypervisor.

Type 2 hypervisors do have some disadvantages. For example, they must depend on the services of a hosting operating system that has not been specifically designed for hosting virtual machines. Also, the larger memory footprint and CPU consumed by unrelated features of a conventional OS may reduce the amount of physical resources remaining for guests.

The primary advantage of Type 2 hypervisors for desktop systems is that the user can continue to run some applications, such as e-mail, word processing, and software development software, using a favorite OS and its tools, running without performance penalty. Other advantages include the ability to leverage features provided by the OS: process abstractions, file systems, device drivers, web servers, debuggers, error recovery, command-line interfaces, and a network stack. Similar advantages apply in server environments: Some applications on a server may run "first level" directly on the OS, whereas other applications are hosted in virtual machines, perhaps to provide increased isolation for security purposes, or to host a different OS version without the disruption of installing a Type 1 hypervisor on the bare metal. These advantages can be compelling enough to compensate for the memory footprint of the hosting OS and the potential performance penalty of the hypervisor. It is sometimes assumed that a Type 2 hypervisor is inherently less efficient than a Type 1 hypervisor, but this need not be the case. Further, a Type 2 hypervisor may benefit from scalability and performance provided by the underlying OS that would be challenging to replicate in a Type 1 hypervisor.

Examples of Type 2 hypervisors include Oracle VM VirtualBox, VMware Server, VMware Fusion, Parallel Inc. Parallels Workstation, and Microsoft Windows Virtual PC.

1.2.2.4 Full Virtualization and Paravirtualization

Another distinction between different forms of hypervisor-based virtualization is whether full virtualization or paravirtualization is used. When full virtualization is used, the hypervisor creates virtual machines that are architecturally consistent with the "bare iron" physical machine. With paravirtualization, the hypervisor provides software interfaces that virtual machines can use to communicate with the hypervisor for requesting services and receiving event notifications.

The advantage of full virtualization is that unmodified operating systems can be run as guests, simplifying migration and technology adoption, albeit at the cost of requiring the hypervisor to implement all platform details. This approach can create substantial overhead depending on the platform, especially for I/O, timer, and memory management.

Paravirtualization offers the opportunity to optimize performance by providing more efficient software interfaces to these and other functions. It can include cooperative processing between guest and hypervisor for memory management (e.g., memory ballooning, shared pages for I/O buffers), shortened I/O path length (e.g., device drivers making direct calls to the hypervisor or combining multiple I/O requests into a single request), clock skew management, and other optimizations. The disadvantage of paravirtualization is that it requires source code to port the guest OS onto the virtualized platform, or at least the ability to add optimized devices drivers.

Examples of paravirtualization include Xen implementations such as Oracle VM Server for x86 and Citrix XenServer, Oracle VM Server for SPARC, the guest/host additions in Oracle VM VirtualBox and VMware ESX, and the Conversational Monitor System (CMS) under VM/370.

1.2.2.5 Relative Strengths of Hypervisors

Hypervisors typically represent a "middle ground" between the isolation of hard partitions and the flexibility of OSV. The additional isolation of separate OS instances compared to OSV allows for the consolidation of completely different operating systems. The hypervisor layer also provides a convenient point of separation for VEs, thereby facilitating and simplifying VE mobility.

Some hypervisors offer optional CPU and I/O partitioning, which can reduce the overhead of the hypervisor significantly. Of course, the scalability of this method is limited by the number of CPUs and I/O buses. Systems with few CPUs must share these resources among the VEs.

1.2.3 Operating System Virtualization

Hardware partitioning and virtual machine technologies share a common trait: Each virtual environment contains an instance of an operating system. Most of those technologies allow different operating systems to run concurrently.

In contrast, operating system virtualization (OSV) uses features of the operating system to create VEs that are not separate copies of an operating system. This approach provides the appearance of an individual operating system instance for each VE. Most OSV implementations provide the same OS type as the hosting OS. Others, such as Oracle Solaris Containers, also have the ability to behave as another operating system.

Figure 1.20 shows the relationship between the hardware, OS, and VEs when using OSV.

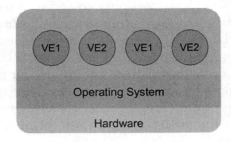

Figure 1.20 Operating System Virtualization

We have already discussed the importance of isolation to virtualization. The isolation between OSV VEs is just as important as the isolation noted in other models. For OSV, this isolation is enforced by the OS kernel, rather than by a hypervisor or hardware.

In the OSV model, all processes share the same operating system kernel, which must provide a robust mechanism to prevent two different VEs from interacting directly. Without this isolation, one VE could affect the operation of another VE. The kernel must be modified so that the typical interprocess communication (IPC) mechanisms do not work between processes in different VEs, at least in a default configuration. The network stack can be modified to block network traffic between VEs, if desired. Existing security features can be enhanced to provide this level of isolation.

OSV implementations are usually very lightweight, taking up little disk space, consuming little RAM, and adding very little CPU overhead. Nevertheless, although they can easily mimic the same operating system, most of them do not provide any ability to appear as another operating system.

Another strength of this model of virtualization relates to the possibility of hardware independence. Because a physical computer is not being simulated, an operating system that runs on multiple CPU architectures can potentially provide the same feature set, including OSV features, on different types of computers.

1.2.3.1 Failure Isolation

All isolation of software and hardware failures must be provided by the operating system, which may utilize hardware failure isolation features if they exist. For example, the operating system may be able to detect a hardware failure and limit the effects of that failure to one VE. Such detection may require hardware features to support this functionality.

The isolation between processes in different VEs can also be used to minimize propagation of software or hardware failures. A failure in one VE should not affect other VEs. This is easier to achieve if each VE has its own network services, such as sshd.

Further, the operating system must prevent any event that is occurring in one VE from affecting another VE. This includes unintentional events such as software failures, or actions taken by a successful intruder.

To be both robust and efficient, these hardware and software features must be tightly integrated into the OS implementation.

1.2.3.2 Operating System Features

All of the necessary functionality of OSV is provided by the OS, rather than by hardware or an extra layer of software. Usually this functionality is provided via features integrated into the core of the OS. In some cases, however, the features are provided by a different organization or community and integrated on-site, with varying levels of application compatibility.

The shared kernel offers the possibility for a privileged user to observe all processes running in all VEs, which simplifies the process of performance analysis and troubleshooting. You can use one tool to analyze resource consumption of all processes running on the system, even though many are in different VEs. After the problem is understood, you can use the same centralized environment to control the VEs and their processes.

This global control and observability is nothing new for consolidated systems, but it provides a distinct advantage over other virtualization models that lack a centralized environment that can inspect the internals of its guests. Analyzing an OSV system is not any more complicated than analyzing a consolidated one.

After the resource usage characteristics of a particular workload are known, resource management tools should be used to ensure that each VE has sufficient access to the resources it needs. Centralized control offers the potential for centrally managed, fine-grained, dynamic resource management. Most operating systems already have sophisticated tools to control the consumption of resources in one or more of these ways:

- Assigning CPU time, which is performed by a software scheduler. This control can be achieved through process prioritization or capping the amount of CPU time that a process uses during an interval of real time.
- Providing exclusive assignment of a group of processes to a group of processors.
- Dedicating a portion of RAM to a group of processes, capping the amount of RAM that a group of processes can use, or guaranteeing that a VE will be able to use at least a specific amount of RAM.
- Dedicating a portion of the network bandwidth of a network port to an IP address or a group of processes, or capping the amount of network bandwidth used during an interval of time.

Because most operating systems already have the ability to control these resources with fine granularity, if these controls are extended to the VEs, their resource consumption can be managed with the same granularity.

Some operating systems include automated features that detect conditions and take actions. For example, system software might detect that a network service such as sshd has failed and attempt to restart that service. In the context of resource management, dynamic resource controls can be used to react to changing processing needs of different workloads by changing resource control values on the fly.

The basic model of OSV assumes that the VEs provide the same operating system interfaces to applications as a non-virtualized environment provided by the host operating system (e.g., system calls). If this similarity can be achieved, applications need not be modified to run correctly.

Additionally, a particular implementation may mimic a different operating system if the two are sufficiently similar. In this case, the functionality of an OS kernel can be represented by its system calls. A thin layer of software can translate the system calls of the expected guest OS into the system calls of the hosting OS. This strategy can allow programs and libraries compiled for one OS to run—unmodified—in a VE that resides on a different OS, as long as they are all compiled for the same hardware architecture.

The extra operations of translating one set of functionality to another will incur a certain amount of CPU overhead, decreasing system performance. Achieving identical functionality is usually challenging, but sufficient compatibility can be achieved to enable common applications to run well.

1.2.3.3 Access to Hardware

OS virtualization features must allow isolated access to hardware so that one VE can make appropriate use of hardware but cannot observe or affect another VE's hardware accesses. Each VE might be granted exclusive access to a hardware resource, or such access might be shared. Existing implementations of OSV provide differing functionality for hardware access.

Figure 1.21 shows most VEs sharing most of the CPUs and a network port. One VE has exclusive access to another port and two dedicated CPUs.

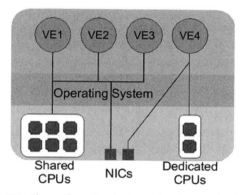

Figure 1.21 Shared or Exclusive Hardware Assignments

1.2.3.4 Software Infrastructure

OSV design engineers decide exactly where to place the division between base OS operations and VEs. A VE may include only the application processes or, alternatively, each VE may include some of the services provided by the operating system, such as network services and naming services.

1.2.3.5 Flexibility and Granularity of Resource Configuration

Because one control point exists for all of the hardware and the VEs, all resource management decisions can be made from one central location. For example, the single process scheduler can be modified to provide new features for the system administrator. These features can be used to ensure that the desired amount of compute power is applied to each VE to meet business needs. Because the scheduler can monitor each process in each VE, it can make well-informed scheduling decisions; it does not need to give control to a separate scheduler per VE.

An alternative method to moderate CPU power as a resource gives one VE exclusive access to a set of CPUs. This approach means that the VE's processes have access to all of the CPU capacity of these CPUs and reduces cache contention. RAM can be treated similarly, either as an assignment of a physical address range or as a simple quantity of memory.

Other resource constraints can include limits or guaranteed minimum amounts or portions.

1.2.3.6 Scalability

Operating system virtualization technologies tend to scale as well as the underlying operating system. From one perspective, all processes in all VEs can be seen as a set of processes managed by one kernel, including inter-VE isolation rules. If the kernel scales well to many processes, the system should scale well to many VEs of this type. At least one implementation of OS virtualization—Solaris Containers—has demonstrated excellent scalability, with more than 100 running VEs on one Solaris instance.

1.2.3.7 Platform Management

Operating system features must provide the ability to create, configure, manage, and destroy VEs. This capability can be extended to remote management.

1.2.3.8 Relative Strengths

Similar to other virtualization models, OSV has its particular strengths. Some of these are specific goals of OSV implementations; others are side effects of the OSV model.

Many of the strengths of OSV implementations are derived from the tight integration between the OSV technology and the OS kernel. Most of these operating systems are mature and have well-developed facilities to install and maintain them and to manage multiple workloads. It is usually possible to extend those features to the environments created via OSV.

A significant strength of OSV is its efficient use of resources. This efficiency applies to the use of CPU time, RAM, and virtual memory.

When implemented correctly, OSV will not add any CPU overhead compared to a consolidated but non-virtualized system. The OS must still perform the same operations for that set of running applications. However, to perform well with more than three or four VEs, the OS must be scalable —that is, able to switch the CPU(s) among the dozens or hundreds of processes in the VEs. It must also be able to efficiently manage the many gigabytes of RAM and swap space used by those processes.

Because OSV VEs do not have a separate OS instance, they do not consume hundreds of megabytes of RAM per VE for each OS kernel. Instead, the amount of RAM needed for multiple VEs typically is limited to the memory footprint of the underlying OS plus the amount of RAM used by each of the consolidated applications. In some implementations, operating systems that reuse a program's text pages can reduce the memory footprint of a VE even further by sharing those text pages across VEs.

Because of the single OS instance of OSV, a centralized point exists for security controls. This arrangement also creates the possibility of per-VE configurable security and centralized auditing, a topic discussed in Chapter 6.

OSV implementations have a primary goal of minimizing the effort needed to maintain many operating systems in a data center environment. Put simply, fewer OS instances means less activity installing, configuring, and updating operating systems. Because the OS is already installed before a VE is created, provisioning VEs is usually very rapid, taking anywhere from a few seconds to a few minutes. The minimalist nature of OSV also reduces the time to boot a VE—if that step is even needed—to a few seconds.

1.2.3.9 Industry Examples

Early examples of OS virtualization include Oracle Solaris Containers, HP-UX Secure Resource Partitions, Linux VServers, and AIX Workload Partitions. Each of these products follows the model described earlier, with differences reflecting their use of network and storage I/O, security methods and granularity, and resource controls and their granularity.

1.3 Summary

Server consolidation improves data center operations by reducing the number of servers, which in turn reduces hardware acquisition costs, hardware and software support costs, power consumption, and cooling needs. Virtualization enables consolidation of workloads that might interfere with one another, and of workloads that should be isolated for other reasons, including business agility and enhanced security.

Three general virtualization models exist. Hardware partitioning separates a computer into separate pools of hardware, each of which acts as its own computer, with its own operating system. Virtual machines rely on a hypervisor to enable multiple operating system instances to share a computer. Operating system virtualization creates virtual OS instances—software environments in which applications run in isolation from one another but share one copy of an OS and one OS kernel.

Each model has both strengths and weaknesses. Each model has been implemented on multiple hardware architectures, with each implementation being most appropriate in certain situations. The more you understand the models and implementations, the more benefit you can derive from virtualization.

2

Hard Partitioning: Dynamic Domains

Hard partitioning—a form of server virtualization—provides the ability to group multiple subsets of resources in the server in such a way that each group is not only software fault isolated, but also fully hardware and electrically fault isolated. It is important to understand how the hardware works and how physical resources are assigned to domains, as both of these factors have a direct impact on the applications running in the domain or in an Oracle Solaris Container.

The implementation of hard partitions differs in important ways from other virtualization technologies. Technologies based on hypervisors and operating system virtualization depend on services running in a special domain to configure the guest virtual environments. The use of virtualized interfaces (e.g., network, disks, CPUs, consoles) means that these interfaces must be routed through the hypervisor, which in turn affects performance. Where there is a requirement for bare-metal performance, high I/O throughput, and large memory footprint, yet flexible configurability is needed, then hard domaining (hard partitions) should be considered.

This chapter covers the fundamental concepts behind Dynamic Domains, including how they are designed, configured, and managed.

2.1 Partitions

2.1.1 Hardware Partitions

The grouping of hardware components is called a *hard partition*, or *domain*, and is an independent system resource that runs its own copy of the Oracle Solaris operating system. Domains divide a system's total resources into separate units that are not affected by the operations of the other units. Instantiating a number of Dynamic Domains on a Sun SPARC Enterprise M-Series server divides the system into multiple electrically isolated partitions. Because the SPARC64 processors do not implement the Hyper Privileged Mode instruction, it is not possible to divide up the resources using a hypervisor. Instead, each Dynamic Domain executes a unique instance of Oracle Solaris. Because each domain has its own Solaris instance, each domain can run a different Solaris 10 update level. Also, because isolation is implemented in the hardware, configurations can be created in which software changes, reboots, and potential faults in one domain do not affect applications running in other domains.

2.1.2 The M-Series

The Sun SPARC Enterprise M-Series uses an embedded computer called the eXtended System Control Facility (XSCF—a service processor) to configure the system and set up the domains. The very nature of hard partitions means elements such as security and data isolation are even more tightly integrated than with other virtualization technologies. All domains are created and altered from the XSCF. A command-line interface (CLI) and a browser user interface (BUI) are available. For CLI, access occurs either over a serial interface or over the network using SSH or Telnet.

2.2 Domain Implementation

A feature of Sun SPARC Enterprise M-Series servers known as Dynamic Reconfiguration (DR) supports the movement of CPU, memory, and I/O resources from one Dynamic Domain to another without the need for downtime. This capability can lead to more flexible and cost-effective management of IT resources.

A domain is an independent system resource that runs its own copy of Oracle Solaris (Solaris 10 10/08 or later). Domains divide a system's total resources into separate units that are not affected by operations of the other units. Each domain uses a separate boot disk with its own instance of Solaris as well as I/O interfaces to network and disk resources. CPU/memory boards and I/O boards can be separately added and removed from running domains using DR, provided they are not already assigned to other domains.

Domains run applications in strict isolation from applications running in other domains. Isolation and security between domains are maintained by an important ASIC called the system controller (SC), which ensures that one domain cannot access data packets from another domain.

The M4000/M5000 block diagram in Figure 2.1 shows how memory accesses and I/O transactions pass through the SC. Because the memory access controller (MAC) is not in the CPU but rather is found in a separate ASIC, a CPU's accesses to memory go through the SC. This arrangement allows it to enforce all domain data pathways for complete domain isolation. The SC is also important in ensuring balanced memory access performance. The physical pages of memory on the board are spread evenly across the SC chips for balanced memory throughput—another reason why the SC chip is one of the most critical ASICs in the system.

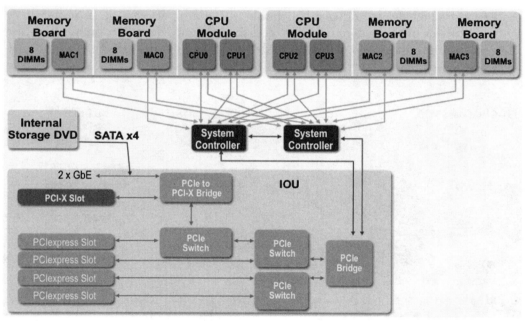

Figure 2.1 Block Diagram of M4000/M5000

The I/O assembly is called the I/O unit (IOU). Also note that there are two PCIe switches per IOU in the M4000/M5000. As a consequence, each IOU can support two domains, but each domain has access to different PCIe slots and storage. (This approach will be explained later when describing the Quad-XSB mode setting for the system board.) The PCIe to PCI-X bridge in the IOU is used to access the two built-in gigabit Ethernet ports and the internal boot drives. If the entire

IOU resides in a single domain, Figure 2.1 shows that the PCIe cards should be installed from the bottom up to reduce any possible bottlenecks with the boot drives and built-in Ethernet.

Because the M5000 can support two IOU trays, it is possible for the number of domains to grow to 4. Thus the first domain assigned to the second IOU is just like the first domain assigned to the first IOU—that is, filled with several interfaces and internal boot drives. The second domain on the second IOU is just like the second domain on the first IOU, which has only two PCIe slots.

The M8000/M9000 block diagram in Figure 2.2 shows similar components to that of the M4000/M5000. The board that contains the CPUs and memory is the CPU/memory unit (CMU). Because the system contains more than two CMU boards, crossbar board units (XBU) are used to provide point-to-point (board-to-board) private communications, depending on the domain configurations. This diagram also shows a slightly different pathway to the SC because of the ability to grow to 4, 8, or 16 system boards. The crossbar allows domain performance to scale as more boards are added to the domain. Domain performance is not affected by the behavior of other domains. The crossbar also provides for domain isolation in the event of faulty CMU or IOU boards. Only the domain with the faulty hardware is affected; the other domains continue to run normally.

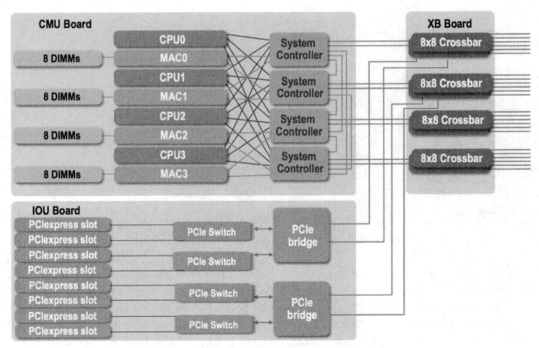

Figure 2.2 Block Diagram of M8000/M9000

Each IOU on the M8000/M9000 has four PCIe switches. This organization provides good performance, as each switch controls only two PCIe slots. It also means each IOU can support as many as four domains; this becomes possible when the board is placed in Quad-XSB mode, as discussed later in this chapter.

Figure 2.3 shows graphical representations of the crossbar interconnects for the M8000, M9000-32, and M9000-64. The crossbar board (XBU) provides a point-to-point communication between boards. It is programmed with a mask so that when the domain is powered on, the firmware identifies the other boards with which each XBU can communicate.

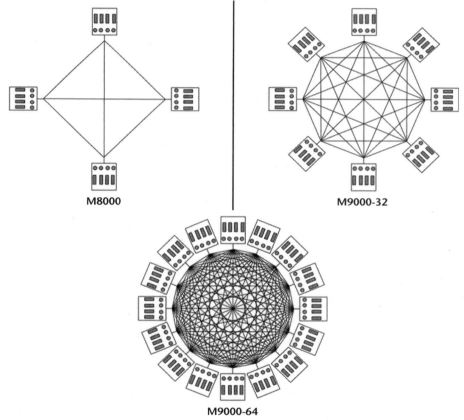

Figure 2.3 Crossbar Diagrams

Important elements when considering a virtualization technology are environment setup (e.g., disk layout, file system, networking), fault isolation, flexible resource management, and extensibility. One major benefit from this design is the ability to physically add or remove boards from a running system without shutting down the domain. Adding a board to the system does not affect other domains or their performance. The abilities to create multiple isolated operating systems, assign a subset of available hardware to each domain, and dynamically change domain resources are key reasons why Dynamic Domains constitute a unique virtualization technology for the data center.

2.2.1 Domain Configurations

Sun SPARC Enterprise M-Series servers have a unique partitioning feature that can divide one physical system board (PSB) into one logical board or four logical boards. The number of physical system boards in the Sun SPARC Enterprise M-Series servers varies from 1 to 16, depending on the model. The I/O varies with the server and can include PCI Express slots, PCI-X slots, and built-in I/O. Except for the M3000, M-Series systems can also extend the number of I/O slots by adding an external I/O expansion unit. This I/O box can add either PCIe or PCI-X slots. Table 2.1 provides the characteristics of each Sun SPARC Enterprise M-Series server.

Table 2.1 Characteristics of Sun SPARC Enterprise M-Series Servers

Server	Processors	Memory	Physical System Boards	I/O Boards	Dynamic Domains
Sun SPARC Enterprise M3000	1 SPARC64 VII	Up to 64 GB	1	4 internal non-hot plug PCIe slots	1
Sun SPARC Enterprise M4000	Up to 4 SPARC64 VI or SPARC64 VII	Up to 256 GB	1	1 I/O tray 4 PCIe and 1 PCI-X slots per tray	Up to 2
Sun SPARC Enterprise M5000	Up to 8 SPARC64 VI or SPARC64 VII	Up to 512 GB	2	Up to 2 I/O trays 4 PCIe and 1 PCI-X slots per tray	Up to 4
Sun SPARC Enterprise M8000	Up to 16 SPARC64 VI or SPARC64 VII	Up to 1TB	Up to 4	Up to 4 IOU 8 PCIe slots per IOU	Up to 16
Sun SPARC Enterprise M9000-32	Up to 32 SPARC64 VI or SPARC64 VII	Up to 2TB	Up to 8	Up to 8 IOU 8 PCIe slots per IOU	Up to 24
Sun SPARC Enterprise M9000-64	Up to 64 SPARC64 VI or SPARC64 VII	Up to 4TB	Up to 16	Up to 16 IOU 8 PCIe slots per IOU	Up to 24

Note: IOU = I/O unit.

To use a PSB in the system, the hardware resources on the board must be logically divided and reconfigured as eXtended System Boards (XSBs) which support two types: Uni-XSB and Quad-XSB:

- Uni-XSB
  - A PSB logically undivided and configured into one XSB.
  - The XSB contains all the resources on the board: 4 CPUs, 32 DIMMs, and all I/O.
  - Memory mirroring always supported in Uni mode.
- Quad-XSB
  - A PSB logically divided and configured into four XSBs.
  - Each of the four XSBs contains one-fourth of the total board resources: 1 CPU, 8 DIMMs, and 2 PCIe slots. On M4000/M5000 servers, only two XSBs have I/O.
  - Memory mirroring in quad mode is supported on only the M4000 and M5000 systems.

A domain consists of one or more XSBs. Each domain runs its own copy of Oracle Solaris and must have a minimum of one CPU, eight DIMMs, and I/O. The number of domains allowed depends on the server model (refer to Table 2.1). The default is 1 domain and the maximum number of domains is 24. The maximum number of XSBs in a domain is 16. Domains can be set up to include both Uni-XSBs and Quad-XSBs.

These XSBs can be combined freely to create domains. It is important to note that each of the CPU, memory, and I/O components are present in a single PSB and, therefore, in an XSB. When assigning an XSB to a domain, you must always add all three. It is not possible just to add I/O or just memory, although the domain can be instructed to ignore the memory, the I/O, or both in a specific XSB. For example, when adding an XSB (either Uni-XSB or Quad-XSB) to a domain, the user has the choice of using only the CPUs. Although the memory and I/O in an XSB can be ignored, it will still be assigned to the domain and cannot be assigned to other domains. The ability to ignore memory and I/O allows an XSB to be used for CPU load balancing, because it can be added, or removed, from a domain in the least amount of time.

Even if the domain is instructed to ignore memory in a specific XSB, the memory must still be present in that XSB. This requirement exists because the system needs memory to load the test program that the CPUs will run to verify the integrity of the XSB. For maximum flexibility, this can be done on a board-by-board basis.

Let's see some examples of PSBs and how they relate to an XSB.

2.2.1.1 Uni-XSB

Because Uni-XSBs constitute physical domaining with boundaries at the board level, a Uni-XSB provides the best fault isolation. If a board fails in a configuration that utilizes Uni-XSBs, only one domain is affected. Figures 2.4 and 2.5 show system boards in Uni-XSB mode for the M4000/5000 and M8000/M9000, respectively.

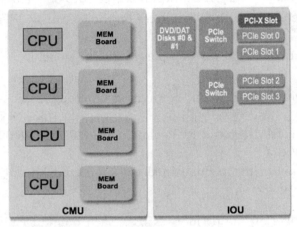

Figure 2.4 M4000/M5000 System Board PSB

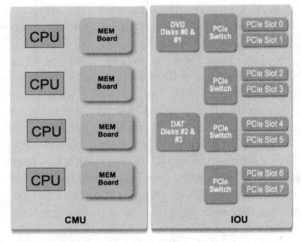

Figure 2.5 M8000/M9000 CMU/IOU PSB

Placing CMU/IOU boards in Uni-XSB mode offers the following advantages:

- Memory performance can be maximized to eight-way interleaving.

- Only one active CPU is required to allow use of all of the memory and I/O in the XSB.
- If service is required, only one domain is affected.

For environments requiring that no failure affect more than one domain, placing system boards in Uni-XSB is the preferred mode. In general, the number of domains possible is half of what would be possible for each system. For example, a CMU/IOU board set on the M8000/M9000 could support four domains, because there are four PCIe switches on the IOU. Ensuring redundancy across two PCIe switches reduces the maximum number of domains on a single CMU/IOU board set to two. Such a decision reflects a trade-off between domain isolation and domain density.

When a system board or CMU is placed in Uni-XSB mode, it is identified as XSBxx-0, where xx is the board slot position. On the M4000, there is only one system board, so it is identified as XSB00-0. On the M5000, there are two system boards, so they are identified as XSB00-0 and XSB01-0. On the M8000/M9000, the physical slot positions determine the XSB numbers: CMU#0 is identified as XSB00-0, CMU#1 is identified as XSB01-0, and so on.

2.2.1.2 Quad-XSB

Although a PSB configured into Quad-XSB mode can have all four XSBs in different domains, the SC chip continues to fully enforce data packet isolation between CPUs and memory on the same CMU. Figures 2.6 and 2.7 show a single PSB configured in Quad-XSB mode for the M4000/M5000 and M8000/M9000, respectively. Each Quad-XSB is completely independent from the other Quad-XSBs on the same PSB. This SC strictly enforces this isolation.

When a system board or CMU is placed in Quad-XSB mode, it is identified as XSBxx-0 to XSB00-3, where xx is the board slot position. On the M4000, there is only one system board, so it is identified as XSB00-0 to XSB00-3. On the M5000, there are two system boards, so they are identified as XSB00-0 to XSB00-3 and XSB01-0 to XSB01-3. On the M8000/M9000, the physical slot positions determine the XSB numbers: CMU#0 is identified as XSB00-0 to XSB00-3, CMU#1 is identified as XSB01-0 to XSB01-3, and so on.

For the XSB configurations on the M4000/M5000, only the first and second XSBs can be used to host domains, as only they have IO channels, or PCIe switches. The other two XSBs (third and fourth) can be added to only those domains that have at least one of the first two XSBs. The Quad-XSB configurations on the M8000/M9000 are more flexible because each Quad-XSB has a PCIe switch and, therefore, can be host to a domain. Quad 00-0 has the PCI-X slot, two PCIe slots, the DVD drive, and two internal disk drives. Quad 00-1 has just two PCIe slots.

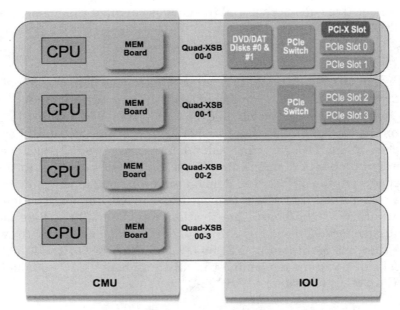

Figure 2.6 Quad-XSB on M4000/M5000

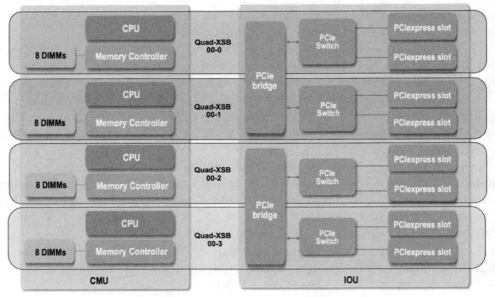

Figure 2.7 Quad-XSB on M8000/M9000

For the XSB configurations on the M8000/M9000, each quad has two PCIe slots, while quads 00-0 and 00-2 are also able to access two disk drives each.

Figure 2.8 shows the complete crossbar interconnect on an M9000-64 with only two domains configured; the specific domain pathways are highlighted. The darker, thicker paths indicate secure and isolated paths for use only by the specific domain. The orange path shows the board-to-board communication of Domain 1. Notice how this configuration utilizes both Uni-XSB and Quad-XSB configured system boards. The board that is configured in Quad-XSB mode has one XSB assigned to Domain 1 and two domains assigned to Domain 2; the fourth XSB is a floater XSB, free to be assigned to any domain. The SC ASICs on that system board ensure the complete isolation and security between each Quad-XSB.

Although Figure 2.8 shows boards spread out across the M9000-64 system, this was done to make it easier to see the unique data pathways on the crossbar interconnect. In practice, domains should be built out of adjacent boards to minimize memory access latency.

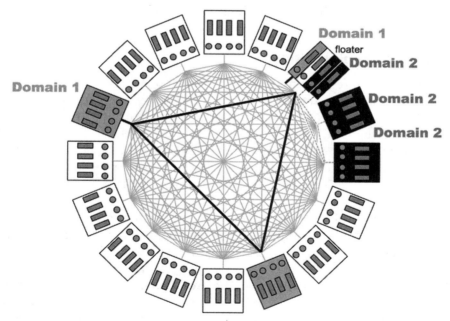

Figure 2.8 Multiple Domains on M9000-64

Table 2.2 shows the minimum and maximum latency for memory access on the M4000 to M9000.

Table 2.2 Memory Access Latency

	M4000	M5000	M8000	M9000-32	M9000-64
Minimum Latency	245 ns	312 ns	342 ns	387 ns	437 ns
Maximum Latency	245 ns	353 ns	402 ns	464 ns	532 ns
Ratio	1	1.13	1.18	1.20	1.22

Minimum latency reflects the amount of time necessary to access the nearest memory, and maximum latency reflects the amount of time necessary to access the farthest memory. As the system size grows, minimum latency increases due to the cache coherency requirements of the system bus. This factor explains the recommendation to choose adjacent boards for a domain.

In the event the system boards are placed in quad mode, the addressing from the XBU is handed off to the SC ASIC. The SC ASICs on each system board are responsible for the data pathway access, and the SC further restricts the data pathways. This constraint applies to other XSBs on the same board, as well as addressing from other XSBs on other boards, with data passed via the XBU.

2.2.2 Domain Combinations

Dynamic Domains offer flexible configuration and assignment of resources. A key requirement of any virtualization solution is the ability to assign the correct resources where they are needed. In the previous examples, I/O was always shown alongside the CPU/memory board. While the IOU will always require the corresponding CMU board, the presence of a CMU board does not require the IOU board. Thus it possible to build CPU-heavy and memory-heavy domains, especially true when specifying CMU boards as floaters, either in Uni-XSB mode or in Quad-XSB mode.

The remainder of this section considers several combinations of system board XSB settings of the M4000 and M5000 and possible domain configurations.

Figure 2.9, top left, is the simple case: The system board is in Uni-XSB mode and supports a single domain. As mentioned earlier, the M4000/M5000 system board can support two and four domains, respectively, and the top right and bottom left diagrams in Figure 2.9 show this in different ways. Although both diagrams depict the system board in Quad-XSB mode, each quad is assigned differently. The diagram on the top right shows XSB00-0 as Domain 1 and XSB00-1 as Domain 2; XSB00-3 and XSB00-4 are not assigned, but rather are floater XSB units. The diagram on the bottom left, in contrast, shows all four quads in use: XSB00-0 and XSB00-3 are in Domain 1 and XSB00-1 and XSB00-2 are in Domain 2. The bottom right diagram shows the possibility of no IOU installed, yet the CPU and memory boards are installed. This setup is possible on the M5000 because it has two system boards available to be populated, and the second system can be used without an IOU tray present.

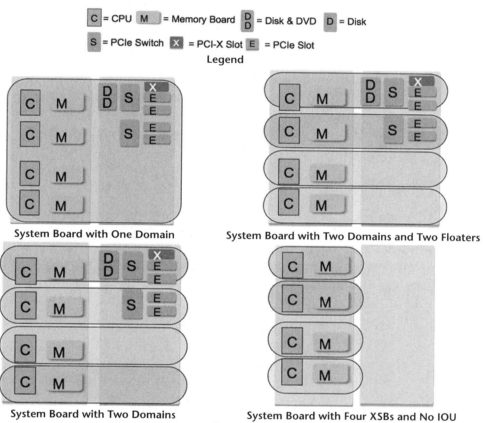

Figure 2.9 System Boards

The lack of an I/O controller for Quads 00-2 and 00-3 limits those quads to use for domain expansion only. This is not the case for the M8000 and M9000, however. The system board design for these high-end servers provides the most flexibility in resource assignment. Because 4 I/O controllers are available on each system board, each system board on the M8000/M9000 can support up to 4 domains, with maximum domain counts of 16 domains on the M8000 and 24 domains on the M9000.

Consider the several system board configurations for the M8000/M9000. Figure 2.10, top left, is the simple case where the system board is in Uni-XSB mode and supports a single domain. Figure 2.10, top right, shows a four-domain configuration on a single system board. Each Quad-XSB is totally independent of the others. Figure 2.10, middle left, shows a two-domain configuration, with Domain 1 owning three of the Quad-XSBs. It just as easily could be configured with Domain 1 and Domain 2 each having two quads. The middle right and bottom diagrams in Figure 2.10 each show a PSB with no IOU present. The XSBs that are configured can only be added to other existing domains.

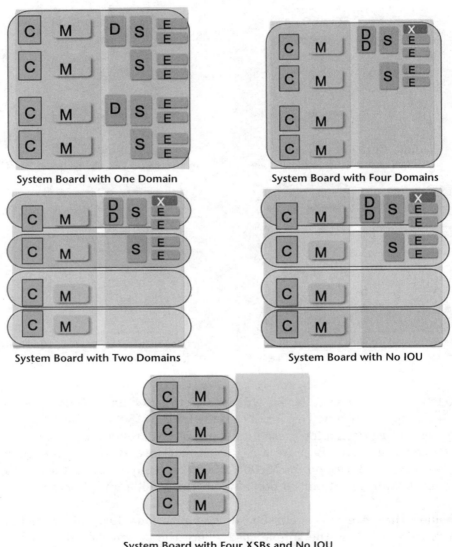

System Board with One Domain   System Board with Four Domains

System Board with Two Domains   System Board with No IOU

System Board with Four XSBs and No IOU

Figure 2.10 System Boards

It should be clear now that the M-Series offers highly configurable systems, allowing the user to configure domains in many different ways.

2.2.3 Domain Availability

Given that many consolidation efforts use virtualization tools to aid in the reduction of server sprawl, the uptime of the systems and of the individual guest environments is critical. Many aspects of the M-Series contribute to domain availability and uptime. While elements such as processor instruction retry, L1 and L2 cache dynamic degradation, memory Extended-ECC, and partial ASIC failure recovery automatically benefit all domains, some features are configurable by the administrator to improve availability:

- **Memory Mirroring.** The M-Series implements true memory mirroring, which means that half of the memory on a system board is visible to the domain. This happens because the Memory Access Controller (MAC) will write and read from two memory locations at the same time. The M4000/M5000 mirrors memory in a different way than on the M8000/M9000. Figure 2.11 shows how memory is mirrored on the M4000/M5000—namely, it is mirrored between the banks that a single MAC manages. For the M4000 and M5000, memory can be mirrored regardless of the mode of the system board (Uni-XSB or Quad-XSB). There is no trade-off between memory availability and domain granularity.

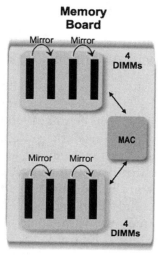

Figure 2.11 Memory Mirroring on M4000/M5000

Figure 2.12 shows how memory is mirrored on the M8000 and M9000. This approach is very different from that taken by the M4000/M5000. Memory is mirrored across adjacent MACs on the same system board, which means memory mirroring is possible only when the system board is configured in Uni-XSB mode. While this will be the most common mode on these higher-end systems, it does require a trade-off between memory availability and domain granularity.

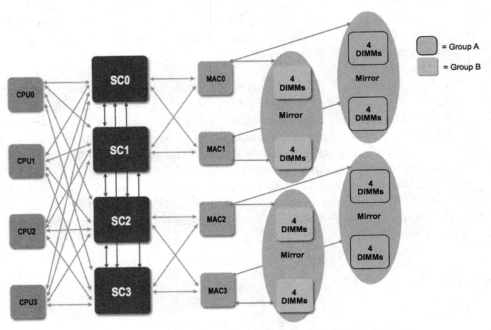

Figure 2.12 Memory Mirroring on M8000/M9000

- **Domain Configuration.** The choices for different ways to create domains are more pronounced on the M8000 and M9000. Improving availability can be achieved in different ways. Consider a configuration of two domains using just two CMU/IOU boards. The model shown at the top of Figure 2.13 shows Domain 1 completely on XSB01 and Domain 2 completely on XSB02. In this model, a failure on a system board affects only a single domain. Likewise, repair will affect only a single domain. If the MAC has a complete failure, it is possible that the domain would be down until repair. Now consider the model shown at the bottom of Figure 2.13. Both domains have the same amount of resources as before, but in a different configuration—namely, the domains are striped across the two boards. Now if the MAC fails on a board, both domains go down, but both will come back up without the XSB that contains the broken MAC. Business uptime requirements will dictate which configuration makes the most sense.

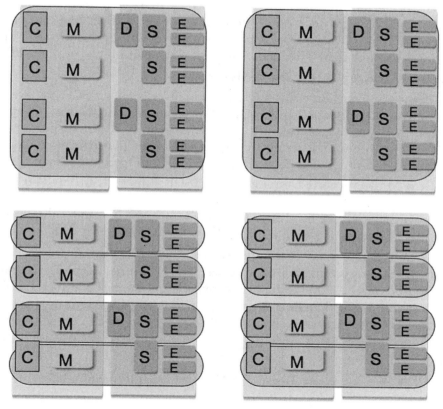

Figure 2.13 Two Domains on Separate PSBs (top); Two Domains Striped Across PSBs (bottom)

2.3 Managing Domains

As mentioned earlier, domains are managed several ways:

- **CLI**
    - **Serial.** Every XSCF is equipped with a dedicated serial port. This port is considered the primary console for the XSCF, and every M-Series server

installation should have a terminal server connected to the serial port. While the serial port on both primary and redundant XSCF is active on the M8000/M9000, only the active XSCF has full platform management capability.

- **Ethernet.** Ethernet communication can be done via Telnet or SSH, but the preferred method is SSH. Because both access protocols are disabled by default, only one should be enabled. Every XSCF has two Ethernet ports, allowing the XSCF to be accessed from different subnets. Full platform management is available only via Ethernet on the primary XSCF.

- **Graphical User Interface (GUI)**

  - **Browser User Interface (BUI).** If enabled, every XSCF has a small secure HTTP server, allowing the M-Series platform to be managed through a browser, such as Firefox, Internet Explorer, or Safari. Aside from a few CLI-only commands, almost every aspect of the platform can be managed through the BUI. This is the preferred method for remote management.

  - **Sun Management Center.** Every XSCF runs the Sun MC 4.0 platform agent. This agent requires an active Sun MC 4.0 server. The Sun MC interface can either be a Java GUI or be accessed through a browser. This interface gives access to most of the same capabilities as the direct BUI.

  - **Oracle Enterprise Manager Ops Center.** Ops Center provides domain creation and configuration, as well as Dynamic Reconfiguration. Ops Center has full Oracle Solaris provisioning support for installation and patching in all domains. A separate add-on package can be used to connect the messages and error report from Ops Center to Oracle Enterprise Manager.

- **SNMP**

  - All M-Series servers support SNMP for basic platform monitoring.

2.3.1 Building Domains Examples

The CLI interface on the XSCF is used in all of the following examples. The first step is determining which resources are available.

```
XSCF> showhardconf -u
SPARC Enterprise M9000; Memory_Size:576 GB;

    +-------------------------------------+------------+
    |                 FRU                 |  Quantity  |
    +-------------------------------------+------------+
    | CMU                                 |     10     |
    |     Type:A;                         |    ( 8)    |
```

```
|         Type:B;                    |  (  2)  |
|         CPUM                       |    40   |
|             Freq:2.280 GHz;        |  ( 16)  |
|             Freq:2.880 GHz;        |  (  8)  |
|             Freq:2.520 GHz;        |  ( 16)  |
|         MEM                        |   224   |
|             Type:2A; Size:2 GB;    |  ( 32)  |
|             Type:2B; Size:2 GB;    |  (128)  |
|             Type:4B; Size:4 GB;    |  ( 64)  |
| IOU                                |    6    |
| IOBOX                              |    1    |
|     IOB                            |    1    |
|     PSU                            |    2    |
| XSCFU_B                            |    2    |
| XSCFU_C                            |    2    |
| XBU_B                              |   16    |
| CLKU_B                             |    4    |
| OPNL                               |    1    |
| PSU                                |   60    |
| FANBP_A                            |    2    |
| FANBP_B                            |    2    |
|     FAN_A                          |   32    |
| SWBP                               |    2    |
| MEDBP                              |    2    |
+-----------------------------------+---------+
```

The `showhardconf -u` command provides a brief description of the contents of this M9000-64. The relevant domain information is outlined here:

- CPUs
  - 16 of the 2.28 GHz CPUs means 4 CMU boards with 4 CPUs each at this clock rate.
  - 8 of the 2.88 GHz CPUs means 2 CMU boards with 4 CPUs each at this clock rate.
  - 16 of the 2.52 GHz CPUs means 4 CMU boards with 4 CPUs each at this clock rate.
  - Total of 10 CMU boards: 8 are type A, or the original CMU boards, and 2 are type B, with the improved MAC ASIC.
- Memory
  - 8 CMU boards have 32×2 GB DIMMs installed on each.
  - 2 CMU boards have 32×4 GB DIMMs installed on each.
  - Memory type is also shown. There are 8 types possible:

- Type 1A = 1 GB / rank1
- Type 1B = 1 GB / rank2
- Type 2A = 2 GB / rank1
- Type 2B = 2 GB / rank2
- Type 4A = 4 GB / rank1
- Type 4B = 4 GB / rank2
- Type 8A = 8 GB / rank1
- Type 8B = 8 GB / rank2
- I/O
  - There are only 6 IOU boards; thus 2 CMU boards have no associated IO availability.

The output is too long to list here, but running just the command showhardconf (no -u option) will give a detailed list of each CMU and IOU board. Here is a summary of what is on each board:

- CMU#0: 4 × 2.28 GHz CPUs and 32 × 2 GB of memory
  IOU#0: Base I/O card in slots 0 and 4, Fiber Channel (FC) card in slot 1
- CMU#1: 4 × 2.28 GHz CPUs and 32 × 2 GB of memory
  IOU#1: Base I/O card in slots 0 and 4
- CMU#6: 4 × 2.88 GHz CPUs and 16 × 2 GB of memory
- CMU#7: 4 × 2.88 GHz CPUs and 16 × 2 GB of memory
- CMU#8: 4 × 2.28 GHz CPUs and 32 × 2 GB of memory
  IOU#0: Base I/O card in slots 0 and 4
- CMU#10: 4 × 2.28 GHz CPUs and 32 × 2 GB of memory
- CMU#12: 4 × 2.52 GHz CPUs and 16 × 4 GB of memory
  IOU#0: Base I/O card in slots 0 and 4, uplink card to IO expansion box in slot 5, and Quad Gigabit Ethernet (QGbE) in slot 7
- CMU#13: 4 × 2.52 GHz CPUs and 16 × 4 GB of memory
  IOU#0: no cards
- CMU#14: 4 × 2.52 GHz CPUs and 16 × 4 GB of memory
- CMU#15: 4 × 2.52 GHz CPUs and 16 × 4 GB of memory
  IOU#0: Base I/O card in slot 0, network card in slot 1

To see how these are assigned to domains, use the showboards command:

```
XSCF> showboards -a
XSB   DID(LSB)  Assignment  Pwr  Conn Conf Test     Fault

----  --------  ----------  ----  ---- ---- -------  --------
00-0  00(00)    Assigned    y     y    y    Passed   Normal
00-1  00(01)    Assigned    y     y    y    Passed   Normal
00-2  00(03)    Assigned    y     y    y    Passed   Normal
00-3  00(04)    Assigned    y     y    y    Passed   Normal
01-0  10(00)    Assigned    y     y    y    Passed   Normal
06-0  14(02)    Assigned    y     y    y    Passed   Normal
07-0  14(03)    Assigned    y     y    y    Passed   Normal
08-0  08(00)    Assigned    y     y    n    Passed   Normal
10-0  SP        Available   n     n    n    Unknown  Normal
12-0  SP        Available   n     n    n    Unknown  Normal
13-0  SP        Available   n     n    n    Unknown  Normal
14-0  SP        Available   n     n    n    Unknown  Normal
15-0  SP        Available   n     n    n    Unknown  Normal
```

CMU/IOU board 0 has been placed in Quad-XSB mode, while CMU/IOU boards 6, 7, 8, 10, and 12 are in Uni-XSB mode. The DID (Domain ID) column shows the assignment of XSBs to domains. All four quads of CMU#0 are in Domain 0. Domains 8 and 10 have just one CMU/IOU board set, while Domain 14 has two CMU/IOU board sets.

Let's create the first domain. It will be Domain 2 and will contain a single board. Because CMU#10 has no corresponding IOU, CMU#12 will be used. In Uni-XSB mode, the board will be identified as XSB12-0. Domain 2 will use the internal disks in slots 0 and 1, and Solaris 10 10/09 (Update 8) has been loaded on the disks. This will require a base I/O card to be installed in PCIe slot#0 of IOU#12. This XSB will occupy the first board position in the domain, or LSB00. We could have chosen positions 0 to 15, or LSB00 to LSB15. Because this is a single-board domain, we use LSB00.

```
XSCF> setupfru -m y -x 1 sb 12
XSCF> setdcl -d 2 -s 00=12-0
XSCF> addboard -y -c assign -d 2 12-0
XSB#12-0 will be assigned into DomainID 2. Continue?[y|n] :y
XSCF> poweron -y -d 2
```

Each command is described below.

```
setupfru -m y -x 1 sb 12
```

CMU#12 (sb 12) has been set to Uni-XSB (the -x -1 option) and memory mirroring has been enabled (the -m y option). Because CMU#12 has 64 GB of memory, Solaris will see only 32 GB available.

```
setdcl -d 2 -s 00=12-0
```

XSB12-0 has been given LSB#0 in Domain 2. The LSB number is the board position order in the domain.

```
addboard -y -c assign -d 2 12-0
```

XSB12-0 has been assigned to Domain 2.

```
poweron -y -d 2
```

Domain 2 is now powering up.

If we later determine that Domain 2 requires more processing resources, another XSB must be added to the domain. Only a single CPU is required, so one of the available boards must be placed in Quad-XSB mode. CMU#10 will be used. To allow the user to create another domain with the other unassigned XSBs from CMU#10, XSB10-1 will be assigned to Domain 2.

```
XSCF> setupfru -x 4 sb 10
XSCF> setdcl -d 2 -s 15=10-1
XSCF> setdcl -d 2 -s no-mem=true 15
XSCF> addboard -y -c configure -d 2 10-1
XSB#10-1 will be configured into DomainID 2. Continue?[y|n] :y
Initial diagnosis started. [1800sec]
    0.....30.....60.....90.....120.....150.....180.....210.....240.....270
.....300.....end
Initial diagnosis has completed.
Start configuring XSB to domain.
Configured XSB to domain.
```

```
XSCF> showboards -v -d 2
XSB  R DID(LSB) Assignment  Pwr  Conn Conf Test    Fault     COD
---- - -------- ----------- ---- ---- ---- ------- --------  ----
12-0  02(00)    Assigned    y    y    y    Passed  Normal    n
10-1  02(15)    Assigned    y    y    y    Passed  Normal    n
XSCF> showdcl -v -d 2
DID  LSB  XSB   Status    No-Mem  No-IO  Float   Cfg-policy
02              Running                          FRU
     00   12-0            False   False  False
     01   -
     02   -
     03   -
     04   -
     05   -
     06   -
```

```
07    -
08    -
09    -
10    -
11    -
12    -
13    -
14    -
15    01-1          True      False      False
```

Each command is described below.

```
setupfru -x 4 sb 10
```

CMU#10 (`sb 10`) has been set to Quad-XSB (`-x -4`).

```
setdcl -d 2 -s 15=10-1
```

XSB10-1 has been given LSB#15 in Domain 2. The LSB number is the board position order in the domain. Because this XSB will most likely be added and removed several times to better balance the load of other domains, XSB10-1 is given the LSB#15 position. This makes it less likely that Solaris kernel pages will be mapped to this XSB.

```
setdcl -d 2 -s no-mem=true 15
```

To allow for faster removal of this XSB from a running domain, the memory on XSB10-1 (16 GB) is not made available to the domain. This attribute applies to any XSB that is assigned the LSB#15 position in Domain 2. In this example, it applies to XSB10-1.

```
addboard -y -c configure -d 2 10-1
```

Because the domain is already running, we must configure the board in, not just assign it. Diagnostics are run first to ensure that the processors and memory work correctly before they are added to the domain. Even though the `no-mem` flag was set to true, memory must still be tested.

```
showboards -v -d 2
```

This command helps verify that the XSB10-1 has, indeed, been added to Domain 2 and is active.

```
showdcl -v -d 2
```

Because XSB10-1 is in Domain 2, this command verifies whether memory is available.

A different configuration becomes possible with the addition of a new CMU board to an active domain without shutting the domain down just to add the new resources. To make this addition, first select the empty CMU slot for the new board. CMU slot 3 is empty, so we will use it.

```
XSCF> addfru
------------------------------------------------------------------
Maintenance/Addition Menu
Please select a type of FRU to be added.

  1. CMU/IOU    (CPU Memory Board Unit/IO Unit)
  2. FAN        (Fan Unit)
  3. PSU        (Power Supply Unit)
------------------------------------------------------------------
Select [1-3|c:cancel] :1


------------------------------------------------------------------
Maintenance/Addition Menu
Please select whether to add a CMU only, an IOU only,
or both a CMU and an IOU.

  1. Add CMU only.
  2. Add IOU only.
  3. Add both CMU and IOU.
------------------------------------------------------------------
Select [1-3|b:back] :1


------------------------------------------------------------------
Maintenance/Addition Menu
Please select a CMU to be added.


                    DomainID
No. FRU            XSB#0 XSB#1 XSB#2 XSB#3 Power Status
--- -------------- --------------------------- ----- ---------------
  1. CMU#0             0     0     0     0  On    Normal
  2. CMU#1            10    10    10    10  Off   Normal
  3. CMU#2            --    --    --    --  ---   Not installed
  4. CMU#3            --    --    --    --  ---   Not installed
  5. CMU#4            --    --    --    --  ---   Not installed
  6. CMU#5            --    --    --    --  ---   Not installed
  7. CMU#6            14    14    14    14  On    Normal
  8. CMU#7            14    14    14    14  On    Normal
  9. CMU#8             8     8     8     8  On    Normal
 10. CMU#9             0     0     0     0  Off   Normal
 11. CMU#10            0     0     0     0  Off   Normal
 12. CMU#11           --    --    --    --  ---   Not installed
 13. CMU#12            0     0     0     0  Off   Normal
 14. CMU#13            0     0     0     0  Off   Normal
 15. CMU#14            0     0     0     0  Off   Normal
 16. CMU#15            0     0     0     0  Off   Normal
------------------------------------------------------------------
```

```
Select [1-4|b:back] :4


You are about to add CMU#3.
Do you want to continue?[a:add|c:cancel] :a


Please install CMU#3.
After installation has been completed, please select[f:finish] :f


-------------------------------------------------------------------
Maintenance/Addition Menu
Please select whether CMU#3 is an Uni- or Quad-XSB and select
whether Memory Mirroring is enabled.

No. Uni/Quad-XSB   Mirror
--- -------------- ----------
 1. Uni-XSB         no
 2. Uni-XSB         yes
 3. Quad-XSB        no
-------------------------------------------------------------------
Select [1-3] :1


-------------------------------------------------------------------
Maintenance/Addition Menu
Uni- or Quad-XSB and Memory Mirror mode of CMU#3.

Uni/Quad-XSB   Mirror
-------------- ----------
Uni-XSB         no
-------------------------------------------------------------------
Is this correct?[y:yes|n:no] :y


To ensure correct operation, diagnostic tests should be run on
CMU#3.[d:diagnose|s:skip] :d


Diagnostic tests for CMU#3 have started.
[This operation may take up to 60 minute(s)]
(progress scale reported in seconds)
    0.....  30.....  60.....  90..... 120..... 150..... 180.....
210..... 240..... 270..... 300..... 330....done


-------------------------------------------------------------------
Maintenance/Addition Menu
Status of the added FRU.


-------------------------------------------------------------------
The addition of CMU#3 has completed normally.[f:finish] :f
XSCF> showboards -a
XSB DID(LSB) Assignment  Pwr  Conn Conf Test     Fault
```

continues

```
---- -------- ----------- ---- ---- ---- ------- --------
00-0 00(00)   Assigned     y    y    y    Passed  Normal
00-1 00(01)   Assigned     y    y    y    Passed  Normal
00-2 00(03)   Assigned     y    y    y    Passed  Normal
00-3 00(04)   Assigned     y    y    y    Passed  Normal
01-0 10(00)   Assigned     y    y    y    Passed  Normal
03-0 SP       Available    n    n    n    Unknown Normal
06-0 14(02)   Assigned     y    y    y    Passed  Normal
07-0 14(03)   Assigned     y    y    y    Passed  Normal
08-0 08(00)   Assigned     y    y    n    Passed  Normal
10-0 SP       Available    n    n    n    Unknown Normal
12-0 SP       Available    n    n    n    Unknown Normal
13-0 SP       Available    n    n    n    Unknown Normal
14-0 SP       Available    n    n    n    Unknown Normal
15-0 SP       Available    n    n    n    Unknown Normal
```

The addfru command has successfully added the CMU in slot 3 to the system. Now the same procedure that was used to add XSB01-1 to Domain 2 can be used to add XSB03-0 to Domain 2.

```
XSCF> setdcl -d 2 -s 01=03-0
XSCF> setdcl -d 2 -s no-mem=false 01
XSCF> addboard -y -c configure -d 2 03-0
XSB#03-0 will be configured into DomainID 2. Continue?[y|n] :y
Initial diagnosis started. [1800sec]
    0.....30.....60.....90.....120.....150.....180.....210.....240.....270.....300
.....end
Initial diagnosis has completed.
Start configuring XSB to domain.
Configured XSB to domain.
XSCF> showboards -v -d 2
XSB  R DID(LSB) Assignment  Pwr  Conn Conf Test    Fault    COD
---- - -------- ----------- ---- ---- ---- ------- -------- ----
12-0   02(00)   Assigned     y    y    y    Passed  Normal   n
03-0   02(01)   Assigned     y    y    y    Passed  Normal   n
10-1   02(15)   Assigned     y    y    y    Passed  Normal   n
XSCF> showdcl -v -d 2
DID  LSB  XSB   Status    No-Mem  No-IO   Float   Cfg-policy
02               Running                           FRU
     00   12-0            False   False   False
     01   03-0            False   False   False
     02   -
     03   -
     04   -
     05   -
     06   -
     07   -
     08   -
     09   -
```

```
        10      -
        11      -
        12      -
        13      -
        14      -
        15      01-1            True      False     False
```

Now combinations of CMU boards in Uni-XSB or Quad-XSB mode can be combined to form domains with different processing capacity. Dynamic Domains also allow for those domains to have more resources added to them without requiring a system shutdown or domain shutdown first. Because the new CMU just added has the newest processors available, the domain is able to stay current with the latest technology without penalty.

2.3.2 View from the Domain

Once the domain is running, the domain administrator needs the ability to view the resources available from the domain's perspective. There are many reasons why domain resources need to be identifiable from within the domain. For example, they enable use of application scripts that perform different operations depending on the number of CPUs, amount of memory, or type of network interface control (NIC) cards available. Moreover, inventory control might need to be performed within the domain, due to different business units in the company owning different domain hardware.

The Solaris `prtdiag` command shows the list of resources in a specific domain.

```
-bash-3.00# prtdiag
System Configuration:   Sun Microsystems   sun4u Sun SPARC Enterprise M8000 Server
System clock frequency: 960 MHz
Memory size: 196608 Megabytes


================================= CPUs =================================

        CPU                 CPU                       Run   L2$  CPU   CPU
LSB Chip                     ID                       MHz    MB  Impl  Mask
--- ----    -------------------------------------     ----  ---  ----  ----
 00   0       0,   1,   2,   3                        2280  5.0    6   146
 00   1       8,   9,  10,  11                        2280  5.0    6   146
 00   2      16,  17,  18,  19                        2280  5.0    6   146
 00   3      24,  25,  26,  27                        2280  5.0    6   146
 15   0     480, 481, 482, 483, 484, 485, 486, 487    2880  6.0    7   160
 15   1     488, 489, 490, 491, 492, 493, 494, 495    2880  6.0    7   160
```

continues

```
15   2   496, 497, 498, 499, 500, 501, 502, 503   2880  6.0      7  160
15   3   504, 505, 506, 507, 508, 509, 510, 511   2880  6.0      7  160


=========================== Memory Configuration =====================

        Memory  Available         Memory   DIMM   # of  Mirror  Interleave
LSB  Group  Size               Status   Size   DIMMs Mode    Factor
---  ------ --------------     -------  ------ ----- ------- ----------
 00   A       32768MB           okay     2048MB    16 no      8-way
 00   B       32768MB           okay     2048MB    16 no      8-way
 15   A       65536MB           okay     4096MB    16 no      8-way
 15   B       65536MB           okay     4096MB    16 no      8-way


========================= IO Cards =========================

LSB      Name            Model
---      ------------    ------------
 00      scsi            LSI,1064
 00      network         N/A
 00      network         N/A
 00      scsi            LSI,1064
 00      network         N/A
 00      network         N/A


=================== Hardware Revisions =====================

System PROM revisions:
----------------------

OBP 4.24.11 2009/04/21 14:53


=================== Environmental Status ===================

Mode switch is in UNLOCK mode
```

This output shows that the domain has two XSBs assigned: LSB#00 and LSB#15. LSB#00 is a CMU in Uni-XSB mode, because there are 4 CPU chips (0 to 3) and 32 DIMMs (16 in Memory Group A and 16 in Memory Group B). There is also a corresponding IOU in LSB#00 that has 2 base I/O cards (LSI-1064), each of which provides 2 network interfaces. LSB#15 is also a CMU in Uni-XSB mode because it has the same number of CPU and DIMM counts as LSB#00. However, LSB#15 has no IOU associated with the CMU.

The LSBs provide CPUs with different speeds and different core counts. This is a key differentiator of the Sun SPARC Enterprise M-Series compared to other major UNIX-based platforms. Each CPU on LSB#00 provides four threads, where each thread is represented by a unique CPU ID. These CPUs are called *virtual CPUs* (or vCPUs) because they are not real CPUs, but rather threads in a core on a real CPU. These vCPUs are found on SPARC64 VI, which is a dual-core processor with two threads per core.

Table 2.3 shows how the vCPU identifiers map to the physical cores and processors on LSB#00. The vCPU IDs jump by a count of 4 when the count continues on to the next CPU because Oracle Solaris assumes each core should have 8 CPU IDs and leaves the empty CPU IDs unused when a SPARC64 VI processor is used in the domain.

Table 2.3 LSB#00 vCPU Mappings to Physical Cores and Processors

	Core 0		Core 1	
CPU#0	vCPU 0	vCPU 1	vCPU 2	vCPU 3
CPU#1	vCPU 8	vCPU 9	vCPU 10	vCPU 11
CPU#2	vCPU 16	vCPU 17	vCPU 18	vCPU 19
CPU#3	vCPU 24	vCPU 25	vCPU 26	vCPU 27

LSB#15 shows the result when a SPARC64 VII processor is used in a domain. Because the SPARC64 VII is a quad-core processor with two threads per core, there are a total of eight threads per CPU, or eight vCPUs. Table 2.4 shows the mapping of vCPUs to the physical cores and processors on LSB15:

Table 2.4 LSB#15 vCPU Mappings to Physical Cores and Processors

	Core 0		Core 1		Core 2		Core 3	
CPU#0	vCPU 480	vCPU 481	vCPU 482	vCPU 483	vCPU 484	vCPU 485	vCPU 486	vCPU 487
CPU#1	vCPU 488	vCPU 489	vCPU 490	vCPU 491	vCPU 492	vCPU 493	vCPU 494	vCPU 495
CPU#2	vCPU 496	vCPU 497	vCPU 498	vCPU 499	vCPU 500	vCPU 501	vCPU 502	vCPU 503
CPU#3	vCPU 504	vCPU 505	vCPU 506	vCPU 507	vCPU 508	vCPU 509	vCPU 510	vCPU 511

Notice that the CPU IDs of LSB#15 start at 480—because room is needed for the IDs of CPUs added later using a lower LSB number. The starting CPU ID of any LSB is always $32 \times$ LSB#. Thus the CPU IDs of LSB#00 start at $32 \times 0 = 0$. The CPU IDs of LSB15 start at $32 \times 15 = 480$. If an LSB#08 were added, the CPU IDs of that board would start at $32 \times 8 = 256$.

This system is very important to understand when using Solaris Containers inside a Dynamic Domain. Assigning vCPUs to a Container, or zone, along core boundaries provides certain benefits. Another goal may be to create a Container that uses only the fastest CPUs available, leaving the slower CPUs for general use in the domain. This approach will be covered in more detail in Chapter 6, "Oracle Solaris Containers."

The command output provided earlier also shows that the domain has 19.7 GB of memory installed, but with different densities on the two LSB boards. LSB#00 is using 32 DIMMs at 2 GB each, whereas LSB#15 is using 32 DIMMs at 4 GB each. Each DIMM is running at 480 MHz, or half the speed of the system clock frequency of 960 MHz. The memory is using the full eight-way interleaving possible on each LSB, because each LSB is configured in Uni-XSB mode. If the LSB boards were in Quad-XSB mode, the memory would use only two-way interleaving.

2.3.2.1 Dynamic Reconfiguration of PCIe Cards

DR can be performed on the individual PCIe cards only from within the domain. The PCIe cards cannot be removed or added via a command on the XSCF. Cards are added or removed by using the Solaris command cfgadm.

```
-bash-3.00# cfgadm
AP_ID           Type        Receptacle    Occupant       Condition
...
iou#0-pci#1     unknown     empty         unconfigured   unknown
iou#0-pci#2     unknown     empty         unconfigured   unknown
iou#0-pci#3     etherne/hp  connected     configured     ok
iou#0-pci#4     fibre/hp    connected     configured     ok
```

The AP_ID comprises the IOU number (iou#0 or iou#1) and the PCI cassette slot number (pci#1, pci#2, pci#3, pci#4). To remove the Ethernet card in slot pci#3, the card must first be unconfigured and then disconnected.

```
-bash-3.00# cfgadm -c unconfigure iou#0-pci#3
-bash-3.00# cfgadm -c disconnect iou#0-pci#3
-bash-3.00# cfgadm
AP_ID           Type        Receptacle    Occupant       Condition
...
iou#0-pci#1     unknown     empty         unconfigured   unknown
iou#0-pci#2     unknown     empty         unconfigured   unknown
iou#0-pci#3     etherne/hp  disconnected  unconfigured   ok
iou#0-pci#4     fibre/hp    connected     configured     ok
```

Because the NIC card in slot 3 is disconnected and powered off, it can now be removed without shutting down the domain, or the system.

When a CMU must be moved from one domain to another, remember that the associated IOU—if one is installed—also moves with it. The administrator must disconnect all of the PCIe cards currently active in the source domain, using the `cfgadm` command on each card. If the XSB that represents the CMU/IOU to be moved has the attribute `no-io=true`, then it is not necessary to run the `cfgadm` command. If the PCIe card is active and has not been disconnected from the domain, the command to remove the source CMU/IOU will fail.

2.3.3 Fault Isolation

Domains are protected against software or hardware failures in other domains. Failures in hardware shared between domains cause failures only in those domains that share the hardware. When a domain encounters a fatal error, a *domainstop* operation occurs that cleanly and quickly shuts down only the domain with the error. Domainstop operates by shutting down the paths in and out of the system address controller and the system data interface ASICs. The shutdown is intended to prevent further corruption of data and to facilitate debugging by preventing the failure from being masked by continued operation.

When certain hardware errors occur in a Sun SPARC Enterprise M-Series server, the system controller performs specific diagnosis and domain recovery steps. The following automatic diagnosis engines identify and diagnose hardware errors that affect the availability of the system and its domains:

- **eXtended System Control Facility (XSCF) diagnosis engine:** Diagnoses hardware errors associated with domains operations.
- **Oracle Solaris operating system diagnosis engine:** Identifies nonfatal domain hardware errors and reports them to the system controller.
- **POST diagnosis engine:** Identifies any hardware test failures that occur when the power-on self-test runs.

In most situations, hardware failures that cause a domain crash are detected and eliminated from the domain configuration either by the power-on self-test (POST) or an OpenBoot PROM during the subsequent automatic recovery boot of the domain.

2.3.4 Dynamic Reconfiguration

Dynamic Reconfiguration (DR) allows resources to be dynamically reallocated or balanced between domains. Utilizing this technology enables a physical or logical restructuring of the hardware components of Sun SPARC Enterprise M-Series servers even as the system continues running and the applications remain available. This high degree of resource flexibility allows the domain or platform administrator to reconfigure the system easily so as to parcel out the resources to meet changing workload demands. Domain configurations can be optimized for workloads that are either compute intensive, I/O intensive, or both. DR can also be used to remove and replace failed or upgraded hardware components while the system is online. This flexible resource allocation technology is critical in ensuring a robust virtualization solution.

The DR functions of Sun SPARC Enterprise M-Series servers are performed on XSB units and managed through the XSCF. The XSCF security management restricts DR operations to administrators who have the proper access privileges. For example, on Sun SPARC Enterprise M8000 and M9000 servers, an IT operator can first use DR to delete a faulty system board and then use the system's hot-plug feature to physically remove it. After plugging in the repaired board or a replacement, DR can be used to add the board into the domain. In addition, combining the capabilities of DR with network and storage multipathing solutions can foster creation of redundant network or storage subsystems with automatic failover, load balancing, and dynamic reconfiguring capabilities.

Figure 2.14 provides an example of DR carried out on a system board for an M9000. In this figure, the floater XSB can be assigned to either Domain 1 or Domain 2. This XSB has 4 CPUs, 32 memory DIMMs, and an optional 8 PCIe

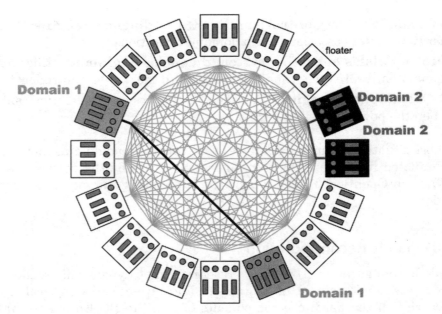

Figure 2.14 Two Domains on M9000-64

slots. When assigning the XSB to a domain, either all of the devices can be configured in to the domain, or only some of them. The floater XSB can be added to a domain while the domain is still running. Although the example shows a system board on an M9000, this same capability exists on the M4000 and M5000. This general form of DR is similar in functionality to the other virtualization technologies used on Oracle VM Server for SPARC (formerly known as Logical Domains) and Solaris Containers.

The ability to physically add or remove CPU/memory system boards while the system is powered up and domains are running is unique to the M8000 and M9000. This additional functionality, which is called *hot plug,* is important in providing improved system uptime and rolling upgrade capability. As potentially faulty components are taken offline by the Solaris Predictive Self-Healing functions in the Solaris Fault Management system, the XSCF (or service processor) can be used to remove the board with the faulty component and add the replacement board back in. This capability has other business benefits. As new processors are developed and released for the M-Series, the M8000 and M9000 can add these new processors in to existing domains. This facilitates rolling upgrades, thereby making a large contribution to the M-Series' high return on investment (ROI) value.

As mentioned earlier, DR of the individual PCIe cards can be performed only from within the domain that is using the PCIe card.

2.3.5 Extending Dynamic Domains

No one product fits all business requirements—and this statement certainly holds true for virtualization technologies. Hybrid virtualization solutions allow multiple technologies to be combined to maximize consolidation and system utilization. Because every domain on a Sun SPARC Enterprise M-Series server runs a separate instance of Oracle Solaris, the Containers features can be used in each domain. While the M-Series has the ability to increment domains by only a CPU and a small amount of memory and I/O, greater utilization can be achieved by using Containers in a domain. This approach allows users to combine the best of both virtualization technologies to meet specific business or technical requirements.

Containers are typically used on the M-Series in a domain that consists of several system boards. This large domain can then be partitioned further with OS virtualization. Certain factors must be taken into account regarding the configuration of system boards that the Containers will run on, however. One consideration is the mode of the system boards. If the boards are in Uni-XSB mode, memory will be accessed using eight-way memory interleaving. If the boards are in Quad-XSB mode, memory will be accessed using two-way interleaving. This configuration could affect the performance of the applications in the Containers. Of course, if a

Quad-XSB needs to be removed from an active Container, only 1 CPU, 8 DIMMs, and 2 PCIe slots will be removed from the Container. Chapter 6 provides details on using Containers as a form of OS virtualization.

2.4 Summary

Dynamic Domains implement hard partitioning with extreme isolation between virtual environments. They are available in mid-range and high-end SPARC systems and provide excellent reliability, availability, and serviceability characteristics. They are appropriate for the most demanding business-critical and mission-critical workloads as well as for consolidation of many smaller workloads.

3

Oracle VM Server for SPARC

Logical Domains (now Oracle VM Server for SPARC) is a virtualization technology that creates SPARC virtual machines, also called domains. This new style of hypervisor permits operation of virtual machines with less overhead than traditional designs by changing the way guests access physical CPU, memory, and I/O resources. It is ideal for consolidating multiple complete Oracle Solaris systems onto a modern powerful, low-cost, energy-efficient SPARC server, especially when the virtualized systems require the capability to have different kernel levels.

The Logical Domains technology is available on systems based on SPARC chip multithreading technology (CMT) processors. These include the Sun SPARC Enterprise T5x20/T5x40 servers, Sun Blade T6320/T6340 server modules, and Sun Fire T1000/T2000 systems. The chip technology is integral to Logical Domains because it leverages the large number of CPU threads available on these servers. At this writing, that number can be as many as 128 threads in a single-rack unit server and as many as 256 threads in a four-rack unit server. Logical Domains is available on all CMT processors without additional license or hardware cost.

3.1 Overview of Logical Domains Features

Logical Domains creates virtual machines, usually called *domains*. Each appears to have its own SPARC server. A domain has the following resources:

- CPUs
- RAM

- Network devices
- Disks
- Console
- OpenBoot environment
- Cryptographic accelerators (optional)

The next several sections describe properties of Logical Domains and explain how they are implemented.

3.1.1 Isolation

Each domain runs its own instance of Oracle Solaris 10 or OpenSolaris with its own accounts, passwords, and patch levels, just as if each had its own separate physical server. Different Solaris patch and update levels run at the same time on the same server without conflict. Some Linux distributions can also run in domains. Logical Domains support was added to the Linux source tree at the 2.6.23 level.

Domains are isolated from one another. Thus each domain is individually and independently started and stopped. As a consequence, a failure in one domain—even a kernel panic or CPU thread failure—has no effect on other domains, just as would be the case for Solaris running on multiple servers.

3.1.2 Compatibility

Oracle Solaris and applications in a domain are highly compatible with Solaris running on a physical server. Solaris has long had a binary compatibility guarantee; this guarantee has been extended to Logical Domains, making no distinction between running as a guest or on bare metal. Solaris functions essentially the same in a domain as on a nonvirtualized system.

3.1.3 Real and Virtual CPUs

One of the distinguishing features of Logical Domains compared to other hypervisors is the assignment of CPUs to individual domains. This approach has a dramatic benefit in terms of increasing simplicity and reducing the overhead commonly encountered with hypervisor systems.

Traditional hypervisors time-slice physical CPUs among multiple virtual machines in an effort to provide CPU resources. Time-slicing was necessary because the number of physical CPUs was relatively small compared to the desired number of virtual machines. The hypervisor also intercepted and emulated privileged instructions that would change the shared physical machine's state (such as interrupt masks, memory maps, and other parts of the system environment), thereby violating the integrity of separation between guests. This process is complex and creates CPU overhead. Context switches between virtual machines can require hundreds or even thousands of clock cycles. Each context switch to a different virtual machine requires purging cache and translation lookaside buffer (TLB) contents because identical virtual memory addresses refer to different physical locations. This scheme increases memory latency until the caches become filled with fresh content, only to be discarded when the next time slice occurs.

In contrast, Logical Domains is designed for and leverages the chip multithreading (CMT) UltraSPARC T1, T2, and T2 Plus processors. These processors provide many CPU threads, also called *strands*, on a single processor chip. Specifically, the UltraSPARC T1 processor provides 8 processor cores with 4 threads per core, for a total of 32 threads on a single processor. The UltraSPARC T2 and T2 Plus processors provide 8 cores with 8 threads per core, for a total of 64 threads per chip. From the Oracle Solaris perspective, each thread is a CPU. This arrangement creates systems that are rich in dispatchable CPUs, which can be allocated to domains for their exclusive use.

Logical Domains technology assigns each domain its own CPUs, which are used with native performance. This design eliminates the frequent context switches that traditional hypervisors must implement to run multiple guests on a CPU and to intercept privileged operations. Because each domain has dedicated hardware circuitry, a domain can change its state—for example, by enabling or disabling interrupts—without causing a trap and emulation. The assignment of strands to domains can save thousands of context switches per second, especially for workloads with high network or disk I/O activity. Context switching still occurs within a domain when Solaris dispatches different processes onto a CPU, but this is identical to the way Solaris runs on a non-virtualized server.

One mechanism that CMT systems use to enhance processing throughput is detection of a cache miss, followed by a hardware context switch. Modern CPUs use onboard memory called a *cache*—a very high-speed memory that can be accessed in just a few clock cycles. If the needed data is present in memory but is not in this CPU's cache, a *cache miss* occurs and the CPU must wait dozens or hundreds of clock cycles on any system architecture. In essence, the CPU affected by the cache miss stalls until the data is fetched from RAM to cache. On most systems, the CPU sits idle, not performing any useful work. On those systems, switching to a different process would require a software context switch that consumes hundreds or thousands of cycles.

In contrast, CMT processors avoid this idle waiting by switching execution to another CPU strand on the same core. This hardware context switch happens in a single clock cycle because each hardware strand has its own private hardware context. In this way, CMT processors use what is wasted (stall) time on other processors to continue doing useful work.

This feature is highly effective whether Logical Domains are in use or not. Nonetheless, a recommendation for Logical Domains is to reduce cache misses by allocating domains so they do not share per-core L1 caches. The simplest way to do so is to allocate domains with a multiple of the CPU threads per core—for example, in units of 8 threads on T2-based systems. This approach ensures that all domains have CPUs allocated on a core boundary and not shared with another domain. Actual savings depend on the system's workload, and may be of minor consideration when consolidating old, slow servers with low utilization.

3.2 Logical Domains Implementation

Logical Domains are implemented using a very small hypervisor that resides in firmware and keeps track of the assignment of logical CPUs, RAM locations, and I/O devices to each domain. It also provides logical channels for communication between domains and between domains and the hypervisor.

The Logical Domains hypervisor is intentionally kept as small as possible for simplicity and robustness. Many tasks traditionally performed within a hypervisor kernel (such as the management interface and performing I/O for guests) are offloaded to special-purpose domains, as described in the next section.

This scheme has several benefits. Notably, a small hypervisor is easier to develop, manage, and deliver as part of a firmware solution embedded in the platform, and its tight focus helps security and reliability. This design also adds redundancy: Shifting functions from a monolithic hypervisor to privileged domains insulates the system from a single point of failure. As a result, Logical Domains have a level of resiliency that is not available in traditional hypervisors of the VM/370, z/VM, or VMware ESX style. Also, this design makes it possible to leverage capabilities already available in Oracle Solaris, providing access to features for reliability, performance, scale, diagnostics, development tools, and a large API set. It has proven to be an extremely effective alternative to developing all these features from scratch.

3.2.1 Domain Roles

Domains are used for different roles, and may be used for Logical Domain infrastructure or applications. The *control domain* is an administrative control point that runs Solaris or OpenSolaris and the Logical Domain Manager services. It has a privileged interface to the hypervisor, and can create, configure, start, stop, and destroy other domains. *Service domains* provide virtualized disk and network devices for other domains. *I/O domains* have direct access to physical I/O devices and are typically used as service domains to provide access to these devices. The control domain also is an I/O domain and can be used as a service domain. Applications generally run in *guest domains,* which are non-I/O domains using virtual devices provided by service domains. The domain structure and the assignment of CPUs are shown in Figure 3.1.

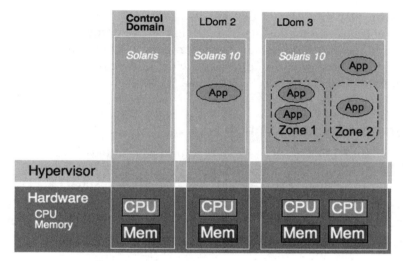

Figure 3.1 Control and Guest Domains

The definition of a domain includes its name, amount of RAM and number of CPUs, its I/O devices, and any optional hardware cryptographic accelerators. Domain definitions are made by using the command-line interface in the control domain, using the Oracle Enterprise Manager Ops Center product, or for the initial configuration, using the Logical Domains Configuration Assistant.

3.2.1.1 Domain Relationships

Each server has exactly one control domain, found on the instance of Solaris that was first installed on the system. It runs Logical Domain Manager services, which are accessed by a command-line interface provided by the ldm command. These Logical Domain Manager services include a "constraint manager" that decides how to assign physical resources to satisfy the specified requirements (the "constraints") of each domain.

There can be as many I/O domains as there are physical PCI buses on the system. An I/O domain is often used as a service domain to run virtual disk services and virtual network switch services that provide guest domain virtual I/O devices.

Finally, there can be as many guest domains as are needed for applications, subject to the limits associated with the installed capacity of the server. At the time of this writing, the maximum number of domains on a CMT system was 128, including control and service domains, even on servers with 256 threads such as the T5440. While it is possible to run applications in control or service domains, it is highly recommended, for stability reasons, to run applications only in guest domains. Applications that require optimal I/O performance can be run in an I/O domain to avoid virtual I/O overhead, but it is recommended that such an I/O domain not be used as a service domain.

A simple configuration consists of a single control domain also acting as a service domain, and some number of guest domains. A more complex configuration could use redundant service domains to provide failover in case of a domain failure or loss of a path to an I/O device.

3.2.2 Dynamic Reconfiguration

CPUs and virtual I/O devices can be dynamically added to or removed from a Logical Domain without requiring a reboot. An Oracle Solaris instance running in a guest domain can immediately make use of a dynamically added CPU for additional capacity and can also handle the removal of all but one of its CPUs. Virtual disk and network resources can also be nondisruptively added to or removed from a domain, and a guest domain can make use of a newly added virtual disk or network device without a reboot.

3.2.3 Virtual I/O

Logical Domains technology abstracts underlying I/O resources to virtual I/O. It is not always possible to give each domain direct access to a bus, an I/O memory mapping unit (IOMMU), or devices, so Logical Domains provides a virtual I/O (VIO) infrastructure to provide access to these resources.

Virtual network and disk I/O is provided to Logical Domains by service domains. A service domain runs Solaris and usually has direct connections to a PCI bus connected to physical network and disk devices. In that configuration, it is also an I/O domain. Likewise, the control domain is typically configured as a service domain. It is also an I/O domain, because it requires access to I/O buses and devices to boot up.

The virtual I/O framework allows service domains to export virtual network and disk devices to other domains. Guest domains use these devices exactly as if they were dedicated physical resources. Guest domains perform virtual I/O to virtual devices provided by service domains. Service domains then proxy guests' virtual I/O by performing I/O to back-end devices, which are usually physical devices. Virtual device characteristics are described in detail later in this chapter.

Guest domains have network and device drivers that communicate with I/O domains through Logical Domain Channels (LDCs) provided by the hypervisor. The addition of device drivers that use LDCs rather than physical I/O is one of the areas in which Solaris has been modified to run in a logical domain—, an example of paravirtualization discussed in Chapter 1, "Introduction to Virtualization." LDCs provide communications channels between guests, and an API for enqueuing and dequeuing messages that contain service requests and responses. Figure 3.2 shows the relationship between guest and service domains and the path of I/O requests and responses.

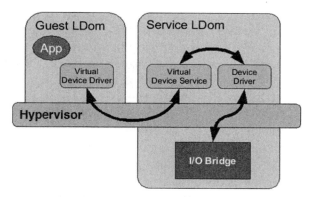

Figure 3.2 Service Domains Provide Virtual I/O

Shared memory eliminates the overhead associated with copying buffers between domains. The processor's memory mapping unit (MMU) is used to map shared buffers in physical memory into the address spaces of a guest and an I/O domain. This strategy helps implement virtual I/O efficiently: Instead of copying the results of a disk read from its own memory to a guest domain's memory, an I/O domain can read directly into a buffer it shares with the guest. This highly secure mechanism is controlled by hypervisor management of memory maps.

I/O domains are designed for high availability. Redundant I/O domains can be set up so that system and guest operation can continue if a path fails, or if an I/O domain fails or is taken down for service. Logical Domains provides virtual disk multipathing, thereby ensuring that a virtual disk can remain accessible even if a service domain fails. Domains can use IP network multipathing (IPMP) for redundant network availability.

3.3 Details of Domain Resources

Logical Domains technology provides flexible assignment of hardware resources to domains, with options for specifying physical resources for a corresponding virtual resource.

3.3.1 Virtual CPUs

As mentioned in the section "Real and Virtual CPUs," each domain is assigned exclusive use of a number of CPUs, also called *threads* or *strands*. Within a domain, these are called *virtual CPUs* (vCPUs).

The granularity of assignment is a single vCPU. A domain can have from one vCPU up to all the vCPUs on the server. On UltraSPARC T1 systems (T1000 and T2000), the maximum is 8 cores with 4 threads, for a total of 32 vCPUs. On UltraSPARC T2 and T2 Plus systems, the maximum is 8 cores with 8 threads each, for a total of 64 vCPUs per chip. Systems with the T2 Plus chip can have multiple chips per server: The T5140 and T5240 servers have 2 T2 Plus chips for a total of 16 cores and 128 vCPUs, while the T5440 has 4 T2 Plus chips with 32 cores and 256 vCPUs.

Virtual CPUs should be assigned to domains on core boundaries. This strategy prevents "false cache sharing," which can reduce performance when multiple domains share a CMT core and compete for the same L1 cache. To avoid this problem, vCPU quantities equivalent to entire cores to each domain should be allocated. For example, you should allocate vCPUs in units of 8 vCPUs on T2 and T2 Plus servers. Of course, this tactic may be overkill for some workloads, and administrators need not excessively concern themselves when defining domains to accommodate the light CPU requirements needed to consolidate small, old, or low utilization servers. Figure 3.3 is a simplified diagram of the threads, cores, and caches in a SPARC CMT chip.

The number of CPUs in a domain can be dynamically and nondisruptively changed while the domain is running. Oracle Solaris commands such as vmstat and mpstat can be used within the domain to monitor its CPU utilization, just as on a dedicated server. The ldm list command can be used in the control domain to display each domain's CPU utilization. A change in the quantity of vCPUs in a running domain takes effect immediately. The number of CPUs can be managed automatically with the Logical Domains Dynamic Resource Manager, which is discussed later in this chapter.

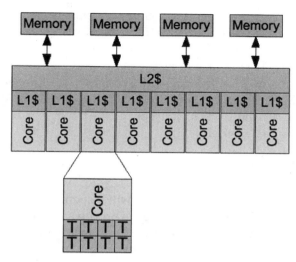

Figure 3.3 CMT Cores, Threads, and Caches

3.3.2 Virtual Network Devices

Guests have one or more virtual network devices connected to virtual Layer 2 network switches provided by service domains. Virtual network devices can be on the same or different virtual switches so as to connect a domain to multiple networks, provide increased availability using IPMP (IP Multipathing), or increase the bandwidth available to a guest domain.

From the guest perspective, virtual network interfaces are named vnet*N*, where *N* is an integer starting from 0 for the first virtual network device defined for a domain. In fact, the simplest way to determine if an Oracle Solaris instance is running in a guest domain (specifically, a domain that is not an I/O domain) is to issue the command ifconfig -a and see if the network interfaces are vnet0, vnet1, and so on, rather than real devices like nxge0 or e1000g0. Virtual network devices can be assigned static IP or dynamic IP addresses, just as with physical network devices.

3.3.2.1 MAC Addresses

Every virtual network device has its own MAC address. This is different from Oracle Solaris Containers, where a single MAC address is usually shared by all Containers in a Solaris instance. MAC addresses can be assigned manually or automatically from the reserved address range of 00:14:4F:F8:00:00 to 00:14:4F:FF:FF:FF. The bottom half of the address range is used for automatic assignments; the other 256K addresses can be used for manual assignment.

The Logical Domains manager implements duplicate MAC address detection by sending multicast messages with the address it wants to assign and listening for a possible response from another machine's Logical Domains manager saying the address is in use. If such a message comes back, it randomly picks another address and tries again. The message time-to-live (TTL) is set to 1, and can be changed by the SMF property `ldmd/hops`. Recently freed MAC addresses from removed domains are used first, to help prevent DHCP servers from exhausting the number of addresses available.

3.3.2.2 Network Connectivity

Virtual switches are usually assigned to a physical network device, permitting traffic between guest domains and the network segment to which the device is connected. Network traffic between domains on the same virtual switch does not travel to the virtual switch or to the physical network, but rather is implemented by a fast memory-to-memory transfer between source and destination domains using dedicated LDCs. Virtual switches can also be established without a connection to a physical network device, which creates a private secure network not accessible from any other server. Virtual switches can be configured for securely isolated VLANs, and can exploit features such as VLAN tagging and jumbo frames.

3.3.2.3 Hybrid I/O

Network Interface Unit (NIU) Hybrid I/O is an optimization feature available on servers based on the UltraSPARC T2 chip, the T5120 and T5220 servers, and the Sun Blade T6320 server module. It is an exception to the normal Logical Domains virtual I/O model, and provides higher performance network I/O. In hybrid mode, DMA resources for network devices are loaned to a guest domain so it can perform network I/O without going through an I/O domain. In this mode, a network device in a guest domain can transmit unicast traffic to and from external networks at essentially native performance. Multicast traffic, and network traffic to other domains on the same virtual switch are handled as described above.

In current implementations, there are two 10 GbE NIU `nxgeN` devices per T2-based server. Each can support three hybrid I/O virtual network devices, for a total of six.

3.3.3 Virtual Disk

Service domains can have virtual disk services that export virtual block devices to guest domains. Virtual disks are based on back-end disk resources, which may be physical disks, disk slices, volumes, or files residing in ZFS or UFS file systems. These resources could include any of the following:

- A physical block device (disk or LUN)—for example, `/dev/dsk/c1t48d0s2`
- A slice of a physical device or LUN—for example, `/dev/dsk/c1t48d0s0`
- A disk image file residing in UFS or ZFS—for example, `/path-to-filename`
- A ZFS volume—for example,

  `zfs create -V 100m ldoms/domain/test/zdisk0`

  creates the back-end `/dev/zvol/dsk/ldoms/domain/test/zdisk0`
- A volume created by Solaris Volume Manager (SVM) or Veritas Volume Manager (VxVM)
- A CD ROM/DVD or a file containing an ISO image

A virtual disk may be marked as read-only. It also can be made exclusive, meaning that it can be given to only one domain at a time. This setting is available for disks based on physical devices rather than files, but the same effect can be provided for file back-ends by using ZFS clones. The advantages of ZFS—such as advanced mirroring, checksummed data integrity, snapshots, and clones—can be applied to both ZFS volumes and disk image files residing in ZFS. ZFS volumes generally provide better performance, whereas disk image files provide simpler management, including renaming, copying, or transmission to other servers.

In general, the best performance is provided by virtual disks backed by physical disks or LUNs, and the best flexibility is provided by file-based virtual disks or volumes, which can be easily copied, backed up, and, when using ZFS, cloned from a snapshot. Different kinds of disk back-ends can be used in the same domain: The system volume for a domain can use a ZFS or UFS file system back-end, while disks used for databases or other I/O intensive applications can use physical disks.

Redundancy can be provided by using virtual disk multipathing in the guest domain, with the same virtual disk back-end presented to the guest by different service domains. This provides fault tolerance for service domain failure. A timeout interval can be used for I/O failover if the service domain becomes unavailable. The `ldm` command syntax for creating a virtual volume lets you specify an MPXIO group. The following commands illustrate the process of creating a disk volume back-end served by both a control domain and an alternate service domain:

```
# ldm add-vdsdev mpgroup=foo \
    /path-to-backend-from-primary/domain ha-disk@primary-vds0
# ldm add-vdsdev mpgroup=foo \
    /path-to-backend-from-alternate/domain ha-disk@alternate-vds0
# ldm add-vdisk ha-disk ha-disk@primary-vds0 myguest
```

Multipathing can also be provided from a single I/O domain with multiplexed I/O (MPXIO), by ensuring that the domain has multiple paths to the same device—for example, two FC-AL HBAs to the same SAN array. You can enable MPxIO in the control domain by running the command `stmsboot -e`. That command creates a single, but redundant path to the same device. The single device is then configured into the virtual disk service. Perhaps most simply, insulation from a path or media failure can be provided by using a ZFS file pool with mirror or RAID-Z redundancy. These methods offer resiliency in case of a path failure to a device, but do not insulate the system from failure of a service domain.

3.3.4 Console and OpenBoot

Every domain has a console, which is provided by a virtual console concentrator (vcc). The vcc is usually assigned to the control domain, which then runs the Virtual Network Terminal Server daemon (`vntsd`) service.

By default, the daemon listens for localhost connections using the Telnet protocol, with a different port number being assigned for each domain. A guest domain operator connecting to a domain's console first logs into the control domain via the `ssh` command so that no passwords are transmitted in cleartext over the network; the `telnet` command can then be used to connect to the console.

Optionally, user domain console authorization can be implemented to restrict which users can connect to a domain's console. Normally, only system and guest domain operators should have login access to a control domain.

3.3.5 Cryptographic Accelerator

The processors in CMT systems are equipped with on-chip hardware cryptographic accelerators that dramatically speed up cryptographic operations. This technique improves security by reducing the CPU consumption needed for encrypted transmissions, and makes it possible to transmit secure traffic at wire speed. Each CMT processor core has its own hardware accelerator unit, making it possible to run multiple concurrent hardware-assisted cryptographic transmissions.

In the T1 processor used on the T1000 and T2000 servers, the accelerator performs modular exponentiation and multiplication, which are normally CPU-intensive portions of cryptographic algorithms. The accelerator, called the *Modular Arithmetic Unit* (MAU), speeds up public key cryptography (i.e., RSA, DSA, and Diffie-Hellman algorithms).

Although the T2 and T2 Plus chips include this function, the accelerator has additional functionality. This cipher/hash unit accelerates bulk encryption (RC4, DES, 3DES, AES), secure hash (MD5, SHA-1, SHA-256), other public key algorithms (elliptical curve cryptography), and error-checking codes (ECC, CRC32).

At this time, a cryptographic accelerator can be allocated only to domains that have at least one virtual CPU on the same core as the accelerator.

3.3.6 Memory

The Logical Domains technology dedicates real memory to each domain, instead of using virtual memory for guest address spaces and swapping them between RAM and disk, as some hypervisors do. This approach limits the number and memory size of domains on a single CMT processor to the amount that fits in RAM, rather than oversubscribing memory and swapping. As a consequence, it eliminates problems such as thrashing and double paging, which are experienced by hypervisors that run virtual machines in virtual memory environments.

RAM can be allocated to a domain in highly granular units—the minimum unit that can be allocated is 4 MB. The memory requirements of a domain running the Oracle Solaris OS are no different from running Solaris on a physical machine. If a workload needs 8 GB of RAM to run efficiently on a dedicated server, it will need the same amount when running in a domain.

3.3.7 Binding Resources to Domains

The Logical Domains administrator uses the `ldm` command to specify the resources required by each domain: the amount of RAM, the number of CPUs, and so forth. These parameters are sometimes referred to as the domain's constraints.

A domain that has been defined is said to be inactive until resources are bound to it by the `ldm bind` command. When this command is issued, the system selects the physical resources required by the domain's constraints and associates them with the domain. For example, if a domain requires 8 CPUs, the domain manager selects 8 CPUs from the set of online and unassigned CPUs on the system and gives them to the domain.

Until a domain is bound, the sum of the constraints of all domains can exceed the physical resources available on the server. For example, one could define 10 domains, each of which requires 8 CPUs and 8 GB of RAM on a machine with 64 CPUs and 64 GB of RAM. Only the domains whose constraints are met can be bound and started. In this example, the first 8 domains to be bound would boot. Additional domains can be defined for occasional or emergency purposes, such as a disaster recovery domain defined on a server normally used for testing purposes.

3.4 Installing Logical Domains and Building a Guest Domain

This section walks through the process of installing Logical Domains on a CMT server, creating a guest domain, and installing Oracle Solaris on it. The installed domain will then be set up as a master image for cloning further domains.

3.4.1 Verifying and Installing Firmware

All CMT servers and Blade Modules ship with firmware support for Logical Domains. Nevertheless, it is important to ensure that the current firmware for the server is installed, matching it to the version of Solaris running in the control domain and the version of Logical Domains management software to be installed. Current information can be obtained from http://docs.sun.com. The Release Notes, Reference Manual, and Administration Guide for Logical Domains software list the firmware levels needed on each server model. Use the instructions in the server's Installation Guide or Administration Guide for verifying and installing the firmware.

3.4.2 Installing Logical Domains Software

Examples in this section are taken from Logical Domains version 1.2. (Note: File names, command syntax, and screen output may vary slightly in future releases.) Logical Domains software can be downloaded from http://www.sun.com/servers/coolthreads/ldoms/. The software is delivered as a .zip file, which can be unpacked by issuing the following command (or something similar):

```
# unzip Ldoms_Manager-1_2.zip
```

Before installing the software, read the README file contained in the opened .zip file. It will describe any prerequisite patches to install. If any patches are required, download them from http://sunsolve.sun.com and install them using patchadd(1M) as directed.

At that point, you can run the install script, responding to any prompts as needed.

```
# cd /ldoms/LDoms1.2/LDoms_Manager-1_2/Install
# ./install-ldm

Welcome to the LDoms installer.

You are about to install the Logical Domains Manager package that will
enable you to create, destroy and control other domains on your
system.  Given the capabilities of the LDoms domain manager, you can
now change the security configuration of this Solaris instance using
the Solaris Security Toolkit.

Select a security profile from this list:

a) Hardened Solaris configuration for LDoms (recommended)
```

```
b) Standard Solaris configuration
c) Your custom-defined Solaris security configuration profile

Enter a, b, or c [a]:
...
...
LOGICAL DOMAINS CONFIGURATION

Once installed, you may configure your system for a basic Logical
Domains deployment. If you select "y" for the following question, the
Logical Domains Configuration Assistant will be launched following a
successful installation of packages.

(You may launch the LDoms Configuration Assistant at a later time with
the command /usr/sbin/ldmconfig, or use the GUI Configuration Assistant
which is bundled in the LDoms zip file - see README.GUI for more
details)

Select an option for configuration:

y) Yes, launch the LDoms Configuration Assistant after install
n) No thanks, I will configure LDoms myself later

Enter y or n [y]: n
Installing LDoms and Solaris Security Toolkit packages.
pkgadd -n -d "/ldoms/LDoms1.2/LDoms_Manager-1_2/Product" -a pkg_admin SUNWldm.v
Copyright 2009 Sun Microsystems, Inc.  All rights reserved.
Use is subject to license terms.
Copyright 2009 Sun Microsystems, Inc.  All rights reserved.
Use is subject to license terms.

Installation of <SUNWldm> was successful.
pkgadd -n -d "/ldoms/LDoms1.2/LDoms_Manager-1_2/Product" -a pkg_admin SUNWjass
Copyright 2005 Sun Microsystems, Inc.  All rights reserved.
Use is subject to license terms.

Installation of <SUNWjass> was successful.

Verifying that all packages are fully installed.  OK.
Enabling services: svc:/ldoms/ldmd:default
Solaris Security Toolkit was not applied. Bypassing the use of the
Solaris Security Toolkit is _not_ recommended and should only be
performed when alternative hardening steps are to be taken.
```

You can then verify that the software is installed and that the Logical Domains
daemon is running. The command-line interface is accessed by issuing the `ldm`

command. At this time, a single domain will be running on the server that owns
all of the installed memory and CPUs.

The following example is taken from a small (6-core) T1000. The warning that
the system is in configuration mode is displayed after each `ldm` command until
the system is rebooted with the new configuration. For brevity, we will omit the
subsequent identical warning messages.

```
# pkginfo -x SUNWldomr
SUNWldomr  Solaris Logical Domains (Root)
           (sparc.sun4v) 11.10.0,REV=2006.10.04.00.26
# pkginfo -x SUNWldomu
SUNWldomu  Solaris Logical Domains (Usr)
           (sparc.sun4v) 11.10.0,REV=2006.08.08.12.13


# ldm -V
--------------------------------------------------------------------
Notice: the LDom Manager is running in configuration mode. Configuration and resource
information is displayed for the configuration under construction; not the current
active configuration. The configuration being constructed will only take effect after it
is downloaded to the system controller and the host is reset.
--------------------------------------------------------------------
Logical Domain Manager (v 1.2)
       Hypervisor control protocol v 1.3
       Using Hypervisor MD v 1.1
System PROM:
       Hypervisor v. 1.7.3   @(#)Hypervisor 1.7.3 2009/06/08 18:00:15
       OpenBoot  v. 4.30.3 @(#)OBP 4.30.3 2009/06/08 13:27
# ldm list
Name       State     Flags  Cons  VCPU  Memory  Util  Uptime
primary    active -n-c--    SP    24    8064M   0.1%  12m
```

3.4.3 Configuring the Control Domain

Because the control domain initially owns all hardware resources, it must be resized to provide the RAM and CPUs to be allocated to guest domains. Essential
services for providing virtual disk, network, and consoles should be defined now as
well. When the domain is rebooted, it will have the specified number of CPUs and
amount of RAM. The remainder of those resources will be available for allocation
to guest domains. The sequence will look similar to this sequence:

```
1    # ldm add-vdiskserver primary-vds0 primary
2    # ldm add-vconscon port-range=5000-5100 primary-vcc0 primary
3    # ldm add-vswitch net-dev=e1000g0 primary-vsw0 primary
```

```
4     # ldm set-mau 1 primary
5     # ldm set-vcpu 4 primary
6     # ldm set-memory 3g primary
7     # ldm add-config initial
8     # ldm list-config
9     factory-default
10    initial [current]
11
12    # shutdown -y  -g0 -i6
```

Line 1 defines a virtual disk server. Notice the naming convention: The name of the server is `primary-vds0`, indicating that the service operates in the domain named `primary` (the control domain) and is the initial virtual disk server (`vds0`). The last token on the line indicates which domain will run this service. While following this convention is not necessary, it is highly recommended, as the name of the service makes its function self-documenting. Note also that this naming convention is separate from Solaris device naming.

Line 2 defines a vcc that will listen for local connections on ports 5000 to 5100. Line 3 defines a virtual Layer 2 switch, `primary-vsw0`, which is associated with the physical NIC device `e1000g0`. Multiple virtual switches can be defined and attached to different NIC devices or to no NIC device at all. Lines 4, 5, and 6 describe the control domain: It has a single cryptographic accelerator, 4 CPUs, and 3 GB of RAM. The remaining lines save this initial configuration in firmware so it will persist after a power cycle and then reboot the server.

3.4.4 Network Connectivity Between Primary and Guest Domains

By default, networking on a virtual switch connecting the control domain and guest domains is disabled. This approach provides an additional layer of security by isolating the control domain from guest domains' network traffic. If this situation is not desired—for example, if the control domain is to be used as a JumpStart server for guest domains—the virtual switch can be configured as a network device and may then be used as the primary interface instead of the physical device to which the switch is assigned.

To configure the virtual switch as a network device, first issue the command `ifconfig -a` to get all the network parameters for the physical device (in the following example, `e1000g0`). Then unplumb the device, and replumb the virtual switch (in this example, `vsw0`) with the same information. When this procedure is complete, guest domains will be able to communicate with the control domain via this network connection.

Important Note!
Before you attempt to reconfigure the virtual switch, you *must* log in from the control domain's console or from a different interface than the interface being unplumbed; otherwise, you will abruptly terminate your session! Terminating the network interface you are using for your login session can be embarrassing.

```
# ifconfig -a
lo0: flags=2001000849<UP,LOOPBACK,RUNNING,MULTICAST,IPv4,VIRTUAL> mtu 8232
        index 1 inet 127.0.0.1 netmask ff000000
e1000g0: flags=201000843<UP,BROADCAST,RUNNING,MULTICAST,IPv4,CoS> mtu 1500 index 3
        inet 10.6.160.125 netmask fffffc00 broadcast 10.6.163.255
        ether 0:14:4f:2b:65:4e
# ifconfig e1000g0 down              #(See important note!)
# ifconfig e1000g0 unplumb
# ifconfig vsw0 plumb
# ifconfig vsw0 10.6.160.125 netmask 255.255.252.0 up
# ifconfig -a
lo0: flags=2001000849<UP,LOOPBACK,RUNNING,MULTICAST,IPv4,VIRTUAL> mtu 8232 index 1
        inet 127.0.0.1 netmask ff000000
vsw0: flags=201000843<UP,BROADCAST,RUNNING,MULTICAST,IPv4,CoS> mtu 1500 index 5
        inet 10.6.160.125 netmask fffffc00 broadcast 10.6.163.255
        ether 0:14:4f:fa:85:bb
```

This change does not persist over a control domain reboot, so you must update `/etc/hostname.*` and `/etc/dhcp/*` to make it permanent. In this example, you would rename the configuration files for `e1000g0` to the equivalent files for `vsw0` by issuing the following commands:

```
# mv /etc/hostname.e1000g0 /etc/hostname.vsw0
# mv /etc/dhcp.e1000g0 /etc/dhcp.vsw0
```

3.4.5 Creating a Domain and Installing Oracle Solaris

In the following example, we create a guest domain imaginatively named `1dom1`, with no cryptographic accelerator, a single virtual network device, and a virtual disk residing in a ZFS file system. The following commands define a ZFS file system and allocate within it an empty 10 GB file that will be used for the Solaris system disk:

```
# zfs create rpool/ldoms
# zfs set mountpoint=/ldoms rpool/ldoms
# zfs set compression=on rpool/ldoms
# zfs create rpool/ldoms/ldom1
# mkfile -n 10g /ldoms/ldom1/disk0.img
```

In the preceding lines, ZFS compression is turned on to save disk space. The option to `mkfile` creates an empty file: No disk blocks are allocated until data is written to them. The file takes up no disk space, even though it is apparently 10 GB in size:

```
# ls -l /ldoms/ldom1/disk0.img
-rw-------T 1 root root 10737418240 2009-10-12 19:32 /ldoms/ldom1/disk0.img
# zfs list rpool/ldoms/ldom1
NAME                 USED  AVAIL  REFER  MOUNTPOINT
rpool/ldoms/ldom1    19K   21.4G   19K   /ldoms/ldom1
```

The virtual disk can also be allocated from other back-ends, such as a physical disk, but ZFS provides operational flexibility.

The following commands create the domain. Lines 2 and 3 set the number of CPUs and cryptographic accelerators. Line 4 sets the amount of RAM assigned to the domain. Line 5 creates the virtual network device using the virtual Layer 2 switch defined previously. Additional network devices could be defined if we wanted the domain to reside on separate networks. Line 6 exports the empty disk image as a virtual volume `vol10@primary-vds0` from the virtual disk service. Line 7 imports this volume as a virtual disk `vdisk10` into the guest domain. The commands for adding a virtual disk are a bit more complicated than the others; they can be interpreted as first defining a resource exported by the virtual disk server and then importing that resource into the domain that uses it. Finally, lines 8 and 9 do the same for a file containing the ISO format image of an Oracle Solaris installation DVD.

```
1   # ldm add-domain ldom1
2   # ldm set-vcpu 4 ldom1
3   # ldm set-mau 0 ldom1
4   # ldm set-mem 4g ldom1
5   # ldm add-vnet vnet1 primary-vsw0 ldom1
6   # ldm add-vdsdev /ldoms/ldom1/disk0.img vol10@primary-vds0
7   # ldm add-vdisk vdisk10 vol10@primary-vds0 ldom1
8   # ldm add-vdsdev /DVD/S10u7/solarisdvd.iso s10u7iso@primary-vds0
9   # ldm add-vdisk vdisk_iso s10u7iso@primary-vds0 ldom1
```

At this point, the domain's definition is complete. We set OpenBoot Prom (OBP) variables to force the domain to come to the `ok` prompt instead of booting an OS by setting the `autoboot?` property so as to demonstrate OBP commands. The "\" in the command line is an escape character, so we can enter the "?" character as a literal value. Then we bind the domain, which assigns the specified resources to the domain. This includes assigning the port used by the virtual console concentrator—5000 in the example. Finally, we start the domain, which has an effect similar to performing a "power on" operation for a real server: It loads the OBP, which then displays its ok prompt.

```
# ldm set-variable autoboot\?=false ldom1
# ldm bind ldom1
# ldm list    #(NOTE: this was done after bind, before start)
NAME        STATE      FLAGS    CONS    VCPU  MEMORY   UTIL  UPTIME
primary     active     -n-cv-   SP      4     3G       1.2%  38m
ldom1       bound      ------   5000    4     1G
# ldm start ldom1
```

It's helpful to bring up a second terminal window to watch this process. The telnet command can be issued after the ldm bind command to do so. At first, no output follows the output coming from the telnet command itself (the line beginning with "Press ~?"). When ldm start ldom1 is issued, OpenBoot is loaded and outputs {0} ok.

```
# telnet localhost 5000
Trying 127.0.0.1...
Connected to localhost....
Escape character is '^}'.
Connecting to console "ldom1" in group "ldom1" ....
Press ~? for control options ..

{0} ok
```

3.4.6 Viewing a Domain

From the ok prompt, we can issue OpenBoot commands and view the domain's devices:

```
Sun Fire(TM) T1000, No Keyboard
Copyright 2009 Sun Microsystems, Inc.  All rights reserved.
OpenBoot 4.30.3, 1024 MB memory available, Serial #xxxxxxxx.
Ethernet address x:xx:xx:xx:xx:xx, Host ID: xxxxxxxx
{0} ok banner
Sun Fire(TM) T1000, No Keyboard
Copyright 2009 Sun Microsystems, Inc.  All rights reserved.
OpenBoot 4.30.3, 1024 MB memory available, Serial #xxxxxxxx.
Ethernet address x:xx:xx:xx:xx:xx, Host ID: xxxxxxxx.
{0} ok show-disks
```

```
a) /virtual-devices@100/channel-devices@200/disk@1
b) /virtual-devices@100/channel-devices@200/disk@0
Enter Selection, q to quit:q
{0} ok show-nets
b) /virtual-devices@100/channel-devices@200/network@0
q) NO SELECTION
Enter Selection, q to quit:q
{0} ok devalias
vdisk_iso       /virtual-devices@100/channel-devices@200/disk@1
vdisk10         /virtual-devices@100/channel-devices@200/disk@0
vnet10          /virtual-devices@100/channel-devices@200/network@0
net             /virtual-devices@100/channel-devices@200/network@0
disk            /virtual-devices@100/channel-devices@200/disk@0
virtual-console /virtual-devices/console@1
name            aliases
```

This output shows that the domain is a virtual machine with its own devices—notice how the device aliases are derived from the `ldm` commands that defined them.

3.4.7 Installing Oracle Solaris into a Domain

Even the thrill of issuing OpenBoot commands at the `ok` prompt can pall after a while, so we will install Solaris 10 in the domain. Installation can be done over the network if a JumpStart or Ops Center infrastructure is available, and works just as on physical machines. For simplicity, we illustrate booting from a Solaris installation DVD image. Except for the device name alias in the boot command, this process is identical to that used when installing from a DVD on a physical machine. Notice the name of the discovered network interface: `vnet0`.

```
{0} ok boot vdisk_iso
Boot device: /virtual-devices@100/channel-devices@200/disk@1:f  File and args:
SunOS Release 5.10 Version Generic_139555-08 64-bit
Copyright 1983-2009 Sun Microsystems, Inc.  All rights reserved.
Use is subject to license terms.
Using RPC Bootparams for network configuration information.
Attempting to configure interface vnet0...
Configured interface vnet0
Reading ZFS config: done.
Setting up Java. Please wait...
Serial console, reverting to text install
Beginning system identification...
Searching for configuration file(s)...
Search complete.
Discovering additional network configuration...
```

The rest of the Solaris installation is as usual, and is not shown here.

The disk space occupied by virtual disks may be smaller than its apparent size. As demonstrated by the following lines, a 10 GB virtual disk containing a newly installed copy of Oracle Solaris takes up only a little more than 2.5 GB of disk space.

```
# ls -l /ldoms/ldom1/
total 5292263
-rw------T  1 root      root       10737418240 Aug 14 16:45 disk0.img
# zfs list rpool/ldoms/ldom1
NAME                USED  AVAIL  REFER  MOUNTPOINT
rpool/ldoms/ldom1   2.52G 61.6G  2.52G  /ldoms/ldom1
```

The disk space consumed will depend on how much of the virtual disk has been populated by the guest operating system and how well the data is compressed if ZFS compression is being used.

3.4.8 Observing Guest Domains from the Control Domain

From the control domain, you can use the `ldm` command to observe the activity of the domain, and to see which CPU, memory, network disk, cryptographic accelerator, and console resources are bound to it. The following example shows the short and long forms of `ldm list`. The control domain's console is SP, indicating that its console is accessed via the service processor, which is typical for Solaris on a SPARC server. The line for the guest domain shows the virtual console service port number used to access the domain's console.

In this example, you can see the number of virtual CPUs and the physical CPUs to which they are bound. For instance, ldom1's virtual CPU 0 is on physical CPU 4. The long listing format shows the utilization of each virtual CPU.

```
# ldm list
NAME           STATE      FLAGS   CONS    VCPU   MEMORY    UTIL   UPTIME
primary        active     -n-cv-  SP      4      3G        1.2%   1h 3m
ldom1          active     -n----  5000    4      1G        29%    22m
# ldm list -l ldom1
NAME           STATE      FLAGS   CONS    VCPU   MEMORY    UTIL   UPTIME
ldom1          active     -n----  5000    4      1G        17%    22m


SOFTSTATE
Solaris running


MAC
    00:14:4f:f9:fe:c8
```

```
HOSTID
    0x84f9fec8

CONTROL
    failure-policy=ignore

DEPENDENCY
    master=

VCPU
    VID    PID    UTIL  STRAND
     0      4     38%   100%
     1      5     51%   100%
     2      6     13%   100%
     3      7    2.6%   100%

MEMORY
    RA             PA              SIZE
    0x8000000      0xc8000000      1G

VARIABLES
    auto-boot?=false

NETWORK
    NAME              SERVICE               DEVICE      MAC          MODE
PVID VID                 MTU
    vnet10            primary-vsw0@primary  network@0
00:14:4f:fb:f8:a4          1                 1500

DISK
    NAME              VOLUME                TOUT DEVICE  SERVER
MPGROUP
    vdisk10           vol10@primary-vds0         disk@0  primary
    vdisk_iso         s10u7iso@primary-vds0      disk@1  primary

VCONS
    NAME              SERVICE               PORT
    ldom1             primary-vcc0@primary  5000
```

The STRAND column indicates the percentage of the physical CPU strand owned by that domain. In the current implementation, that value is always 100% because threads are dedicated to domains. The field is provided so scripts that process command output will continue to work if partial thread allocation is added later. The ldm list -p command option can be used to produce parsable output for easier script writing. In the following listing, ldom2 is a four-vCPU domain running at 25% average CPU utilization. The parsable format output, with or without the awk command, makes it clear that one CPU is fully used while the others are idle.

```
# ldm list ldom2
NAME              STATE        FLAGS    CONS    VCPU   MEMORY    UTIL   UPTIME
ldom2             active       -n----   5001    4      1G        25%    1h 27m
# ldm list -p -1 ldom2|grep strand
|vid=0|pid=12|util=0.4%|strand=100
|vid=1|pid=13|util=0.0%|strand=100
|vid=2|pid=14|util=0.0%|strand=100
|vid=3|pid=15|util=100%|strand=100
# ldm list -p -1 ldom2|grep strand\
    |awk -F'|' '{print $4}'|sed 's/util=//; s/%//'
0.4
0.0
0.1
100
```

3.4.9 Viewing a Domain from the Inside

Once Oracle Solaris is installed in a domain, you can use normal commands to view its configuration. Notice that the domain has four CPUs and a network interface named vnet0 with its own MAC address. A pleasant side effect of running in a domain is that the boot process is very fast, because there is no need to perform a power-on self-test (POST) or probe physical devices.

```
{0} ok boot disk
Boot device: /virtual-devices@100/channel-devices@200/disk@0   File and args:
SunOS Release 5.10 Version Generic_139555-08 64-bit
Copyright 1983-2009 Sun Microsystems, Inc.  All rights reserved.
Use is subject to license terms.
Hostname: t1ldom1
Reading ZFS config: done.
Mounting ZFS filesystems: (5/5)

t1ldom1 console login: root
Password:
Aug 14 16:42:06 t1ldom1 login: ROOT LOGIN /dev/console
Last login: Fri Aug 14 16:35:45 from xxx.xxx.xx.xxx
Sun Microsystems Inc.   SunOS 5.10       Generic January 2005
# ifconfig -a
lo0: flags=2001000849<UP,LOOPBACK,RUNNING,MULTICAST,IPv4,VIRTUAL> mtu 8232 index 1
        inet 127.0.0.1 netmask ff000000
vnet0: flags=201000843<UP,BROADCAST,RUNNING,MULTICAST,IPv4,CoS> mtu 1500 index 2
        inet 192.168.2.101 netmask ffffff00 broadcast 192.168.2.255
        ether 0:14:4f:fb:f8:a4
```

```
# hostid
84f9fec8
# psrinfo
0        on-line     since 08/14/2009 16:40:26
1        on-line     since 08/14/2009 16:40:28
2        on-line     since 08/14/2009 16:40:28
3        on-line     since 08/14/2009 16:40:28
```

At this point, the administrator can install application software and start using the domain.

3.4.10 Dynamic Reconfiguration

The Logical Domains technology lets the system administrator change the CPU and virtual I/O resources made available to guest domains. For example, the domain in the preceding example can be changed to use eight CPUs by issuing either of these commands: `ldm add-vcpu 4 ldom2` or `ldm set-vcpu 8 ldom2`. Each command takes effect immediately without rebooting the guest, and the new CPU resources can be used immediately. The `psrinfo` command in the guest domain shows the new CPU configuration, including the date and time shown for the added CPUs.

```
# psrinfo
0        on-line     since 10/25/2009 11:17:44
1        on-line     since 10/25/2009 11:17:45
2        on-line     since 10/25/2009 11:17:45
3        on-line     since 10/25/2009 11:17:45
4        on-line     since 10/28/2009 09:21:36
5        on-line     since 10/28/2009 09:21:36
6        on-line     since 10/28/2009 09:21:36
7        on-line     since 10/28/2009 09:21:36
```

Virtual I/O devices can also be added via the `ldm add-vnet` and `ldm add-vdisk` commands, and both I/O and CPU resources can be removed using complementary `ldm rm-vnet` and `ldm rm-vdisk` commands. Similarly, cryptographic accelerators can be dynamically added or removed. These commands can easily be scripted to ensure their execution at particular times or as part of a resource manager. At this writing, changing the amount of RAM in a domain requires that the domain be rebooted before the Solaris instance will recognize the change.

3.4.11 Dynamic Resource Management

The Logical Domains technology provides a policy-based resource manager that automatically adds or removes CPUs from a running domain based on its utilization and relative priority. Policies can be prioritized to ensure that important domains obtain preferential access to resources. They can also be enabled or disabled manually or based on time of day for different prime shift and off-hours policies. For example, one domain may have the highest resource needs and priority during the daytime, while a domain running batch work may operate in a more resource-intensive manner at night.

Policy rules specify the number of CPUs that a domain has, bounded by minimum and maximum values, and based on their utilization:

- The number of CPUs is adjusted between vcpu-min and vcpu-max based on util-upper and util-lower CPU busy percentages. (All of these variables are property values associated with the policy.)
- If CPU utilization exceeds the value of util-upper, virtual CPUs are added to the domain until the number is between vcpu-min and vcpu-max.
- If the utilization drops below util-lower, virtual CPUs are removed from the domain until the number is between vcpu-min and vcpu-max.
- If vcpu-min is reached, no more virtual CPUs can be dynamically removed. If vcpu-max is reached, no more virtual CPUs can be dynamically added. Manual changes to the number of CPUs can still be made using the ldm commands shown previously.
- Multiple policies can be in effect, and are optionally controlled by tod-begin and tod-end (time of day) values.

The resource manager includes ramp-up (attack) and ramp-down (decay) controls to adjust the system's response to workload changes, specifying the number of CPUs to add or remove based on changes in utilization, and how quickly the resource manager responds. Resource management is disabled in elastic power management mode, in which unused CPUs are powered down to reduce power consumption. The following is an example of a command creating a policy:

```
# ldm add-policy tod-begin=09:00 tod-end=18:00 util-lower=25 \
    util-upper=75 vcpu-min=2 vcpu-max=16 attack=1 \
    decay=1 priority=1 name=high-usage ldom1
```

This policy controls the number of CPUs for domain ldom1, is named high-usage, and is in effect between 9 A.M. and 6 P.M. The lower and upper CPU utilization settings are 25% and 75% CPU busy, respectively. The number of CPUs is adjusted between 2 and 16: One CPU is added or removed at a time (the attack and decay values). For example, if the CPU utilization exceeds 75%, a CPU is added unless `ldom1` already has 16 CPUs.

The resource manager provides flexible and powerful policy-driven dynamic CPU resource management for Logical Domains that can automatically adjust CPU assignments based on CPU resource requirements and domain priorities.

3.4.12 Cloning a Domain

The Logical Domains technology makes it easy to clone systems, especially when using virtual disks residing in ZFS. A golden image instance of Oracle Solaris can be installed, patched, and customized, and then used as a master copy for multiple domains.

ZFS makes this process efficient by letting the administrator take a snapshot of a virtual disk and then create clones from it. Snapshots are read-only images of data in a ZFS file system at the time the `zfs snapshot` command is executed, while clones are read/write images based on the snapshot. ZFS saves disk space because only changed data takes up additional space on disk. For example, if a snapshot is made of a ZFS file system with 100 GB of data and 5 MB of data is changed, only 5 MB of additional disk space is consumed by the snapshot. Both a snapshot and the file system it is based on use common disk locations for data that is common to both. The same is true with clones: Space is consumed only for changed disk contents. At first, the disk footprint of the new domain will be negligible, as shown in the following example, but eventually it may increase if the contents of the Solaris instance diverge from the master image.

Virtual disks based in a different file system, such as UFS, can be easily replicated by using the low-tech `cp` command. With this approach, however, each copy of a disk will require the same disk space as the original. Given that ZFS is much more space efficient, it is the recommended technique for cloning a domain.

Before cloning a domain, be sure to shut it down to ensure that all buffers have been written and that its disk contents are stable. You may also wish to unbind the domain if its purpose is to be a template for other domains.

Then, assuming use of the same domain as in the previous example, we could issue the following commands:

```
# zfs snapshot tank/ldoms/ldom1@initial
# zfs list
NAME                          USED  AVAIL  REFER  MOUNTPOINT
...
rpool/ldoms/ldom1             2.52G  61.6G  2.52G  /ldoms/ldom1
rpool/ldoms/ldom1@initial         0      -  2.52G  -
```

continues

```
# zfs clone rpool/ldoms/ldom1@initial  rpool/ldoms/ldom2
# zfs list
NAME                                  USED  AVAIL  REFER  MOUNTPOINT
...
rpool/ldoms/ldom1                     2.52G 61.6G  2.52G  /ldoms/ldom1
rpool/ldoms/ldom2                         0 61.6G  2.52G  /ldoms/ldom2
rpool/ldoms/ldom1@initial                 0     -  2.52G  -
# ls -l /ldoms/ldom2
-rw------T  1 root      root      10737418240 Jan  2 23:19 disk_ldom.img
{Issue ldm commands to define the domain.}
{The OS is already installed; just boot it.}
{When it has finished booting: }
# zfs list
...
rpool/ldoms/ldom2                     11.2M 60.6G  2.25G  /ldoms/ldom2
```

Once you've issued the ldm commands needed to define domain ldom2, you can simply bind and boot the guest domain—Oracle Solaris is already installed on the virtual disk.

A cloned Solaris instance has the same IP address and host name as the system it was cloned from. You can choose from several methods to give it a unique identity. One strategy is to configure the guest to use DHCP at boot. Another technique is to issue the /usr/sbin/sys-unconfig command before shutting down and cloning the golden image. The first boot of the cloned image will then prompt (at the guest console) for system identification data, such as the time zone, IP address, and so on. Alternatively, you can configure the golden image domain with a unique host name and IP address that will not be given to any other domain. After booting a domain cloned from it, simply log into the clone via SSH, and change its host name and IP address via standard Solaris administrator commands. An advantage of this method is that it avoids the use of the guest console.

3.5 Domain Mobility

Domains can be installed on one CMT server (the source host) and migrated to a different, compatible CMT server (the target host) for planned workload migration. Doing so can free up memory and CPUs on a server, or vacate it for planned maintenance. At the time of this writing, Logical Domains supported two forms of domain migration, both invoked by the ldm migrate command. The following command migrates a domain to the host at the specified address. The command will prompt for the root password of the control domain on the target system.

```
# ldm migrate ldg1 root@192.168.1.12
```

The `ldm migrate` command can be issued with the option `-n` to request a dry run that tests whether the migration is possible but does not actually migrate the domain.

In *cold* migration, the domain must be stopped. It must also be in the *bound* or *inactive* state on the source machine. Cold migration consists of verifying access to the domain's I/O resources. In particular, the virtual disks must be accessible to both the source and the target. This step also ensures there are sufficient resources to bind the domain after migration, and then transmits the domain's description to the target machine. Once the domain is migrated, the domain on the source machine is unbound (if it is currently bound to resources) and removed from the source domain configuration. Cold migration applies only to domains that are not running, but can be very helpful for planned migration of workloads that can tolerate an outage with a shutdown and reboot. It is very fast, as only descriptive information is transmitted between servers.

In *warm* migration, a running domain is suspended on the source machine and resumed on the target machine without a reboot. Domain execution is suspended while it is being migrated. This process may take a number of seconds or a few minutes, depending on domain memory size and network speed, and on whether the control domain has access to a cryptographic accelerator.

First, the domain managers on both source and target machines verify that sufficient capacity to bind the domain on the target is available. Then, the target system creates and binds a single-CPU version of the guest domain, and the source machine removes all but one CPU from the running domain. Next, the source machine suspends the domain and removes its last CPU. The domain's memory contents and state are then compressed, encrypted (using the cryptographic accelerator if one is associated with the control domain), and transmitted from the source to the target.

Processing is multithreaded and takes advantage of the CPU threads in the control domain; it also exploits the cryptographic accelerator to ensure better performance. Domain memory contents are always encrypted before transmission, as it would be a significant security exposure to transmit a domain's memory contents (which might include passwords or private information) as cleartext. The domain is then restored on the target system and its remaining CPUs added. The Oracle Solaris instance continues execution on the target machine with the same disk storage, IP addresses, and MAC addresses as before, and applications resume processing. Finally, the domain is unbound and removed from the source host's domain configuration.

Warm migration is suitable for planned migration of any workload that can be paused for a number of seconds.

A *live* migration capability is anticipated, in which a migrating domain will be unresponsive for only a very small interval.

3.6 Physical to Virtual Conversion

Logical Domains provides a Physical to Virtual (P2V) tool to automate conversion of physical Oracle Solaris systems into guest Logical Domains. This tool moves file system contents from a physical server to a Logical Domain on the CMT server, and if necessary, replaces packages geared toward the sun4u architecture platform (all UltraSPARC and SPARC64 systems) with packages for the sun4v architecture provided by the CMT platform. The physical system can be running Solaris 8 or later on a sun4u system, or Solaris 10 running outside of a domain.

P2V migration consists of three phases, which are carried out under the control of the ldmp2v command:

1. *Collection*: Runs on the physical machine and collects a file system image and configuration data using ufsdump or flarcreate. The resulting file can be transmitted to the target system's control domain or stored on an NFS server that is available to both the physical system and the control domain.

2. *Preparation*: Runs on the control domain of the target platform. It creates a guest domain, and restores the contents of the collected file system into virtual disks.

3. *Conversion*: Runs on the control domain of the target platform. It upgrades the guest domain to prepare it to run as a domain. This process removes packages, replacing sun4u packages with their corresponding sun4v versions.

If the physical system is running Solaris 8 or Solaris 9, the P2V process installs the system image in a Solaris Container using a Solaris 8 Container or Solaris 9 Container under the guest domain's Solaris 10 kernel. That practice lets the migrated image appear to be the same Solaris version as on the physical machine. The P2V process can optionally preserve the physical system's network identity by reusing its MAC address.

The P2V process requires Solaris 10 system images to be available in either Solaris installation DVD or network install format, with the package SUNWldmp2v being installed in the control domain. The file /etc/ldmp2v.conf must be populated with variables indicating the names of the default virtual switch and virtual disk servers, and the type of disk back-ends to use for virtual disks. The P2V command must be made available to the physical system, either by NFS mount or by copying the command to a local disk.

Once these setup tasks are complete, a set of commands can be executed like those shown in the following example. In this case, sparcules indicates the login session on the physical server, and primary indicates the control domain login session. The collect phase writes a collected image to an NFS-mounted directory that is also accessed by the control domain. The preparation phase creates a domain and imports the collected file system image into virtual disks. The conversion phase boots the

guest domain with an Oracle Solaris installation image to upgrade the system image
to a software level that is compatible with the Logical Domains technology.

```
sparcules# ldmp2v collect -x /export/home -d /home/p2v
Collecting system configuration …
Archiving file systems ...
  DUMP: Date of this level 0 dump: Sun Oct 25 11:46:32 2009
  DUMP: Date of last level 0 dump: the epoch
  DUMP: Dumping /dev/rdsk/c0d0s0 (sparcules:/) to /home/p2v/ufsdump.0.
  DUMP: Mapping (Pass I) [regular files]
  DUMP: Mapping (Pass II) [directories]
  DUMP: Writing 63 Kilobyte records
  DUMP: Estimated 5576806 blocks (2723.05MB).
  DUMP: Dumping (Pass III) [directories]
  DUMP: Dumping (Pass IV) [regular files]
  DUMP: Dumping (Pass III) [directories]
  DUMP: Dumping (Pass IV) [regular files]
  DUMP: 64.06% done, finished in 0:05
  DUMP: 5576758 blocks (2723.03MB) on 1 volume at 3064 KB/sec
  DUMP: DUMP IS DONE
sparcules#
{...now we move to the control domain...}

primary# ldmp2v prepare -d /home/p2v -o keep-mac sparcules
Creating vdisks ...
Creating file systems ...
Populating file systems ...
Modifying guest domain OS image ...
Removing SVM configuration ...
Unmounting guest file systems ...
Creating domain sparcules ...
Attaching vdisks to domain sparcules
primary # ldmp2v convert -i /DVD/S10u7/solarisdvd.iso \
     -d /home/p2v sparcules
Testing original system status ...
LDom sparcules started
Waiting for Solaris to come up ...
Select 'Upgrade' (F2) when prompted for the installation type.
Disconnect from the console after the Upgrade has finished.
Trying 0.0.0.0...
Connected to 0.
Escape character is '^]'.
Connecting to console "sparcules" in group "sparcules" ....
Press ~? for control options ..
Configuring devices.
Using RPC Bootparams for network configuration information.
Attempting to configure interface vnet0...
{… many lines of a typical Solaris upgrade dialogue omitted.}
```

Once this process is complete, the guest domain has the same system identity and applications as it did on the original physical server. The amount of time to complete the process depends on the size of the file systems being copied and the network bandwidth available for its transmission to the control domain. The amount of administrator effort is dramatically reduced, with only a few commands needed to carry out a complete system migration.

3.7 Ease-of-Use Enhancements

The preceding examples manage Logical Domains with a command-line interface. This strategy is traditional and scriptable—but also requires prerequisite skills, can be error-prone, and is intimidating for the occasional user. It also does not scale well when many machines are involved.

These limitations can be addressed by using scripts and by making appropriate use of standards and automation in an enterprise. They are also addressed by the Logical Domains Configuration Assistant, which provides a graphical user interface (GUI) for the initial installation and configuration of Logical Domains software and guest domains on a server. The Configuration Assistant is a Java application that is provided with the Logical Domains install software. To start it, issue the following command:

```
$ java -jar /path/Configurator.jar
```

This command launches a GUI that steps the user through a set of panels, such as the one shown in Figure 3.4.

The GUI steps through a series of panels that let the user specify the number of domains to be created and the paths to their virtual disks. The last step lets the user save a script to run at a later time on one or more servers or, if the appropriate host name and password are provided, to run on a target CMT server. The Logical Domains package also includes the ldmconfig command, a text-mode tool that prompts the administrator for information about the domains and then generates the commands to build those domains according to best-practice naming conventions and a template of where the virtual disk back-ends are stored.

A more comprehensive solution is based on the Oracle Enterprise Manager Ops Center licensed product, described at http://www.sun.com/software/products/opscenter/. This product provides full life-cycle support for provisioning, and managing systems in a data center from a single user interface and screen, for both real and virtual systems. Ops Center can create, delete, configure, boot, and shut down Logical Domains. It also provides monitoring and management, showing utilization charts for CPU, memory, and file systems. In addition, the Ops Center manages resource pools, permitting dynamic reallocation of resources based on policies, and provides a graphical interface for controlling domain migration. Figure 3.5 shows several physical nodes that are visible in the assets tab of the Ops Center, with details illustrating resources used by several domains.

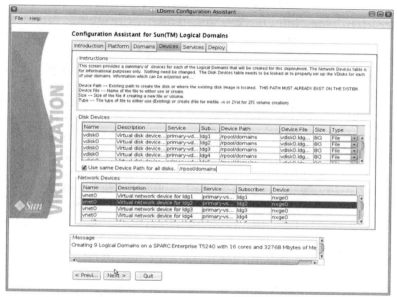

Figure 3.4 Logical Domains Configuration Assistant

Figure 3.5 Oracle Enterprise Manager Ops Center Display for Logical Domains

3.8 Comparison with Oracle Solaris Containers

Oracle Solaris Containers and Logical Domains provide alternative and complementary methods to virtualize Solaris systems, so it is natural to compare them.

Solaris Containers provide ultra-lightweight OS virtualization with excellent isolation, security, observability, fast deployment, resource granularity, and native performance. However, because many Containers run on a single Solaris instance, they do not permit multiple kernel patch levels to be used. Solaris Containers also have a few restrictions, such as the inability to run an NFS server.

In contrast, Logical Domains are more like "business as usual" for system administrators and application planners. They are individually installed, patched, used, and managed, much like physical servers. Oracle Solaris can be installed in a domain via a JumpStart or by booting from a DVD device, just like on a physical server. Like Containers, domains can also be cloned from previously installed and customized instances. However, unlike Containers, a running domain can be migrated from one server to another even without rebooting the domain.

Logical Domains are available only on CMT servers, whereas Containers are available on any platform that supports Solaris. Also, because domains host full OS instances on dedicated CPUs and RAM, they have a larger resource footprint than Containers. Many more virtualized instances can be hosted on the same platform by using Containers than by using domains.

Solaris Containers and Logical Domains are complementary virtualization technologies. They can be combined without adding overhead by running Containers within domains to achieve the highest degree of flexible virtualization. Separate OS instances can be configured when different OS kernel levels are required, with each OS instance hosting many lightweight, virtualized Container environments.

3.9 Summary

Logical Domains provide low-cost, efficient virtualization on UltraSPARC T1, T2, and T2 Plus processors. Each domain is a separate, independent virtual machine with its own OS instance. Hardware resources are dedicated to each domain through a highly granular and dynamic resource allocation scheme.

Compared to other virtualization technologies, Logical Domains provide an extremely efficient hypervisor implementation that avoids the overhead inherent in traditional hypervisors, and avoids the license costs of commercial virtualization products.

Logical Domains is an ideal technology for migrating from older platforms to current hardware in a consolidated, energy-efficient platform. Oracle Solaris systems can be easily moved to a domain using the Logical Domains P2V tool, thereby leveraging Solaris and SPARC binary compatibility. Workloads from other operating systems and platforms can also be migrated to provide an efficient virtualized solution that reduces both energy costs and server sprawl.

4

Oracle Solaris 10 as an x86 Guest

As we will discuss in Chapter 6, "Oracle Solaris Containers," an Oracle Solaris Container is a virtualized operating system (OS) environment created within a single instance of the Oracle Solaris operating system. Today, many people also want to run Solaris 10 as a full instance of an operating system in a virtual machine (VM) of an x86 (or x64) computer. It is anticipated that the number of users seeking this capability will increase in the future, and that the use of Solaris 10 as an x86 guest will expand into other virtualization technologies as well.

This chapter discusses the use of Solaris 10 as an x86 guest running on Type 1 hypervisors only. Oracle's Type 2 hypervisor, Oracle VM VirtualBox (covered in Chapter 5, "Oracle VM VirtualBox") is capable of running Solaris 10 as an x86 guest and other x86 guests such as Linux distributions and Windows.

This chapter discusses the use of Solaris 10 as an x86 guest with respect to certification and support. In some cases, the OS is known to work but is not certified for those circumstances. Each virtualization technology is covered at a high level with respect to architecture and features. A comparison of each technology's features and architecture is beyond the scope of this chapter.

This chapter provides information on running the Solaris 10 release as an x86 guest on the following virtualization technologies:

- *Oracle VM Server for x86*
- *xVM hypervisor*

- *Citrix XenServer*
- *VMware ESX*
- *Microsoft Windows Server 2008 Hyper-V*
- *Red Hat Enterprise Virtualization (Kernel-Based Virtual Machine [KVM])*

Oracle provides a central point of reference for support of Solaris in the Hardware Compatibility List (HCL). The HCL is available at `http://www.bigadmin.com/hcl.`

4.1 Overview

This section provides a quick description of the HCL and then discusses Type 1 hypervisors, including those based on the Xen open-source project.

4.1.1 Overview of the Hardware Compatibility List

The HCL identifies hardware, servers, desktops, laptops, and a selection of peripherals that are compatible with Oracle Solaris and OpenSolaris releases; it also provides information about available software support. The December 2009 HCL section on virtualization is the reference point for this chapter.

4.1.2 Type 1 Hypervisor Overview

All of the virtualization technologies listed earlier are Type 1—that is, "bare metal"—hypervisors and are classified by each vendor as operating at the enterprise level. A virtual machine monitor (VMM) or hypervisor is a host program that allows a single computer to support multiple execution environments. Users see their virtual machines as self-contained computers isolated from other users, even though every user is served by the same physical machine. A Type 1 hypervisor runs directly on the hardware platform and sits between the guest operating system in the virtual machine and the host computer's hardware. The primary function of the hypervisor is to monitor and prevent a guest operating system from accessing resources outside its privilege scope. Multiple virtual machines can be run on a single physical system. Each virtual machine (known as a *guest domain*) runs its own complete and distinct operating environment with its own I/O devices, CPUs, memory, and network interfaces. Thus the hypervisor enables the transparent sharing and partitioning of system resources.

As of December 2009, the majority of Type 1 hypervisors were 64-bit rather than 32-bit based. A 32-bit hypervisor can access up to 4 GB of memory. However, using Physical Address Extensions (PAE), it becomes possible to access as much as 64 GB. With a 64-bit hypervisor, it is possible to access even more than 64 GB of memory and, therefore, to support a greater number of virtual machines.

4.1.3 Xen Open-Source Project-Based Hypervisors

The following technologies are derived from the work of the open-source Xen project:

- Oracle VM Server for x86
- xVM hypervisor
- Citrix XenServer

For further details on the Xen project, see `http://www.xen.org`.

Xen is open-source software that was released under the terms of the GNU General Public License. Its hypervisor uses a combination of paravirtualization and hardware-assisted virtualization. Paravirtualization allows for collaboration between the operating environment and the virtualization platform, which in turn enables the creation of a simple and lightweight hypervisor. For guest operating environments that are not fully paravirtualized, the Xen-based hypervisor uses hardware virtualization assist technologies.

Two types of domains are supported: the privileged domain 0 (also referred to as dom0) and unprivileged guest domains (referred to as domU).

While the hypervisor performs low-level virtualization functionality, it relies on dom0 for the following functions:

- Creating guest domains
- Controlling access to system resources by the guest domains
- Controlling the amount of memory allocated to a guest domain
- Determining which real physical devices a guest domain can access

Because Xen-based hypervisors do not include any device drivers, the hypervisor delegates control of the machine's physical devices to dom0. That domain must work closely with the hypervisor layer; therefore, dom0 is always paravirtualized. The hypervisor boots before dom0 and then boots dom0 as its first guest domain. Thus this domain is, in effect, a special-purpose paravirtualized guest that provides the control of the virtualization functionality.

A guest domain can be either paravirtualized (PV) or a hardware virtual machine (HVM).

In *paravirtualization*, the guest operating environment is aware that it is running on top of a hypervisor and has additional features that can expedite device access and support the concept of stable devices. Stable devices free the guest from the need to be aware of the physical devices underneath, and the dependencies to physical device drivers are removed. Paravirtualized guest domains can run on either 32- or 64-bit platforms.

In the fully virtualized HVM model, the guest domain is completely unaware that it is being virtualized and acts as if it has exclusive access to the devices and resources presented to it. HVM guest domains depend on the HVM extensions to the x86 instruction set, which are currently provided by AMD with AMD Virtualization Technology (AMD-V) and by Intel with Intel Virtualization Technology (VT) processors. Note that HVM guest domains require either AMD-V technology or Intel VT processor systems.

HVM guests require exclusive hypervisor interaction as well as a dedicated QEMU process for each guest. QEMU is a processor emulator that provides a set of device models, which in turn allow it to run a variety of unmodified guest operating systems. Using QEMU, the virtual machine can be equipped with many types of hardware. Examples include hard disks, CD-ROM drives, network cards, sound chips, and some USB devices. QEMU is also capable of simulating multiple CPUs within a guest domain. It does not depend on the presence of graphical output methods on the host system, but rather allows the user to access the console of the guest operating system via Virtual Network Computing (VNC).

For Xen-based hypervisors, QEMU does not provide emulated CPUs for either HVM or paravirtualized guests. Instead, the hypervisor schedules actual CPUs to run the guest domains. QEMU provides network and disk device emulation for HVM guest domains when paravirtualized drivers are not in use. It also provides emulation of the rest of the devices commonly found on a PC platform (e.g., interrupt controller, timer, serial port). QEMU device support is not dependent on whether the platform supports AMD-V/Intel-VT.

In summary, both types of guest domains are being fooled into believing they have exclusive access to the system resources presented to them. The difference is that a paravirtualized guest is aware that it is being fooled, whereas the HVM is not.

Paravirtualization offers near-native performance, in contrast to HVM. HVM has a higher overhead due, in part, to the use of device emulation and the use of the CPU virtualization extensions. Even so, it is able to support a broader array of guest operating systems.

4.2 Oracle VM Server for x86

Oracle VM Server for x86 (previously known as Oracle VM) is a low-cost server virtualization and management solution from Oracle utilizing the Xen hypervisor. Oracle VM's dom0 was specifically designed to provide the best performance for high I/O workloads. The Oracle VM dom0 is a paravirtualized Oracle Enterprise

Linux guest kernel. The dom0 hypervisor is able to run on 64- or 32-bit CPUs and, therefore, is capable of supporting 64- or 32-bit guests, respectively. Oracle considers the control domain to be an appliance, which is completely maintained by Oracle.

Oracle VM provides a browser-based management solution for creating, cloning, sharing, configuring, booting, and migrating VMs within pools of Oracle VM servers.

Oracle VM is the only Oracle-certified hypervisor solution for 32- or 64-bit x86 platforms for Oracle software. Oracle products such as Oracle Database, Oracle Real Application Clusters (RAC), Oracle Enterprise Manager Grid Control, Application Server, Hyperion, JD Edwards, Berkeley DB, TimesTen, Oracle E-Business Suite, Siebel, PeopleSoft, Oracle Retail, Oracle Financial Services Software Limited, Oracle Weblogic Platform, and so on are officially supported when running in Oracle VM-based environments. Customers who obtain paid support for Oracle VM receive access to patches, fixes, and updates through the Unbreakable Linux Network (ULN).

4.2.1 Oracle VM Key Features

Oracle VM key features include the following:

- Windows, Linux, and Solaris guests
- Rapid Oracle application deployment using preconfigured virtual machine templates
- Advanced high-availability features such as guest and VM Manager HA, secure live migration, and server pool load balancing
- Virtual Machine I/O resource management features
- P2V (Physical to Virtual) and V2V (Virtual to Virtual) conversion
- Official Oracle product certification based on real-world testing
- Full-stack enterprise-class support
- Centralized multiserver management with Oracle VM or Oracle Enterprise Manager
- Shared SAN, iSCSI, and NAS storage

4.2.2 Oracle Solaris PV Drivers

Oracle VM provides guest paravirtualized drivers for Windows and Oracle Enterprise Linux.

4.2.3 Oracle VM Support for Oracle Solaris

Table 4.1 describes the certification for Solaris as an x86 guest running on Oracle VM on an Oracle VM-supported host.

Table 4.1 Support for Oracle Solaris as a Guest of Oracle VM

Oracle VM Version	Guest OS	Certified	Tested	PV/HVM
2.2	Solaris 10 10/09	Yes	Yes	HVM with PV drivers

4.3 xVM Hypervisor

The xVM hypervisor is a free server virtualization platform for the OpenSolaris operating system derived from the work of the Xen community. This hypervisor contains features such as live migration, snapshots, shared storage support, and V2V machine guest migration at no cost. The product is free to download and use.

To download the latest supported OpenSolaris release, which includes the xVM hypervisor, visit http://www.opensolaris.com/get/index.jsp.

For further information about the features and support of OpenSolaris, visit http://www.opensolaris.com/learn/faq/.

Oracle Solaris 10 distributions for x86, starting with Solaris 10 10/08 and OpenSolaris 2008.11, offer integrated paravirtualization support for the xVM hypervisor. Both Solaris 10 and OpenSolaris can also be run as an HVM guest. Red Hat Enterprise Linux and CentOS distributions (versions 5.2 and 5.3) are known to work as both PV and HVM guests. Fedora 10, Ubuntu Linux 7.04, and OpenSuSE 11.1 are known to work as HVM guests.

Table 4.2 details xVM hypervisor capabilities in OpenSolaris 2009.06 and the version of Xen on which it is based.

Table 4.2 xVM Hypervisor Capabilities in OpenSolaris 2009.06

Hypervisor 32-/64-Bit	dom0 32-/64-Bit	Xen Version
64-bit	64-bit	3.1.4

4.3.1 xVM Hypervisor Key Features

xVM Hypervisor key features include the following:

- Oracle Solaris 10, OpenSolaris, Windows, and Linux guests.
- V2V tools for importing VMware, Microsoft, Oracle VM VirtualBox (previously called Sun VirtualBox), and OVF file types via Oracle VM VirtualBox

guest images. For more information about OVF (Open Virtualization Format), see `http://www.dmtf.org/standards/published_documents/DSP0243_1.0.0.pdf`.

- Shared SAN, iSCSI, and NAS storage.
- Live migration.
- Virtual networking and VLAN support.
- ZFS file system.
- Carrier-grade security.
- Fault Management Architecture (FMA) .
- Dynamic Tracing (DTrace) hypervisor probes.

4.3.2 Oracle Solaris PV Drivers

The xVM hypervisor paravirtualized drivers are automatically loaded and installed on Solaris 10 10/08 and later releases. They are available for Solaris 10 05/08 as patch 137112-06 or later. In Table 4.3, the reference to HVM and PVIO is a variation on an HVM guest that uses paravirtualized network and disk drivers for improved performance. In the case of OpenSolaris, the guest can either be a paravirtualized or HVM guest; in either case, paravirtualization drivers are loaded and installed automatically.

4.3.3 xVM Hypervisor Support for Oracle Solaris

Table 4.3 outlines the certification for the Solaris and OpenSolaris operating systems as x86 guests running xVM hypervisor on a supported host.

Table 4.3 xVM Hypervisor Support of Oracle Solaris and OpenSolaris

xVM Hypervisor Version	Guest OS	Certified	Tested	PV/HVM
2009.06	Solaris 10 10/09	Yes	Yes	HVM and PVIO
2009.06	Solaris 10 05/09	Yes	Yes	HVM and PVIO
2009.06	Solaris 10 10/08	Yes	Yes	HVM and PVIO
2009.06	Solaris 10 05/08	Yes	Yes	HVM and PVIO with patch 137112-06 (or later)
2009.06	OpenSolaris 2009.06	Yes	Yes	HVM or PV
2009.06	OpenSolaris 2008.11	Yes	Yes	HVM or PV

4.4 Citrix XenServer

Citrix XenServer is a server virtualization platform derived from the work of the Xen community. Modifications and additions include features such as live migration (XenMotion), centralized multiserver management (XenCenter), virtual machine templates, snapshots, shared storage support, and resource pools. The product is free to download and use.

Citrix XenServer supports paravirtualization with Windows and Linux distributions such as Red Hat Enterprise Linux, Novell SuSE, Debian, Oracle Enterprise Linux, and CentOS.

Table 4.4 details Citrix XenServer 5.5 U1 capabilities and the Xen version on which it is based.

Table 4.4 Citrix XenServer 5.5 U1 Capabilities

Hypervisor 32-/64-Bit	dom0 32-/64-Bit	Xen Version
64-bit	32-bit	3.3

4.4.1 Citrix XenServer Key Features

Citrix XenServer key features include the following:

- Windows, Linux, and Solaris guests
- Unlimited servers, virtual machines, and memory
- P2V and V2V conversion
- Shared SAN, iSCSI, and NAS storage
- Centralized multiserver management
- Resilient distributed management architecture
- Live motion (live migration)
- Shared virtual machine template library
- Centralized configuration management with Citrix XenCenter
- Virtual infrastructure patch management

4.4.2 Oracle Solaris PV Drivers

Citrix XenServer provides guest paravirtualized drivers for Microsoft Windows and utilities for Linux called Citrix Tools for Virtual Machines. At the time of this writing, no Citrix XenServer supplied Solaris 10 or OpenSolaris paravirtualized drivers were available.

4.4.3 Citrix XenServer Support for Oracle Solaris

Table 4.5 describes the certification for Solaris as an x86 guest running on Citrix XenServer on a Citrix XenServer supported host.

Table 4.5 Support for Oracle Solaris as a Guest of Citrix Xen Server

Citrix XenServer Version	Guest OS	Certified	Tested	PV/HVM
5.5 U1	Solaris 10 10/09	No	Yes	HVM

4.5 VMware ESX

VMware ESX is a component of both VMware Infrastructure (VI) version 3.x and vSphere version 4.x. Each is a suite of products that adds management and reliability services to the core server product. The basic server requires persistent storage, typically hard disk based, for storing the virtualization kernel and support files. The use of centralized shared storage enables the use of features such as VMotion (live migration). The ESXi product offers a small-footprint hypervisor on the host with a simple configuration console primarily for network configuration and the remote-based VMware Infrastructure Client Interface. This approach allows for more resources to be dedicated to guest environments and offers the option to place this small-footprint hypervisor on a dedicated hardware device. ESX and ESXi basically consist of the same code; however, ESX includes a service console operating system (COS) that is a standard Linux environment through which a user has privileged access to the VMware ESX kernel. This Linux-based privileged access allows the user to customize the environment by installing agents and drivers, and by executing scripts and other Linux-environment code.

VMware ESX supports full virtualization using the combination of binary translation and direct execution techniques. Binary translation replaces the instructions that are not able to be virtualized with new sequences of instructions that have the same effect on the virtual hardware. Also, guest user-level code is directly executed on the processor for high-performance virtualization. The VMM provides each virtual machine with all the services of a physical system, such as BIOS, virtual devices, and virtualized memory management. Using these techniques, the virtual machine is fully abstracted from the underlying hardware.

The operating environment within the virtual machine is unaware that it is being virtualized and, therefore, can remain unmodified.

A fully virtualized approach negates the need for using hardware virtualization assistance. Nevertheless, to support 64-bit guests, ESX requires the use of AMD-V or Intel-VT CPUs. ESX also uses the hardware-assisted memory management capabilities provided by AMD Rapid Virtualization Index (RVI) and Intel Extended Page Table (EPT) to improve performance. In the case of ESX 4.x, the use of these features plus the use of large memory pages further increases performance. VMware ESX 4.0 installs and runs only on servers with 64-bit x86 CPUs; in other words, it does not work on 32-bit systems.

4.5.1 VMware vSphere Key Features

VMware vSphere key features include the following:

- VMFS high-performance concurrent (cluster-aware) file system
- Shared SAN, iSCSI, and NAS storage
- Network virtualization
- VMotion (live migration)
- Storage VMotion
- High availability
- Dynamic resource scheduling
- Centralized multiserver management with Virtual Center and VI Client
- Fault-tolerant VMs on ESX 4.x
- Update Manager

The availability of many of these features depends on the type of distribution purchased: VMware Infrastructure Foundation, Standard or Enterprise for V3.x and Essentials, Standard, Advanced, Enterprise or Enterprise Plus for V4.x. Virtual Center or vCenter is required to take advantage of some of the more advanced features; these tools must be purchased separately.

4.5.2 Oracle Solaris PV Drivers

VMware ESX provides guest paravirtualized drivers called VMware Tools. In the case of Solaris, the installation of these tools enhances graphics and mouse operation. The first step in the installation of the tools is via the VMware Virtual Infrastructure Client console, where the VMware Tools CD image is extended to

Solaris. The image is then copied to a temporary install directory, unpacked, and then installed. The guest must be rebooted to ensure that the changes take hold.

4.5.3 ESX Support for Oracle Solaris

Table 4.6 outlines the certification for Solaris as an x86 guest running on VMware ESX 4.0 on a VMware-supported host. For earlier VMware versions, visit the following website:

```
http://www.bigadmin.com/hcl/data/v12n/views/v12n_vmware.page1.html
```

For information about VMware support, select the Guest/Host OS tab at the following website:

```
http://www.vmware.com/resources/compatibility/search.php
```

Table 4.6 Support for Oracle Solaris as a Guest of VMWare ESX 4.0

ESX Version	Guest OS	Certified	Tested
4.0	Solaris 10 05/09	Yes	Yes
4.0	Solaris 10 05/08	Yes	Yes
4.0	Solaris 10 08/07	Yes	Yes
4.0	Solaris 10 11/06	No	Yes
4.0	Solaris 10 06/06	No	Yes
4.0	Solaris 10 03/05	No	Yes

4.6 Microsoft Windows Server 2008 Hyper-V

Microsoft Hyper-V Server is a dedicated stand-alone product that contains only the Windows hypervisor, Windows Server driver model, and virtualization components. It offers the advantages of a small footprint and minimal overhead. Microsoft Hyper-V Server is designed to easily integrate into a customer's existing Microsoft management frameworks and tools.

Microsoft Hyper-V Server supports isolation through the use of a *partition*. A partition is a logical unit of isolation in which a guest operating system executes. A hypervisor instance must have at least one parent partition that is running Windows Server 2008. The Hyper-V hypervisor is a 64-bit application that is loaded after the parent partition has booted. The virtualization stack runs in the parent partition and has direct access to the hardware devices. The parent partition creates the child partitions, which in turn host the guest operating systems.

Child partitions do not have direct access to hardware resources, but instead have a virtual view of the resources. Any request to the virtual devices is redirected via the VMBus to the physical devices in the parent partition. The VMBus is a logical channel that enables inter-partition communication. The response is also redirected via the VMBus. The parent partitions run a virtualization service provider (VSP), which connects to the VMBus and handles device access requests from child partitions. Virtual devices of child partitions run a virtualization service client (VSC), which redirects the requests to VSPs in the parent partition via the VMBus. This entire process is transparent to the guest operating systems.

The distribution in the parent partition can be either a full distribution of Windows Server 2008 or a Core version. The Core version is limited to a CLI, where server configuration is performed using shell commands. A menu-driven CLI interface (SCONFIG) is available that simplifies the initial server configuration. Once initial configuration is complete, it is possible to use the Microsoft Management Console tools, Windows PowerShell, or Microsoft System Center Virtual Machine Manager (SCVMM) to manage the server more extensively.

4.6.1 Microsoft Windows Server 2008 R2 Hyper-V Key Features

Microsoft Windows Server 2008 R2 Hyper-V key features include the following:

- Windows, Solaris, and Linux guests
- Live migration
- High-availability, cluster-shared volumes
- Shared SAN, iSCSI, and NAS storage
- Dynamic VM storage
- Network load balancing and virtualized network enhancements
- Virtual machine snapshots
- P2V and V2V via the System Center SCVMM tool set
- Centralized multiserver management with Microsoft System Center

4.6.2 Oracle Solaris PV Drivers

As with Oracle Solaris, paravirtualized drivers have been integrated into Microsoft Windows. For details on Microsoft Windows Support as a guest on Hyper-V Server R2, visit the following website:

```
http://www.microsoft.com/windowsserver2008/en/us/hyperv-
supported-guest-os.aspx
```

Microsoft Windows Server 2008 Hyper-V R2 provides guest paravirtualized drivers in the form of Linux integration components for SuSE Linux Enterprise Server 10, both 32- and 64-bit editions. These integration components enable Xen-enabled Linux to take advantage of the VSP/VSC architecture and provide improved performance.

At the time of this writing, no Microsoft supplied Solaris 10 or OpenSolaris paravirtualized drivers were available.

4.6.3 Microsoft Windows Server 2008 Hyper-V R2 Support for Oracle Solaris

Table 4.7 summarizes the certification for Solaris as an x86 guest running on a supported Microsoft Windows Server 2008 Hyper-V R2 host.

Table 4.7 Microsoft Windows Server 2008 Hyper-V R2 Support for Oracle Solaris

Microsoft Windows Server 2008 Hyper-V Version	Guest OS	Certified	Tested
R2	Solaris 10 10/09	No	Yes

4.7 Red Hat Enterprise Virtualization

The Red Hat Enterprise Virtualization (RHEV) portfolio of products consists of two components: the Red Hat Enterprise Virtualization Hypervisor (RHEV-H) and the Red Hat Enterprise Virtualization Manager for Servers (RHEV-M Server).

The Red Hat Enterprise Virtualization Hypervisor is based on Kernel-based Virtual Machine (KVM) virtualization technology. It can be deployed with Red Hat Enterprise Linux 5.4 and later, installed as a hypervisor host, and managed through RHEV-M Server. The Red Hat Enterprise Virtualization Manager (RHEV-M) product provides management of virtual machines and their associated infrastructure (e.g., images, network and storage connections).

The KVM project represents the most recent generation of open-source virtualization. KVM is implemented as a loadable kernel module that converts the Linux kernel into a bare metal hypervisor. Because KVM was designed after the advent of hardware-assisted virtualization, it did not have to implement features that were provided by hardware. Instead, KVM depends on Intel VT-X or AMD-V enabled CPUs and uses those features to virtualize the CPU. It can run on either 32- or 64-bit hosts. KVM supports 32-bit virtual machines on 64-bit hosts; however, it does not support 64-bit virtual machines on 32-bit hosts. For more information, see `http://www.linux-kvm.org`.

Within the KVM architecture, a virtual machine is implemented as a Linux process and, therefore, is scheduled by the Linux scheduler. Device emulation is handled by a modified version of QEMU that provides an emulated BIOS, PCI bus, USB bus, and a standard set of devices such as IDE and SCSI disk controllers and network cards.

To provide the security and isolation for the virtual machine running as a Linux process, the standard Linux security model is used. The Linux kernel uses Security-Enhanced Linux (SELinux) to add mandatory access controls and multilevel and multicategory security as well as provide policy enforcement. The sVirt project (`http://selinuxproject.org/page/SVirt`) builds on SELinux to provide an infrastructure that allows an administrator to define policies for virtual machine isolation. The default state of sVirt ensures that a virtual machine's resources cannot be accessed by any other process or virtual machine. This default state can be extended by the administrator to define fine-grained permissions—for example, to group virtual machines together to share resources.

4.7.1 Red Hat Enterprise Virtualization Key Features

Red Hat Enterprise Virtualization key features include the following:

- Windows, Solaris, and Linux guests
- Live migration
- High availability
- Dynamic system scheduling
- Power-saving features
- Maintenance manager
- Image and template manager
- Thin provisioning for server and desktop guests
- Shared SAN, iSCSI, and NAS storage
- Centralized multiserver management with Red Hat Enterprise Virtualization Manager

4.7.2 Oracle Solaris PV Drivers

KVM paravirtualized drivers are automatically loaded and installed on Red Hat Enterprise Linux 4.8, 5.3, and later. The KVM hypervisor uses the VirtIO community standard for paravirtualized drivers and provides drivers for Microsoft Windows XP, Server 2003, Vista, and Server 2008.

At the time of writing, Red Hat did not offer Solaris 10 or OpenSolaris paravirtualized drivers.

4.7.3 Red Hat Enterprise Virtualization Support for Oracle Solaris

Table 4.8 summarizes the certification for Solaris as an x86 guest running on a supported Red Hat Enterprise Virtualization Hypervisor host.

Table 4.8 Support for Solaris as a Guest of Red Hat Enterprise Virtualization

Red Hat Enterprise Virtualization	Guest OS	Certified	Tested
5.4	Solaris 10 10/09	No	Yes

4.8 Summary

For people who want to virtualize Oracle Solaris releases on Sun platforms, a plethora of options are available: Oracle Solaris Containers, Oracle VM Server for x86, Oracle VM Server for SPARC (previously called Sun Logical Domains), Sun Dynamic System Domains, Oracle VM VirtualBox, and xVM hypervisor. Oracle Solaris runs very well as a guest of several x86 hypervisors. Its functionality, scalability, and thousands of certified applications make it an excellent choice as a virtual machine operating system.

5

Oracle VM VirtualBox

Oracle VM VirtualBox ("VirtualBox") is a high-performance, cross-platform virtualization engine for use on computers running Microsoft Windows, the most popular Linux distributions, Oracle Solaris, or MacOS. Designed for use on Intel and AMD x86 systems, Oracle VM VirtualBox can be deployed on desktop or server hardware. As a hosted hypervisor, it extends the existing operating system installed on the hardware rather than replacing it.

VirtualBox includes a hypervisor for the host platform, an application programming interface (API) and software development kit (SDK) for managing guest virtual machines, a command-line tool for managing guests locally, a web service for remote management of guests, a wizard-style graphical tool to manage guests, a graphical console for displaying guest applications on the local host, and a built-in Remote Desktop Protocol (RDP) server that provides complete access to a guest from a remote client.

As shown in Figure 5.1, VirtualBox can run on a wide variety of host platforms. Binaries are available for these operating systems, most of them in 32-bit and 64-bit versions:

- Solaris 10 5/08 and newer, and OpenSolaris 2008.05 and newer
- Oracle Enterprise Linux (32-bit)
- Microsoft Windows (XP, Vista, 7) and Windows Server 2003 and 2008
- Mac OS X 10.5 and newer (Intel only)
- Linux distributions, including SuSE 9 and newer, Ubuntu, Red Hat Enterprise Linux 4 and newer, and others

There are no specific limitations on the guest operating system, but supported guests include all of the host operating systems plus FreeBSD, OS/2, and legacy Windows versions (NT, Windows 98, Windows 3.1, DOS). No special hardware is required to run VirtualBox, other than an Intel x86-compatible system and adequate memory to run the guests. If the system has Intel VT-x or AMD-V hardware virtualization extensions and they are enabled in the BIOS, VirtualBox can take advantage of these items and provide even better guest operational behavior.

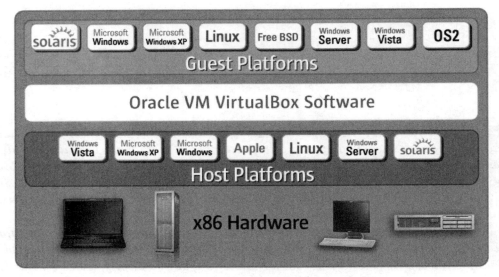

Figure 5.1 Platforms Supported by Oracle VM VirtualBox

The modular design of VirtualBox provides a consistent set of features across a wide range of host platforms. As a consequence, a virtual machine or disk image created on one host can be loaded and run on any supported host. In addition, a user or administrator who is familiar with managing guest virtual machines on one type of host can manage guests on any of the other supported systems.

Advanced desktop features such as Seamless Mode and Shared Clipboard give users a uniquely intimate experience when interacting with locally running guests. The built-in Remote Desktop Protocol (RDP) server makes VirtualBox ideal for consolidating and hosting remote desktop systems. Recent improvements in disk and network performance, especially when combined with the advanced resource management features available in Oracle Solaris, make VirtualBox an excellent choice for hosting server workloads.

This chapter assumes general knowledge of PC hardware. It also assumes the use of VirtualBox version 3.1.4.

5.1 How Oracle VM VirtualBox Works

Virtualizing an operating system on an x86 processor is a difficult task, especially without Intel VT-x or AMD-V hardware features. Before describing how VirtualBox works, a quick review of the x86 storage protection model is necessary.

The Intel x86 architecture defines four levels of storage protection called *rings*, which are numbered from 0 (the most privileged) to 3 (the least privileged). These rings are used by operating systems to protect critical system memory from programming errors in less-privileged user applications. Of these four levels, ring 0 is special in that it allows software to access real processor resources such as registers, page tables, and service interrupts. Most operating systems execute user programs in ring 3 and their kernel services in ring 0.

VirtualBox runs a single process on the host operating system for each virtual guest. All of the guest user code is run natively in ring 3, just as it would be if it were running in the host. As a result, user code will perform at native speed when running in a guest virtual machine.

To protect the host against failures in the guest, the guest kernel code is not allowed to run in ring 0 but instead runs in ring 1 if there is no hardware virtualization support, or in a VT-x ring 0 context if such support is available. This presents a problem because the guest may be executing instructions that are permitted only in ring 0 while other instructions behave differently when run in ring 1. To maintain proper operation of the guest kernel, the VirtualBox Virtual Machine Monitor (VMM) scans the ring 1 code and either replaces the troublesome code paths with direct hypervisor calls or executes them in a safe emulator.

In some situations, the VMM may not be able to determine exactly what the relocated ring 1 guest code is doing. In these cases, VirtualBox makes use of a QEMU emulator to achieve the same general goals. Examples include running BIOS code, real-mode operations early during guest booting when the guest disables interrupts, or when an instruction is known to cause a trap that may require emulation.

Because this emulation is slow compared to the direct execution of guest code, the VMM includes a code scanner that is unique for each supported guest. As mentioned earlier, this scanner will identify code paths and replace them with direct calls into the hypervisor for a more correct and efficient implementation of the operation. In addition, each time a guest fault occurs, the VMM will analyze the cause of the fault to see if the offending code stream can be replaced by a less expensive method in the future. As a consequence of this approach, VirtualBox performs better than a typical emulator or code recompiler. It can also run a fully virtualized guest at nearly the same speed as one that is assisted by Intel VT-x or AMD-V features.

Some operating systems may run device drivers in ring 1, which can cause a conflict with the relocated guest kernel code. These types of guests will require hardware virtualization.

5.1.1 Oracle VM VirtualBox Architecture

VirtualBox uses a layered architecture consisting of a set of kernel modules for running virtual machines, an API for managing the guests, and a set of user programs and services. At the core is the hypervisor, implemented as a ring 0 (privileged) kernel service. Figure 5.2 shows the relationships between all of these components. The kernel service consists of a device driver named vboxsrv, which is responsible for tasks such as allocating physical memory for the guest virtual machine, and several loadable hypervisor modules for things like saving and restoring the guest process context when a host interrupt occurs, turning control over to the guest OS to begin execution, and deciding when VT-x or AMD-V events need to be handled.

The hypervisor does not get involved with the details of the guest operating system scheduling. Instead, those tasks are handled completely by the guest during its execution. The entire guest is run as a single process on the host system and will run only when scheduled by the host. If they are present, an administrator can use host resource controls such as scheduling classes and CPU caps or reservations to give very predictable execution of the guest machine.

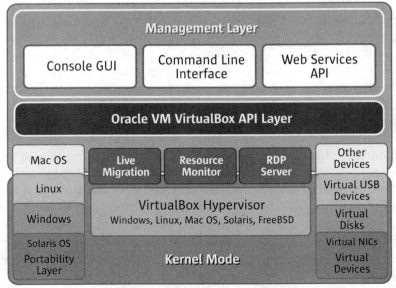

Figure 5.2 Oracle VM VirtualBox Architecture

Additional device drivers will be present to allow the guest machine access to other host resources such as disks, network controllers, and audio and USB devices. In reality, the hypervisor actually does little work. Rather, most of the interesting work in running the guest machine is done in the guest process. Thus the host's resource controls and scheduling methods can be used to control the guest machine behavior.

In addition to the kernel modules, several processes on the host are used to support running guests. All of these processes are started automatically when needed.

- `VBoxSVC` is the VirtualBox service process. It keeps track of all virtual machines that are running on the host. It is started automatically when the first guest boots.

- `vboxzoneacess` is a daemon unique to Solaris that allows the VirtualBox device to be accessed from an Oracle Solaris Container.

- `VBoxXPCOMIPCD` is the XPCOM process used on non-Windows hosts for interprocess communication between guests and the management applications. On Windows hosts, the native COM services are used.

- `VirtualBox` is the process that actually runs the guest virtual machine when started. One of these processes exists for every guest that is running on the host. If host resource limits are desired for the guest, this process enforces those controls.

5.1.2 Interacting with Oracle VM VirtualBox

There are two primary methods for a user to interact with VirtualBox: a simple graphical user interface (GUI) and a very complete and detailed command-line interface (CLI). The GUI allows the user to create and manage guest virtual machines as well as set most of the common configuration options. When a guest machine is started from this user interface, a graphical console window opens on the host that allows the user to interact with the guest as if it were running on real hardware. To start the graphical interface, type the command `VirtualBox` at any shell prompt. On Oracle Solaris, this command is found in `/usr/bin` and is available to all users.

The CLI is the `VBoxManage` command. `VBoxManage` has many subcommands and options, some of which are discussed in the following sections. To get a list of all `VBoxManage` options, just type `VBoxManage` at any shell prompt. Without any command arguments, `VBoxManage` will respond with a list of all valid options. When a `VBoxManage` command successfully completes, it will print out a banner similar to the one in the following example:

```
% VBoxManage list vms
Sun VirtualBox Command Line Management Interface Version 3.1.4
(C) 2005-2010 Sun Microsystems, Inc.
All rights reserved.

"Windows XP" {4ec5efdc-fa76-49bb-8562-7c2a0bac8282}
```

If the banner fails to print, an error occurred while processing the command. Usually, diagnostic information will be displayed instead of the banner. If the banner is the only output, the command successfully completed. In the examples in the remainder of this chapter, the banner output has been omitted for the sake of brevity.

5.2 Oracle VM VirtualBox Guest Platform

VirtualBox supports the execution of guest operating systems in fully virtualized machines—a capability that allows the guest to run without requiring any special software or device drivers. The guest operating system is presented with a virtual motherboard with the following features.

- 1 to 32 CPUs
- Up to 32 GB of memory
- A dual-channel IDE disk controller with up to four devices
- An optional Serial ATA (SATA) disk controller with up to 30 attached devices
- An optional SCSI controller with up to 16 attached devices
- Up to 8 PCI network host adapters
- Keyboard, video, and mouse (KVM) console
- Either a legacy BIOS or EFI firmware

The next several sections describe details of the VirtualBox guest platform.

5.2.1 Virtual CPUs

Unlike Oracle VM Server for SPARC (previously called Sun Logical Domains), VirtualBox does not directly assign CPU resources to the guest domain. Instead, virtual CPUs are presented to the guest and time-sliced on real CPUs using the host system's scheduling facilities. The number of CPUs allocated for each guest can be specified in the Processor tab of the guest machine's System settings, as shown in Figure 5.3.

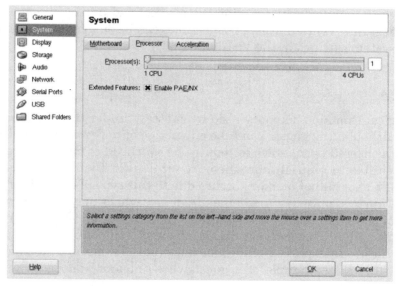

Figure 5.3 Configuring Virtual Processors

If you try to specify more CPUs than are present on the system, the VirtualBox graphical interface will display a warning. The guest will run but the performance of the guest is likely to be significantly degraded.

The number of CPUs can also be specified using the VBoxManage modifyvm command. VBoxManage will not issue a warning if the number of CPUs exceeds the capacity of the host.

```
% VBoxManage showvminfo "Solaris 10" | grep CPU
Number of CPUs:   1
CPUID overrides: None
% VBoxManage modifyvm "Solaris 10" --cpus 8
% VBoxManage showvminfo "Solaris 10" | grep CPU
Number of CPUs:   8
CPUID overrides: None
```

VirtualBox offers support for non-executable pages (NX). This feature enables guest operating systems to mark a page that is used for data so that it cannot be executed. This technique can help reduce the chance that a buffer overflow type of attack from a worm or virus against the guest will be successful. If the guest supports the NX feature, it is recommended that it be enabled in the CPU settings.

Although a guest does not require hardware virtualization assistance to perform well, if the host platform supports nested page tables, enabling this feature for a guest will provide a significant improvement in performance because most of the memory management functions can be carried out by the guest without requiring host intervention. Nested page tables can be enabled in the Acceleration tab of the system settings in the VirtualBox GUI.

5.2.2 RAM

Unlike Logical Domains, memory used by guests is under the control of the host platform. Although the guests can take advantage of hardware virtualization features such as nested page tables to reduce the overhead of memory management, it is still possible to request more memory for a guest than the host system has available. If a shortfall of memory occurs due to this type of oversubscription, the host operating system will start demand paging, which may drag down the performance of the guest machines and other applications and services running on the host. VirtualBox does not yet provide a memory ballooning feature that would enable the host to take pages back from a guest in the event of a memory shortfall. Figure 5.4 shows an example of a guest whose memory allocation exceeds the recommended maximum.

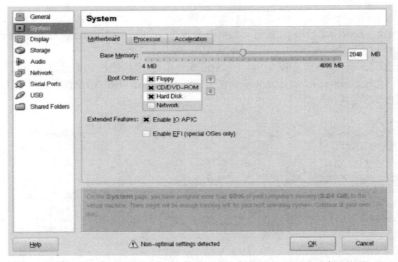

Figure 5.4 Setting Memory for an Oracle VM VirtualBox Guest

To help prevent overallocation of the host memory, the VirtualBox GUI will display a warning if it thinks that too much memory is being configured for a guest. In doing so, it considers only the total amount of memory on the system, not how much of that is actually free. It will display a warning if more than 50% of memory is allocated to a guest and a stronger warning if more than 80% is reserved for a guest.

If sufficient free memory is not available at the time, a guest machine may fail to start with an out-of-memory error, even if it will consume only a small amount of the memory allocated for its use.

Most guest systems run only a few applications or services. Because the host system performs most of the real operations on behalf of the guest, smaller memory allocations for the guest can still produce excellent results. Running a guest desktop with 512 MB or less may work well as long as enough memory is allocated for the guest system to boot.

5.2.3 Virtual Disk

Because a guest operating system needs persistent storage, VirtualBox can make several different types of host storage available to the guest in the form of virtual disks:

- A file that contains a disk image
- A real disk device
- An iSCSI target
- A CD-ROM/DVD or file containing an ISO image
- A file containing a floppy disk image

All of these storage options must be presented to the guest OS using a virtual disk. To facilitate this sharing, the VirtualBox virtual platform can have up to three disk controllers. Each of these controllers can have attached devices that provide access to the host storage.

Each virtual motherboard has a dual-channel IDE controller. Each of the two channels has two devices: a master and a slave. By convention, the master device on the first IDE channel is the boot disk and the master device on the second IDE channel is a CD-ROM/DVD. Many IDE chipsets are available, and VirtualBox can emulate an Intel PIIX3, PIIX4, or ICH6. There is no difference in the performance between these options, but if an operating system is expecting a particular IDE controller and sees a different one, it may not operate properly. This situation happens most often when importing a virtual machine from another virtualization product. To prevent this problem, set the IDE controller type to match that of the other virtualization product.

A virtual motherboard may also have a Serial ATA (SATA) controller. Such a controller can support up to 30 disk devices. By default, the first 4 devices operate in legacy IDE mode, meaning that the BIOS can use them just like any other IDE device. Once the guest operating system is up and running and has loaded the SATA drivers for these devices, they can then be accessed in SATA mode. In addition to supporting a larger number of devices, SATA is a more efficient interface both on the guest and in the emulation layer. SATA devices are preferred if the operating system supports them.

VirtualBox can also provide an LSI Logic or BusLogic SCSI controller, if necessary. Such a controller supports up to 16 devices. It is intended to facilitate use of legacy operating systems that do not support SATA and need more than the 4 devices provided by the IDE controller. This controller can also be used to attach more than the 30 disks supported by the SATA controller.

Guest hard disks are generally mapped to files on the host platform that contain a complete image of the guest disk, including the boot sector and partition table. The disk images have a fixed geometry based on their total size. Once the disk image is created, its size cannot be altered. When a guest reads from or writes to the disk, VirtualBox redirects the I/O to the native file system services on the host.

VirtualBox supports four disk image file formats.

- VDI, the native VirtualBox disk format. It is the default when you create a new virtual machine or disk image.
- VMDK, a popular disk format used by VMware.
- VHD, the format used by Microsoft.
- Parallels version 2 HDD format. VirtualBox does not support newer formats, but those can be converted to version 2 using tools supplied by Parallels.

With each of these formats, VirtualBox can create fixed-size or dynamically expanding disk images. Fixed-size image files are completely allocated at creation time. This type of image file will take longer to create, because it is dependent on the write performance of the host file system. Once in use, it will be more efficient, as the system does not need to get new blocks as the guest writes to new storage areas. In contrast, dynamically expanding disk images start off small and will grow as the guest writes to new blocks on the virtual disk. These are faster to create, but additional work is required by the host to find new blocks the first time a guest accesses a particular part of the disk. Host file system caching strategies can hide most of the difference in performance, especially on a host that is not heavily loaded. For performance-critical applications that perform many disk writes, fixed-size disk images are recommended. For all other uses, the convenience of dynamically allocated images makes this approach the preferred method.

VirtualBox maintains a library of disk, CD-ROM, and floppy disk images. Before a disk or CD-ROM image can be used by a guest, it must be registered in the Virtual Media Manager. This can be done in the VirtualBox GUI or via the VBoxManage openmedium command. Once an image is registered, it can be assigned to an open port on any guest. Although a disk image may be connected to more than one guest, it can be used by only one guest at a time. A guest will fail to start if one of its disk images is connected to another guest that is currently running.

Using the VBoxManage command line, the following example creates a 16 GB dynamically expanding disk image and attaches it to port 3 of the SATA controller in the guest named Windows 7.

```
% VBoxManage createhd --filename /vbox/HardDisks/Windows7-user.vdi  \
       --size 16000 --format VDI --variant Standard --remember


0%...10%...20%...30%...40%...50%...60%...70%...80%...90%...100%


Disk image created. UUID: 4a0ef971-13d1-428b-aded-5f8720155e0a

% VBoxManage showhdinfo 4a0ef971-13d1-428b-aded-5f8720155e0a
UUID:                 4a0ef971-13d1-428b-aded-5f8720155e0a
Accessible:           yes
Description:
Logical size:         16000 MBytes
Current size on disk: 0 MBytes
Type:                 normal (base)
Storage format:       VDI
Location:             /vbox/HardDisks/Windows7-user.vdi


% VBoxManage storageattach "Windows 7" --storagectl "SATA Controller" \
       --port 3 --device 0 -type hdd   \
       --medium /vbox/HardDisks/Windows7-user.vdi
```

The results of this command can be seen in the Storage settings of this Windows 7 guest, as shown in Figure 5.5.

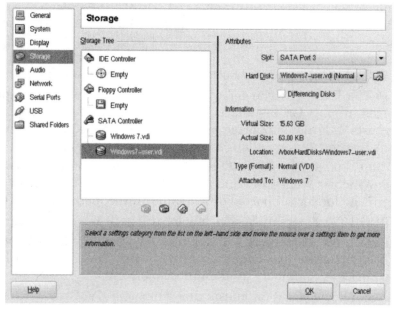

Figure 5.5 Selecting a Guest Disk Image

Note that the actual size of the disk image is only 63KB. To create a fixed-size image, add `--variant Fixed` to the `createhd` step in the preceding example.

CD-ROM images are treated in a similar fashion. The Virtual Media Manager maintains a list of registered images. Because CD-ROM images are not writable by the guest, they can be used by more than one guest at a time. One special image is `VBoxGuestAdditions.iso`, which can be found in the directory `/opt/VirtualBox/additions`. It contains all of the guest drivers and configuration tools that match the version of VirtualBox installed on the host. This image is automatically added by the installation program and is available to all guests.

In addition to a CD-ROM image, a guest can access real media in a CD-ROM or DVD drive on the host. By default, the guest is only allowed to read from the drive. To give the guest write access or to allow special I/O operations required by some multimedia players, enable the Passthrough setting on the CD-ROM device.

5.2.4 Virtual Network Devices

VirtualBox provides up to eight Ethernet PCI devices to each guest virtual machine. The user can select the type of virtual devices that are presented to the guest as well as what the host will do with the associated network I/O. The guest adapter does not need to be the same type as that on the host. For example, a Realtek Ethernet interface on the host can be virtualized as an Intel PRO/1000 on a guest. The first four virtual network adapters can be configured using the Network settings in the GUI. All eight of the devices can be configured using the `VBoxManage` command.

VirtualBox can present any of the following virtual devices to the guest operating system.

- AMD PCNet PCI II: A legacy host adapter for older guest operating systems.
- AMD PCNet FAST III: The default for most guests. This host adapter is well supported in most OS installation media, which makes it a good choice for most guests. It is also supported by the GNU GRUB bootloader, which allows network booting and installation of a guest operating system.
- Intel PRO/1000 MT Desktop: The default for newer guest operating systems such as Windows Vista and Windows Server 2008. Use this where the PCNet adapter is no longer supported or available on the installation media.
- Intel PRO/1000 T Server: Specifically for use with Windows XP guests.
- Intel PRO/1000 MT Server: A driver that allows guests to be imported from other virtualization products such as VMware. The PRO/1000 MT Server virtual device is commonly used on those platforms.
- `Virt-io`: A device used for guests that support a KVM paravirtualized (PV) network interface. Because this device is designed for virtualization, it may

offer performance advantages over the other emulated devices. PV drivers are available in 2.6.25 or later Linux kernels. They can be downloaded for other operating systems at the KVM project page.

In addition to choosing the virtual device for the guest, the user must configure a host networking mode to use for each device. Five different modes are available, each of which offers some interesting benefits.

Not attached is a mode similar to a network adapter that doesn't have a network cable attached. The device is present in the guest machine but is not reporting a positive link status. Traffic will not flow through this device in this mode.

Network Address Translation (NAT) will hide the guest's interface behind a network tunnel. This mode is often used when the guest is a desktop system and primarily a consumer of network resources rather than a provider. To assist guests that automatically detect their network settings, VirtualBox provides a DHCP server, router, and DNS proxy to resolve network names and correctly route packets. NAT has a few limitations that may cause applications to behave differently than they would on a real system. For example, ping may not work across the NAT tunnel. Some VPN products use this method to determine if a network is reachable, so these products would not work with a virtual NIC in NAT mode. In addition, jumbo frames are not reliable when using NAT.

Because external systems cannot communicate directly with a guest using NAT mode, VirtualBox can provide port redirection using the host's IP address. External systems connect to the specified port on the host; VirtualBox then redirects all of the packets to the guest. There are a few restrictions on the use of port forwarding. For example, you cannot redirect a port that is already in use by the host. Ports with numbers less than 1024 require the requester to be running as root or with the `net_privaddr` privilege. Because neither of these is a recommended practice for otherwise unprivileged users, you should choose a port on the host with a number greater than 1024. The most common use of NAT mode is to forward guest port 22, which allows an external system to access the guest using SSH. The following example establishes an SSH port from the first network adapter (an Intel Pro/1000 MT Desktop) on the guest named `Solaris 10` to port 2222 on the host:

```
% VBoxManage setextradata "Solaris 10" \
      "VBoxInternal/Devices/e1000/0/LUN#0/Config/s10ssh/Protocol" TCP

% VBoxManage setextradata "Solaris 10" \
      "VBoxInternal/Devices/e1000/0/LUN#0/Config/s10ssh/GuestPort" 22

% VBoxManage setextradata "Solaris 10" \
      "VBoxInternal/Devices/e1000/0/LUN#0/Config/s10ssh/HostPort" 2222
```

The guest can be accessed by using `ssh -p 2222 user@host`.

Bridged is a more advanced network mode. When working in this mode, VirtualBox installs a software network that allows the guest to share a specific host interface. A randomly generated MAC address is assigned to the guest adapter and its full network stack is visible to external systems. All of the network operations are available to the guest, including ping and jumbo frames. The bridged mode is the recommended setting for guests running server applications and desktops requiring a VPN connection into another network.

Internal mode is used to communicate between virtual machines on the same host. It is similar to bridged mode except that all communications stay internal to the host platform. Traffic over the internal mode software network is also invisible to the host. Internal mode is the fastest and most secure method of communication between guests. The most common use for this mode is to establish a private secure channel for guests to share that cannot be observed by any external system or other applications on the host system. Examples include an internal NFS server or a content provider for an externally facing web service.

Host only mode is similar to *internal mode* except that the host is able to communicate with the guests. All communications are internal to the host, but applications and users on the host can observe and use network services on the guests.

Basic network settings for the first four adapters, as shown in Figure 5.6, can be specified on the Network settings screen in the VirtualBox graphical interface.

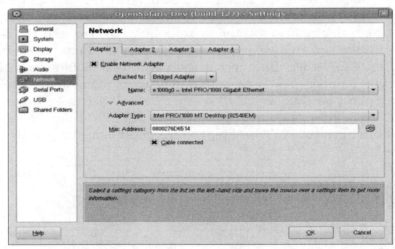

Figure 5.6 Oracle VM VirtualBox Guest Network Configuration Settings

5.2.5 BIOS and EFI

VirtualBox provides a virtual standard BIOS firmware that is used by the guest virtual machine during the boot process. Through the user interface, the user can select options such as boot order and support for I/O APIC.

VirtualBox also provides an Extended Firmware Interface (EFI) for operating systems such as Mac OS X that use EFI instead of the legacy BIOS. Newer versions of Windows and some Linux distributions can use either the legacy BIOS or EFI. The type of firmware is selected in the Motherboard part of the System settings. Figure 5.7 shows the BIOS and boot order settings for a guest machine.

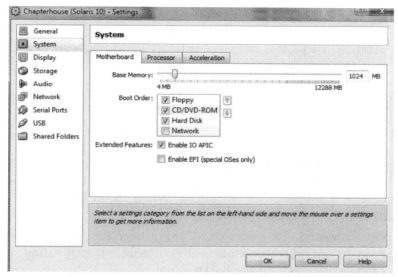

Figure 5.7 Selecting the Guest BIOS Type and Boot Order

You can also set the type of BIOS firmware by using the VBoxManage modifyvm command:

```
# VBoxManage modifyvm "Solaris 10" --firmware bios
```

These are just the basic features of the VirtualBox guest platform. For a complete list of all configuration options, see the *VirtualBox User Manual*, which is available in PDF format in the installation directory /opt/VirtualBox/ UserManual.pdf. This document can be found at http://www.virtualbox. org/wiki/Downloads.

5.2.6 Guest Additions

Although guest operating systems do not need any special software or drivers to operate correctly, the host platform includes many features that a guest can utilize if they are available. Specifically, VirtualBox provides a special set of drivers and utilities that can be used by the guest once the operating system has been installed. These "Guest Additions" are provided in a CD-ROM disk image that is always available to the guest.

You can use one of two methods to install the Guest Additions. The first method is to attach the disk image file `VBoxGuestAdditions.iso` to one of the available virtual CD-ROM devices. The second method is to use the VirtualBox graphical console and choose Devices → Install Guest Additions from the guest console window. If the guest operating system does not automatically mount the media, this step can be done manually from the guest.

Once the virtual media has been mounted, run the appropriate installer for your guest platform. A reboot of the guest is required only if you are upgrading an older version of the guest additions that are already installed. For a new installation, all that is required is to log out of the guest and log back in again to use the Guest Additions.

Once installed, the Guest Additions provide several new features:

- **Integrated keyboard and mouse.** The guest no longer requires a captive keyboard and mouse. When the guest window receives focus, the keyboard and mouse are automatically attached. When the window loses focus, they are automatically released by the guest.

- **Shared clipboard.** This feature allows a user to copy an object from an application in one guest and paste it into another application on a totally different guest, or even on the host system.

- **Resize guest display.** This feature enables the user to resize the guest display. VirtualBox will notify the guest of the resolution changes, and the drivers inside the guest will handle the changes.

- **Seamless mode.** VirtualBox can hide the guest display background, only displaying application windows on the host. When used with the shared clipboard, this feature will hide the fact that applications are being run in virtual machines. Instead, all applications appear to be running together in a single environment—a uniquely integrated desktop experience.

- **Time synchronization.** This feature keeps the guest clock synchronized with that of the host, thereby avoiding the type of clock skewing that is common in virtualized environments.

- **High-performance graphics.** If this feature is enabled in the Display settings of the guest machine, VirtualBox will allow the guest operating system to pass OpenGL and Direct3D graphics commands directly to the host's graphics adapter. The guest can then perform 3D graphics operations at nearly the same speed as if they were running on the host. For Windows guests, 2D graphics acceleration is also available.

- **Shared folders.** Shared folders allow the guest to access the host file systems as if they were local file systems. For Windows guests, these appear as network shares. For all other guests, a special file system driver is used to access the shared folders.

5.3 Oracle Solaris as an Oracle VM VirtualBox Host

VirtualBox supports Solaris 10 5/09 and later as a host platform with a few restrictions:

- There is no support for USB. VirtualBox uses a newer USB device management system that was introduced into OpenSolaris build 124 and is not available in Solaris 10.
- ACPI information, such as battery status and power source, is not reported to guest operating systems.
- Wireless network adapters cannot be used for bridged networks.

VirtualBox can run in either the global zone or a Solaris Container. Running in a Container provides several interesting benefits. It may be easier to place resource controls on an entire Container than an arbitrary workload, especially if different people are tasked with these functions. The global zone administrator can place resource policies on the Container that the VirtualBox user may not be aware of or have sufficient privilege to set. Migrating a Container by detaching it from one host and attaching it to another host can greatly simply the task of relocating a guest. Most of the configuration settings needed for proper operation of the guest are contained in the Container configuration file, so any changes that need to be made can be done in one place. Finally, the ability to clone a Container that contains a guest and its associated data makes it easier to rapidly deploy several copies of the same machine on the host.

To enable VirtualBox operation in a Container, just add the device /dev/vboxdrv to the Container. For OpenSolaris hosts for which you want to enable USB support, add the device /dev/vboxusbmon in addition to /dev/vboxdrv. The following example shows the creation of a Container called WinXP that could be used to run VirtualBox guests. A more detailed example is provided in Chapter 8, "Applying Virtualization."

```
# zonecfg -z WinXP
WinXP: No such zone configured
Use 'create' to begin configuring a new zone.
zonecfg:WinXP> create
zonecfg:WinXP> set zonepath=/zones/WinXP
zonecfg:WinXP> add device
zonecfg:WinXP:device> set match=/dev/vboxdrv
zonecfg:WinXP:device> end
zonecfg:WinXP> add net
zonecfg:WinXP:net> set physical=e1000g0
zonecfg:WinXP:net> set address=192.168.1.41/24
zonecfg:WinXP:net> end
zonecfg:WinXP> exit

# zoneadm -z WinXP install
Preparing to install zone <WinXP>.
Creating list of files to copy from the global zone.
Copying <35929> files to the zone.

# zoneadm -z WinXP boot
# zlogin -C WinXP
```

Finish the installation as you would any other Container by answering the Solaris system identification questions. Once this step is complete, you can use the VirtualBox graphic or command-line tools just as you would in the global zone. Some of the host networking modes may require the use of exclusive IP for configuration of the guest's virtual network interface.

Another Oracle Solaris feature that can be used by VirtualBox is ZFS. Although VirtualBox has a host-independent disk cloning feature, it works by copying entire disk images—an approach that doubles the amount of storage required for the duplicated clone and places a heavy load on the host system during the copying operation. By comparison, ZFS has a fast cloning capability that takes significantly less time to complete; the cloned disk image needs to store only those blocks that are different from the blocks in the original image. This strategy is very efficient for deploying many copies of the same type of guest.

When running VirtualBox on a Solaris host that is also using ZFS, limiting the size of the adaptive replacement cache (ARC) is recommended. By default, ZFS can use most of the physical memory on the system: up to three-fourths on systems with 4 GB or less and up to maxphys-1 GB on larger systems. A guest may demand memory faster than ZFS is able to free it, which would produce one of the memory shortfall situations we are trying to prevent. The solution is to limit the amount of memory that ZFS is able to use for the ARC. This cap can be set with the zfs_arc_max Solaris tunable parameter, which you can set in /etc/system.

The following setting will limit the ARC to 1 GB, which is a reasonable value for a 4 GB desktop hosting several virtual machines:

```
set zfs:zfs_arc_max = 0x40000000
```

As a general rule, do not set `zfs_arc_max` equal to more than three-fourths of the physical memory that is left after allocating memory for all of your guests.

See Chapter 8, "Applying Virtualization," for an example of using both ZFS and Containers for rapid provisioning of guests on an Oracle Solaris host.

5.3.1 Installing Oracle VM VirtualBox

The VirtualBox software can be downloaded from `http://virtualbox.org/downloads`. The Oracle Solaris version is provided in a single SVR4 data stream package that includes both the 32-bit and 64-bit versions of the software as well as a `README` text file describing the installation process and a package answer file named `autoresponse` for non-interactive installations. Because the package installation scripts load kernel modules, the installation must be done in the global zone and carried out either by root or by a user or role that has the `Software Installation` execution profile.

If an older version of VirtualBox is installed on the host, it must be removed before installing the new version. For versions prior to 3.1, two packages must be uninstalled: `SUNWbox` and `SUNWvboxkern`. Starting with version 3.1, there is just a single package: `SUNWvbox`. It is not necessary to reboot the Solaris host after the old version of VirtualBox is removed or the new version is installed.

In the next example, a new version of VirtualBox is installed on a system that is already running an older release. Note the use of the included `autoresponse` file for unattended package operations.

```
# ls
VirtualBox-3.1.4-57640-SunOS.tar.gz


# /usr/sfw/bin/gtar xpzf VirtualBox-3.1.4-57640-SunOS.tar.gz


# ls
ReadMe.txt
VirtualBox-3.1.4-57640-SunOS.tar.gz
VirtualBox-3.1.4-SunOS-r57640.pkg
autoresponse


# pkgrm -n -a autoresponse  SUNWvbox

Removing VirtualBox drivers and services...
   - Unloaded: Web service
```

continues

```
    - Unloaded: Zone access service
    - Unloading: USB  ...FAILED!
    - Removed: USB module
    - Unloaded: USBMonitor module
    - Removed: USBMonitor module
    - Unloaded: NetFilter module
    - Removed: NetFilter module
    - Unloaded: NetAdapter module
    - Removed: NetAdapter module
    - Unloaded: Host module
    - Removed: Host module
Done.


# pkgadd -n -a autoresponse -d VirtualBox-3.1.4-SunOS-r57640.pkg all
Checking for older bits...
Installing new ones...

Loading VirtualBox kernel modules...
    - Loaded: Host module
    - Loaded: NetAdapter module
    - Loaded: NetFilter module
    - Loaded: USBMonitor module
    - Loaded: USB module


Configuring services...
    - Loaded: Web service
    - Loaded: Zone access service


Installing Python bindings...
    - Installed: Bindings for Python 2.4
    - Installed: Bindings for Python 2.5
    - Installed: Bindings for Python 2.6


Updating the boot archive...


Installation of <SUNWvbox> was successful.
```

The default directory for the VirtualBox components is /opt/VirtualBox.
The user commands VirtualBox, VBoxManage, VBoxSDL, VBoxHeadless, and
VBoxQtconfig are all symbolically linked into /usr/bin so that they are available
for all users on the system. In general, no special privileges are required to run
VirtualBox on Solaris other than appropriate file permissions to devices and disk
images. The privilege net_priv_addr would be required to forward a host port
number less than 1024 to a guest, but this configuration is strongly discouraged.

When a user runs VirtualBox, all of the machine definitions and private disk
images are stored by default in a directory named .VirtualBox in the user's

home directory. Although the machine configuration files are small, disk images can grow quite large. To change the locations where these files are stored, click File → Preferences in the VirtualBox graphical interface or use the `VBoxManage setproperty` command. Figure 5.8 shows how to change those preferences to a different location.

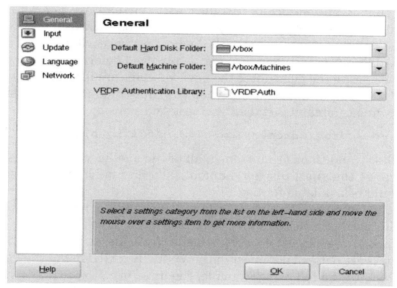

Figure 5.8 Changing the Location of Guest Disks and Machine Definitions

VirtualBox disk images and machine configurations can be shared among many users. All that is required to share machine configurations and disk images is read and write file permissions to the associated files.

5.4 Oracle Solaris as an Oracle VM VirtualBox Guest

Solaris 10 is a fully supported guest OS for VirtualBox. A full complement of Guest Additions is available, including seamless mode and accelerated 3D graphics. For optimal performance, the following settings are recommended for a Solaris guest:

- Boot disk: SATA (one of the first four ports with IDE compatibility mode enabled)
- CD-ROM: Master device on the second IDE channel (the default)

- Network: Intel Pro/1000MT Desktop
- Hardware acceleration: Enabled if supported by the host
- Nested page tables: Enabled if supported by the host
- PAE/NX: Enabled

As with all supported guests, the Guest Additions are provided on a CD-ROM image file that is automatically installed with VirtualBox. The Oracle Solaris Guest Additions are included in a single SVR4 data stream package named VBoxSolarisAdditions.pkg. As with the host packages, if a previous release of the Guest Additions is installed, it must be removed before a new version can be installed. Rebooting the guest after the new additions are installed is strongly recommended; this step is not required when the Guest Additions are first installed.

The following command installs the Guest Additions on a new Solaris guest:

```
# pkgadd -d /cdrom/cdrom0/VBoxSolarisAdditions.pkg all
```

Once the Guest Additions are installed, all of the ancillary features—such as the ability to resize the guest display automatically and implement the shared clipboard—should be available for use.

One special feature of the Guest Additions is shared folders. It allows the guest to share files with other guests and the host via the host's native file system. In Oracle Solaris, the shared folders are made available as a vboxfs file system. Shared folders are defined per guest in the VirtualBox GUI or via the VBoxManage command line. In the following example, the directory /export/iso on the host is shared as /iso with a Solaris 10 guest. On the host platform, issue the following command to create the shared folder. In this example, the guest is named Solaris10.

```
Host% VBoxManage sharefolder add Solaris10 --name iso \
    --hostpath /export/iso
```

Now the guest can mount and access the file system, as in the following example:

```
# mkdir /iso
# mount -F vboxfs -o uid=1234,gid=5678 iso /iso
# ls -la /iso

total 19720801

drwxrwxrwx   1 1234      5678       4096 Dec  1 16:02 .
```

```
drwxr-xr-x  34 root     root          35 Feb 12 20:51 ..
drwxrwxrwx   1 1234     5678        4096 Sep  9 08:43 centos
drwxrwxrwx   1 1234     5678        4096 Aug 27 13:22 fedora
drwxrwxrwx   1 1234     5678        8192 Feb  1 12:20 opensolaris
drwxrwxrwx   1 1234     5678        4096 Oct 25 10:29 oracle
drwxrwxrwx   1 1234     5678        8192 Aug 31 13:44 redhat
drwxrwxrwx   1 1234     5678        4096 Sep  9 08:56 rescue
drwxrwxrwx   1 1234     5678        4096 Feb  3 16:12 s10
drwxrwxrwx   1 1234     5678        8192 Feb  3 21:57 s11
drwxrwxrwx   1 1234     5678           0 Aug 31 13:31 suse
drwxrwxrwx   1 1234     5678           0 Aug  9  2009 ubuntu
drwxrwxrwx   1 1234     5678        8192 Feb 13 00:38 windows
```

Because the file permission and ownership abstractions may not translate directly between the host operating system and that of the guest, the user starting the virtual machine in the host must have appropriate access to the files being shared. Inside the guest, the owner and group are set by mount options—in this case, user `1234` and group `5678`.

5.5 Creating and Managing Oracle VM VirtualBox Guests

After you have installed VirtualBox, you can create guests. While this can be accomplished using command-line tools, the first example given here uses the VirtualBox GUI installation wizard.

5.5.1 Creating the Guest Machine

You can start to install a guest machine by launching the VirtualBox tool:

```
% VirtualBox &
```

Figure 5.9 shows the initial VirtualBox screen.

To begin creating the first virtual machine, click the New button. This will launch the New Virtual Machine Wizard.

The first step is to name the new virtual machine and choose the operating system of the guest. The name of the guest is unrelated to its actual host name or network identity; those identities will be set later, once the guest is running. The guest name is only used by VirtualBox to identify the guest being managed. The operating system type determines how VirtualBox will emulate devices and which code scanning techniques to use when running the guest kernel code. The name of the guest can be changed later, but the OS type should be correct before creating the guest.

Figure 5.9 VirtualBox Main Window

For this example, the guest will be named `Windows XP` and will run the Windows XP operating system, as shown in Figure 5.10.

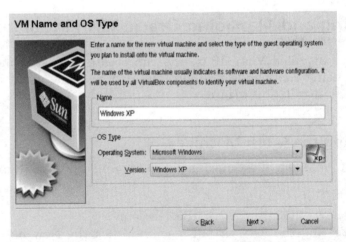

Figure 5.10 Choosing the Guest Operating System Type

The next step is to assign the amount of memory to be allocated for the guest. The amount needed is usually less than needed for a physical system. Many operating systems manage a file cache to improve performance of disk reads. If the host OS has a file cache, the guests will not need much of a file cache to maintain reasonable performance, so you can allocate less memory to guests. The installation wizard will suggest a minimum memory size based on the operating system type chosen in the previous step. Figure 5.11 shows the allocation of 512 MB for the Windows XP guest—more than enough for typical virtual desktop needs.

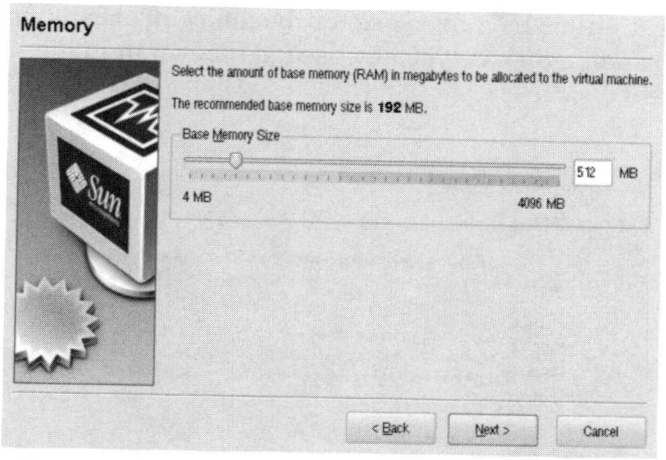

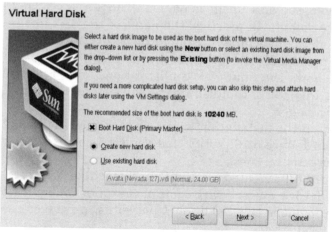

Figure 5.11 Setting the Amount of Guest Memory

Every guest needs a boot disk. For simplicity, the New Virtual Machine Wizard allows you to create only a single boot disk image. It will always assign this disk as the master device on the first IDE controller. If you need a different configuration, use the VBoxManage command. At this point in the guest installation, you can choose whether to create a new disk image or use one that is already registered in the Virtual Media Manager. There aren't any virtual disks on this system yet, so select Create new hard disk as shown in Figure 5.12. Note that VirtualBox suggests a size for the disk based on the operating system that was chosen in the previous step.

Figure 5.12 Virtual Hard Disk Wizard

This disk must either be a fixed size or dynamically expanding disk image. A dynamically expanding disk is typically used, as shown in Figure 5.13, because it doesn't waste real disk space.

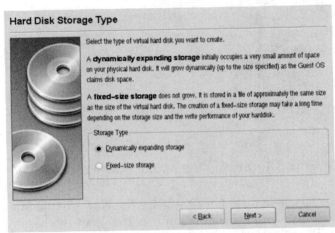

Figure 5.13 Choosing the Disk Image Type

The next screen allows you to name the disk image and specify its size. By default, this disk image is stored in your home directory in a hidden directory named .VirtualBox. If not enough space is available there, you can click the icon to the right of the image name and tell VirtualBox where to place the image. You will need read and write access to the directory holding the disk images.

In this example, the disk image is named Windows 7.vdi and has a size of 10 GB, which is the default. In practice, the name of the disk image should indicate not only which virtual machine is using it, but also how that disk is used. Figure 5.14 shows the name and size of the guest boot disk.

Figure 5.15 shows the final disk configuration. After reviewing the settings, click Finish. At this point, the disk image will be created and registered in the Virtual Media Manager.

The final step in the installation wizard is to review the final guest configuration, as shown in Figure 5.16. Verify that the settings are what you desired and click Finish to create the guest.

You have successfully created your first guest machine. You can click the Settings button and familiarize yourself with some of the other configuration options, such as audio, video memory size, additional networks, processor accelerations, and shared folders.

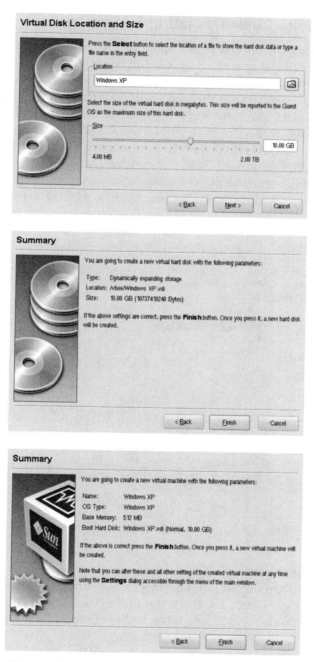

Figure 5.14 Choosing the Name and Size of the Guest Disk Image (top)
Figure 5.15 Reviewing the Guest Disk Settings (center)
Figure 5.16 Final Review of the Guest Configuration (bottom)

5.5.2 Installing the Guest Operating System

Once you are satisfied that the guest machine configuration is suitable for your needs, you can install the operating system on the guest boot disk. The most common method of doing so is to attach a CD-ROM disk image to one of the available virtual CD-ROM devices so that the guest will boot from that device. To attach the CD-ROM image, select the guest machine and click Settings. Then select Storage and a window similar to Figure 5.17 will be displayed.

When you click the CD-ROM device, you will see that it is the master device on the secondary IDE channel. This device also happens to be second device in the BIOS boot order, right behind the floppy disk, which is rarely used. Also note that the device is currently empty, meaning that no virtual or real media has been inserted.

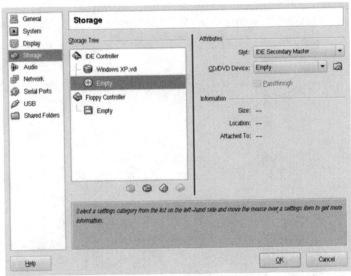

Figure 5.17 Guest Storage Configuration Before Attaching the Installation Media

To attach the installation media, you must first register it with the Virtual Media Manager. In this example, the media is found in the file `/export/iso/windows/winxp_sp3_x86.iso`. Click the folder icon to the right of the CD/DVD Device pull-down menu, which will launch the Virtual Media Manager, as shown in Figure 5.18.

Because this is the first guest in a new VirtualBox installation, the only CD-ROM disk image present is `VBoxGuestAdditions.iso`, which contains the Guest Additions. To add the Windows installation media, click the Add button, navigate to the directory where the CD-ROM image is stored, and select it, as shown in Figure 5.19. Then you can highlight the appropriate disk image and click the Select button to insert it into the virtual CD-ROM device. Once registered, you can select this media in any guest from the CD/DVD Device pull-down menu on the guest Storage settings without having to start the Virtual Media Manager.

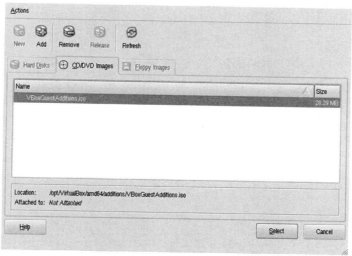

Figure 5.18 Virtual Media Manager

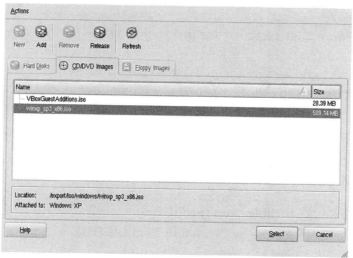

Figure 5.19 Virtual Media Manager After Adding the Windows Installation Media

After the CD-ROM disk image is registered with the Virtual Media Manager, it should be available as a CD-ROM device selection on the guest storage settings, as shown in Figure 5.20. Alternatively, if you start the guest with a new boot disk and fail to assign a CD-ROM, VirtualBox will launch the Virtual Media Manager so that you can select an existing image or register a new one. When this process is complete, the image will automatically be attached to the CD-ROM device and the guest will continue the booting process.

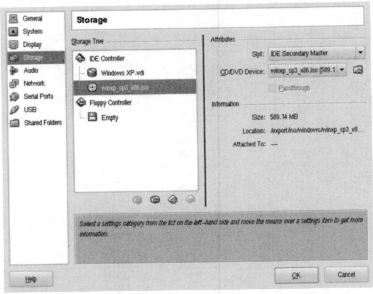

Figure 5.20 Selecting the Installation Media for the Guest

All that is left to do is start the guest machine. However, first we will show the creation of a guest using the VBoxManage command line.

5.5.3 Creating a Guest Machine Using the Command Line

The command-line interface (CLI) for VirtualBox is more complicated to use than the GUI, but it offers several advantages:

- The CLI is more flexible than the GUI.
- The CLI offers features not available from the GUI.
- The CLI can be used to script guest creation.
- Scripts using the CLI can be used to build an automated guest creation system.

As in the previous example, the first step is to create and register the guest virtual machine. If you don't know which OS type to select when creating your virtual machine, giving the command `VBoxManage list ostypes` will produce a list of supported options. For this example, `WindowsXP_64` is the correct choice.

```
% VBoxManage createvm --name "Windows XP" \
      --ostype WindowsXP_64 --register
Virtual machine 'Windows XP' is created and registered.
UUID: 4ec5efdc-fa76-49bb-8562-7c2a0bac8282


Settings file: '/vbox/Machines/Windows XP/Windows XP.xml'

% VBoxManage showvminfo "Windows XP"
Name:              Windows XP
Guest OS:          Windows XP (64 bit)
UUID:              4ec5efdc-fa76-49bb-8562-7c2a0bac8282
Config file:       /vbox/Machines/Windows XP/Windows XP.xml
Hardware UUID:     4ec5efdc-fa76-49bb-8562-7c2a0bac8282
Memory size:       128MB
VRAM size:         8MB
Number of CPUs:    1
Synthetic Cpu:     off
CPUID overrides:   None
Boot menu mode:    message and menu
Boot Device (1):   Floppy
Boot Device (2):   DVD
Boot Device (3):   HardDisk
Boot Device (4):   Not Assigned
ACPI:              on
IOAPIC:            on
PAE:               on
Time offset:       0 ms
Hardw. virt.ext:   on
Hardw. virt.ext exclusive: on
Nested Paging:     on
VT-x VPID:         on
State:             powered off (since 2010-02-14T23:05:30.798000000)
Monitor count:     1
3D Acceleration:   off
Teleporter Enabled: off
Teleporter Port: 0
Teleporter Address: <NULL>
Teleporter Password: <NULL>
NIC 1:             MAC: 0800270213D4, Attachment: NAT, Cable connected: on, Trace: off
(file: none), Type: 82540EM, Reported speed: 0 Mbps
NIC 2:             disabled
NIC 3:             disabled
```

continues

```
NIC 4:              disabled
NIC 5:              disabled
NIC 6:              disabled
NIC 7:              disabled
NIC 8:              disabled
UART 1:             disabled
UART 2:             disabled
Audio:              disabled
Clipboard Mode:     Bidirectional
VRDP:               disabled
USB:                disabled
USB Device Filters:     <none>
Shared folders:     <none>
Guest:
Statistics update:                  disabled
```

This guest should need about 512 MB of memory, and you may want to use the audio device. Also, 8 MB is not enough video RAM, and 3D acceleration is supported with the Guest Additions.

```
% VBoxManage modifyvm "Windows XP" --memory 512 --vram 32 \
    --accelerate3d on --audio oss
```

Storage configuration requires a few commands to complete. First you must create the IDE controller and the boot disk image, and attach them together. Then you must register and attach the CD-ROM image of the boot media. Finally, the BIOS boot order must be set to boot from CD-ROM before the disk. Note that because the image file name is specified as a relative path name, it is relative to the VirtualBox settings, not your current working directory.

```
% VBoxManage storagectl "Windows XP" --name "IDE Controller" \
    --add ide --controller ICH6

% VBoxManage createhd --filename "Windows XP.vdi" --size 10240 \
    --format VDI --remember

0%...10%...20%...30%...40%...50%...60%...70%...80%...90%...100%

Disk image created. UUID: 388311ed-b303-4405-8689-3dee5abc8f68

% VBoxManage storageattach "Windows XP" \
    --storagectl "IDE Controller" --port 0 --device 0 \
    --type hdd --medium «Windows XP.vdi»
```

```
% VBoxManage openmedium dvd /export/iso/windows/winxp_sp3_x86.iso

% VBoxManage storageattach "Windows XP"     \
    --storagectl "IDE Controller" --port 1 --device 0    \
    --medium "/export/iso/windows/winxp_sp3_x86.iso"   \
    --type dvddrive

% VBoxManage modifyvm "Windows XP" --boot1 dvd --boot2 disk
```

At this point, the virtual machine is configured and ready to boot.

5.5.4 Starting a Virtual Machine

Oracle VM VirtualBox provides three different methods for starting a virtual machine. The most common method is from inside the VirtualBox graphical tool itself. Select the guest and click the Start button. When the guest machine starts, a fully featured console window is opened on the host. Until the Guest Additions are installed, keyboard and mouse operations are captive. In other words, once you click inside the guest window, it will restrict your cursor to its window and will continue to receive all keyboard input until told to release the focus, usually achieved by clicking the Host key. The current Host key is displayed at the lower-right corner of the guest console window. Once the Guest Additions are installed, however, the keyboard and mouse will be seamlessly attached and detached as your mouse moves over the window.

Using this method, the user on the host can control many of the operations of the guest, such as changing the size of the window, attaching CD-ROM media, or turning seamless mode on or off.

If a less complicated console is desired, a simple window with no menu decorations can be used to start a guest. Give the command /usr/bin/VBoxSDL to start the guest. Instead of a fully featured window, a simple window is displayed. This approach is primarily used for debugging purposes but can be used if a simple console is required.

A more interesting start method is a headless system. In this case, the guest machine is started by the /usr/bin/VBoxHeadless command. This command starts the guest machine but does not display the console on the host system. Instead, the built-in Virtual Remote Desktop Protocol (VRDP) server starts. A remote system can then access the guest console using any RDP client program. For Oracle Solaris, one such program is rdesktop, which can be found on the Solaris Companion Software CD.

The following example demonstrates starting a guest machine in headless mode on a host system. This is just the type of operation that the Solaris Service Manage Facility (SMF) could easily automate.

```
% VBoxHeadless --startvm "Windows XP"
Sun VirtualBox Headless Interface 3.1.4
(C) 2008-2010 Sun Microsystems, Inc.
All rights reserved.

Listening on port 3389.
```

To connect to this guest from a remote system, we will use an RDP client. This example shows the use of rdesktop on an Oracle Solaris system to connect to the newly created Windows XP guest machine, which is running on a host named pandora.

```
% rdesktop pandora:3389
```

On the remote system, a new window is opened showing the guest desktop that is running on pandora. Figure 5.21 shows the guest desktop running the Windows XP installation program.

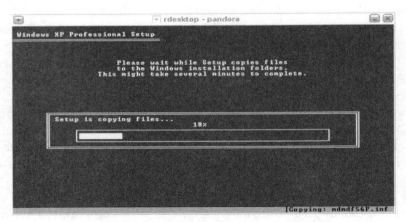

Figure 5.21 Displaying the Remote Desktop

5.5.5 Stopping a Virtual Machine

A guest is typically shut down by using its native method. Nevertheless, other options for stopping a virtual machine are available. Regardless of the method used to create the guest, it can be stopped from the host either through the command line or via the VirtualBox GUI. Both of these methods provide several mechanisms that can stop a guest.

- **An ACPI shutdown signal.** This is the recommended method. A shutdown signal is sent to the guest and, if that signal is supported, the guest will begin a normal shutdown. This process includes tasks such as flushing disk caches and unmounting file systems. An ACPI signal is the safest of the external shutdown methods.

- **Snapshot.** The guest machine's current state will be saved and can be restarted from this point in the future. The snapshot approach is similar to a hibernation feature found on modern laptops, but you can save many snapshots and roll them back as desired. This flexibility enables you to test the effects of various operations, starting with a consistent state each time.

- **Reset.** This "hard stop" will cause a machine reset; it is recommended only when the ACPI shutdown does not work. In this case, the guest disk buffers are not flushed, and some of the uncommitted disk data may be corrupted. Most modern operating systems feature some form of recovery in the event of a power loss, so the chances of corruption are small, but this approach is recommended only when no other method works.

- **Pause.** This option causes a virtual machine to stop execution. The guest remains in memory, however, and its operation can be resumed. The state is not saved by a pause operation.

Here is an example of a safe external host-initiated shutdown for the guest named `Windows XP`:

```
% VBoxManage controlvm "Windows XP" acpipowerbutton
```

This command sends an ACPI shutdown signal to the guest, which will start an orderly shutdown process.

5.5.6 Cloning a Virtual Machine

Although VirtualBox does not currently feature complete cloning of a virtual machine, it does provide a host-agnostic method of cloning disk images. This is done via the `VBoxManage clonehd` command. The source disk image is copied in its entirety and a new UUID is assigned. The disk can be registered in the user's Media Manager or copied to another system to be used elsewhere. All that is required to complete the cloning of the virtual machine is to create the new guest configuration, using either the command line or the GUI as shown before.

If the host system is running Oracle Solaris, ZFS data set cloning can be used instead of cloning the virtual disk device with VBoxManage. The result is much faster cloning time. Because ZFS needs to allocate space only for the additional blocks that are changed in the clone, this approach also results in a smaller total storage requirement for the new guest.

To use ZFS cloning, two steps must be completed. The first step is the creation of the ZFS clone, which requires two commands. Because ZFS cloning occurs on a data set level, you should place the guest disk images in separate ZFS file systems. If a guest machine has several disks and they will always be used together, place them all in the same ZFS file system so that one ZFS operation can manage all of them.

The second step is the creation of a new UUID for the cloned virtual disk. Without this step, the cloned disk image would have the same UUID as a disk that is already registered. VirtualBox provides a method of creating a new UUID that must be used after completing the ZFS cloning operation.

The following example compares the time and space required to clone a disk image. The source is a 5 GB Solaris 10 boot disk. To simplify management of virtual disk devices, the source disk image is placed in a ZFS file system named pandora/HardDisks/s10guest1, which is mounted on the host as /vbox/HardDisks/s10guest1.

We first clone the disk image into the directory /vbox/HardDisks/s10guest2-trad using the VirtualBox clonehd method. For a consistent comparison of used space, the target directory is also a ZFS file system.

```
# time VBoxManage clonehd       \
     "/vbox/HardDisks/s10guest1/Solaris 10 boot disk.vdi"  \
     "/vbox/HardDisks/s10guest2-trad/Solaris 10 boot disk.vdi" \
     --remember

0%...10%...20%...30%...40%...50%...60%...70%...80%...90%...100%

Clone hard disk created in format 'VDI'. UUID: 19fb45a2-3773-4580-9e85-bb54af784d9a

real    9m40.680s
user    0m2.233s
sys     0m2.352s
```

Now we can clone the disk image using ZFS. The specific steps to do so are shown below. To record the total time of this operation, these commands were run from a script. The resulting time is indicated after the commands.

```
# zfs snapshot pandora/vbox/HardDisks/s10guest1@s10guest2-zfs

# zfs clone pandora/vbox/HardDisks/s10guest1@s10guest2-zfs  \
      pandora/vbox/HardDisks/s10guest2-zfs

# VBoxManage internalcommands sethduuid    \
      "/vbox/HardDisks/s10guest2-zfs/Solaris 10 boot disk.vdi"
UUID changed to: f06b5f4e-805e-4e74-8345-de9a22e39e81

# VBoxManage openmedium disk    \
      "/vbox/HardDisks/s10guest2-zfs/Solaris 10 boot disk.vdi"

real     0m1.288s
user     0m0.087s
sys      0m0.132s
```

Using `VBoxManage`, virtual disk cloning took nearly 10 minutes, and the ZFS method just slightly more than 1 second. Although all directories indicate that they are 5 GB in size, the ZFS space listing shows how much space is *actually* consumed.

```
# du -h /vbox/HardDisks
 5.0G    /vbox/HardDisks/s10guest2-zfs
 5.0G    /vbox/HardDisks/s10guest1
 5.0G    /vbox/HardDisks/s10guest2-trad
 15 G    /vbox/HardDisks

# zfs list -r -o space pandora/vbox/HardDisks
NAME                                         AVAIL    USED   USEDSNAP
pandora/vbox/HardDisks                       57.0G   10.0G          0
pandora/vbox/HardDisks/s10guest1             57.0G   5.00G          0
pandora/vbox/HardDisks/s10guest2-trad        57.0G   4.99G          0
pandora/vbox/HardDisks/s10guest2-zfs         57.0G    164K          0
```

The traditional method of using the VirtualBox copy method consumed an additional 5 GB of disk space, which was expected. However, the ZFS clone consumed only 164KB of space. Of course, as the cloned guest machine starts writing to the disk, additional space will be required for storage of its data. For the parts of the disk that are not written, only one copy of the data will be kept across all of the cloned images, which represents a significant storage savings opportunity achieved by using ZFS for guest disk images.

5.5.7 Live Migration of a Guest

Beginning with version 3.1, VirtualBox includes a feature called *teleportation* that allows a guest machine to move from one host to another while the guest machine is running. Except for some rare cases, the source and destination hosts need not run the same operating system or even the same type of hardware. In other words, you can migrate a guest running on an Oracle Solaris host to a Linux or Windows host.

The following steps are required to migrate a guest machine:

1. Ensure there is a TCP/IP network connection between the source and target hosts. The migration will occur over a TCP connection.

2. Configure the original guest to use some sort of shared storage (NFS, SMB, CIFS, or iSCSI) for all of its disk, CD-ROM, and floppy images.

3. On the target system, create a guest configuration that exactly matches the hardware settings (e.g., processor, memory, network) of the guest that is currently running on the source host.

4. On the target host, the guest machine must start listening for a teleportation connection request instead of actually starting. The VBoxManage modifyvm --teleporter command will perform this task.

5. Start the guest machine on the target host. Instead of starting, it will display a progress bar while waiting for the teleportation request from the source.

6. Initiate the live migration by issuing a VBoxManage controlvm teleport command on the source host system.

In this example, a guest machine named Solaris10 migrates from a host named source to one named target. The Solaris10 guest configurations on both hosts meet the guidelines listed above. On the target, place Solaris10 in teleportation mode and start it. Because it is not currently in use, port 6000 will be used for the teleportation connection.

```
target% VBoxManage modifyvm Solaris 10 --teleporter on    \
    --teleporter 6000
target% VBoxManage startvm Solaris10
```

On the host source where the guest Solaris10 is currently running, initiate the live migration with the following command:

```
source% VBoxManage controlvm Solaris10 teleport --host source \
    --port 6000
```

The state of the guest `Solaris10` will be transferred to the host `target` and the guest will resume execution on the new host. For more information on guest teleportation, see the *VirtualBox User Manual*.

5.6 Summary

Oracle VM VirtualBox is a compact and efficient virtualization solution for Intel and AMD x86 systems. Each guest runs in a separate virtual machine and needs no additional software or drivers to run. To improve performance and allow the guests greater access to resources within the host platform, Guest Additions are provided for all supported guest operating systems.

While not as efficient as Oracle Solaris Containers, VirtualBox can take advantage of many of the resource management facilities available in Oracle Solaris to provide an excellent and well-managed environment for hosting a wide variety of applications. While features such as the internal RDP server and seamless mode make VirtualBox an obvious choice for virtualizing desktops, its performance and use of advanced virtualization features in modern hardware also make it a good choice for handling server workloads.

6

Oracle Solaris Containers

Operating system virtualization was virtually unknown in 2005 when Solaris 10 was released. That release of Solaris introduced Solaris Containers—also called Solaris Zones, now called Oracle Solaris Containers—making it the first fully integrated, production-ready implementation of OS virtualization. In response, several other implementations have been developed or are planned for other operating systems. Containers use a basic model similar to an earlier technology called Jails.

Chapter 1 provided a complete description of operating system virtualization (OSV). To summarize the key points here, OSV creates virtual OS instances, which are software environments in which applications run, isolated from each other but sharing one copy of an OS and one OS kernel.

Oracle Solaris Containers provide a software environment that appears to be a complete OS instance from within the Container. To a process running in a Container, the only differences are side effects of the robust security boundary around each Container, and a few limitations of the Oracle Solaris operating system.

Containers offer a very rich set of features, most of which were originally features of Solaris, which were then applied to Containers. This tight level of integration between Containers and the rest of Solaris minimizes software incompatibility and improves the overall "feel" of Containers. Containers provide the following capabilities:

- Configurable isolation and security boundary
- Multiple namespaces—one per Container

- Software packaging, deployment, and flexible file system assignments
- Resource management controls
- Resource usage reporting
- Network access
- Optional access to devices
- Centralized or localized patch management
- Management of Containers (e.g., configure, boot, halt, migrate)

This chapter describes the most useful features that can be used with Containers. Although a complete description of the use of all of these features is beyond the scope of this book, more details can be found at `http://docs.sun.com`. The next few sections describe features and provide simple command-line examples of their usage. Unless otherwise noted, these features are available in Solaris 10. Most of them are also available in OpenSolaris, which also offers new features not found in Solaris 10.

The command examples in this chapter use the prompt `GZ#` to indicate a command that must be entered by the root user in the global zone. The prompt `zone1#` indicates that a command will be entered as the root user of the Container named `zone1`.

6.1 Feature Overview

The Containers feature set was introduced in the initial release of Solaris 10, in 2005. The Containers implementation of operating system virtualization (OSV) includes a rich set of capabilities. This section describes the features of Containers and provides brief command-line examples demonstrating the use of those features.

Containers are characterized by a high degree of isolation, with the separation between them enforced by a robust security boundary. They serve as the underlying framework for the Solaris Trusted Extensions feature set. Trusted Extensions have achieved the highest commonly recognized global security certification, which is a tribute to the robustness of the security boundary around each Container.

The Solaris 10 documentation uses two different terms to refer to its OSV feature set: Containers and zones. Within the Oracle Solaris development community, the word "zones" refers to the isolation and security features. A Container is a zone that uses resource management features. However, making a distinction between those two terms is rarely worth the effort. Indeed, most people use them interchangeably. In this book, we use the word "Containers" exclusively, even if resource management features are not in use.

The examples shown here were taken from a Solaris 10 10/09 system. Some of the features described in this section—for example, CPU caps—did not exist in early updates to Solaris 10. To determine feature availability of a particular Solaris 10 update, see the "What's New" document for that update at `http://docs.sun.com/app/docs/prod/solaris.10`.

Later in this chapter, the section "Network Virtualization in OpenSolaris," applies only to OpenSolaris 2009.06 and newer releases.

6.1.1 Basic Model

When you install Oracle Solaris 10 on a system, the original operating environment—a traditional UNIX-like system—is also called the *global zone*. A sufficiently privileged user running in the global zone can create Containers but they cannot be nested: A Container cannot contain other Containers, as shown in Figure 6.1.

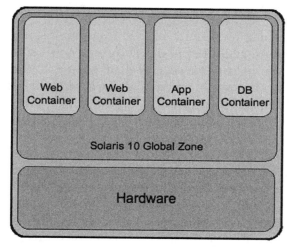

Figure 6.1 Structure of an Oracle Solaris System with Containers

In a system with Containers, the global zone is usually the platform management area with the sole purpose of managing Containers and the system's hardware and software resources. This is similar to the control domain of hypervisor-based system, for two reasons:

- The global zone requires resources to operate, such as CPU cycles and RAM. If an application running in the global zone consumes too much of a resource that the global zone's management tools need, it may become difficult or impossible to manage the system.

- Users and processes in the global zone aren't subject to all of the rules of Containers. One example is process observability. A process in one Container cannot detect processes in other Containers. As with a one-way mirror, processes in the global zone, even nonprivileged ones, can see processes in the Containers, even though users in the Containers cannot see processes in the global zone.

Although a Container is a slightly different environment from a normal Oracle Solaris system, a basic design principle underlying all Containers is software compatibility. A good rule of thumb is this: "If an application runs as a nonprivileged user in a Solaris 10 system that doesn't have Containers, it will run properly in a Container." Nevertheless, some applications must run with extra privileges—traditionally, applications that must run as the root user. These applications may not be able to gain the privileges they need and, therefore, may not run correctly in a Container. In some cases, it is possible to enable such applications to run in a Container by adding more privileges to that Container, a topic discussed later in this chapter.

Containers have their own life cycle, which remains largely separate from the life cycle of the base instance of Solaris. After Solaris has been installed and booted, Containers can be configured, installed, booted, and used as if they were discrete systems. They can easily and quickly be booted, halted, and rebooted. In fact, booting or halting a Container takes less than five seconds, plus any time to start or halt applications running in the Container. When you no longer need a Container, you can easily destroy it.

Containers are very lightweight, because they are not an entire operating system instance. They do not need to test the hardware or load a kernel or device drivers. The base OS instance does all that work once—and each Container then benefits from that work when it boots.

Given these characteristics, Containers, by default, use very few resources. A default configuration uses approximately 100 MB of disk space, and approximately 40 MB of RAM when running. When it is not running, a Container does not use any RAM at all. Further, because there is no virtualization layer to run on a CPU, Containers have negligible performance overhead (which is a trait all OSV technologies should have). In other words, a process in a Container follows the same code path that it would outside of a Container unless it attempts to perform an operation that is not allowed in a Container. Because it follows the same code path, it has the same performance.

Although Containers are primarily intended for use in Solaris virtual environments (VEs), a framework exists to provide a translation layer from another operating system to the Oracle Solaris kernel. This framework has been used to enable the migration of Solaris 8 and Solaris 9 environments into Solaris 8 Containers and Solaris 9 Containers. These VEs operate like Solaris 8 and Solaris 9 systems, respectively. Each of these non-native models is called a "brand." A brand for Red Hat Enterprise Linux 3 was also created.

Recently, the brand framework has been used to provide other functionality, such as Oracle Solaris Cluster, in Containers. In that case, and in some others, the brand marks the Container so that the kernel or other software handles it differently than a native Container. For those special Containers, a translation layer is not necessary.

6.1.2 Isolation

The primary purpose of Containers is to isolate workloads that are running on one Oracle Solaris instance. Although this functionality is typically used when consolidating workloads onto one system, placing a single workload in a single Container on a system has a number of benefits. By design, the isolation provided by Containers includes the following factors:

- Each Container has its own objects: processes, file system mounts, network interfaces, and System V IPC objects.
- Processes in one Container are prevented from accessing objects in another Container.
- Processes in different Containers are prevented from directly communicating with each other, except for typical intersystem network communication.
- A process in one Container cannot obtain any information about a process running in a different Container—even confirmation of the existence of such a process.
- Each Container has its own namespace and can choose its own naming services, mostly configured in /etc. For example, each Container has its own set of users (via LDAP, /etc/passwd, and other means) and root user.
- Architecturally, the model of one application per OS instance maps directly to the model of one application per Container while reducing the number of OS instances to manage.

In addition to the functional or security isolation constraints listed above, Containers provide for resource isolation, as discussed in the next section.

6.1.2.1 Containers Security Boundary

The basis for a Container's security boundary is Solaris 10 privileges. Thus understanding the robust security boundary around Containers starts with an understanding of Solaris privileges.

Oracle Solaris implements two sorts of rights management. User rights management determines which privileged commands a nonprivileged user might execute. Consider the popular `sudo` program as an example of this kind of rights management. Process rights management determines which low-level, fine-grained, system-call-level actions a process can carry out.

Oracle Solaris privileges implement process rights management. Privileges are associated with specific actions—usually actions that are not typically permitted for non-root users. For example, there is a Solaris privilege associated with modification of the system's time clock. Normally, only the root user is permitted to change the clock. Solaris privileges reduce security risks: Instead of giving a person the root password just so that the person can modify the system time clock, that person's user account is given the appropriate privilege. The user is not permitted to perform any other actions typically reserved for the root user. Instead, the Solaris privileges allow the system administrator to grant a process just enough privilege to carry out its function but no more, thereby reducing the system's exposure to security breach or accident.

Thus, in contrast to the situation noted with earlier versions of Solaris and with many other UNIX-like operating systems, the root user in Oracle Solaris is able to perform any operation not because its UID number is zero, but rather because it has the required privileges. However, the root user can grant privileges to another user, enabling specific users to perform specific tasks or sets of tasks.

When a process attempts to perform a privileged operation, the kernel determines whether the owner of the process has the privilege(s) required to perform the operation. If the user, and therefore the user's process, has that privilege, the kernel permits that user to perform the associated operation.

A Container has a specific configurable subset of all privileges. The default subset provides normal operations for the Container, and prevents the Container's processes from learning about or interacting with other Containers' users, processes, and devices. The root user in the Container inherits all of the privileges that the Container has. Non-root users in a Container have, by default, the same set of privileges that non-root users of the global zone have.

The platform administrator—normally the root user of the global zone—can configure Containers as necessary, including increasing or decreasing the maximum set of privileges that a Container has. No user in that Container can exceed that maximum set—not even the Container's root user. The root user of a Container can modify the set of privileges of users in that Container, but cannot modify the set of privileges that the Container can have. In other words, the maximum set of privileges that a Container has cannot be escalated from within the Container.[1] At the same time, processes with sufficient privileges, running in the global zone, can interact with processes and other types of objects in Containers. This type of interaction is necessary for the global zone to manage Containers. For example, the root user in the global zone must be able to diagnose a performance issue caused by a process in one Container. It can use DTrace to accomplish this task because privileged processes in the global zone can interact with processes in Containers in certain ways.

Also, nonprivileged users in the global zone can perform some operations that are commonplace on UNIX systems, but that are unavailable to nonprivileged users in a Container. A simple example is the ability to list all processes running on the system, whether they are running in Containers or not. For some systems, this capability is another reason to prevent user access to the global zone.

The isolation of Containers is very thorough in Oracle Solaris. The Containers feature set is the basis for the Solaris Trusted Extensions feature set, and the capabilities of Solaris Trusted Extensions are appropriate for systems that must compartmentalize data. Solaris 10 11/06 with Solaris Trusted Extensions achieved Common Criteria Certification for the Labeled Security Protection Profile (LSPP) at Evaluation Assurance Level (EAL) 4+, the highest commonly recognized global security certification. This certification allows Solaris 10 to be deployed when multi-level security (MLS) protection and independent validation of an OS security model is required. Solaris 10 achieved this certification for SPARC and x86-based systems, for both desktop and server functionality, and also received Common Criteria Certification for the Controlled Access Protection Profile (CAPP) and Role-Based Access Control Protection Profile (RBACPP).

The isolation of Containers is implemented in the Oracle Solaris kernel. As described earlier, this isolation is somewhat configurable, enabling the global zone administrator to customize the security of a Container. By default, the security boundary around a Container is very robust. This boundary can be further hardened by removing privileges from the Container, which effectively prevents the Container from using specific features of Solaris. The boundary can be selectively enlarged by enabling the Container to perform specific operations such as setting the system time clock.

The entire list of privileges appears on the `privileges`(5) man page. Table 6.1 shows the privileges that are most commonly used to customize a Container's security boundary. The third column indicates whether the privilege is in the default privilege set for Containers. Note that nondefault settings described elsewhere, such as `ip-type=exclusive`, change the list of privileges automatically.

---

1. For more details on Solaris privileges, see the book *Solaris Security Essentials* or *Solaris 10 System Administration Guide: Security Services*, which can be obtained at `http://docs.sun.com/app/docs/prod/solaris.10`.

Table 6.1 Privileges for Containers

Privilege	The privilege gives a process the ability to . . .	Default?
dtrace_proc	Use DTrace process-level tracing	No
dtrace_user	Use DTrace user-level tracing	No
net_icmpaccess	Send and receive ICMP packets	Yes
net_privaddr	Bind to privileged ports	Yes
net_rawaccess	Have raw network access, which is necessary to use snoop	No
proc_clock_highres	Allow the use of high-resolution timers	No
proc_info	Examine /proc for other processes in the same Container	Yes
proc_lock_memory	Lock pages in physical memory	Yes
proc_owner	See and modify other process states	Yes
proc_priocntl	Increase your priority or modify your scheduling class	No
proc_session	Send signals or trace processes outside your session	Yes
sys_acct	Enable, disable, and manage accounting via acct(2)	Yes
sys_admin	Set nodename, domainname, and nscd settings; use coreadm(1M)	Yes
sys_audit	Start the audit daemon	Yes
sys_ipc_config	Increase the size of the System V IPC message queue buffer	No
sys_ip_config	Configure a system's NICs, routes, and other network features (a privilege automatically given to exclusive-IP Containers)	No
sys_resource	Exceed the resource limits of setrlimit(2) and setctl(2)	Yes
sys_time	Change the system time clock via stime(2), adjtime(2), and ntp_adjtime(2)	No

Whereas some privileges can be added to a Container, other privileges can *never* be added to a Container. These privileges control hardware components directly (e.g., turning a CPU off or controlling access to kernel data). The latter action is prevented to prohibit one Container from examining or modifying data about another Container. Table 6.2 lists these privileges.

Table 6.2 Privileges Not Allowed in Containers

Privilege	The privilege gives a process the ability to . . .
dtrace_kernel	Use DTrace kernel-level tracing
proc_zone	Signal or trace processes in other zones
sys_config	Perform file system-specific operations, quota calls, and creation and deletion of snapshots
sys_devices	Create device special files; override device restrictions

Table 6.2 Privileges Not Allowed in Containers, *continued*

Privilege	The privilege gives a process the ability to . . .
sys_linkdir	Link and unlink directories
sys_mount	Mount and unmount file systems; add and remove swap devices
sys_res_config	Administer CPUs, processor sets, and resource pools
sys_suser_compat	Manage third-party modules' use of the kernel suser() function

The configurable security of Containers is a core component of Immutable Service Containers. ISCs are an architectural deployment pattern used to describe a platform for highly secure service delivery. They provide a security-reinforced Container into which a specific service (i.e., an application) or a set of services is deployed. For more information, see http://hub.opensolaris.org/bin/view/Project+isc.

6.1.3 Namespaces

Each Container has its own *namespace*. A namespace is the complete set of recognized names for entities such as users, hosts, printers, and others. In other words, a namespace represents a mapping of human-readable names to names or numbers that are more appropriate to computers. The user namespace maps user names to user identification numbers (UIDs). The host name namespace maps host names to IP addresses. As in any Oracle Solaris system, namespaces in Containers can be managed using the /etc/nsswitch.conf file.

One simple outcome of having an individual namespace per Container is separate mappings of user names to UIDs. When managing Containers, remember that a user in one Container with UID 238 is a different user from UID 238 in another Container.

Also, each Container has its own Service Management Facility (SMF). SMF starts, monitors, and maintains network services such as sshd. As a consequence, each Container appears on the network just like any other Solaris system, using the same well-known port numbers for common network services.

6.1.4 Brands

Each Container includes a property called its *brand*. A Container's brand determines how it interacts with the Oracle Solaris kernel. Most of this interaction occurs via Solaris system calls. Some brands call for system calls to be used without modification; other brands add a layer of software that translates the Container's system call definitions into the system calls provided by the kernel for that Solaris distribution.

Each Solaris distribution—for example, Solaris 10—has a default brand for its Containers. The default brand for Solaris 10 is called `native`, but other brands exist for Solaris 10, too. The default brand for OpenSolaris is called `ipkg`.

Table 6.3 lists the current brands.

Table 6.3 Brands

Purpose	Brand Name	Base OS	System Call Layer?	Description
Solaris 8 Containers	`solaris8`	Solaris 10	Yes	A Solaris 8 (or 9) environment on a Solaris 10 system, with P2V tools
Solaris 9 Containers	`solaris9`	Solaris 10	Yes	
Solaris Cluster Nodes	`cluster`	Solaris 10	No	Assists with cluster functions
Solaris Trusted Extensions	`labeled`	Solaris 10	No	Enables data compartmentalization
Red Hat EL 3	`lx`	Solaris 10	Yes	A Linux environment on a Solaris 10 system
Solaris 10 on OpenSolaris	`s10brand`	OpenSolaris	Yes	A Solaris 10 environment on an OpenSolaris system*

* The s10brand is under development at `http://opensolaris.org`.

6.1.5 Packaging, Deployment, and File Systems

A Container's directory structure is a subset of the global zone's directory tree. When you create a Container, Oracle Solaris creates a new directory in which all of the Container's directories and files reside. That directory, which is owned by the global zone's root user, is chosen as the Container's `zonepath`, which in turn contains a directory named `root`. The latter directory is known by two names, as shown in Figure 6.2. If you are in the global zone, its name is simply `root`; if you are in the Container, that directory has the usual name for a system's root directory: '/'. A process in the Container cannot change its current working directory above that directory, nor can it reference any part of the global zone's directory structure above the Container's root directory. Thus, by default, a process in one Container cannot access a file in another Container.

By default, a Container inherits all of the Solaris programs installed in the global zone, including programs and some other files in `/sbin`, `/usr`, `/lib`, and `/platform`. These directories are mounted onto a Container's directories of the same names. These are read-only mounts, so as to prevent processes running in the Container from modifying the Solaris binaries. Figure 6.2 shows two of these read-only loopback mounts, which makes the commands and libraries in /usr and /lib available to the Container.

These directories are called package directories because they contain the contents of packages. A package from another software vendor can also be inherited by specifying the directory containing that software. During Container configuration, you can specify additional, non-Solaris package directories.

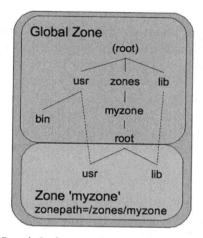

Figure 6.2 Read-Only Loopback Mount into Container

This design, called the "sparse-root" model, has several benefits. By sharing mounts with the global zone, it significantly decreases the amount of disk space used by a Container, shrinking it to less than 100 MB. It also reduces the amount of RAM used by the Container when it is running because a Solaris program running in multiple Containers requires only one set of memory pages for the program instructions, not one set per Container. In most cases, use of the sparse-root model minimizes the effort required to administer Containers. Packages and patches can be deployed once in the global zone, then become immediately available to all Containers using the sparse-root model.

The last benefit of this model is security enhancement. Occasionally, intruders have taken advantage of application software on a UNIX-like system to gain access to the system as a privileged user. Once they have done so, they can replace an existing operating system binary with a program that performs some malicious task when it is run (a "Trojan horse"). An unsuspecting user who runs that program at a later date may inadvertently cause difficult-to-diagnose problems. If the Trojan horse program is run regularly, it can send data updates from the system to a remote user on the Internet. A sparse-root zone significantly minimizes the risk from this type of attack through the read-only mounts of Solaris programs.

If a Container needs the ability to modify the package directories that are normally inherited, it can instead be configured using the "whole-root" model. Such a Container can add programs and files to those directories, but uses much more disk space. This approach is useful if you want to install additional software into the /usr and /lib directories.

6.1.6 Patching

A Solaris 10 package can be updated by applying a patch. Oracle Solaris provides some flexibility regarding the patching of systems that have Containers.

You should choose a sparse-root Container if you want to get the most benefit from the lightweight nature of Containers. Because it inherits almost all of its packages from the global zone, the amounts of disk space and RAM used by Oracle Solaris binaries are minimized. A package can be present at only one patch level, however, so all sparse-root Containers will be at the same patch level as the global zone in regard to those packages. This includes any non-Solaris packages installed in the global zone.

By comparison, a whole-root Container can more easily maintain its own unbundled and third-party software packages. This increases the flexibility and potential complexity for diverse environments.

Typically, you apply Oracle Solaris patches to the global zone and to Containers by using the patchadd(1M) command in the global zone. That command first patches the global zone, and then automatically patches each Container. Patches for Solaris packages will be applied in this way. If you choose to install non-Solaris packages from the global zone, those packages will, with a few exceptions, also be made available to the Containers.

By default, patchadd patches each Container in sequence. Systems with sufficient compute capacity can use the "parallel patching" feature to reduce the elapsed time needed to patch many Containers. To use this feature, while working in the global zone, edit the file /etc/patch/pdo.conf and change the value of num_proc to a value other than 1, which is the default. That number represents the desired level of parallelization. Ideally, you should choose a number close to the number of CPUs that are not in use. For example, an 8-CPU system running at 50% CPU utilization should be able to support patch parallelization of 4 without reducing the performance of workloads. If you are patching a system in single-user mode, you can set num_proc to the number of CPUs in the system. You may further reduce the elapsed patching time by increasing num_proc to 1.5 times the number of CPUs.

You can install third-party software packages and patches in whole-root Containers; these packages and patches can be different from the packages and patches installed in the global zone. To do so, use the patchadd command when logged into that Container. Note that this action is not permitted for packages marked "SUNW_PKG_ALLZONES=true" in the pkginfo(4) file.

It is also possible to apply a patch to a package in the global zone but modify only the contents of the global zone. The patchadd command has a -G option that means "apply the patch only to the current zone." This option is occasionally useful for patching a package that delivers content only into the global zone.

6.2 Feature Details

Features that can be applied to Containers include all of the configuration and control functionality you would expect from an operating system *and* from a visualization solution. Fortunately, almost all of the features specific to Containers are optional. You can learn each set of features separately from the others.

The features can be assigned to these categories:

- Creation and basic management, such as booting
- Packaging
- File systems
- Security
- Resource controls
- Networking
- Device access

The following sections demonstrate the use of these features.

6.2.1 Container Creation

The first step in creating a Container is configuring it with at least the minimum information. All initial Container configuration is performed with the zonecfg(1M) command, as in this example. The first command merely shows that there are no Containers on the system yet.

```
GZ# zoneadm list -cv
  ID NAME      STATUS      PATH                    BRAND    IP
   0 global    running     /                       native   shared
GZ# zonecfg -z myzone
myzone: No such zone configured
Use 'create' to begin configuring a new zone.
zonecfg:myzone> create
zonecfg:myzone> set zonepath=/zones/roots/myzone
```

continues

```
zonecfg:myzone> exit
GZ# zoneadm list -cv
   ID NAME        STATUS       PATH                      BRAND    IP
    0 global      running      /                         native   shared
    - myzone      configured   /zones/roots/myzone       native   shared
GZ# zonecfg -z myzone info
zonename: myzone
zonepath: /zones/roots/myzone
brand: native
autoboot: false
bootargs:
pool:
limitpriv:
scheduling-class:
ip-type: shared
inherit-pkg-dir:
        dir: /lib
inherit-pkg-dir:
        dir: /platform
inherit-pkg-dir:
        dir: /sbin
inherit-pkg-dir:
        dir: /usr
```

The output from the `info` subcommand of `zonecfg` shows all of the global properties of the Container as well as some default settings. Table 6.4 lists the global properties and their meanings.

Table 6.4 Global Properties of Containers

Property	Meaning
zonename	Name of the Container; cannot be changed
zonepath	Directory that contains all of the Container's files
brand	Type of Container: `native` for most; non-native brands include `solaris8` and others
autoboot	Determines whether the Container should be booted when the system boots
bootargs	Arguments to be used with zoneadm(1M) when the Container boots
pool	Resource pool of CPUs that this Container will use for its processes
limitpriv	The set of `privileges`(5) that this Container can have; if this field is empty, the Container has the default set of privileges
scheduling-class	The default scheduling class for this Container; one of TS (the default), IA, FSS, RT
ip-type	Type of IP networking which this Container will use; can be "shared" or "exclusive." Shared-IP Containers can share one or more NICs with other shared-IP Containers. Exclusive-IP Containers have exclusive access to their NICs.

A Container can be reconfigured after it has been configured, and even after it has been booted. However, a change in configuration does not take effect until the next time the Container boots. The next example changes the Container so that the next time the system boots, the Container boots automatically.

```
GZ# zonecfg -z myzone
zonecfg:myzone> set autoboot=true
zonecfg:myzone> exit
```

As mentioned earlier, package directories contain Solaris 10 package contents. The package and patch tools need to know where packages are stored. The property `inherit-pkg-dir` tells the operating system where packages are stored.

Software that is not part of the OS can be inherited as well, using the `inherit-pkg-dir` resource. You can modify the configuration of a Container that has already been configured. The following commands add the directory `/opt` as a directory that contains software packages to be made available to this Container:

```
GZ# zonecfg -z myzone
zonecfg:myzone> add inherit-pkg-dir
zonecfg:myzone:inherit-pkg-dir> set dir=/opt
zonecfg:myzone:inherit-pkg-dir> end
zonecfg:myzone> exit
```

After the Container has been installed, the set of `inherit-pkg-dir` resources cannot be modified.

As you might have guessed, a whole-root Container is simply one that doesn't inherit `/sbin`, `/usr`, `/lib`, and `/platform`. The process of configuring a whole-root Container begins with these commands to create a different Container:

```
GZ# zonecfg -z mywholerootzone
zonecfg:mywholerootzone> create
zonecfg:mywholerootzone> remove inherit-pkg-dir dir=/lib
zonecfg:mywholerootzone> remove inherit-pkg-dir dir=/platform
zonecfg:mywholerootzone> remove inherit-pkg-dir dir=/sbin
zonecfg:mywholerootzone> remove inherit-pkg-dir dir=/usr
zonecfg:mywholerootzone> set zonepath=/zones/roots/mywholerootzone
zonecfg:mywholerootzone> exit
```

6.2.1.1 Adding File Systems

In addition to the ability to mount file systems that contain packages, any arbitrary directory that exists in the global zone can be mounted into a Container, either as read-only or as read-write. This requires the use of a loopback mount, as shown in the next example for yet another Container. The programs in non-Solaris packages installed in such a file system would be available to the zone, but package and patch tools used in the zone will not recognize those packages.

```
GZ# zonecfg -z myufszone
zonecfg:myzone> add fs
zonecfg:myzone:fs> set dir=/shared
zonecfg:myzone:fs> set special=/zones/shared/myzone
zonecfg:myzone:fs> set type=lofs
zonecfg:myzone:fs> end
zonecfg:myzone> exit
```

In the preceding example, the `special` parameter specifies the global zone's name for that directory. The `dir` parameter specifies the directory name in the Container on which to mount the global zone's directory.

A brief diversion is warranted here. When managing Containers, you must keep in mind the two different perspectives on all objects such as files, processes, and users. In the most recent example, a process in the global zone would normally use the path name `/zones/shared/myzone` to refer to that directory. A process in the Container, however, must use the path `/shared` instead. While the Container is running, a privileged user of the global zone can also use the path `/zones/roots/myzone/root/shared`, as shown in Figure 6.3.

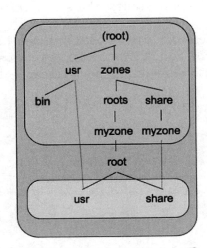

Figure 6.3 Loopback Mounts into a Container

Also, an entire file system can be configured into a Container so that only the Container can access it. Processes in other Containers cannot use that file system, and only privileged users in the global zone can access the file system. In this example, `dir` has the same meaning as in the previous example, but `special` indicates the name of the device that contains the file system.

```
GZ# zonecfg -z myufszone
zonecfg:myzone> add fs
zonecfg:myzone:fs> set dir=/mnt/myfs
zonecfg:myzone:fs> set special=/dev/dsk/c1t0d0s5
zonecfg:myzone:fs> set type=ufs
zonecfg:myzone:fs> end
zonecfg:myzone> exit
```

Storage managed by ZFS can be added in two different ways. In the next example, the first method is similar to the previous examples. Processes running in the Container can access the storage available to the ZFS file system `rpool/myzone1`. We recommend setting a quota on all file systems assigned to Containers so that one Container does not fill up the pool and prevent other workloads from using the pool.

The second method assigns a ZFS data set to the Container.[2] This method delegates administration of the data set to the Container. A privileged user in the Container, such as the root user, can control attributes of the data set and create new ZFS file systems in it. That user also controls attributes of those file systems, such as quotas and access control lists (ACLs).

```
GZ# zonecfg -z myzfszone
zonecfg:myzone> add fs
zonecfg:myzone:fs> set dir=/mnt/myzfs1
zonecfg:myzone:fs> set special=rpool/myzone1
zonecfg:myzone:fs> set type=zfs
zonecfg:myzone:fs> end
zonecfg:myzone> add dataset
zonecfg:myzone:dataset> set name=rpool/myzone2
zonecfg:myzone:dataset> end
zonecfg:myzone> exit
```

All of these mounts—UFS, lofs, ZFS, and others—are created when the Container is booted. For more information on types of file systems that can be used within a Container, see the Oracle Solaris 10 documentation at `http://docs.sun.com/app/docs/prod/solaris.10`.

---

2. See the ZFS documentation at `http://docs.sun.com/app/docs/doc/819-5461` for details regarding ZFS data sets.

6.2.1.2 Modifying Container Privileges

Earlier in this chapter, we discussed Oracle Solaris privileges, including the fact that you can modify the set of privileges that a Container can have. If you change the privileges that a Container can have, you must reboot the Container before the changes will take effect. The following example depicts the steps to add the sys_time privilege to an existing Container.

```
GZ# zonecfg -z web
zonecfg:web> set limitpriv="default,sys_time"
zonecfg:web> exit
GZ# zoneadm -z web boot
```

6.2.1.3 Installing and Booting the Container

After you have configured the Container, you can install it, making it ready to run.

```
GZ# zoneadm -z myzone install
Preparing to install zone <myzone>.
Creating list of files to copy from the global zone.
Copying <7503> files to the zone.
Initializing zone product registry.
Determining zone package initialization order.
Preparing to initialize <1098> packages on the zone.
Initialized <1098> packages on zone.
Zone <myzone> is initialized.
The file </zones/roots/myzone/root/var/sadm/system/logs/install_log> contains a log of
the zone installation.
GZ# zoneadm list -cv
  ID NAME      STATUS      PATH                     BRAND   IP
   0 global    running     /                        native  shared
   - myzone    installed   /zones/roots/myzone      native  shared
```

During the installation process, zoneadm creates the directories required by the Container. For directories that hold system packages, the appropriate files and directories are either copied or loopback-mounted from the global zone, depending on whether the Container uses the sparse-root or whole-root model. Directories that contain system configuration information, such as /etc, are created in the Container's file structure and populated with configuration files.

Containers boot much faster than virtual machines, mostly because there is so little to do. The global zone sets up the security boundary and then creates a zinit process that starts the Container's Services Management Facility (SMF) and creates a few other processes. At that point, the Container is ready for use.

```
GZ# zoneadm -z myzone boot
GZ# zoneadm list -cv
  ID NAME      STATUS       PATH                    BRAND     IP
   0 global    running      /                       native    shared
   1 myzone    running      /zones/roots/myzone     native    shared
```

The first time the Container boots after installation, it needs system configuration information, which is usually collected by Solaris systems when you are installing Solaris. You can provide this information via the `zlogin(1)` command, which provides access for privileged global zone users into a Container. With just one argument—the Container's name—it enters a shell in the Container as the root user. Arguments after the Container's name are passed as a command line to a shell in the Container, and the output is displayed to the user of `zlogin`. One important option is `-C`, which provides access to the Container's virtual console. The root user in the global zone can use that console whenever it is not already in use.

Because this is the first time the Container is booting, it immediately issues its first prompt to the Container's virtual console. After connecting to the virtual console, you might need to press Return once to get a new terminal type prompt.

```
GZ# zlogin -C myzone
[Connected to zone 'myzone' console]
<RETURN>
What type of terminal are you using?

  1) ANSI Standard CRT
  2) DEC VT52
  3) DEC VT100
  4) Heathkit 19
  5) Lear Siegler ADM31
  6) PC Console
  7) Sun Command Tool
  8) Sun Workstation
  9) Televideo 910
 10) Televideo 925
 11) Wyse Model 50
 12) X Terminal Emulator (xterms)
 13) CDE Terminal Emulator (dtterm)
 14) Other
Type the number of your choice and press Return: 13

<Enter Host Name>
<Choose Time Zone>
<Enter Root Password>
```

```
System identification is completed.

rebooting system due to change(s) in /etc/default/init

[NOTICE: Zone rebooting]

SunOS Release 5.10 Version Generic_141445-09 64-bit
Copyright 1983-2009 Sun Microsystems, Inc.  All rights reserved.
Use is subject to license terms.

Hostname: myzone
Reading ZFS config: done.

myzone console login:
```

Instead of providing the system configuration information manually, you can use the method used by Solaris administrators for years: place the information in the /etc/sysidcfg file. The difference in these two approaches relates to the location of that file: It must be the *Container's* /etc/sysidcfg file, not the *system's* /etc/sysidcfg file. Extending the earlier examples, the Container's file is located at /zones/roots/myzone/root/etc/sysidcfg. You can use this method to completely automate the creation of Containers. If the necessary information resides in the Container's sysidcfg file, the Container will use it before completing the boot process.

6.2.1.4 Halting a Container

Not only does the zoneadm command install and boot Containers, but it also halts them.

The halt subcommand simply kills the processes in the Container. It does not run scripts that gracefully shut down the Container. As you might suspect, however, it is faster.

GZ# **zoneadm -z myzone halt**

Usually, however, you should gracefully stop a Container by using the zlogin command to run the shutdown program in the Container.

```
GZ# zlogin myzone shutdown -i 0

Shutdown started.    Fri Oct 30 15:00:52 EDT 2009

Do you want to continue? (y or n):   y
Changing to init state s - please wait
Standard input not a tty line
```

Figure 6.4 shows the entire life cycle of a Container, along with the commands you can use to manage one.

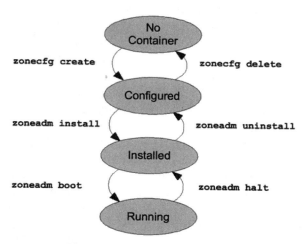

Figure 6.4 Container States

6.2.2 Resource Management

The Containers feature set includes comprehensive resource management features, also called *resource controls*. These controls allow the platform administrator to manage those resources that are typically controlled in VEs. Use of these controls is optional, and most are disabled by default. We highly recommend that you take advantage of these features. They can prevent many problems caused by one workload consuming more resources than it should.

The following resources were mentioned in Chapter 1, "Introduction to Virtualization":

- CPU capacity—that is, the portion of a CPU's clock cycles that a VE can use
- Amount of RAM used
- Amount of virtual memory or swap space used
- Network bandwidth consumed
- Use of kernel data structures—both structures of finite size and ones that use another finite resource such as RAM

This section describes the implementation of resource controls for Containers. It also demonstrates the use of Solaris tools to monitor resource consumption by Containers.

The zonecfg command is the most useful tool to set resource controls on Containers, but its settings do not take effect until the next time the Container boots. Other useful commands include prctl(1) and rcapadm(1M), both of which have an immediate effect on a Container. Resource control settings can be viewed with the commands prctl, rcapstat(1), and poolstat(1M).

Oracle Solaris 10 includes a wide variety of tools that report on resource consumption, including prstat, poolstat(1M), mpstat(1M), rcapstat, and kstat(1M). Many of these features can be applied to Containers using command-line options or other methods. In addition, a few companies produce excellent software products designed for monitoring resource consumption by the global zone and by individual Containers—for example, Oracle Enterprise Manager Ops Center, BMC Patrol, CA Unicenter, HP Operations Manager, TeamQuest, and others. This section discusses only those tools that are included with Oracle Solaris 10. Chapter 9, "Virtualization Management," discusses Ops Center.

One of the greatest strengths of Containers is common to most OSV implementations but absent from other forms of virtualization—namely, the ability of tools running in the management area to provide a holistic view of system activity (all VEs) as well as a detailed view of activity in each VE. The monitoring tools described in this section are common Solaris tools that provide either a holistic view, a detailed view, or options to do both.

6.2.2.1 CPU Controls

Oracle Solaris offers three methods of controlling a Container's use of CPU time. First, the Fair Share Scheduler is the most flexible, allowing multiple Containers to share the system's CPUs, or a subset of them. Second, Dynamic Resource Pools create subsets of CPUs, and allow you to exclusively assign a Container to a subset called a *pool*. Third, CPU caps enforce a maximum amount of computational ability on a Container. Although you can use a Container without any CPU controls, we recommend using these controls to improve performance predictability.

Fair Share Scheduler   The best all-around mechanism is the Fair Share Scheduler (FSS), which was discussed earlier in Chapter 1. FSS can control the allocation of available CPU resources among workloads based on their importance. This importance is expressed by the number of cpu-shares that you assign to each workload. The FSS compares the number of shares assigned to a particular workload to the aggregate number of shares assigned to all workloads. If one workload has 100 shares and the total number of shares assigned to all workloads is 500, the scheduler will ensure that the workload receives one-fifth of the available CPU resources at a minimum.

The last point is very important. A key advantage of this CPU control mechanism over the other options is that it does not waste idle CPU cycles. With FSS, any workload can use idle CPU cycles as long as each workload receives its guaranteed minimum resources. The FSS method does not force any process to wait if a CPU is available, unlike the other methods of CPU control. Even so, a more important workload may wait while a less important task finishes its time slice on a CPU.

To use the FSS with Containers, first enable it for use across the Solaris instance. As is often the case, one command is needed to tell Solaris to change a specific setting the next time Solaris boots, and a different command is needed to tell Solaris to begin changing its behavior now. The dispadmin(1M) command shown here changes the default scheduler to be used the next time that Solaris boots. The priocntl(1) command changes the default scheduler that Solaris is using now for all existing processes.

```
GZ# dispadmin -d FSS
GZ# priocntl -s -c FSS -i all
```

Now that FSS is the default scheduler, you must assign sufficient shares to the global zone to ensure that its processes get sufficient CPU time. Choose a value that is of the same magnitude as the values used for the other Containers. Set a value with zonecfg for the next time the system boots. Also, use prctl to set a value for right now. The order of execution does not matter.

```
GZ# zonecfg -z global
zonecfg:web> set cpu-shares=100
zonecfg:web> exit
GZ# prctl -t privileged -n zone.cpu-shares -v 100 -i zone global
```

The next step is the allocation of 100 cpu-shares to a Container, using the following command:

```
GZ# zonecfg -z web
zonecfg:web> set cpu-shares=100
zonecfg:web> exit
GZ# zoneadm -z web reboot
```

After the zone is rebooted, this value can be queried with the following command:

```
GZ# prctl -n zone.cpu-shares -t privileged -i zone web
zone: 6: web
NAME             PRIVILEGE  VALUE   FLAG   ACTION        RECIPIENT
zone.cpu-shares  privileged  100     -      none           -
```

This resource constraint can also be dynamically changed for a running zone:

`GZ# prctl -n zone.cpu-shares -r -v 200 -i zone web`

Whenever share assignments are changed or Containers using FSS are added or removed, the proportion of CPU time allowed for each Container changes to reflect the new total number of shares.

A final note on efficiency and FSS: Although this method does not leave idle CPU cycles when a workload might use them, the presence of a large number of Containers on a busy system will tax the scheduler. Its algorithm will use a measurable amount of CPU cycles. On medium and large systems, dozens of running Containers would be needed for the effect to be noticeable.

Dynamic Resource Pools   Use of the Fair Share Scheduler assumes that multiple Containers should share the system's processors, or a specific set of those processors. An alternative—Solaris Dynamic Resource Pools—ensures that a workload has exclusive access to a set of CPUs. When this feature is used, typically a Container is configured to have its own pool of CPUs reserved for its exclusive use. Processes in the global zone and in other Containers never run on that set of CPUs. This type of resource pool is called a *temporary* pool, because it exists only when the Container is running. It is also sometimes called a *private* pool because those CPUs are dedicated (private) to that one Container and its processes.

A resource pool can be of fixed size, or it can be configured to vary in size within a range that you choose. In the latter situation, the OS will shift CPUs between pools as their needs change, as shown in Figure 6.5. Each CPU is assigned to either a (nondefault) resource pool or the default pool. CPUs in the default pool are used by global zone processes and processes in Containers that are not configured to use a pool.

A private pool is not created until its Container boots. If sufficient CPUs are not available to fulfill the configuration, the Container will not boot, and a diagnostic message will be displayed. In that case, one of the following steps can be taken to enable the Container to boot:

- Reconfigure the Container with fewer CPUs
- Reconfigure the Container to share CPUs with other Containers
- Shift CPUs out of the private pools of other Containers into the default pool
- Move the Container to a system with sufficient CPUs.

For example, consider Figure 6.5, which shows a 32-CPU system with a default pool of 4–32 CPUs and with Containers Web, App, and DB, which are configured with pools of 2–6 CPUs, 8–16 CPUs, and 8–12 CPUs, respectively. Solaris will attempt to assign each pool its maximum quantity of CPUs while leaving the default pool with its minimum quantity of CPUs. By default, Solaris will balance the quantity of CPUs assigned to each pool within the configuration constraints. In this example, Web will get 6 CPUs, and App and DB will each get 11 CPUs, leaving 4 CPUs for the default pool. After the Containers have been running for a while, if the CPU utilization of one pool exceeds a configurable threshold, Solaris will automatically shift one CPU into it from an under-utilized pool.

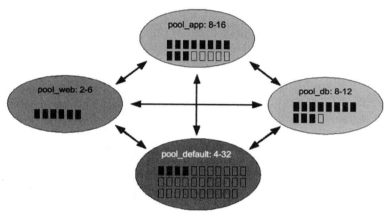

Figure 6.5 Dynamic Resource Pools

Figure 6.6 shows graphs of CPU allocation and utilization for three different Containers and the system's default pool. As the workloads become more active, they need more processing capacity, and Solaris dynamically provides this resource as necessary.

For example, "Web CPUs" is the number of CPUs configured in the Web Container's pool as time passes. As the utilization of one pool grows beyond a configurable threshold, Solaris shifts a CPU into the pool. As the workload increases, Solaris shifts more CPUs until it has reached the maximum quantity configured for that pool, or until there are no more CPUs that can be shifted to the pool. After the utilization of a pool has decreased below the threshold for a suitably long period, Solaris shifts a CPU out of the Container's pool and back into the default pool.

Note that the App Container's pool and the DB Container's pool have a minimum of 8 CPUs each. During at least some periods of time, these pools have excess capacity that other Containers cannot use. The advantage in maintaining that excess capacity is that those Containers can use it instantly when they need it, without waiting for Solaris to shift a CPU to their own pools. In other words, they can react more quickly to changing needs for processor time.

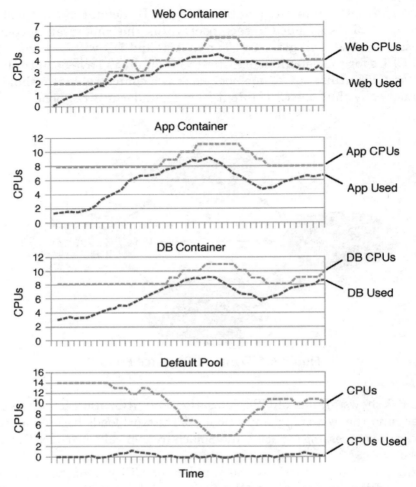

Figure 6.6 Dynamic Resource Pools: CPU Allocation and Utilization Rates

Configuring Dynamic Resource Pools   Configuring a Container to use a private pool is very easy. To dedicate two processors to a Container named web, run the following commands:

```
GZ# zonecfg -z web
zonecfg:web> add dedicated-cpu
zonecfg:web:dedicated-cpu> set ncpus=2
zonecfg:web:dedicated-cpu> end
zonecfg:web> exit
GZ# zoneadm -z web reboot
```

Global zone administrators can view the current configuration of pools with the `poolstat` command. A private pool has a name beginning with `SUNWtmp_` followed by the name of the Container:

```
GZ# poolstat
                          pset
   id pool          size used load
    1 SUNWtmp_web      2 0.00 0.00
    0 pool_default     2 0.00 0.24
```

Note that the pool is associated with a processor set that contains the CPUs.

To change the pool size to a dynamic quantity for the next time the Container boots, you can run the following commands to allocate between two and four processors to the Container. The first command enables the service `poold`. This service is aware of resource pools that have been configured with a variable quantity of CPUs. It tracks CPU utilization of those pools and, if one is over-utilized, shifts a CPU to it from an under-utilized pool. If multiple pools are over-utilized, the `importance` parameter informs the OS of the relative importance of this pool compared to other pools.[3]

```
GZ# svcadm enable pools/dynamic
GZ# zonecfg -z web
zonecfg:web> select dedicated-cpu
zonecfg:web:dedicated-cpu> set ncpus=2-4
zonecfg:web:dedicated-cpu> set importance=5
zonecfg:web:dedicated-cpu> end
zonecfg:web> exit
GZ# zoneadm -z web reboot
```

The size of a pool can be changed while the Container runs by manually shifting CPUs from one pool to another. This manipulation requires learning the name of the processor set.

```
GZ# poolstat -r pset
   id pool          type rid rset          min max size used load
    1 SUNWtmp_web   pset   1 SUNWtmp_web      2   2    2 0.00 0.00
    0 pool_default  pset  -1 pset_default     1 66K    1 0.00 0.24
```

---

3. For more information on the ability to load balance by automatically shifting CPUs from one pool to another, see *Solaris 10 Administration Guide: Solaris Containers: Resource Management and Solaris Zones* at `http://docs.sun.com/app/docs/prod/solaris.10`.

The column labeled `rset` lists the processor set's name. The quantity of CPUs in the processor set can be changed with the following command:

```
GZ# poolcfg -dc 'transfer 1 from pset pset_default to pset SUNWtmp_web'
```

Before leaving the topic of resource pools, let's consider the acronym "CPU" and the kernel's interpretation of it. For decades, "CPU" meant the chip that ran machine instructions, one at a time. The operating system created a process, branched execution to it, and cleaned up when it was done. A multiprogramming OS ran one process for a small period of time, then switched the CPU to another process if one was ready to run.

Multiprocessing systems required a more sophisticated scheduler because that tool was responsible for choosing a CPU for the next runnable process on the run queue.

Now we have multicore processors and multithreaded cores. Multicore processors are simply multiple CPUs implemented on one piece of silicon, although some models provide some shared resources for those cores, such as a large bank of shared cache. Multithreaded cores improve throughput performance by duplicating some—but not all—of a core's circuitry within the core. To take the most advantage of those hardware threads, the operating system must be able to efficiently schedule processes onto the threads, preferably with some knowledge of the CPU's internal workings and memory architecture.

Oracle Solaris has a long history of efficiently scheduling hundreds of processes on dozens of processors, going back to the E10000 with its 64 single-core CPUs. Because of its scalability, Solaris was modified to schedule processes on any hardware thread in the system, maximizing the total throughput of the platform. Unfortunately, this scheme can be a bit confusing when configuring resource pools, because each type of CPU has its own type and amount of hardware threading. Each also has its own per-thread performance characteristics.

Table 6.5 lists various CPUs that will run Oracle Solaris 10 and core and thread data. It also shows some sample systems.

Table 6.5 Multithreaded CPUs

CPU	No. Cores per Chip	No. Threads per Core	Sample Systems			
			Model	Max. No. CPU Chips	Max. No. Threads	Form Factor
SPARC64-VII	4	2	Sun M9000	64	512	Multicabinet server
UltraSPARC-T2+	8	8	Sun T5440	4	256	4RU server
Opteron 8384	4	1	Sun X4600	8	32	4RU server
Xeon X5570	4	2	Sun X4270	2	16	2RU server
Xeon W3580	4	1	Sun Ultra 27	1	4	Workstation

Because Solaris identifies each hardware thread as a CPU, you can create very flexible resource pools. For example, on a Sun T5440 you can create seven 32-CPU pools and still have 32 CPUs left for the global zone! Most multithreaded CPUs have some shared cache, so if you want to optimize performance you should configure CPU quantities in multiples of 4 or 8, depending on the architecture of that CPU.

Finally, the kernel does not enforce a limit on the total number of CPUs configured in different pools or Containers until they are actually running. Thus you can configure and install ten 128-CPU Containers on a T5440 as long as you run only one at a time. Alternatively, you could configure and run 10 Containers, each with 20–128 CPUs. In other words, you can over-subscribe CPUs.

Oracle Solaris CPU Caps   The final CPU resource control available for Containers is the *CPU cap*. You can use such a cap to tell Solaris that the processes of a specific Container should not be allowed to use more than a certain amount of CPU time, over a small sampling period. This cap allows granularity to be specified in hundredths of a CPU—for example, 5.12 CPUs.

For example, to assign a CPU cap equivalent to $4\frac{1}{3}$ CPUs, use the following command:

```
GZ# zonecfg -z web
zonecfg:web> add capped-cpu
zonecfg:web:capped-cpu> set ncpus=4.33
zonecfg:web:capped-cpu> end
zonecfg:web> exit
GZ# zoneadm -z web reboot
```

After the zone is rebooted, this value can be queried with the following command:

```
GZ# prctl -n zone.cpu-cap -i zone web
zone: 6: web
NAME            PRIVILEGE    VALUE    FLAG    ACTION      RECIPIENT
zone.cpu-cap system         4.33     inf     deny        -
```

Similarly, this resource constraint can be dynamically changed for a running Container:

```
GZ# prctl -n zone.cpu-cap -t privileged -v 300 -i zone web
```

Note that the `prctl` command requires an integer value representing hundredths of a CPU. In the example command, 300 means "300 hundredths of one CPU," which is equivalent to 3.00 CPUs.

Although `prctl` will display the setting and `prstat` will display the CPU utilization rate, the `kstat` command will display both pieces of information, if you first determine the Container's ID number with `zoneadm`.

```
GZ# zoneadm list -cv
   ID NAME       STATUS     PATH                    BRAND    IP
    0 global     running    /                       native   shared
    1 myzone     running    /zones/roots/myzone     native   shared
GZ# kstat  'caps:1:cpucaps_zone_1'

module: caps                            instance: 1
name:   cpucaps_zone_1                  class:      zone_caps
        above_sec                       0
        below_sec                       7
        crtime                          115643.232135332
        maxusage                        111
        nwait                           0
        snaptime                        115650.048256739
        usage                           14
        value                           300
        zonename                        myzone
```

The output of `kstat` shows that the Container is currently using approximately 14% of a CPU, and has used as much as 111% of a CPU during one measurement sample.

You can combine a CPU cap with FSS to ensure that a Container receives a specific minimum amount of compute time, but no more than another amount. It does not make sense to apply both a CPU cap *and* a pool to a Container, and the kernel does not allow it.

CPU controls should be used to prevent one workload from using more CPU time than it should, either accidentally or intentionally as a result of a denial-of-service attack.

Choosing a CPU Control   Each of those CPU controls affects processing in different ways. Which one should you use? Every situation is different, but some general statements can be made:

- FSS is the best all-around CPU control. All Containers can access all of the CPUs, so there are never idle CPU cycles that cannot be used by a Container that is trying to use more—which is sometimes a problem with dedicated CPUs or a CPU cap. A new Container can be added without reassigning CPUs, which may be required when using dedicated CPUs. However, the FSS algorithm can consume an unacceptable amount of CPU time if dozens of Containers must be scheduled.

- Dedicated CPUs allow you to minimize software licensing costs for some software. Instead of licensing the software for all 256 CPU cores in an M9000, you may be able to assign a much smaller number (e.g., 16) to a Container and pay for only a 16-core software license. When configured correctly, dedicated CPUs also maximize performance of the associated Container because its processes are more likely to return to the same CPU every time it gets a time slice, thereby reducing the effects of cache eviction and maintaining data in memory attached to that CPU.

- A CPU cap is useful to set user expectations among early users of a system. Otherwise, users may become accustomed to the response time they observe when they can use all of the CPUs in the system, only to be disappointed later by the system's response time when they are sharing the CPUs. Service providers also use CPU caps to ensure that their users can use only the compute capacity they paid for.

CPU Usage Monitoring Tools   Oracle Solaris 10 includes some CPU monitoring tools that are available on most UNIX-like operating systems as well as some that are unique to Solaris. These include ps, prstat, poolstat, and mpstat.

The ps command has two new options to help observe Containers:

- -z: Adds a new column of output labeled ZONE (the name of the Container in which the process is running)

- -z <name>: Limits the output to processes in the Container specified by <name>

The following example shows ps output limited to one Container's processes. Notice that zsched has a parent PID of 1, which is the global zone's init process. Also, note that zsched is the parent of the Container's init process, and the Container's svc.startd and svc.configd services have also been inherited by the global zone's init process.

```
GZ# ps -fz myzone
    UID    PID  PPID  C    STIME TTY     TIME  CMD
   root   1076     1  0 18:15:15 ?      0:00  zsched
   root   1089  1076  0 18:15:16 ?      0:00  /sbin/init
   root   1091     1  0 18:15:16 ?      0:06  /lib/svc/bin/svc.startd
   root   1093     1  0 18:15:16 ?      0:08  /lib/svc/bin/svc.configd
...
```

Of course, users of the Container can use the ps command. As mentioned earlier, the zlogin command can be issued from the global zone to run a program in the Container—in this case, ps -ef.

```
GZ# zlogin myzone ps -ef
    UID   PID  PPID  C    STIME TTY        TIME  CMD
   root  1335  1331  0 15:22:51 ?         0:00  ps -fz myzone
   root  1076  1076  0 18:15:15 ?         0:00  zsched
   root  1089  1076  0 18:15:16 ?         0:00  /sbin/init
   root  1091  1076  0 18:15:16 ?         0:06  /lib/svc/bin/svc.startd
   root  1093  1076  0 18:15:16 ?         0:08  /lib/svc/bin/svc.configd
...
```

In the previous output, note that from within the Container, we are not allowed to know anything about the outside world. Even the PID number of the global zone's init process remains hidden from us. The kernel replaces that forbidden information with safe information—in this case, the PID of the Container's zsched process. Any process that would normally be inherited by init is, seemingly, inherited by zsched. Note also that the parent PID of zsched is hidden—by displaying a PPID equal to its PID!

The -Z option adds the ZONE column to ps output. This column is very helpful when you are trying to understand the relationship between processes and the Container with which they are associated.

```
GZ# ps -efZ
     ZONE      UID   PID  PPID  C    STIME TTY      TIME CMD
   global     root     0     0  0 15:24:18 ?       0:25 sched
   global     root     1     0  0 15:24:20 ?       0:00 /sbin/init
   ...
   myzone     root  1076     1  0 18:15:15 ?       0:00 zsched
   global     root  1075     1  0 18:15:15 ?       0:00 zoneadmd -z myzone
   global     root  1500  1042  0 21:46:19 pts/3   0:00 ps -efZ
```

Another very useful command for examining processes and Containers is prstat. At the first sign of trouble, or when you are examining the system out of curiosity, prstat will help you determine which Containers are busy and which are not. It can provide both a holistic view and a detailed view, even doing both at the same time. For the first release of Solaris 10, a pair of new options were added just for Containers:

- -Z: Splits the terminal window into an upper section and a lower section. The upper section lists processes as if no options were used. The lower section shows the same information, but for entire Containers—the aggregate of all of the processes in each Container. As with the default output, the upper and lower sections are each sorted; the sort order is by CPU utilization rate by default, but you can choose another sort key with -s.

- -z <name>: Lists information about processes in the specified Container or Containers.

In the following example, notice that the output is arranged in two sections. The upper section provides the default output of prstat. The lower section sums up data from each Container, including the amount of virtual memory (SIZE) and RAM (RSS) used by the Container's processes.

```
GZ# prstat -z
   PID USERNAME   SIZE   RSS STATE   PRI NICE     TIME  CPU PROCESS/NLWP
 25586 root      9760K 8944K sleep    59    0  0:00:07 4.2% svc.configd/15
 25506 root      9728K 8920K sleep    59    0  0:00:07 3.8% svc.configd/13
 25583 root      7576K 6608K sleep    59    0  0:00:02 0.7% svc.startd/14
 25504 root      7488K 6488K sleep    59    0  0:00:01 0.5% svc.startd/12
 25948 root      4984K 3760K sleep    59    0  0:00:00 0.2% inetd/4
 25646 root      4984K 3760K sleep    59    0  0:00:00 0.2% inetd/4
 25538 root      5808K 3080K sleep    59    0  0:00:00 0.0% zoneadmd/4
 25487 root      5808K 3080K sleep    59    0  0:00:00 0.0% zoneadmd/4
     1 root      2472K  424K sleep    59    0  0:00:18 0.0% init/1


ZONEID    NPROC   SIZE   RSS MEMORY       TIME  CPU ZONE
   246       22    84M   51M   0.4%    0:00:09 5.3% ProdWeb1
   245       22    84M   51M   0.4%    0:00:08 4.6% DevApp1
     0       47   235M   54M   0.4%    1:41:59 0.2% global
Total: 91 processes, 359 lwps, load averages: 0.55, 0.13, 0.04
```

The next example limits the output to just those processes that belong to a specific Container.

```
GZ# prstat -z myzone
   PID USERNAME   SIZE   RSS STATE   PRI NICE     TIME  CPU PROCESS/NLWP
 10702 root         0K    0K sleep    60    -  0:00:00 0.0% zsched/1
 10829 root      4952K 3084K sleep    59    0  0:00:01 0.0% nscd/22
 10872 root      1960K 1392K sleep    59    0  0:00:00 0.0% ttymon/1
 10761 root      3892K 1660K sleep    59    0  0:00:00 0.0% svc-dlmgmtd/1
 10756 root      8460K 6880K sleep    59    0  0:00:01 0.0% svc.startd/11
 10870 root      1640K  852K sleep    59    0  0:00:00 0.0% utmpd/1
 10736 root      2352K 1312K sleep    59    0  0:00:00 0.0% init/1
 10792 daemon    1888K 1176K sleep    59    0  0:00:00 0.0% kcfd/2
 10758 root        10M 9468K sleep    59    0  0:00:03 0.0% svc.configd/14

Total: 9 processes, 54 lwps, load averages: 1.44, 1.37, 1.35
```

If you use the dedicated-cpu feature of zonecfg, or if you use poolcfg to create processor sets and pools for Containers, poolstat and mpstat will be useful.

The former provides on-demand information about processor set populations, whereas the latter provides synchronous notices about population changes.

The `poolstat` program lists the resource pools, their associated processor sets, and the population of each pool/processor set combination.

```
GZ# poolstat -r pset
id pool            type rid rset              min  max size used load
1  SUNWtmp_zone1   pset   1 SUNWtmp_zone1       4    6    4 0.35 0.45
0  pool_default    pset  -1 pset_default        1  66K    1 0.14 0.01
3  SUNWtmp_zone2   pset   3 SUNWtmp_zone2       2    2    2 0.00 0.25
2  SUNWtmp_zone3   pset   2 SUNWtmp_zone3       6    8    8 0.21 0.40
```

In the preceding example, three Containers are using the `dedicated-cpu` feature of `zonecfg`. The output from `poolstat` provides the mapping between the pool name, processor set, and processor set identification number. For example, the Container `zone1` has been assigned to pool `SUNWtmp_zone1`, which uses the processor set `apppset` (identified by the number 1). Its number can be used to cross-reference the data provided by `poolstat` with data provided to other commands, such as `mpstat`.

The `mpstat` command does not have options specific to Containers, but it does report information specific to processors, processor sets, and changes in their state and processor set membership. You can watch the output from `mpstat` for changes in processor set population as they occur.

```
GZ# mpstat -ap 5
SET minf mjf xcal intr ithr csw icsw migr smtx srw syscl usr sys wt idl sze
  0    6   0  355  291  190  22    0    0    0   0    43   0   2  0  43   1
  1   24  17  534  207  200  70    1    0    2   0   600   4   1  0  84   2
  2   19   7  353  325  318  44    0    0    5   0   345   1   1  0  94   3
  3   36   2  149  237  236  14    0    0    4   0    97   0   0  0  98   2
...
     <<processor 3 moved from pset: -1 to: 1>>
     <<pset destroyed: 1>>
     <<pset created: 1>>
     <<processors added: 1, 3>>
     <<processors removed: 1, 3>>

SET minf mjf  xcal intr ithr csw icsw migr smtx srw syscl usr sys wt idl sze
  0    1   0   720  405  304  55    0    0   18   0    12   0  15  0  81   1
  1    0  69  1955  230  200 313   33    4   41   9  7086  34  10  0  19   2
  2    0  46   685  314  300 203   11    0   54   1  5287  36   6  0  28   3
  3    0   0    14  386  384   0    0    0    0   0     0   0   0  0 100   2
```

The messages in angle brackets indicate that the configuration of one or more processor sets changed between reporting samples.

6.2.2.2 Memory Controls

Containers also offer several memory controls. Each control can be configured separately, or various controls can be used in any combination. Some constrain the use of a physical resource, such as the RAM cap or the virtual memory cap. The latter is a physical resource because it is the sum of RAM and swap space.

Other memory controls limit the use of special types of memory resources that the kernel provides, including locked memory and shared memory. The virtual memory system does not page those memory pages out to the swap device. If one Container allocates a lot of locked memory or shared memory, it can prevent other Containers from allocating sufficient memory to run well. The ability to lock down pages must be limited to prevent one Container from locking down all of its memory pages, thereby potentially starving other Containers and preventing them from using RAM. This feat can be accomplished through the proper use of resource controls.

Virtual Memory Tools   A virtual memory cap prevents one Container from using more swap space than it should. Over-utilization of this resource can happen when a workload grows too quickly, or it can be caused by an application that "leaks" memory. It may also result from a denial-of-service attack that tries to starve the system of swap space. A system that runs out of swap space has little recourse, and will either crash, stop itself gracefully, or forcefully halt processes in an attempt to free up swap space.

The virtual memory cap that can be assigned to each Container is called a "swap cap." That name is a bit misleading, because it really limits the amount of virtual memory (physical RAM plus swap disk usage). The following command can be used to limit a zone to 4 GB of virtual memory:

```
GZ# zonecfg -z web
zonecfg:web> add capped-memory
zonecfg:web:capped-memory> set swap=4g
zonecfg:web:capped-memory> end
zonecfg:web> exit
GZ# zoneadm -z web reboot
```

This limit can be queried using the following command:

```
GZ# prctl -n zone.max-swap -i zone web
zone: 6: web
NAME            PRIVILEGE       VALUE     FLAG   ACTION    RECIPIENT
zone.max-swap   privileged      4.0GB      -     deny         -
                system          16.0EB    max    deny         -
```

After the zone has been rebooted, the processes running in that Container will be able to use only 4 GB of virtual memory, in aggregate. The first attempt by one of those processes to use more virtual memory will fail with the same error code as if the virtual memory had been exhausted on the system:

```
web# ls
bash: fork: Not enough space
```

In other words, an application in that Container will behave as if it was running on a non-virtualized system that had exhausted its virtual memory (i.e., filled up the swap partitions). Unfortunately, some applications do not handle this condition gracefully. For this and other reasons, caution should be used to avoid this situation in normal operating situations. Choosing a reasonable quantity for this cap is similar to sizing swap space for a non-virtualized system.

This limit can also be changed while the Container is running. The following command changes the Container's virtual memory limit (swap cap) to 6 GB without requiring a reboot for the change to take effect:

```
GZ# prctl -n zone.max-swap -v 6g -t privileged -r -e deny -i zone web
```

Virtual Memory Usage Monitoring Tools You can monitor the amount of virtual memory used by each zone with the prstat command.

```
GZ# prstat -Z
  PID USERNAME  SIZE  RSS STATE  PRI NICE    TIME  CPU PROCESS/NLWP
25586 root     9760K 8944K sleep  59    0 0:00:07 4.2% svc.configd/15
25506 root     9728K 8920K sleep  59    0 0:00:07 3.8% svc.configd/13
25583 root     7576K 6608K sleep  59    0 0:00:02 0.7% svc.startd/14
25504 root     7488K 6488K sleep  59    0 0:00:01 0.5% svc.startd/12
25948 root     4984K 3760K sleep  59    0 0:00:00 0.2% inetd/4
25646 root     4984K 3760K sleep  59    0 0:00:00 0.2% inetd/4
25538 root     5808K 3080K sleep  59    0 0:00:00 0.0% zoneadmd/4
25487 root     5808K 3080K sleep  59    0 0:00:00 0.0% zoneadmd/4
    1 root     2472K  424K sleep  59    0 0:00:18 0.0% init/1

ZONEID   NPROC  SIZE  RSS MEMORY      TIME  CPU ZONE
   246      22   84M  51M   0.4%   0:00:09 5.3% ProdWeb1
   245      22   84M  51M   0.4%   0:00:08 4.6% DevApp1
     0      47  235M  54M   0.4%   1:41:59 0.2% global
Total: 91 processes, 359 lwps, load averages: 0.55, 0.13, 0.04
```

The amount of virtual memory used by a Container is shown in the SIZE column. In the same output, the RSS column shows the amount of RAM used by the Container's processes. Notice how little RAM and virtual memory Containers need.

Another tool, kstat, will display both the VM cap and usage of a Container. To use it, first you must obtain the Container's ID number from zoneadm, as shown earlier.

```
GZ# kstat 'caps:1:swapresv_zone_1'
module: caps                   instance: 1
name:   swapresv_zone-1        class: zone_caps
        crtime                 112164.799153163
        snaptime               112174.884801884
        usage                  23638016
        value                  2147483648
        zonename               myzone
```

The `value` field is the cap you set. The `usage` field is the amount in use.

Physical Memory Tools Other Containers, including the global zone, will not be directly affected if one Container has reached its virtual memory cap. Nevertheless, they might be affected if most or all of the RAM is consumed as a side effect. Whether there is a shortage of virtual memory or not, the over-consumption of RAM will cause excessive paging, which might affect all Containers on the system.

To protect against over-consumption of RAM by one Container, you can establish a memory cap for physical memory. To add a memory cap to the Container configured earlier, enter the following command:

```
GZ# zonecfg -z web
zonecfg:web> select capped-memory
zonecfg:web:capped-memory> set physical=2g
zonecfg:web:capped-memory> end
zonecfg:web> exit
GZ# zoneadm -z web reboot
```

Note that the `zonecfg` subcommand `add capped-memory` may be used only to add the first memory cap. Subsequent modifications to memory capping, including adding a different type of memory cap, must use the subcommand `select capped-memory`. To verify that a physical memory cap is in place, enter the following command:

```
GZ# rcapstat -z 5
   id zone       nproc    vm   rss   cap   at avgat    pg avgpg
    6 web           24  123M   96M    2G 140M    0K   98M    0K
    6 web            -  123M   96M    2G   0K    0K    0K    0K
```

Also, this physical memory cap can be modified while the Container is running:

GZ# **rcapadm -z web -m 3g**

As with all other resource controls, the Container's resource limits will revert back to the values set with zonecfg after reboot.

How should the OS enforce a RAM cap? If a process running in a memory-capped Container attempts to exceed its limit, the application behavior should be consistent with application behavior in a non-virtualized system with insufficient RAM. Put simply, the operating system should begin forcing memory pages out to swap space. Other than the performance penalty of paging, this action should be transparent to the application. However, performance would become inconsistent if the application was temporarily suspended while memory pages were paged out. Because paging takes time, it should be possible for the application to continue to allocate RAM while the pager tries to catch up.

Oracle Solaris uses the resource capping daemon, a program named rcapd(1M). If a Container's processes begin to use more memory than the physical memory cap, rcapd will begin to force memory pages associated with that Container out to the swap disk(s). To maintain consistency with non-capped behavior, the application is allowed to continue running while paging occurs. As a result, a Container's processes may temporarily exceed its physical memory cap.

Care should be taken when setting this cap. Caps that are set too low will cause excessive paging, which can drag down overall system performance. This is especially true if other Containers are also causing paging or are using the same disk or storage I/O connection.

Also, the program that enforces the RAM cap, rcapd, uses some CPU cycles to track memory usage of processes. This effect will become noticeable on larger systems with hundreds of processes.

Physical Memory Usage Monitoring Tools   If you use the resource capping feature, you should monitor the use of RAM by all Containers on a regular basis. You can use the rcapstat command with its -z option to accomplish this goal:

```
GZ# rcapstat -z 5
id zone     nproc    vm    rss   cap   at avgat   pg avgpg
 1 ProdWeb1    30    0K    0K    8G   0K    0K    0K    0K
 1 ProdWeb1     -  644M  454M   8G   0K    0K    0K    0K
 1 ProdWeb1     -  966M  908M   8G   0K    0K    0K    0K
 1 ProdWeb1     - 1610M 1362M   8G   0K    0K    0K    0K
 1 ProdWeb1     - 2568M 1702M   8G   0K    0K    0K    0K
```

This output shows that the Container never uses more than roughly 2.5 GB of RAM, well under the cap of 8 GB. If any paging activity (values greater than zero) appears in the four columns on the right, their presence indicates that the Container's processes are paging. A small amount of infrequent paging is normal for operating systems with virtual memory, but frequent paging or infrequent paging of large amounts of memory is a sign of a problem. In that situation, the Container is using more RAM than you expected, either because there is a problem with the workload or because you chose a value that is too low for normal operations.

If you didn't use the resource capping feature, you can still get a reasonable estimate of memory consumption per Container with prstat as shown in earlier examples.

Another Solaris command that can report information on a per processor set basis is vmstat. The default output reports basic paging activity, which is collected separately for each processor set. If you run vmstat in a Container, the paging activity reported is that of the processors in the Container's processor set. The -p option to vmstat reports details of paging activity. When that option is used with vmstat in a Container that is running in a processor set, the paging activity information reported is that of the Container's processors.

An even better tool for providing visibility into per-Container paging is zvmstat, a tool in the DTrace Toolkit. Its output provides similar information to the vmstat command, but the data is aggregated per Container. The DTrace Toolkit can be found at opensolaris.org.

```
GZ# zvmstat 3
   ZONE re    mf   fr     sr   epi epo epf api apo apf fpi fpo fpf
 global 43   431 1766 16760   65   0 678   0 378 378   1   4 710
myzone2  0     1    0      0    0   0   0   1   0   0   0   0   0
myzone2  0     0    0      0    0   0   0   0   0   0   0   0   0

   ZONE re    mf   fr     sr   epi epo epf api apo apf fpi fpo fpf
 global  0     0    4      0    0   0   0   0   0   0   0   4   4
myzone2 25   276    0      0    5   0   0  45   0   0  57   0   0
myzone2  0     0    0      0    0   0   0   0   0   0   0   0   0

   ZONE re    mf   fr     sr   epi epo epf api apo apf fpi fpo fpf
 global  0     1   12      0    0   0   0   1   0   0   0  12  12
myzone2  1    17    0      0    0   0   0  10   0   0   0   0   0
myzone2  0     0    0      0    0   0   0   0   0   0   0   0   0
```

Shared Memory and Locked Memory Tools   Some applications use shared memory so that multiple processes can access one set of data. For example, database software uses shared memory to store table indexes. Database performance will be severely affected if that data is paged out to disk. When applications use shared memory pages via Solaris ISM (Intimate Shared Memory) or DISM (Dynamic ISM), those memory pages are locked into memory and cannot be paged out by the operating system.

Overly aggressive software could use more shared memory than is appropriate. Also, this functionality could be used to craft a denial-of-service attack. Although a RAM cap will prevent some of these problems, virtual memory systems were designed with the assumption that most of a workload's memory pages can be paged out.

Under normal operations, a workload that needs 30 GB of RAM in a 32 GB system may need to lock down only 2 GB. Allowing its processes to lock all 30 GB may reduce the RAM available to other Containers to the point that they cannot function normally. To prevent a Container from allocating so much shared memory that other workloads suffer, a resource cap for shared memory also exists. Enter the following command to set a shared memory cap of 2 GB for the Container:

```
GZ# zonecfg -z web
zonecfg:web> set max-shm-memory=2g
zonecfg:web> exit
GZ# zoneadm -z web reboot
```

After the Container is rebooted, this value can be verified with the following command:

```
GZ# prctl -n zone.max-shm-memory -t privileged -i zone web
zone: 6: web
NAME                  PRIVILEGE      VALUE    FLAG   ACTION   RECIPIENT
zone.max-shm-memory   privileged     2.0GB     -     deny      -
```

Just as with the other examples, this resource constraint can be dynamically changed for a running Container:

```
GZ# prctl -n zone.max-shm-memory -v 4g -t privileged -r -e deny \
    -i zone web
```

In addition to shared memory, a program can lock down other memory pages. Oracle Solaris provides this functionality for well-behaved applications so as to improve their performance. Of course, this ability can be abused—just as shared memory can be. To limit the amount of memory that a Container can lock down, enter the following command:

```
GZ# zonecfg -z web
zonecfg:web> select capped-memory
zonecfg:web:capped-memory> set locked=2g
zonecfg:web:capped-memory> end
zonecfg:web> exit
GZ# zoneadm -z web reboot
```

After the Container is rebooted, this value can be queried with the following command:

```
GZ# prctl -n zone.max-locked-memory -t privileged -i zone web
zone: 6: web
NAME                      PRIVILEGE      VALUE    FLAG  ACTION    RECIPIENT
zone.max-locked-memory privileged      20.0MB     -    deny          -
```

This resource constraint can also be dynamically changed for a running Container:

```
GZ# prctl -n zone.max-locked-memory -v 4g -t privileged -r -e deny \
   -i zone web
```

Because the `proc_lock_memory` privilege is included in a Container's default privilege set, we strongly encourage the use of this memory cap.

You can view the current amount of memory that a Container has locked with `kstat`:

```
GZ# zoneadm list -cv
  ID NAME         STATUS        PATH                        BRAND     IP
   0 global       running       /                           native    shared
   1 myzone       running       /rpool/Zones/myzone         native    shared

GZ# kstat 'caps:1:lockedmem_zone_1:usage'
module: caps                            instance: 1
name:     lockedmem_zone_1              class:      zone_caps
          usage                         4096
```

6.2.2.3 Miscellaneous Controls

One method that is well known for over-consuming system resources is a fork-bomb. This method does not necessarily consume a great deal of memory or CPU resources, but rather seeks to use up all of the process slots in the kernel's process table. In Oracle Solaris, a running process starts with just one thread of execution, also called a lightweight process (LWP). Many programs generate new threads, becoming multithreaded processes. By default, Solaris systems with a 64-bit kernel can run more than 85,000 LWPs simultaneously. A zone that has booted but is not yet running any applications will have between 100 and 150 LWPs. To prevent a Container from creating too many LWPs, a limit can be set on their use. The following command sets a limit of 300 LWPs for the Container:

```
GZ# zonecfg -z web
zonecfg:web> set max-lwps=300
zonecfg:web> exit
GZ# zoneadm -z web reboot
```

This parameter should not be set so low that it detracts from normal application operation. Instead, an accurate baseline for the number of LWPs for a given Container should be determined and this value then set at an appropriate level.

This resource constraint can also be dynamically changed for a running Container:

```
GZ# prctl -n zone.max-lwps -v 500 -t privileged -r -e deny -i zone web
```

Unless you trust the users of the Container and their applications, we encourage the use of this cap to minimize the impact of fork-bombs.

The number of LWPs used by a Container can be monitored using the following command:

```
GZ# prstat -LZ
[...]
ZONEID     NLWP  SWAP   RSS MEMORY      TIME  CPU ZONE
     0      248  468M  521M   8.6%   0:14:18 0.0% global
    37      108   76M   61M   1.0%   0:00:00 0.0% web



Total: 122 processes, 356 lwps, load averages: 0.00, 0.00, 0.01
[...]
```

In this example, the Web Container currently has 108 LWPs. This value can and will change as processes are created or exit. It should be inspected over a period of time to establish a more reliable baseline and updated when the software, requirements, or workload change.

To maximize the benefit of max-lwps, you should also use a CPU control—for example, FSS or resource pools. Implementation of such a control will slow the rate of LWP creation. Sufficient CPU power must be available to global zone processes so that the platform administrator can fix the problem.

6.2.2.4 Container Dashboard

Because it can be cumbersome to use the set of Solaris commands needed to monitor all resource usage of Containers, one of the authors of this book (Victor) wrote an open-source tool that displays current usage and controls for the most commonly controlled resources. An example of its use is shown here.

```
GZ# zonestat 3
          |----Pool-----|------CPU-------|--------------Memory---------------|
          |---|--Size---|-----Pset-------|---RAM---|---Shm---|---Lkd---|---VM---|
Zonename| IT| Max| Cur| Cap|Used|Shr|S%| Cap| Use| Cap| Use| Cap| Use| Cap| Use
-----------------------------------------------------------------------------
  global  0D  66K    2       0.1  1 33       985M       139K  18E   2M  18E 754M
      z3  0D  66K    2       0.0  1 33  1G  122M 536M       536M    0   1G 135M
   web02  0D  66K    2 0.42  0.2  1 33 100M 100M  20M        20M    0 268M 112M
  --------
  global  0D  66K    2       0.1  1 33       984M       139K  18E   2M  18E 754M
      z3  0D  66K    2       0.0  1 33  1G  122M 536M       536M    0   1G 135M
   web02  0D  66K    2 0.42  0.3  1 33 100M 112M  20M        20M    0 268M 117M
```

The output is very dense because the goal is to provide as much information as possible, although the output can be customized. The `Pool` columns provide information about the resource pool in which the Container's processes are running. The `I` column shows the pool ID number, and the `T` column indicates the type of resource pool: `D` for the default pool, `P` for private (using the `dedicated-cpu` feature), or `S` for shared (using a pool configured with `poolcfg`).

The `Size` columns tell you about the quantity of CPUs in the resource pool, both the maximum configured amount and the current amount. If you are using dynamic resource pools, you will occasionally see these values change as `poold` shifts CPUs in and out of pools.

The `CPU` columns provide data about the other CPU resource controls: CPU caps and FSS. `Cap` is the configured CPU cap, if one has been set. `Used` shows you how much processing power the Container has used recently, in terms of the number of CPUs. In the example, the global zone recently used one-tenth of one CPU. `Shr` is the number of FSS shares the Container has been assigned, and `S%` is the percentage of the total shares assigned to workloads in that pool.

The `Memory` section includes columns for RAM, shared memory, locked memory, and virtual memory. Each of those pairs of columns shows the cap that has been set, if any, and the amount of that resource that is currently being used by that Container.

The `zonestat` tool is available at `http://opensolaris.org/os/project/zonestat/`.

6.2.2.5 DTrace and Holistic Observability

DTrace is a feature set of Oracle Solaris that enables you to gather specific or aggregated data that is available to the kernel. Short DTrace commands or scripts specify exactly which pieces of data or aggregations of data you want. DTrace collects only the requested data, and then presents it to you. This parsimonious behavior minimizes the amount of CPU time that the kernel spends gathering the data you want. The design of DTrace makes it inherently safe to use: It is impossible to create an infinite loop in DTrace, and it is impossible to dereference an invalid pointer. For these and other reasons, it is safe to use DTrace on production systems (which you should not do with a kernel debugger).

OSV implementations include just one OS kernel, which is shared by all of the VEs. This facet of the OSV model enables you to use OS tools such as DTrace to look at all of the VEs as entities, or to peer into each VE and view its constituent parts.

Earlier we saw how DTrace can be used to examine aggregate memory usage, with the zvmstat script. You can also use this tool to gather and report data for a single Container. For example, if vmstat showed an unusually high system call rate, you could use these DTrace commands to determine which Container is causing these calls, which system call is being made most often, and which program is issuing them.

```
GZ# dtrace -n 'syscall:::entry { @num[zonename] = count(); }'
dtrace: description 'syscall:::entry' matched 234 probes
^C


  appzone                 301
  global                11900
  webzone               91002


GZ# dtrace -n 'syscall:::entry/zonename=="webzone"/ \
{ @num[probefunc] = count(); }'
dtrace: description 'syscall:::entry' matched 234 probes
^C
  exece                     1
  fork1                     1
...
  fstat6                 9181
  getdents64             9391
  lstat64               92482
GZ# dtrace -n 'syscall::lstat64:entry/zonename=="webzone"/ \
{ @num[execname] = count(); }'
dtrace: description 'syscall::lstat64:entry' matched 1 probe
^C


  find                107277
GZ# dtrace -n 'syscall::lstat64:entry/zonename=="webzone" && \
execname=="find"/ { @num[uid] = count(); }'
dtrace: description 'syscall::lstat64:entry' matched 1 probe
^C

  1012                  16439
```

Based on the output, we know that the user with a UID of 1012 was running the find program in Container webzone, which was causing most of those system calls.

When used in combination, DTrace and Containers can solve problems that are otherwise difficult or impossible to solve. For example, when troubleshooting a three-tier architecture, you might want to collect a chronological log of events on the three different systems. Each system has its own time clock, making this feat impossible. To gather the needed data, you could re-create the three tiers as three Containers on the same system. Because the three Containers share the kernel's time clock, a DTrace script can collect data on processes in the three different tiers, using one time reference.

6.2.3 Networking

Almost all Containers need access to a network to be useful. A Container can have network access via one or more physical network ports (NICs). By default, Containers have shared access to a NIC, an approach called "shared-IP." Instead of accepting this default, you can configure a Container to have exclusive access to one or more NICs. That type of network configuration, referred to as "exclusive-IP," prevents any other Container, or the global zone, from using that NIC.

6.2.3.1 Shared-IP Containers

All network controls, including routing, for shared-IP Containers are managed from the global zone. Exclusive-IP Containers manage their own networking configuration, including the assignment of IP addresses, routing table management, and bringing their network interfaces up and down.

Configuring network access for a shared-IP Container looks like this:

```
GZ# zonecfg -z myzone
zonecfg:myzone> add net
zonecfg:myzone:net> set physical=e1000g0
zonecfg:myzone:net> set address=192.168.1.10/24
zonecfg:myzone:net> end
zonecfg:myzone> exit
```

You can use the same syntax to add access to additional NICs.

You can modify an existing resource with the select subcommand of zonecfg. In the following example, select is used to establish a specific default router for a Container.

```
GZ# zonecfg -z myzone
zonecfg:myzone> select net physical=e1000g0
zonecfg:myzone:net> set defrouter=192.168.1.1
zonecfg:myzone:net> end
zonecfg:myzone> exit
```

6.2.3.2 Exclusive-IP Containers

Because exclusive-IP Containers manage their own networking configuration, fewer parameters are needed to configure them.

```
GZ# zonecfg -z exipzone
zonecfg:myzone> set ip-type=exclusive
zonecfg:myzone> add net
zonecfg:myzone:net> set physical=e1000g0
zonecfg:myzone:net> end
zonecfg:myzone> exit
```

You can manage networking in an exclusive-IP Container with the same methods and commands as a non-virtualized system. To perform those steps, you must first log in to the Container and become the root user.

You can monitor network usage of individual NICs with the kstat command. The name of the kstat may be different for different types of NICs.

```
GZ# kstat -p 'e1000g:0:mac:*bytes'
e1000g:0:mac:obytes     2509466
e1000g:0:mac:rbytes     4702845
GZ# kstat -p 'e1000g:0:mac:*packets'
e1000g:0:mac:opackets      13306
e1000g:0:mac:rpackets      14426
```

Those commands can be used for shared-IP as well as exclusive-IP Containers.

To increase the availability of Containers' network access, you can use the IP Multipathing feature. IP Multipathing (IPMP) allows you to configure multiple NICs into a group. IPMP detects the failure of a network cable or NIC in the group and circumvents this failure by continuing to use the other NIC(s) for network transport.

For shared-IP Containers, you manage IPMP groups from the global zone. The Containers benefit from IPMP without even knowing it is there. Exclusive-IP Containers with multiple NICs can maintain their own IPMP groups using the same commands.

6.2.3.3 Networking Summary

The default network type (shared-IP) is appropriate unless a Container needs to manage its own networking configuration or needs specific forms of network isolation. Exclusive-IP Containers severely restrict the number of Containers per system because of the limited number of NICs in the computer.

6.2.4 Direct Device Access

The security boundary around a Container prevents direct access to devices, in recognition of the fact that many types of device access would allow one Container to affect other Containers. One form of enforcement is the minimal list of device entries available to the Container. By default, a Container has very few entries in its /dev directory, and it doesn't have a /devices directory at all. The entries in /dev are limited to pseudo-devices that are considered safe and necessary, such as /dev/null.

Sometimes, however, you might want to give a Container direct access to a device. For example, you might want to test some software in a Container in a lab environment, but the test might require creating and destroying a file system from within the Container. To do this, the Container needs device entries for the disk device that will contain the file system.

You can accomplish this task with the add device subcommand, as shown in the following example:

```
GZ# zonecfg -z zone1
zonecfg:zone1> add device
zonecfg:zone1:device> set match=/dev/rdsk/c1t0d0s6
zonecfg:zone1:device> end
zonecfg:zone1> add device
zonecfg:zone1:device> set match=/dev/dsk/c1t0d0s6
zonecfg:zone1> end
GZ# zlogin zone1
zone1# newfs /dev/rdsk/c1t0d0s6
zone1# mount /dev/dsk/c1t0d0s6 /opt/local
```

The direct device method gives a Container's privileged users direct control over a file system's devices, thereby facilitating direct management of the file system. At the same time, these users gain greater control over the system's components, which may enable them to affect other Containers. For example, just as the root user in a non-virtualized system can use device access to panic a UNIX system, so assigning direct device access to a Container may give users the ability to panic the system, stopping all of the Containers. Be very cautious when adding devices to a Container.

6.2.5 Virtualization Management Features

Life-cycle management of Containers involves very few commands. You have already seen the two commands used to create, boot, and halt a Container. One of them, zoneadm, is also used to move a Container's root directory within the same system, and to move the Container to a different system.

In addition to the zoneadm subcommands discussed earlier, three other subcommands can be used to simplify and accelerate the provisioning of Containers. These subcommands, which are not necessary for basic management of Containers, are discussed in the next two sections.

6.2.5.1 Cloning Containers

Installing a Container takes time, and it always results in a Container that is ready to be customized. Not surprisingly, if you are creating many similar Containers, it is easier to perform those customizations just once. The command zoneadm has a subcommand clone to do just that.

The original Container should be configured, installed, and then tailored for the needs of the application. Doing so might require setting up application configuration files, adding resource controls with zonecfg, and testing the application.

Once the original Container can successfully run the application, the Container must be stopped before cloning it. At that point, the following commands can be used. The export subcommand to zonecfg includes resource controls.

```
GZ# cd /zones/configs
GZ# zonecfg -z web01 export -f web01.cfg
GZ# cp web01.cfg web02.cfg
{edit web02.cfg, changing the zonepath and other properties such as the IP address}
GZ# zonecg -z web02 -f web02.cfg
GZ# zoneadm -z web02 clone web01
Copying /zones/roots/web01...
```

After cloning is complete, the new Container is almost ready to boot. First, though, you must deal with the fact that the sys-unconfig(1M) command has been run on it, removing information such as its host name. You can use zlogin -C as before to answer the prompts, providing this information, but the goal of cloning is streamlining and automating the process of creating multiple Containers. All of the answers to those prompts can be found in the Container's /etc/sysidcfg file. As mentioned in the section "Installing and Booting the Container," if you are in the global zone the full path name is <zonepath>/root/etc/sysidcfg.

The next example shows an /etc/sysidcfg file and its placement in a Container, followed by its first boot. Note that the statement network_interface=NONE does *not* imply that there are no network interfaces.

```
GZ# cat /tmp/sysidcfg
system_locale=C
terminal=dtterm
network_interface=NONE { hostname=web01 }
security_policy=NONE
name_service=NONE
nfs4_domain=domain.com
timezone=US/Eastern
root_password=m4qtoWN
GZ# cp /tmp/sysidcfg /zones/roots/web01/root/etc/sysidcfg
GZ# zoneadm -z web01 boot
GZ# zlogin -C web01
[Connected to zone 'web01' console]

[NOTICE: Zone booting up]

SunOS Release 5.10 Version Generic_141445-09 64-bit
Copyright 1983-2009 Sun Microsystems, Inc. All rights reserved.
Use is subject to license terms.
Hostname: web01
. . .
web01 console login:
```

It was not necessary to log in to the Container's console, but by doing so we were able to note that the Container was being configured with the information. The Container can be further customized before or after its first boot.

Although the process of cloning a Container can be accomplished in as little time as 1 or 2 minutes, this operation can be accelerated further by using ZFS. If the original Container resides on a ZFS file system, zoneadm clone will automatically make a ZFS clone of the original file system. Creating a ZFS clone takes just a few seconds and uses almost no disk space at first. As the clone is modified, disk space will be allocated to store the file system modifications. This method maximizes both the time and disk savings.

6.2.5.2 Migrating Containers

Containers offer the ability to migrate a Container from one instance of Oracle Solaris to another. In this context, an *instance* can be a computer running a copy of Solaris, or it can be a VE running Solaris in a Dynamic Domain, Logical Domain, or on another hypervisor. Two zoneadm subcommands implement this functionality.

The detach subcommand prepares a Container for migration and removes it from the list of Containers that can be booted. The contents of the Container, underneath its zonepath, are then ready for transfer to the destination system using common file transfer methods. If the Container's root directory resides on storage space that is shared with the system to which it is being moved, the Container can be "attached" and booted on the new system immediately.[4]

Obviously, shared storage for the Container or the data of its workload smoothes Container migration considerably. Ops Center can manage multiple Containers whose contents are shared among systems via NFS.[5]

Migrating a Container is usually a straightforward process. The "How to Move a Solaris Container" guide, available at `http://www.sun.com/software/so-laris/howto_guides.jsp`, describes the possibilities in more detail. Here is an example session:

```
hostA-GZ# zoneadm -z twilight detach
hostA-GZ# cd /zones/roots/twilight
hostA-GZ# pax -w@f /tmp/twilight.pax -p e *
hostA-GZ# scp /tmp/twilight.pax root@hostB:/tmp/twilight.pax


hostB-GZ# mkdir -m 700 -p /zones/roots/dusk

hostB-GZ# cd /zones/roots/dusk
hostB-GZ# pax -r@f /tmp/twilight.pax -p e
hostB-GZ# zonecfg -z dusk
zonecfg:dusk> create -a /zones/roots/dusk
zonecfg:dusk> exit
hostB-GZ# zoneadm -z dusk attach
```

At this point, the new Container can be reconfigured with its new IP address and any resource controls you want to set. When it is ready, you can boot it. Of course, all of that activity can be automated.

The destination system must be configured to have the same update of Oracle Solaris, or a newer update, than the original system. If the destination is newer, you should use the `-u` option to the `attach` subcommand.

The `-u` option can also be used when patching or upgrading a system that includes Containers to minimize the time it takes to complete those tasks. The first step is detaching all of the Containers, followed by patching or upgrading the system. When those steps are complete, the Containers may be quickly reattached to the system with the `attach -u` subcommand to `zoneadm`.

If the Container's `zonepath` resides on shared storage—for example, on a SAN—the step that transfers the archived Container can be changed to a series of steps that make the file system unavailable to the original host and available to the destination host. If you use Ops Center 2.5 or newer, the Container's zone-

---

4.   See the "How to Move a Solaris Container" guide at `http://www.sun.com` for various configurations.

5.   Chapter 9, "Virtualization Management," discusses Ops Center.

path can be on NFS, and that step can be changed to a mount command on the destination host.

6.3 Solaris 8 Containers and Solaris 9 Containers

Thousands of SPARC systems are currently running the Solaris 8 and Solaris 9 operating systems. In most cases, the desire to take advantage of innovations in Oracle Solaris 10 can be fulfilled by migrating the workload to a native Container on a Solaris 10 system. This process is usually straightforward because of the binary compatibility from one version of Solaris to the next, backed by the Solaris Binary Compatibility Guarantee. People often place these workloads into Containers.

In other situations, such migration proves difficult or uncertain. Perhaps the workload includes shell scripts that work correctly on Solaris 8 but not on Solaris 10. Perhaps your organization tuned the workload for Solaris, but retuning for Solaris 10 would require recompiling the software and the source code is no longer available. Perhaps redeployment in a Solaris 10 environment would require recertification, which is impractical for hundreds of systems that will be replaced within the next year anyway. Whatever the reason, you might strongly prefer to maintain a Solaris 8 environment for the workload, but new SPARC systems will not run Solaris 8. This raises a key question: Are other options available?

In fact, two related products meet this need: Solaris 8 Containers and Solaris 9 Containers.[6] Each replicates a Solaris 8 (or Solaris 9) environment within a Container on a Solaris 10 system. All of the software from the original system runs on the Solaris 10 system without translation or emulation of binary instructions; the only translations required involve the system calls.

To simplify this process, each product includes a P2V tool that uses an archive of the file system of the original computer to populate the file system of the new Container. The entire process typically takes 30–60 minutes to complete and can be automated. After archiving the original system with flar, tar, cpio, or pax, only four commands are needed to create, boot, and log in to the Container. The following example assumes that the Solaris 8 system is named sol8 and that the Solaris 8 and Solaris 10 systems use /net/server as mount points for a shared NFS file system:

```
sol8# flarcreate -S -n mys8 /net/server/balrog.flar
...
Archive creation complete.
```

---

6. When this book went to print, Solaris 8 Containers and Solaris 9 Containers required a combination support contract and software license. A no-cost download for evaluation is available at http://www.sun.com/software/solaris/containers/getit.jsp.

Before booting the Solaris 8 Container, the original Solaris 8 system should be halted because it contains the same configuration information, including the same IP address.

```
GZ# zonecfg -z balrog
zonecfg:balrog> create -t SUNWsolaris8
zonecfg:balrog> set zonepath=/zones/roots/balrog
zonecfg:balrog> add net
zonecfg:balrog:net> set physical=vnet0
zonecfg:balrog:net> set address=10.1.1.9/24
zonecfg:balrog:net> end
zonecfg:balrog> exit

GZ# zoneadm -z balrog install -p -a /net/server/balrog.flar
    Source: /net/server/balrog.flar
...
    Result: Installation completed successfully.

GZ# zoneadm -z balrog boot
GZ# zlogin -C balrog
[Connected to zone 'balrog' console]

SunOS Release 5.8 Version Generic_Virtual 64-bit
Copyright 1983-2000 Sun Microsystems, Inc. All rights reserved

Hostname: balrog
The system is coming up.  Please wait.
NIS domainname is sun.com
starting rpc services: rpcbind keyserv ypbind done.
syslog service starting.
Print services started.
The system is ready.

balrog console login:
```

Multiple Solaris 8 Containers and Solaris 9 Containers can be hosted on the same system. When the migration is complete, a system has the structure shown in Figure 6.7.

Solaris 8 Containers and Solaris 9 Containers can also take advantage of other Solaris 10 innovations. For example, they can be placed on a ZFS file system and gain the benefits of ZFS, particularly its robustness due to its checksummed data blocks and metadata blocks. You can also use DTrace to examine programs running in these Containers.

Solaris 8 Containers and Solaris 9 Containers are excellent tools to move older Solaris workloads to newer, consolidated systems. Following such migrations, the workloads benefit from the increased robustness and performance of Solaris 10.

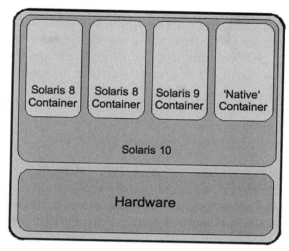

Figure 6.7 Structure of a System with Solaris 8 Containers and Solaris 9 Containers

6.3.1 Oracle Solaris Trusted Extensions

Some data center workloads require or benefit from strict compartmentaliza-tion of different categories of data and users. This statement has been true for certain government organizations for decades, but in recent years governments have required that corporations protect data in new ways. Some users are allowed access to only one category of data, whereas other users need access to multiple categories.

In the past, government and corporate organizations have used customized versions of operating systems, such as Trusted Solaris 8. That functionality was integrated into Solaris 10 as a feature set that can simply be enabled or disabled. The feature set that provides this strict compartmentalization is called Oracle Solaris 10 Trusted Extensions.

As mentioned earlier, Trusted Extensions achieved Common Criteria Certification for the Labeled Security Protection Profile (LSPP) at Evaluation Assurance Level (EAL) 4+, the highest commonly recognized global security certification. This achievement allows Solaris 10 to be deployed when multilevel security (MLS) pro-tection and independent validation of an OS security model is required. Solaris 10 achieved this certification for SPARC and x86-based systems, for both desk-top and server functionality, and also received Common Criteria Certification for the Controlled Access Protection Profile (CAPP) and Role-Based Access Control Protection Profile (RBACPP). Because of this certification, you can deploy systems

using Trusted Extensions to meet the needs of sensitive data environments, including corporate financial transaction systems and medical record systems.

The Trusted Extensions feature set uses Containers to compartmentalize
data and processing. A key factor in its ability to achieve the Common Criteria
Certification described earlier is the robust security boundary that exists around
individual Containers.

The features of Oracle Solaris Trusted Extensions are described in detail in the
book *Solaris Security Essentials*.

6.4 Network Virtualization in OpenSolaris

OpenSolaris offers some features that are not available in Solaris 10. These features include network virtualization features originally called Project Crossbow.
Each of these feature sets is described in detail at `http://opensolaris.org`
and in the `man` pages for OpenSolaris. The network virtualization features are
described in this section.

Network virtualization makes it possible to implement traditional network architectures within a computer without losing any flexibility in network design. The new
network virtualization features in OpenSolaris enable you to create these objects:

- Virtual network interface connectors (VNICs), which can be used with
  Containers to increase the isolation between Containers without losing
  scalability
- Virtual switches (vSwitches), which can be used in the same way as physical
  switches—that is, to connect VEs to each other and to a physical network port

The use of virtual networks starts with a network design. The simplest practical use of virtual network components is to create multiple VNICs so that two
Containers can share a physical NIC. In Figure 6.8, one VNIC has been created for
each of two Containers. Each VNIC uses a physical NIC for communication with
network devices outside of this computer.

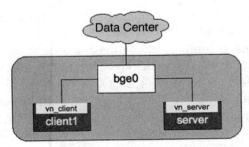

Figure 6.8 Virtual NICs

Figure 6.9 shows a slightly more complicated version: the virtualization of a lab network. It includes two Containers running web client software, one running web server software, and a special Container acting only as a router between the other Containers and the corporate network.

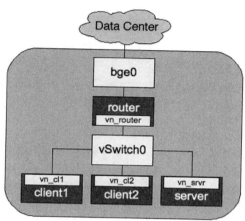

Figure 6.9 Network Layout Using OpenSolaris Network Virtualization

Implementing that architecture starts with creation of the network components. One command creates a vSwitch in OpenSolaris:

```
GZ# dladm create-etherstub vSwitch0
```

Just like a physical switch, a vSwitch does nothing by itself. It becomes useful only when you attach things to it, as in the following example, which creates and connects a VNIC for each Container, including the router Container:

```
GZ# dladm create-vnic -l vSwitch0 vn_cl1
GZ# dladm create-vnic -l vSwitch0 vn_cl2
GZ# dladm create-vnic -l vSwitch0 vn_srvr
GZ# dladm create-vnic -l vSwitch0 vn_router
```

The system now has four virtual NICs, which will communicate via a virtual switch. The vSwitch receives packets from only those four VNICs, and it sends the packet to the appropriate VNIC for receipt at the packet's destination.

Now that the virtual network gear exists, you can create all of the Containers. We will show only the commands pertaining to the Container that will act as the router.

```
GZ# zonecfg -z router
zonecfg:router> create
zonecfg:router> set zonepath=/rpool/zones/roots/router
zonecfg:router> set autoboot=true
zonecfg:router> set ip-type=exclusive
zonecfg:router> add net
zonecfg:route:net> set physical=bge0
zonecfg:router:net> end
zonecfg:router> add net
zonecfg:router:net> set physical=vn_router
zonecfg:router:net> end
zonecfg:router> exit
GZ# zoneadm -z router install
```

The `router` Container is simply a Solaris Container acting as a router, forwarding packets, and, if desired, filtering out packets that should not be forwarded. It must be configured to perform IP forwarding. The IP Filter features can be used to limit the types of traffic that can flow between the lab systems and the rest of the corporate data center. Routing is enabled by default, so there is no need to enable routing in the router Container. After booting the Container, the following steps are needed:

```
router# echo > /etc/resolv.conf
  domain xyz.com
  nameserver 192.99.99.99
  nameserver 192.99.99.9
^D
router# svcadm enable svc:/network/ipv4-forwarding
router# ifconfig bge0 plumb inet 192.168.10.10 up
router# ifconfig vn-router plumb inet 192.168.11.1 up
```

Because of the importance of the router, you should improve security by disabling all unnecessary services. You can easily disable all unnecessary network services with a single command:

GZ# **zlogin router netservices limited**

If you would like to further simplify the router Container, you can disable other unnecessary services with the `svcadm`(1M) command.

The preceding example shows a limited set of OpenSolaris networking features. You can, of course, use other network features, such as the firewall features and network address translation (NAT) features that are managed with the `ipf`(1M) and `ipnat`(1M) commands.

In addition to virtual analogues of physical network devices, OpenSolaris provides the ability to constrain the amount of network bandwidth used by a Container. You can set a bandwidth limit for each network interface—even virtual ones.

```
GZ# dladm set-linkprop -p maxbw=50m vn_cl1
GZ# dladm set-linkprop -p maxbw=50m vn_cl2
GZ# dladm show-linkprop -p maxbw
LINK        PROPERTY  PERM  VALUE   DEFAULT   POSSIBLE
bge0        maxbw     rw    --      --        --
vn_srvr     maxbw     rw    --      --        --
vn_router   maxbw     rw    --      --        --
vn_cl1      maxbw     rw    50m     --        --
vn_cl2      maxbw     rw    50m     --        --
```

6.5 Strengths of Oracle Solaris Containers

Containers provide all of the strengths of the OSV model:

- **Compute efficiency.** Containers have almost zero overhead, giving them an advantage over hypervisors, which use CPU cycles for I/O transactions, and over-partitioning, which leaves CPU cycles unused even when another workload could use those resources.

- **Storage efficiency.** A Container can use as little as 100 MB of disk space and as little as 40 MB of RAM.

- **Hardware independence.** Containers do not depend on any hardware features and do not have any code specific to one instruction set. They are currently supported on x86/x64 and SPARC architectures, with ports of OpenSolaris to other CPU types under way.

- **Observability.** The kernel controls access to all information regarding its Containers, so tools such as DTrace can simultaneously view internal details of multiple Containers and their processes.

In addition, Containers have advantages over other forms of OSV:

- Solaris 8 Containers and Solaris 9 Containers allow you to run all of the software from an older system on a system running Solaris 10.

- The `solaris10` brand allows you to run Solaris 10 software on OpenSolaris.
- The `lx` brand allows you to run some Linux software on a Solaris 10 system.
- The flexible and dynamic resource controls can automatically adapt to the changing needs of one or more workloads.
- A configurable security boundary provides the ability to relax or strengthen the privileges of each Container individually.
- Containers are a tightly integrated feature of Oracle Solaris, and can benefit from innovations in Solaris such as ZFS and DTrace.

6.6 Summary

Containers are a very popular and feature-rich form of system virtualization that are used in production environments in data centers all over the world. In practice, the more common uses of Containers include the following situations:

- Consolidating applications from multiple servers to fewer servers, especially as a no-cost virtual server.
- Hardening an OS environment with read-only mounts and minimal privileges, especially for Internet-facing environments.
- Migrating and consolidating workloads from earlier versions of Solaris to Oracle Solaris 10, using Solaris 8 Containers and Solaris 9 Containers.
- Hosting environments such as cloud computing, ISPs, and web hosting, where a homogeneous environment is preferred by the hosting organization, and where quick provisioning is important. Each customer can be configured on multiple systems, ready to boot on the most lightly loaded system.
- Software development environments, which also benefit from rapid provisioning and homogeneity, giving each developer full privileges in that Container.
- Rapid provisioning for short-lived environments—for example, functionality testing. A cloned Container provides a well-defined starting point.
- High-scale virtualization, in which dozens or hundreds of VEs reside in one computer, because of the superior efficiency of Containers.

Released as a feature set of Solaris 10 in early 2005, Containers have achieved broad support from independent software vendors (ISVs). Network virtualization adds a new dimension to their usefulness for OpenSolaris and the future.

Choosing a Virtualization Technology

The preceding chapters described different forms of server virtualization, each with its own strengths and limitations. But which is the right combination to use?

No one answer applies equally well in all situations. Each form of virtualization has strengths and weaknesses. One approach might provide great value in one situation, but offer little value in another. Some virtualization solutions can be combined, making it possible to benefit from the advantages of more than one virtualization technology at the same time.

This chapter discusses potential advantages and disadvantages of layering virtualization technologies. It also provides guidelines for selecting the right virtualization technologies for different requirements.

7.1 Review of Strengths and Limitations

This section summarizes distinguishing characteristics of the technologies discussed previously, focusing on aspects that are central to the selection process. First we will discuss the benefits of these characteristics.

A key component of virtualization is workload isolation. This takes three forms: hardware, software, and security isolation. Hardware isolation prevents a hardware failure from affecting more than one virtual environment (VE). Software isolation prevents a software failure from affecting multiple environments; it also provides separate namespaces for files, users, and processes. Security isolation permits separate security contexts (with separate user identities, roles, and authentication and authorization mechanisms) for each virtual environment, which means that intrusion into one environment does not make it easier to penetrate a different one on the same system. Although security isolation often focuses on web-facing workloads exposed to public networks and on systems housing sensitive financial, medical, or government data, it is important to secure all environments in a computing infrastructure to prevent attacks on the weakest link. It is best to architect and integrate security on a systematic basis, rather than reserving it for "high-value" targets.

System features providing the most isolation can add to the costs of a system. Nevertheless, business-critical workloads have the strongest need for comprehensive isolation and can often justify the extra expense of supporting independent VEs. Any additional expenses may be offset by the savings provided by consolidation.

Different forms of virtualization offer differing levels of software compatibility. With some approaches, there are few or no incompatibilities: Software runs essentially the same in a virtualized environment as in a non-virtualized system, except potentially in terms of some differences in timing. With others, the virtualization infrastructure performs some operations on behalf of a VE that are implemented differently than on non-virtualized systems, or functionality is limited in some way. These considerations were discussed in previous chapters and will be recapped later in this chapter as needed. Where applicable, incompatibilities should be analyzed and software retested.

Recertification of software products, if necessary, should be performed by the software vendor. In such cases, in-house testing should be minimal. Software developed in-house should be analyzed or retested if it is to be used on the types of virtualization that affect program behavior.

Most forms of virtualization create performance overhead. This overhead is caused by modification of the application code that is running, lengthening the code path, or virtualization software using CPU cycles. The amount of overhead depends on the type of virtualization and on the workload. CPU-intensive workloads are the least affected because they make the least use of state-changing operations that require intervention from virtualization technology. In the simplest cases, a VE gets a time slice on a CPU without needing assistance from the virtualization technology. By comparison, I/O-intensive workloads experience performance overhead in some virtualization solutions due to resource contention and increased number of state-changing operations, especially when I/O devices are shared.

Latency-sensitive workloads that cause such performance overhead should not be installed on systems without testing to ensure they can still meet their performance objectives.

VE scalability is a related performance topic. Some types of virtualization can host only a limited number of VEs. Most can theoretically run dozens or hundreds of VEs. In practice, however, most of those do not scale well: They may need terabytes of RAM, they may be limited by the scalability limits of the hardware architecture to which they are tied, or their current implementation may create so much performance overhead that they can scale to only 10–20 VEs. Others can effectively handle more than 100 VEs. This effect is often mitigated by the common practice of consolidating physical systems from old, slow, low-utilization platforms onto new processors. In such circumstances, the modest resource requirements and the difference in processor speed may compensate for the possible overhead. To maximize the cost savings achieved from consolidation, choose the most scalable virtualization solution.

Many workloads change their resource requirements over short or long periods of time. The ability to dynamically change the amount of resources available to those VEs is necessary to maintain appropriate throughput and response times.

Most applications are able to run on more than one version of an operating system (OS). Some are tied to a specific version or to a specific version of an OS package or a patch level. Such applications can benefit from the freedom to run different VEs at different OS levels, thereby permitting applications with different OS requirements to coexist on the same server. Also, VEs with independent OS levels can use different patch windows for updating system software. Virtual environments that share a common OS software level may need a synchronized patch window. Unfortunately, this strategy may be difficult to realize when different applications and different application owners share the same physical system.

Similarly, while many applications can run on different operating systems, others are available only for a particular OS. The ability to run different operating systems at the same time (e.g., Microsoft Windows and Apple MacOS) also has value, and in some situations is an absolute necessity.

Some virtualization features enhance business agility and operational flexibility—key considerations that are discussed in Chapter 9, "Virtualization Management." Dynamic data centers, whose workloads regularly grow and shrink, benefit the most from these features. Cloning is the ability to create an exact copy of a VE. It accelerates provisioning when many similar workloads will exist, and can even be done as a programmed response to a request for a new instance of an application. VE mobility can be used to move an application from one computer to another. This capability is very valuable in dynamic data centers whose workloads grow and shrink regularly, and it facilitates ongoing application availability during physical server hardware maintenance.

Architects choosing virtualization technologies to meet an application's requirements take all of the previously mentioned factors into consideration, mapping requirements onto the combinations of technologies that best meet them. The following sections describe the virtualization technologies under discussion in this context.

7.1.1 Hard Partitioning and Dynamic Domains

As described in Chapter 2, "Hard Partitioning: Dynamic Domains," Dynamic Domains are a feature of the Sun SPARC Enterprise M9000 servers providing isolated hardware environments, each of which runs its own copy of the Oracle Solaris operating system. This technology has the following strengths:

- **Best fault isolation.** No failure in one domain or in its infrastructure can affect another. Other solutions carry with them the risk that a failure occurring in one VE will affect other VEs, perhaps even causing them all to halt.
- **Security isolation.** A security penetration or compromise in one domain has no effect on other domains.
- **Complete compatibility in every respect with non-domained environments.** There is no concern about incompatibility or non-supportability of software.
- **Native performance compared to non-domained environments.** There is no virtualization layer. The CPU code path of an application is not elongated by virtualization, and no additional firmware is needed to assist with virtualization. This advantage, compared to software hypervisors, is greatest for I/O intensive applications.

  However, domain scalability is limited by hardware capabilities. The highest scalability is provided by Sun M9000 systems, which currently can have a maximum of 24 Dynamic Domains.

- **Completely separate Oracle Solaris instances.** Each instance can potentially have its own OS version, patch levels, and maintenance windows without any conflict or interference. Management of a single domain is the same as management of a single system. This is similar to hypervisor solutions, but is often an advantage compared to OS virtualization (OSV).
- **No extra license fees needed.** This technology is included with all domain-capable systems. Some hypervisors require a fee for use, or a fee for support in addition to support fees for the guest operating systems.
- **Well-established and -accepted history.** There is more than a decade of deployment and experience with hard partitioning in the SPARC product line.

Dynamic Domains are widely deployed in enterprise environments, especially for large applications where scale and the highest degree of isolation and availability are necessary for a relatively small number of vertically scaled virtualized environments.

7.1.2 Oracle VM Server for SPARC

As described in Chapter 3, "Oracle VM Server for SPARC," Oracle VM Server for SPARC (previously called Logical Domains or LDoms) is a SPARC virtual machine capability available on chip multithreading (CMT) servers. Like Dynamic Domains, each domain runs its own instance of Oracle Solaris. This technology offers several advantages:

- **Strong fault isolation.** A software failure in one Logical Domain cannot affect another Logical Domain, and domains are insulated from failure of CPU threads and other hardware resources assigned to other domains. The fault isolation characteristics of Logical Domains are better than those of both software-based hypervisors and OSV, as they permit redundancy with multiple service domains. Nevertheless, this level of fault isolation is not as good as that offered by hardware partitioning, especially when shared I/O resources are in use. Even so, the level of fault isolation available with Logical Domains is appropriate for almost all workloads.

- **Security isolation.** A security penetration or compromise in one domain has no effect on other domains. Logical Domains can be used to store sensitive data.

- **An extremely high level of compatibility with non-domained environments.** Only a few incompatibilities exist, such as the specific behavior of a virtual disk or network device, as documented in the current version of the Logical Domains reference material. Except for those differences, software performs the exact same steps as on a standalone system.

- **Native CPU performance compared to non-domained environments.** I/O performance does suffer under shared-I/O configurations, which can reduce scalability for some workloads.

   CPU threads are assigned to each Logical Domain, so scalability is limited by the number of available threads on the CMT server model. Logical Domains premiered on the Sun Fire T1000 and T2000 (no longer available), which had a single CPU chip with 8 cores and 4 threads per core, for a total of 32 addressable CPU threads; thus at most 32 domains were possible, including the Control Domain. Newer products such as the Sun SPARC Enterprise T5440 Server can run as many as 128 Logical Domains per system.

The Logical Domains' exclusive CPU assignment eliminates the need to time-slice guest environments onto CPUs, avoiding the performance penalty seen in other hypervisors.

- **A large number of completely separate Oracle Solaris instances.** Each domain can have its own patch levels and maintenance windows without conflict or interference with other domains. This approach compares favorably to most OS virtualization (OSV) configurations, which may require keeping patch levels synchronized across some or all guests.

- **High resource granularity.** Logical Domains permit fine-grained assignment of CPU threads and RAM. Granularity is more flexible than with hardware partitions but not as good as with OS virtualization.

- **No extra license fees needed.** This technology is included with all SPARC CMT systems. Some hypervisors require a fee for use or support in addition to acquisition and support fees for the operating systems and hardware.

- **Excellent support for business agility and operational efficiencies.** The advanced features of Logical Domains, such as domain cloning and mobility, support both flexibility and cost-effectiveness.

Logical Domains have proven to be one of the most popular features of the CMT server product line, with rapid uptake in adoption and feature growth occurring since their introduction. This technology is widely used for server consolidation, especially when replacing multiple small, horizontally scaled servers from previous SPARC product families.

7.1.3 x86 Hypervisors

The previously mentioned technologies support virtualized SPARC environments. Oracle Solaris and OpenSolaris also run on the x86 platform on Intel and AMD processors, and can run as guest virtual machines on a wide range of hypervisors, including Oracle VM VirtualBox, Oracle VM Server for x86, VMware, xVM hypervisor, and Microsoft's Hyper-V Server. This technology class provides the following advantages:

- **Fault isolation.** No software failure in virtual machine can affect another domain, although a failure of the hypervisor may halt all of the VEs.

- **Security isolation.** A security penetration or compromise in one guest has no effect on other guests. Given that most hypervisors are managed across a network, however, this creates an opportunity for an intruder to access a hypervisor directly; penetration of the hypervisor could theoretically give access to each guest.

- **An extremely high level of compatibility with native (non-virtual machine) environments.** Depending on the specific hypervisor and x86 processor in use, there may be incompatibilities compared to native execution regarding timer skew and accuracy, number of guest CPUs, or the ability to emulate or pass through features for all I/O devices.

- **Large number of completely separate instances of Oracle Solaris and other operating systems.** Each instance potentially can maintain its own patch levels and maintenance windows without conflict or interference.

- **High resource granularity compared to hardware partitions, permitting fine-grained assignment.** Hypervisors often permit oversubscription of CPU threads and RAM for enhanced consolidation ratios.

- **Coexistence of multiple operating environments that run on the x86 platform.** This provides an opportunity to leverage infrastructure investments for more heterogeneous OS mixtures. In contrast, most OS virtualization implementations support only guests of the same OS type, version, and patch level. Solaris 10 is an exception: It supports Solaris 8 Containers and Solaris 9 Containers—virtual environments that mimic different versions of Solaris.

- **Excellent support for business agility and operational efficiency.** Advanced features include VE cloning, mobility, and dynamic resource management.

This category of virtualization has drawn the largest amount of popular attention owing to the vast size of the x86 market. The large number of non-virtualized, low-utilization x86 systems, mostly running a single application under Windows, provide many candidates for consolidation and make this style of virtualization economically important. The ability to concurrently run different x86 operating systems on the same physical server also offers cost savings and operational flexibility.

7.1.4 Oracle Solaris Containers

The technologies discussed previously provide SPARC or x86 virtual machine or domain environments that can run independent Solaris instances. As described in Chapter 6, "Oracle Solaris Containers," Oracle Solaris provides OS virtualization (OSV) in the form of Solaris Containers, also called zones. Containers provide multiple virtual Solaris environments within a single Solaris instance. This technology offers the following advantages:

- **Fault isolation.** Service and application failures in one container have no effect on other Containers.

- **Security.** Containers remain securely isolated from one another. This separation permits extremely granular privilege assignments, and has provisions for providing immutable containers for "locked-down" environments that are protected from modification. Tamper-proof execution environments are very difficult to achieve with other virtualization methods.

- **A high level of compatibility with native (non-Container) Solaris environments.** Containers do have some functional limitations. For example, a Container cannot currently be an NFS server, though it can be an NFS client. An up-to-date list of exceptions, and other useful information, is maintained at the Zones and Containers FAQ at `http://hub.opensolaris.org/bin/view/Community+Group+zones/faq`.

- **Native performance compared to non-virtualized environments.** Containers require no hypervisor or other virtualization software, and the code paths of the OS and applications are unchanged.

- **Maximum scalability, permitting the largest number of VEs per computer.** The theoretical maximum is 8191 Containers per OS instance. Production systems with more than 100 running Containers exist in data centers.

- **Highest resource granularity.** This characteristic permits fine-grained assignment of CPU capacity, RAM use, and allocation of other system resources.

- **Low overhead.** Only hardware partitions have less overhead than containers.

- **More predictable performance than hypervisors.** Because only one scheduler is making scheduling decisions, predictability is enhanced.

- **Independence from any processor family.** Containers are available on any SPARC-, Intel-, or AMD-based computer that runs Solaris 10 or OpenSolaris. This platform independence lets planners select a virtualization architecture without being locked into a chip family.

- **Centralized observability.** Solaris tools enable you to examine all activities of all processes in all Containers without buying or learning new tools. This is not possible with other virtualization methods.

- **Coexistence.** Solaris 10 environments can coexist with virtual environments at the Solaris 8 or Solaris 9 levels.

- **No extra license fees needed.** Containers are simply a feature of the OS. Some hypervisors require a fee for use, or a fee for support in addition to the support fees for the operating systems.

- **Business agility and operational efficiency.** Containers' features and flexibility exceed those of hardware partitions, owing to their advanced features such as VE cloning, mobility, and dynamic resource management.

Solaris Containers were introduced with Solaris 10, and have been continually enhanced and widely adopted since then. They permit robust, scalable, and highly flexible virtualization without committing to a particular chip architecture.

An additional strength is that Containers can be used in conjunction with any of the other technologies to create highly flexible virtualization architectures. When an Oracle Solaris system is hosted in a Dynamic Domain, Logical Domain, or virtual machine, deploying application environments inside Containers nested within those virtual environments provides additional benefits. Security is enhanced by Containers' ability to provide a locked-down environment. Containers can be quickly and easily cloned, which simplifies the provisioning of additional virtual environments. Perhaps most important, the low resource requirements and scalability make it possible to locate many isolated virtual environments within the same domain or virtual machine, providing better scalability than would be possible with domains or hypervisor technology alone.

One way to realize the most benefits from this combination is to deploy a new domain or virtual machine when a virtual environment needs a dedicated operating system instance, and to deploy Containers within the virtual environment for Solaris virtual environments with compatible OS software levels. That combination exploits the advantages of both forms of virtualization.

7.2 Choosing the Technology: Start with Requirements

Application and organizational requirements drive virtualization technology selection, just as with any architectural decision. The process of choosing any technology should start by assessing the required systemic properties. Each of these requirements can suggest or preclude one or more virtualization technologies:

- Does the solution require a large number of virtualized environments with highly granular resource assignment, or are only a few environments required?

- Are workloads dynamic in nature, requiring the ability to easily change resource assignments?

- Are full fault and service isolation needed with no single points of failure?

- Is maximum performance needed? This consideration is important for workloads that are I/O intensive or make many system calls, because some virtualization technologies introduce performance penalties for those aspects of system behavior.

- What are the availability requirements of the workloads being virtualized?

- Is there a need for automation and sophisticated management such as cloning and mobility?
- Is there additional budget for licensing add-on virtualization technologies?
- Is an automated process needed for migrating from legacy unconsolidated environments or older operating system levels to a more current system?
- Is the processor chip architecture or operating system environment already dictated by application or business requirements?

The last question is a popular starting point: Because virtualization provides virtual platforms for applications to run on, an obvious consideration is whether the application requires a particular platform architecture or operating system. Is a SPARC solution needed, or an x86 solution? Or is the chip architecture unspecified? Is the operating system environment exclusively Oracle Solaris or a mix of operating systems? If Solaris is the sole operating system, is there a need to support multiple kernel update levels?

While platform architecture may drive virtualization choices, this is not a one-way process. The virtualization capabilities of each platform can influence platform selection as well. For example, standardizing on Solaris makes it possible to leverage Containers regardless of the chip architecture employed. This approach provides a no-extra-cost solution that takes advantage of the best resource granularity and scalability of the available technologies, and makes it possible to use either SPARC or x86 systems. Conversely, selecting SPARC makes it possible to leverage the built-in domaining capabilities of modern SPARC processors without incurring additional licensing expenses.

7.3 Virtualization Decision Tree

The following simple decision tree may be useful when you are trying to select a virtualization technology, based on the preceding considerations. Actual decisions will probably be more complex than this decision tree suggests, of course, and external factors such as existing company standards may dictate some choices. Nevertheless, these questions can help frame the considerations, leading to a better choice.

7.3.1 SPARC Environments

Consider using the SPARC environment:

- If the highest priorities include vertical scale, single-thread performance, and complete fault isolation for separate Oracle Solaris instances, then use M-series' Dynamic Domains.

- If the highest priorities include granular, dynamic, resource allocation for multiple Solaris instances, then use CMT servers' Logical Domains.

- If the maximum number of virtual instances with the most flexible resource control is important within a single Solaris kernel environment, then use Solaris Containers as the primary virtualization technology.

- If you are using Dynamic Domains or Logical Domains, deploy applications in Containers within each domain. This approach increases operational flexibility without adding cost, and it permits multiple Solaris virtual environments to reside within a single domain. You can also use Containers to harden the operating environment of the workload against intruders.

7.3.2 x86 Environments

Consider using the x86 environment:

- If different operating systems are used, or different Solaris kernel levels, use virtual machines hosted by an x86 hypervisor such as Oracle VM VirtualBox, Oracle VM Server for x86, xVM hypervisor, VMware, or Microsoft Windows Server 2008 Hyper-V.

- If the maximum number of virtual instances with the most flexible resource control is important, use Containers as the primary virtualization technology.

- If you are using virtual machines, deploy Solaris applications in Containers within each guest. This approach provides operational flexibility without adding cost, and it permits multiple Solaris VEs to reside within a single domain.

7.4 Choosing the Technology: Examples

Let's use the decision tree method described previously with some examples.

7.4.1 Consolidating Large Workloads

In your data center, you need to increase the workload density of high-scale, mission-critical workloads (20 or more cores per workload). This situation has the following specific needs:

- Mission-critical workloads should be placed in the lowest-risk environments. Consolidation adds risk, while isolation reduces it, with isolation being a primary factor in determining the level of risk. Hard partitions are strongly suggested, and perhaps required.

- High-scale workloads need high-scale hardware. x86 systems may not scale high enough, while SPARC systems are ideal. A high-scale operating system, such as Oracle Solaris, will also play a key role.

- Consolidated systems benefit from dynamic resource flexibility. The flexibility of Dynamic Domains will meet this need. A mid-range or high-end SPARC system with 30 or more CPU cores is the ideal solution in this scenario. The amount of RAM in the system should be slightly more than the sum of RAM needed by all of the workloads.

7.4.2 Hosting an ISP Web Service

As an ISP, you want to sell the service of web servers. The business model states a desire to maximize the density of customers and minimize acquisition and maintenance costs. The customer service contract indicates an intent to achieve 99.9% uptime, but includes a "best effort" clause regarding service uptime. Several configurations will be offered, distinguished by CPU capacity and RAM ("cost units" show the relative user cost per year):

- Very small: 0.1 CPU core, 100 MB RAM, 1 GB disk: 1× cost units
- Small: 0.3 CPU core, 200 MB RAM, 2 GB disk: 2× cost units
- Medium: 0.7 CPU core, 300 MB RAM, 4 GB disk: 4× cost units
- Large: 1.5 CPU cores, 512 MB RAM, 8 GB disk: 20× cost units
- Very large: 3.5 CPU cores, 2 GB RAM, 16 GB disk: 50× cost units

These factors will help you choose:

- The highest density of VEs per server requires the greatest efficiency—that is, the least RAM and disk space per VE, and the least performance overhead per VE. Containers provide the highest density of virtualization solutions and are a good choice. With applications running, the Oracle Solaris kernel will use hundreds of megabytes of RAM, but each VE will consume only dozens of megabytes, plus the memory needed for the web server applications. A two-socket, quad-core CPU, either x86 or SPARC, can easily handle 50 small customers, or two very large customers.

- Sparse-root Containers share OS binaries. Instead of potentially needing 50 copies of operating systems, which could use 200–300 GB of disk space, 50 Containers would need roughly 2.5 GB if you use ZFS clones. Customers will appreciate the fact that the disk space they are renting can be used almost entirely for their web server content.

- System memory is a significant portion of the cost of the system. Maximizing customer density means reducing RAM needs as much as possible and, therefore, reducing acquisition costs. This consideration also leads to the choice of Containers. Let's ignore the memory needed for the web server software, which is independent of virtualization technology. Instead of a minimum of 500 MB RAM being required for each VE, only approximately 50 MB is needed for each guest OS. Instead of a total of 25 GB RAM, plus memory for the applications, the system will need only 2.5 GB RAM plus application space.

7.4.3 Diverse OS Consolidation

You have a few racks full of old x86 systems, which run a variety of operating systems: Microsoft Windows, SuSE Linux, and Oracle Solaris. You have been told to move all of the workloads to new systems that fit into one rack because new workloads are arriving that will need their own computers and consume their own portion of the available electric current. While you're at it, you want to implement VE mobility so that when this migration happens again, it will be much simpler.

An x86 hypervisor is the only solution here, unless you have the option to re-implement the workloads on one OS that has sufficient OS virtualization features. Any of the popular x86 hypervisors would work in this scenario. VirtualBox, Oracle VM, VMware, and Microsoft Windows Server 2008 Hyper-V all have the necessary multi-OS and guest mobility capabilities. A virtualization management tool such as Oracle Enterprise Manager Ops Center will make that next consolidation even easier.

7.5 Summary

A wide range of virtualization technologies can be used to provide more efficient, agile, and lower-cost computing infrastructure. This chapter summarized some of the important distinguishing characteristics of the virtualization technologies described in this book, and offered a methodology for selecting the best choices to meet your business and technical requirements.

Applying Virtualization

Previous chapters described the methods of workload isolation via virtualization. Chapter 1, "Introduction to Virtualization," described the need for isolation and the methods that can be used to achieve it. Chapters 2 through 6 detailed the features of several virtualization implementations, particularly those provided by Oracle Solaris 10 or that can host Solaris 10 guests. Chapter 7, "Choosing a Virtualization Technology," offered a strategy for choosing one or more of those technologies in a particular situation.

This chapter demonstrates the use of these virtualization solutions with real-world examples. Each example describes a goal and details the steps you can use to replicate the example. The features used in these examples were discussed in previous chapters; this chapter combines them in interesting ways.

8.1 How to Configure for Dynamic Domains

A basic requirement for Dynamic Domains is the ability to create new operating environments for new services with no detrimental effect on end users or other applications. Moving existing resources to new domains, or adding new hardware to the system that can later be used to create new domains, accomplishes this goal. Although adding hardware makes creating new domains easier, reallocating or reconfiguring existing boards can achieve the same goal with a little preplanning effort.

The discussion here assumes that you have reviewed Chapter 2, "Hard Partitioning: Dynamic Domains," before you read this example. Also note that the concept of a CPU is defined as a physical CPU socket, which is the primary definition used for Dynamic Domains. This is not the definition used by Oracle Solaris when it numbers and counts CPUs.

8.1.1 M9000 Configuration Example

Although the M9000 is the largest M-Series server in the series, it is actually easier to configure than the M5000 due to the smaller number of memory configuration permutations possible. This advantage is balanced by the less flexible memory population rules, which dictate only 16 or 32 DIMMs per CMU. These trade-offs will become more obvious while working through the example.

The desired outcome of this exercise is as follows:

- Configure an M9000 with five domains.
    - Two domains should have 6 CPUs, 128 GB of memory, 4 Gigabit Ethernet (GbE) ports, and 2 8 Gb Fiber Channel (FC) cards, and should use internal boot disks. Call these Domains 1 and 2.
    - Two domains should have 4 CPUs, 256 GB of memory, 4 GbE ports, and 2 8 Gb FC cards, and should use internal boot disks. Call these Domains 3 and 4.
    - One domain should have 4 CPUs, 64 GB of memory, and 2 GbE ports, and should use internal boot disks. Call this Domain 5. Some resources from this domain must be available for the other domains on an as-needed basis.
- The domains with 4 CPUs must be able to have CPUs removed without having to shut down first.
- Provide room for 25% growth.

Domains requiring 6 CPUs can be configured in two different ways:

- A four-CPU CMU in Uni-XSB mode along with two XSBs from a four-CPU CMU in Quad-XSB mode
- A four-CPU CMU in Uni-XSB mode along with a two-CPU CMU in Uni-XSB mode

There are trade-offs between these two options. Sharing a four-CPU CMU board reduces the solution cost, but creates a single point of failure for two domains. Combining the four-CPU and two-CPU CMU boards is more expensive, but does provide for complete hardware isolation between the domains. Both options will be discussed here.

8.1.1.1 Option 1: Domains Sharing a CMU

Configuring a CMU to support more than one domain does provide for less over-provisioning of resources to a domain, but sets up possible scenarios in which problems might affect multiple domains. Processor faults will be isolated, but SC or MAC chip faults would impact all domains using the resources on the affected CMU. Assuming a clustering software solution is used to maintain data services, multiple domains sharing a CMU is a good balance of cost against risk.

Step 1: Configure the CPUs   Each CMU can have either 4 or 2 CPUs. We need a total of $6 + 6 + 4 + 4 + 4 = 24$ CPUs. This equates to 6 CMUs with 4 CPUs each.

- Domain 1: 1½ CMUs (CMU#0 and ½ CMU#1).
- Domain 2: 1½ CMUs (CMU#2 and ½ CMU#1). Because Domains 1 and 2 will share a CMU, the shared memory should be as close as possible to both domains. This means CMU#1 will be the shared board.
- Domain 3: 1 CMU (CMU#5).
- Domain 4: 1 CMU (CMU#4).
- Domain 5: 1 CMU (CMU#3). Because other domains may use some of the resources from this CMU, it should be in the middle of all domain boards so there is a better balance of memory access latency.

Step 2: Configure the Memory   Because each CMU can have either 16 or 32 DIMMs, assume 16 DIMMs each. This gives us room to grow.

- Domain 1: Because this domain requires 1½ CMUs, memory must be spread across two CMUs. That yields a total of $16 + 8 = 24$ DIMMs. If 4 GB DIMMs are used on CMU#1 and 8 GB DIMMs are used on the shared CMU, that gives $16 \times 4 + 8 \times 8 = 64 + 64 = 128$ GB. CMU#0 has 16 4 GB DIMMs and CMU#1 has 16 8 GB DIMMs.
- Domain 2: This domain shares the same ½ CMU as Domain 1, so configure it the same way. CMU#2 has 16 4 GB DIMMs and uses the second half of CMU#1, for a total of 128 GB of memory.
- Domain 3: 256 GB in 16 DIMMs = 16 GB/DIMM. This configuration is not supported on the M-Series, so this domain must use 8 GB DIMM modules in all 32 slots. This gives CMU#5 a total of 256 GB.
- Domain 4: This domain must be configured the same way as Domain 3. CMU#4 must have 32 8 GB DIMMs.
- Domain 5: CMU#3 should have 16 4 GB DIMMs for a total of 64 GB of memory.

Step 3: Configure the I/O   Because none of the domains requires many I/O cards, the most any domain needs is a single IOU board. Domains 3, 4, and 5 will have one IOU to match the CMU. Domains 1 and 2 are not as simple. Because the shared board is needed only for memory and CPUs, the shared CMU does not require that the associated IOU be present.

- Domain 1: Needs only IOU#0, which will house the boot disks. Cards should be placed to get their own PCIe switch, if possible. Place the same type of card in different IO bays in the IOU. This gives redundancy across the Oberon ASICs: one for the top four slots, the second for the bottom four slots.
  - PCIe#0: Base I/O card (part **SEMY7BSIZ**). This provides control of Disks 0 and 1, and access to the internal DVD. This card also provides two GbE ports.
  - PCIe#1: Empty.
  - PCIe#2: Dual-port 8 Gb FC Card (part **SG-XPCIE2FC-QF8-Z**).
  - PCIe#3: Empty.
  - PCIe#4: Dual-port GbE Card (part **7281A-2**).
  - PCIe#5: Empty.
  - PCIe#6: Dual-port 8 Gb FC Card (part **SG-XPCIE2FC-QF8-Z**).
  - PCIe#7: Empty.
- Domain 2: Needs only IOU#2, which will house the boot disks. Cards should be placed to get their own PCIe switch, if possible. Place the same type of card in different IO bays in the IOU. This gives redundancy across the Oberon ASICs: one for the top four slots, the second for the bottom four slots.
  - PCIe#0: Base I/O card (part **SEMY7BSIZ**). This provides control of Disks 0 and 1, and access to the internal DVD. This card also provides two GbE ports.
  - PCIe#1: Empty.
  - PCIe#2: Dual-port 8 Gb FC Card (part **SG-XPCIE2FC-QF8-Z**).
  - PCIe#3: Empty.
  - PCIe#4: Dual-port GbE Card (part **7281A-2**).
  - PCIe#5: Empty.
  - PCIe#6: Dual-port 8 Gb FC Card (part **SG-XPCIE2FC-QF8-Z**).
  - PCIe#7: Empty.
- Domain 3: Needs only IOU#5, which will house the boot disks. Cards should be placed to get their own PCIe switch, if possible. Place the same type of card

in different IO bays in the IOU. This gives redundancy across the Oberon ASICs: one for the top four slots, the second for the bottom four slots.

- PCIe#0: Base I/O card (part **SEMY7BSIZ**). This provides control of Disks 0 and 1, and access to the internal DVD. This card also provides two GbE ports.
- PCIe#1: Empty.
- PCIe#2: Dual-port 8 Gb FC Card (part **SG-XPCIE2FC-QF8-Z**).
- PCIe#3: Empty.
- PCIe#4: Dual-port GbE Card (part **7281A-2**).
- PCIe#5: Empty.
- PCIe#6: Dual-port 8 Gb FC Card (part **SG-XPCIE2FC-QF8-Z**).
- PCIe#7: Empty.

- Domain 4: Needs only IOU#4, which will house the boot disks. Cards should be placed to get their own PCIe switch, if possible. Place the same type of card in different IO bays in the IOU. This gives redundancy across the Oberon ASICs: one for the top four slots, the second for the bottom four slots.
  - PCIe#0: Base I/O card (part **SEMY7BSIZ**). This provides control of Disks 0 and 1, and access to the internal DVD. This card also provides two GbE ports.
  - PCIe#1: Empty.
  - PCIe#2: Dual-port 8 Gb FC Card (part **SG-XPCIE2FC-QF8-Z**).
  - PCIe#3: Empty.
  - PCIe#4: Dual-port GbE Card (part **7281A-2**).
  - PCIe#5: Empty.
  - PCIe#6: Dual-port 8 Gb FC Card (part **SG-XPCIE2FC-QF8-Z**).
  - PCIe#7: Empty.

- Domain 5: Needs only IOU#3. This will house the boot disks. Only the base I/O card is needed.
  - PCIe#0: Base I/O card (part **SEMY7BSIZ**). This provides control of Disks 0 and 1, and access to the internal DVD. This card also provides two GbE ports.
  - PCIe#1: Empty.
  - PCIe#2: Empty.
  - PCIe#3: Empty.
  - PCIe#4: Empty.
  - PCIe#5: Empty.

- PCIe#6: Empty.
- PCIe#7: Empty.

Step 4: Configure the Domains   Now the domains can be configured. CMUs 0, 2, 4, and 5 can be placed in Uni-XSB mode. All of the memory will be used at the same time, and there is no need to share resources. CMU#1 must be placed in Quad XSB mode so two of the XSB units can be assigned to Domains 1 and 2. CMU#3 should also be placed in Quad-XSB mode just in case any of its CPU, memory, or PCIe capacity is required on other domains.

- Domain 1:
  1. `setupfru -m n -x 1 sb 0` (Uni-XSB mode and no memory mirroring)
  2. `setupfru -m n -x 4 sb 1` (Quad-XSB mode and no memory mirroring)
  3. `setdcl -d 1 -s 00=00-0 01=01-0 02=01-1` (XSB00-0 gets LSB#0, XSB01-0 gets LSB#1, XSB01-1 gets LSB#2)
  4. `addboard -y -c assign -d 1 00-0 01-0 01-1`

- Domain 2:
  1. `setupfru -m n -x 1 sb 2` (Uni-XSB mode and no memory mirroring)
  2. `setdcl -d 2 -s 00=02-0 01=01-2 02=01-3` (XSB02-0 gets LSB#0, XSB01-2 gets LSB#1, XSB01-3 gets LSB#2)
  3. `addboard -y -c assign -d 2 02-0 01-2 01-3`

- Domain 3:
  1. `setupfru -m n -x 1 sb 5` (Uni-XSB mode and no memory mirroring)
  2. `setdcl -d 3 -s 00=05-0` (XSB05-0 gets LSB#0)
  3. `addboard -y -c assign -d 3 05-0`

- Domain 4:
  1. `setupfru -m n -x 1 sb 4` (Uni-XSB mode and no memory mirroring)
  2. `setdcl -d 4 -s 00=04-0` (XSB04-0 gets LSB#0)
  3. `addboard -y -c assign -d 4 04-0`

- Domain 5:
  1. `setupfru -m n -x 4 sb 3` (Quad-XSB mode and no memory mirroring)
  2. `setdcl -d 5 -s 00=03-0 01=03-1 02=03-2 03=03-3` (XSB03-0 gets LSB#0, XSB03-1 gets LSB#1, XSB03-2 gets LSB#2, XSB03-3 gets LSB#3)
  3. `addboard -y -c assign -d 5 03-0 03-1 03-2 03-3`

Figures 8.1 and 8.2 show the hardware configurations.

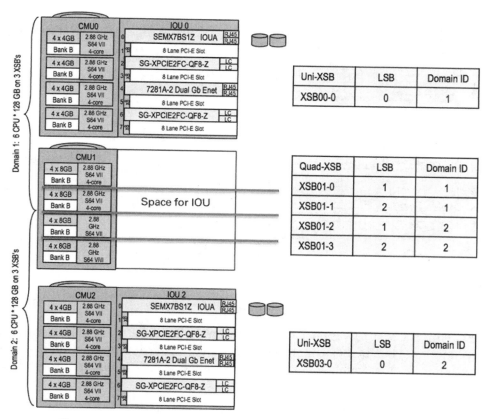

Figure 8.1 Hardware Assignments for Domains 0, 1, and 2

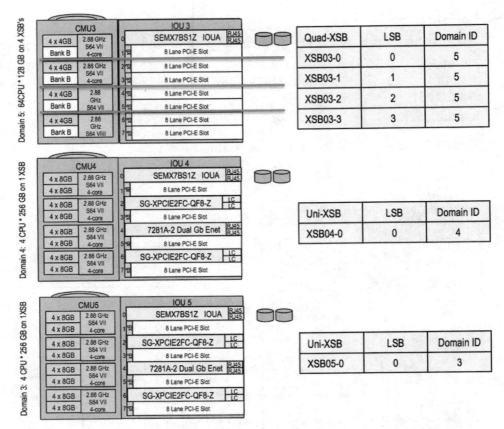

Figure 8.2 Hardware Assignments for Domains 3, 4, and 5

8.1.1.2 Option 2: Completely Isolated Domains

Configuring a CMU to support only one domain provides the most isolation be-tween domains, but brings the possibility of over-provisioning domain resources. This scheme is most viable where the additional cost is less important than com-plete domain isolation.

Step 1: Configure the CPUs   For this option, the four-CPU and two-CPU CMU boards will be combined. For most domains, the four-CPU version will be used.

- Domain 1: 2 CMUs (CMU#0 has four CPUs, CMU#1 has two CPUs).
- Domain 2: 2 CMUs (CMU#2 has four CPUs, CMU#3 has two CPUs).

- Domain 3: 1 CMU (CMU#6).
- Domain 4: 1 CMU (CMU#5).
- Domain 5: 1 CMU (CMU#4). Because other domains may use some of the resources from this CMU, it should be in the middle of all domain boards so there is a better balance of memory access latencies.

Step 2: Configure the Memory   Because each CMU can have either 16 or 32 DIMMs, assume 16 DIMMs each. This provides room to grow.

- Domain 1: It would be best to split the 128 GB across both CMU boards, with 64 GB per CMU. This is done using 16 4 GB DIMMs on both CMU boards. CMU#0 has 16 4 GB DIMMs and CMU#1 has 16 4 GB DIMMs.
- Domain 2: Same as Domain 1. CMU#2 has 16 4 GB DIMMs and CMU#3 has 16 4 GB DIMMs.
- Domain 3: 256 GB/16 DIMMs = 1 GB/DIMM. This setup is not supported on the M-Series, so this domain must use 8 GB DIMM modules in all 32 slots. This gives CMU#6 a total of 256 GB.
- Domain 4: This domain must be configured the same way as Domain 3. CMU#5 must have 32 8 GB DIMMs.
- Domain 5: CMU#4 should have 16 4 GB DIMMs for a total of 64 GB of memory.

Step 3: Configure the I/O   Because none of the domains require many I/O cards, each domain needs only a single IOU board.

- Domain 1: Needs only IOU#0, which will house the boot disks. Cards should be placed to get their own PCIe switch, if possible. Place the same type of card in different IO bays in the IOU. This gives redundancy across the Oberon ASICs: one for the top four slots, the second for the bottom four slots.
  - PCIe#0: Base I/O card (part **SEMY7BSIZ**). This provides control of Disks 0 and 1, and access to the internal DVD. This card also provides two GbE ports.
  - PCIe#1: Empty.
  - PCIe#2: Dual-port 8 Gb FC Card (part **SG-XPCIE2FC-QF8-Z**).
  - PCIe#3: Empty.
  - PCIe#4: Dual-port GbE Card (part **7281A-2**).
  - PCIe#5: Empty.

- PCIe#6: Dual-port 8 Gb FC Card (part **SG-XPCIE2FC-QF8-Z**).
- PCIe#7: Empty.

- Domain 2: Needs only IOU#2, which will house the boot disks. Cards should be placed to get their own PCIe switch, if possible. Place the same type of card in different IO bays in the IOU. This gives redundancy across the Oberon ASICs: one for the top four slots, the second for the bottom four slots.
  - PCIe#0: Base I/O card (part **SEMY7BSIZ**). This provides control of Disks 0 and 1, and access to the internal DVD. This card also provides two GbE ports.
  - PCIe#1: Empty.
  - PCIe#2: Dual-port 8 Gb FC Card (part **SG-XPCIE2FC-QF8-Z**).
  - PCIe#3: Empty.
  - PCIe#4: Dual-port GbE Card (part **7281A-2**).
  - PCIe#5: Empty.
  - PCIe#6: Dual-port 8 Gb FC Card (part **SG-XPCIE2FC-QF8-Z**).
  - PCIe#7: Empty.

- Domain 3: Needs only IOU#6, which will house the boot disks. Cards should be placed to get their own PCIe switch, if possible. Place the same type of card in different IO bays in the IOU. This gives redundancy across the Oberon ASICs: one for the top four slots, the second for the bottom four slots.
  - PCIe#0: Base I/O card (part **SEMY7BSIZ**). This provides control of Disks 0 and 1, and access to the internal DVD. This card also provides two GbE ports.
  - PCIe#1: Empty.
  - PCIe#2: Dual-port 8 Gb FC Card (part **SG-XPCIE2FC-QF8-Z**).
  - PCIe#3: Empty.
  - PCIe#4: Dual-port GbE Card (part **7281A-2**).
  - PCIe#5: Empty.
  - PCIe#6: Dual-port 8 Gb FC Card (part **SG-XPCIE2FC-QF8-Z**).
  - PCIe#7: Empty.

- Domain 4: Needs only IOU#5, which will house the boot disks. Cards should be placed to get their own PCIe switch, if possible. Place the same type of card in different IO bays in the IOU. This gives redundancy across the Oberon ASICs: one for the top four slots, the second for the bottom four slots.

- PCIe#0: Base I/O card (part **SEMY7BSIZ**). This provides control of Disks 0 and 1, and access to the internal DVD. This card also provides two GbE ports.
- PCIe#1: Empty.
- PCIe#2: Dual-port 8 Gb FC Card (part **SG-XPCIE2FC-QF8-Z**).
- PCIe#3: Empty.
- PCIe#4: Dual-port GbE Card (part **7281A-2**).
- PCIe#5: Empty.
- PCIe#6: Dual-port 8 Gb FC Card (part **SG-XPCIE2FC-QF8-Z**).
- PCIe#7: Empty.

- Domain 5: Needs only IOU#4, which will house the boot disks. Only the base I/O card is needed.
  - PCIe#0: Base I/O card (part **SEMY7BSIZ**). This provides control of Disks 0 and 1, and access to the internal DVD. This card also provides two GbE ports.
  - PCIe#1: Empty.
  - PCIe#2: Empty.
  - PCIe#3: Empty.
  - PCIe#4: Empty.
  - PCIe#5: Empty.
  - PCIe#6: Empty.
  - PCIe#7: Empty.

Step 4: Configure the Domains   Now the domains can be configured. CMUs 0–3, 5, and 6 will be placed in Uni-XSB mode. All the memory will be used at the same time, and there is no need to share resources. CMU#4 should also be placed in Quad-XSB mode, just in case any of the CPU, memory, or PCIe is required on other domains.

- Domain 1:
  1. `setupfru -m n -x 1 sb 0` (Uni-XSB mode and no memory mirroring)
  2. `setupfru -m n -x 1 sb 1` (Uni-XSB mode and no memory mirroring)

3. `setdcl -d 1 -s 00=00-0 01=01-0` (XSB00-0 gets LSB#0, XSB01-0 gets LSB#1)

4. `addboard -y -c assign -d 1 00-0 01-0`

- Domain 2:
  1. `setupfru -m n -x 1 sb 2` (Uni-XSB mode and no memory mirroring)
  2. `setupfru -m n -x 1 sb 3` (Uni-XSB mode and no memory mirroring)
  3. `setdcl -d 2 -s 00=02-0 01=03-0` (XSB02-0 gets LSB#0, XSB03-0 gets LSB#1)
  4. `addboard -y -c assign -d 2 02-0 03-0`

- Domain 3:
  1. `setupfru -m n -x 1 sb 6` (Uni-XSB mode and no memory mirroring)
  2. `setdcl -d 3 -s 00=06-0` (XSB06-0 gets LSB#0)
  3. `addboard -y -c assign -d 3 06-0`

- Domain 4:
  1. `setupfru -m n -x 1 sb 5` (Uni-XSB mode and no memory mirroring)
  2. `setdcl -d 4 -s 00=05-0` (XSB05-0 gets LSB#0)
  3. `addboard -y -c assign -d 4 05-0`

- Domain 5:
  1. `setupfru -m n -x 4 sb 4` (Quad-XSB mode and no memory mirroring)
  2. `setdcl -d 5 -s 00=04-0 01=04-1 02=04-2 03=04-3` (XSB04-0 gets LSB#0, XSB04-1 gets LSB#1, XSB04-2 gets LSB#2, XSB04-3 gets LSB#3)
  3. `addboard -y -c assign -d 5 04-0 04-1 04-2 04-3`

Figures 8.3, 8.4, and 8.5 show the hardware configurations.

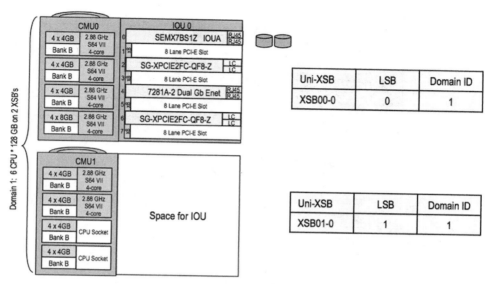

Figure 8.3 Hardware Assignments for Domain 1

Uni-XSB	LSB	Domain ID
XSB00-0	0	1

Uni-XSB	LSB	Domain ID
XSB01-0	1	1

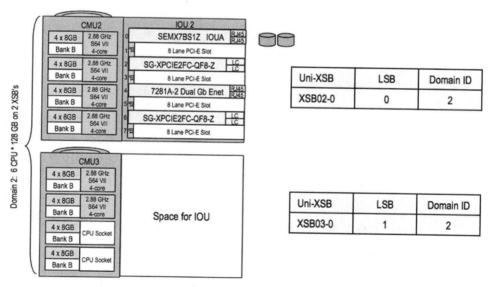

Figure 8.4 Hardware Assignments for Domain 2

Uni-XSB	LSB	Domain ID
XSB02-0	0	2

Uni-XSB	LSB	Domain ID
XSB03-0	1	2

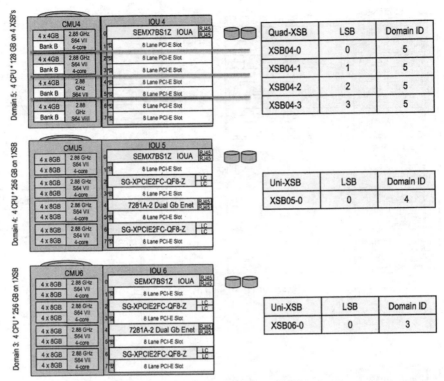

Figure 8.5 Hardware Assignments for Domains 3, 4, and 5

8.1.2 Summary

There are many ways to configure the M-Series servers. Configuring these systems requires understanding and balancing trade-offs. Configuring for higher availability increases costs, but also greatly improves application service uptime. All domains are not equal in importance. It is often appropriate to use shared resources for domains that run less important workloads.

8.2 Consolidating with Oracle VM Server for SPARC (Logical Domains)

Oracle VM Server for SPARC (also called Logical Domains) provides the most direct way to consolidate complete Solaris SPARC instances from multiple servers onto a single hardware platform. Each domain hosts a private Oracle Solaris environment with its own accounts, passwords, and patch levels—just as if each had its own separate physical server. Logical Domains also provides a "physical to virtual" (P2V) tool, further simplifying the process of moving from separate servers to a consolidated environment.

This capability will be demonstrated here with an example based on a real-world scenario. This data center used 16 servers: a combination of Sun Fire V490, V880, and V890 servers, plus one Sun Enterprise 6500 occupying more than 80 rack units. It ran a combination of an Oracle database, SAP R/3, J2EE, portal, and web applications, in both production and test environments.

These aging machines took up a substantial space and energy footprint that could be reduced by the use of modern T-Series servers, which could offer improved total cost of ownership (TCO). Logical Domains would provide a one-to-one correspondence of physical server to virtual server, permitting different kernel patch levels and maintenance windows. Each domain would have the same RAM as the original physical machine, and sufficient CPU threads to meet or exceed the previously consumed CPU capacity.

This example uses concepts and features described in Chapter 3, "Oracle VM Server for SPARC."

8.2.1 Planning

The first step was to enumerate the existing applications, the servers that they ran on, and their capacity requirements. It was determined that the system included 10 production servers and 6 test and development servers. Planning also established network and storage requirements.

Based on available performance data, it appeared that a single T5240 would have approximately enough capacity to handle the entire workload. That would cut the margin of available capacity too close for comfort, however, so a pair of identical T5240s was chosen as a better solution. A second server would provide sufficient capacity headroom and redundancy in case the other server failed or needed to be taken down for maintenance. Production and test domains would be split over the servers, avoiding a single point of failure. If necessary, test workloads could be shed during emergency situations if one server had to do the work of two. Domain isolation was considered to be adequate for securely separating test from production workloads. Because use of the pair of machines provided application redundancy, there was no need in the original implementation to use redundant service domains.

Networks were configured similar to the physical environments, with virtual network devices replacing physical network devices in a one-for-one manner. Separate virtual switches and VLANs could have been used to isolate production networks from test, but were not needed because a single shared network was in use in the existing environment. Storage was split between operating system images residing on internal disk, and application data residing on physical disks.

Separate disks were used for the domained environments, with file system–based disk images for the OS virtual disks, and physical disk back-ends for application data. This scheme provided flexibility for managing the OS environments while providing optimal performance for application data.

8.2.2 Configuring Logical Domains

In this example, the Logical Domains software is installed as described in Chapter 3, with the exception that the control domain is given additional CPU and RAM capacity. Note that eight CPU threads are used to allocate an entire CPU core to the control domain.

```
# ldm add-vdiskserver primary-vds0 primary
# ldm add-vconscon port-range=5000-5100 primary-vcc0 primary
# ldm add-vswitch net-dev=e1000g0 primary-vsw0 primary
# ldm set-mau 1 primary
# ldm set-vcpu 8 primary
# ldm set-memory 6g primary
# ldm add-config initial
# shutdown -y  -g0 -i6
```

8.2.3 Creating Domains

Once Logical Domains has been installed on each new system, each individual domain can be installed, one for each original physical server. Physical servers providing application redundancy in the original configuration are mapped to domains in different T5240s in the new configuration so as to retain the original environment's "no single point of failure" availability. The process of installing each domain follows the same pattern as described in Chapter 3, with the differences reflecting the need to accommodate the specific resource requirements.

In this example, for simplicity, we do fresh installs of Solaris 10 in each domain using the current Solaris 10 update level. Alternatively, the ldmp2v tool illustrated in Chapter 3 could have been used to replicate the existing systems. This is an implementation choice: One can view the move to new hardware as an opportunity to do fresh system installs, or one can replicate the existing systems with as little change as possible. Both alternatives are available with Logical Domains.

In the following example, a ZFS data set is created for storing virtual disks, and a domain is defined with 16 virtual CPUs, 8 GB of RAM, a single virtual network device, and a virtual boot disk and DVD image for installing Oracle Solaris. This replaces one of the application server environments, and provides ample CPU and memory headroom. It has a virtual boot volume with a ZFS back-end, a physical disk for data, and a virtual DVD image for OS installation. Cryptographic accelerators are assigned to the domain to provide hardware-accelerated encryption. Other domains are defined in similar fashion on the two servers, albeit with variations in their names and the assignment of virtual disks, RAM, and CPUs. Installation of Oracle Solaris in each domain proceeds as described in Chapter 3. Alternatively, the initial domain could have been cloned to create each of the additional domains.

```
# zfs create rpool/ldoms
# zfs set mountpoint=/ldoms rpool/ldoms
# zfs set compression=on rpool/ldoms
# zfs create rpool/ldoms/ldom1
# mkfile -n 20g /ldoms/ldom1/disk0.img
# ldm add-domain ldom1
# ldm set-vcpu 16 ldom1
# ldm set-mau 2 ldom1
# ldm set-mem 8gb ldom1
# ldm add-vnet vnet1 primary-vsw0 ldom1
# ldm add-vdsdev /ldoms/ldom1/disk0.img vol10@primary-vds0
# ldm add-vdisk vdisk10 vol10@primary-vds0 ldom1
# ldm add-vdsdev /dev/dsk/c1t48d0s2 c1t48d0@primary-vds0
# ldm add-vdisk vdisk11 c1t48d0@primary-vds0
# ldm add-vdsdev /DVD/solarisdvd.iso s10iso@primary-vds0
# ldm add-vdisk vdisk_iso s10iso@primary-vds0 ldom1
```

8.2.4 Testing

After defining each domain and installing Solaris, applications can be installed and tested, just as if they were on individual servers.

8.2.5 Summary

This example shows how 16 prior-generation SPARC servers can be consolidated onto 2 current chip multithreading servers using Logical Domains, thereby achieving a substantial reduction in power consumption and rack space.

8.3 Deploying Oracle Solaris 10 with Oracle VM Server for x86

Oracle VM for x86 is Oracle's x86 virtual machine solution, derived from the work of the open-source Xen project. Oracle VM supports a variety of different brands of guest virtual machines, including Oracle Enterprise Linux, Red Hat Enterprise Linux, Oracle Solaris 10, and Microsoft Windows. Oracle VM (OVM) consists of three main components:

- Oracle VM Server: A self-contained virtualization environment made up of a reduced installation of Oracle Enterprise Linux and the tools necessary to support guest virtual machines.
- Oracle VM Manager: A centralized, web-based management interface to provision and manage Oracle VM servers and server pools, virtual machines, and the assets required to create virtual machines such as installation media, templates, and saved VM images. While the Oracle VM Manager can be run within a virtual machine hosted on an Oracle VM Server, typically the VM Manager runs on a separate management system running Oracle Enterprise Linux. Oracle VM Manager is capable of managing virtual machines spanning multiple pools of Oracle VM Servers.
- Oracle VM Agent: A software agent that runs on an Oracle VM server and communicates with the Oracle VM Manager.

Details and information about Oracle VM Server and its components can be found at `http://download.oracle.com/docs/cd/E15458_01/index.htm`. At the time of this book's writing, the current release of this product was Oracle VM 2.2.

8.3.1 Prerequisites for Installing Oracle Solaris 10 in an Oracle VM Environment

In this brief example, we demonstrate how to install Solaris 10 in an Oracle VM environment.

The following example uses the Oracle VM Manager to provision a Solaris 10 guest virtual machine. It is assumed that an Oracle VM environment has already been established. As a starting point, the following tasks must have been completed. Details on how to accomplish them can be found in the Oracle VM documentation referenced previously.

- Oracle VM Manager must have been installed on a management system.
- Oracle VM Server must have been installed on at least one system.

- A server pool must have been created in the Oracle VM Manager. This could include the creation of a shared storage repository for a server pool supporting high availability.
- Installation media for Solaris 10 10/09 must have been added to the Oracle VM Manager.

Chapter 4, "Oracle Solaris 10 as an x86 Guest," provides additional details on the Xen hypervisor and lists the Solaris 10 updates that have the necessary device drivers for operation within the Oracle VM.

8.3.2 Creating an Oracle Solaris 10 Guest Virtual Machine

This example guides you through the process of creating a Solaris 10 guest virtual machine in an Oracle VM environment and includes screen shots of the process.

8.3.2.1 Step 1: Creating the Virtual Machine

With a browser, navigate to the Oracle VM Manager. From the Virtual Machines panel, shown in Figure 8.6, click the Create Virtual Machine button to begin. Look for this button in the lower-right corner of the screen.

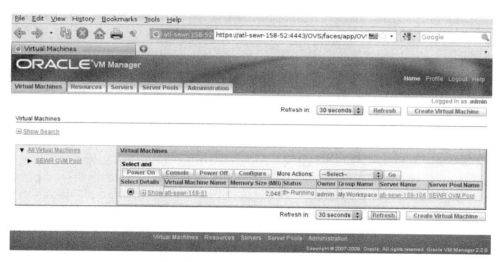

Figure 8.6 Creating the Virtual Machine

On the next panel, select Create from installation media—we are going to install the software from a copy of the installation DVD. On the next screen, select the server pool that will contain the virtual machine. Here, you can also select whether you want Oracle VM Manager to select a preferred server for deployment of the VM or whether you would like to select it yourself.

8.3.2.2 Step 2: Selecting the Installation Media and Virtualization Method

On the next screen, shown in Figure 8.7, select the Solaris 10 installation media from which to install the virtual machine. An image of the Solaris 10 10/09 installation DVD must already have been uploaded into the Oracle VM repository. Here, you also select whether this VM is to be fully virtualized or paravirtualized. Create the Solaris VM as a fully virtualized VM. Select the installation media and Fully Virtualized as the virtualization method and click Next.

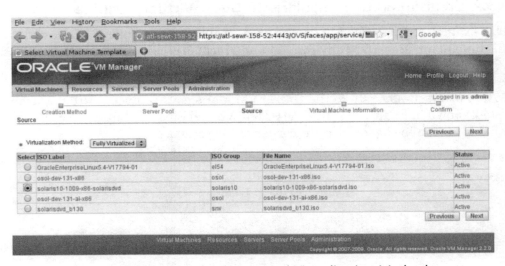

Figure 8.7 Setting the Source and Virtualization Method

8.3.2.3 Step 3: Providing the Virtual Machine Information

At this point, you must select the details of the virtual machine itself—in particular, the name, operating system, CPU, and memory and virtual disk sizes. On this panel, assign a name to the virtual machine; Oracle VM Manager and Oracle VM Server will use this name to refer to this guest virtual machine. There is no absolute requirement for the new name to be associated with the host name or node name of the operating system running inside the VM, but linking them together is likely to lead to less confusion. Select Sun Solaris 10 as the type of operating system to be installed. Oracle VM has some knowledge of various operating systems, so if a known operating system is to be installed, it should be selected; otherwise, select Other.

Oracle VM supports multiple processors for a virtual machine, and this configuration can be selected at the time the virtual machine is created. As a best practice, select a single processor while installing the guest VM and then alter this choice to the desired number of processors once installation is complete. The number of processors in a virtual machine can be changed when a VM is powered off.

Select the amount of memory and the size of the virtual disk to be used for this VM. Memory and disk requirements for a VM are not substantially different from those required for a stand-alone installation of Oracle Solaris on a physical server. Remember that swap and dump space are allocated out of the virtual disk. In this case, we allocated 2 GB of memory and a 16 GB disk. Refer to the Solaris 10 release notes and system requirements documents for specific recommendations for minimum memory and disk requirements. The virtual disk is a file residing on the Oracle VM Server that acts as the disk for the virtual machine; additional disks and storage connections can be made to the VM after it is created. The disk specified here is where the operating system will be installed.

VNC (Virtual Network Computing) is a graphical desktop sharing system. Oracle VM presents the console of its virtual machines using protocols accessible by VNC. The console, keyboard, and mouse of the virtual machine are all made available through VNC as if the VM had actual devices connected. A number of different VNC clients are available for many different operating systems.

Once the virtual machine is created, VNC will be used to access its console, and a password must be used to authenticate access to that console. Select the password you want to use for the VNC console. This is not the password for the Solaris root login, but rather the password used to access the console where you can then log in to the VM.

An Oracle VM Server Pool can be created with high-availability enabled. This choice allows for automatic migration and restart of a virtual machine from a failed physical node to a remaining, running physical server node. Because the pool in this case has this feature enabled, we will choose to use it. This decision is determined by your own requirements and pool configuration.

Lastly, we create the virtual network interfaces. Two types of network interfaces are supported: `ioemu` and `netfront`. The `ioemu` interface is a fully virtualized interface and is presented to the operating system as the `rtls` Ethernet driver (`rtls0`, for example). The `netfront` interface is a paravirtualized interface, which presents itself as the `xnf` network driver (`xnf0`, for example). Oracle Solaris 10, while a fully virtualized VM, provides paravirtualized drivers for network and disk that may be used—an arrangement referred to as an HVM+PV virtual machine. In the present release of Oracle VM 2.2, the network type can be changed once the system has been installed. In this example, we will initially configure the system with an `ioemu` fully virtualized network interface. Once Solaris has been installed, we will then convert it to a `netfront` paravirtualized interface.

Notice the Bridge pull-down menu, which specifies the physical interface on the host that should be associated with this virtual interface. In this example, all of the host Oracle VM Server nodes have their networks connected to their first network (instance 0), so the device xenbr0 is selected. Any other physical connection on the Oracle VM Server node could be selected for association with the virtual network. If a network connection plumbed on the third interface was the desired association, for example, you would select xenbr2.

As previously mentioned, it is often a good idea to tie the name of the VM to the host name of the operating system running within the VM. This convention might require using the MAC address provided for the primary network to reserve a predetermined IP address. In this example, this has been done by reserving the IP address for this network interface in the local DHCP server.

To complete this step, review the summary page, shown in Figure 8.8, and click the Confirm button.

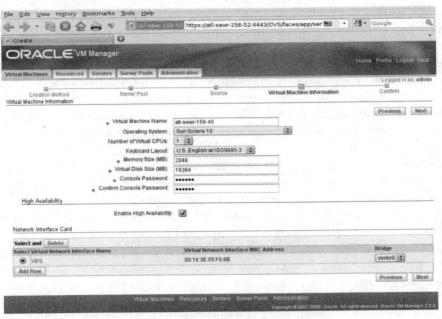

Figure 8.8 Virtual Machine Information

8.3.2.4 Step 4: Provisioning the Oracle Solaris Virtual Machine

At this point, Oracle VM will begin the provisioning process for this VM. Refresh the Oracle VM Manager screen to follow its progress. Figure 8.9 shows the status of the partially installed guest. Once the Oracle VM Manager Virtual Machine indicates that the VM is running, click the Console button to initiate a VNC connection to the console of the VM.

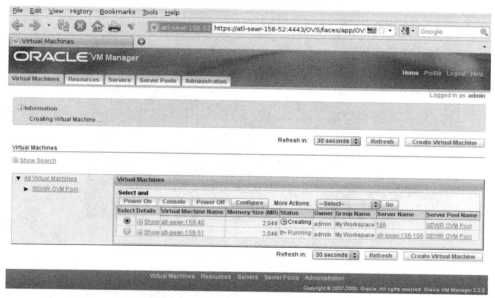

Figure 8.9 Oracle Solaris Virtual Machine

8.3.2.5 Step 5: Performing an Oracle Solaris Interactive Installation

Oracle VM Manager includes a Java-based VNC client. This built-in client provides a relatively low-resolution display—a lower resolution, in fact, than is used for the standard Solaris desktop, and one that limits the visibility of the entire Solaris desktop. In addition to the built-in-VNC client, you can use any other VNC client of your choosing. Click the Show link in the Details column for the virtual machine to find out which VNC port to use. Connect to that port on the server listed in the Server Name column. Although the widely used `vncviewer` may provide an even better experience than the Java VNC client based on its higher screen resolution, the Java client is always available.

Once you connect via VNC using the password you selected earlier as the console password, you are presented with a standard Solaris interactive installation, as shown in Figure 8.10. As a best practice, use the Interactive Text (Console Session) selection to realize the most efficient installation experience. While it is possible to do a graphical installation via VNC, it can be an unsatisfactory experience, especially with a slow network connection.

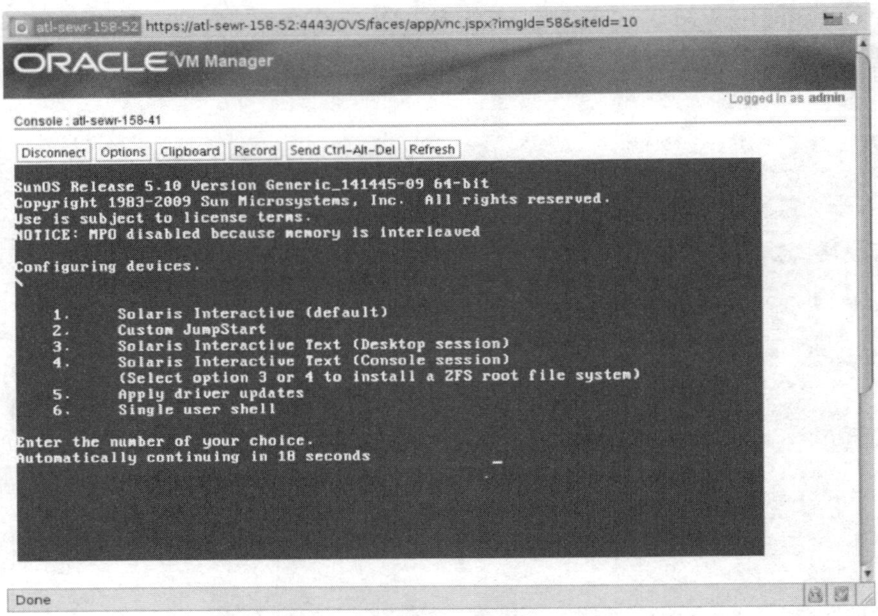

Figure 8.10 Oracle Solaris Interactive Installation

Network devices are not discovered during the installation of Solaris with Oracle VM 2.2. As a consequence, during the interactive installation, no network questions will be asked, addresses will not be assigned, and naming services will not be assigned. Additionally, because no networks are discovered, Solaris JumpStart cannot be used to install the virtual machine. Also, the data for the actual installation cannot be fetched via HTTP or NFS; it must be read from the installation media. Once a single virtual machine has been created, it can be used as a template and instantiated with different qualities as many times as required and much more rapidly than is possible for even a network installation. This limitation during installation does not mean that there will never be network access to the VM. In fact, after the virtual machine is installed, network access can be enabled.

If the installation boot archive included both fully virtualized and paravirtualized drivers, there is no need to change the network type after the installation. This practice allows for network-based installation because networks will be discovered automatically when the VM boots at the beginning of the installation.

8.3.2.6 Step 6: Reconfiguring the Network Interface

After the installation is complete, a few steps remain to create a fully functional Solaris 10 guest VM. Most important among these steps for Solaris 10 10/09 is to reconfigure the network interface and make it available to the VM.

Once the installation process has completed, Oracle VM will shut down the guest. Select Power On for the virtual machine and use VNC to connect again to the console. When you power on the VM using the Oracle VM Manager, Solaris will go through its typical first boot process—importing all of the SMF manifests, discovering devices, asking for information about the connected keyboard, and then presenting a graphical login. Note that when the graphical console is presented via the Java VNC client, it is clipped on the right and bottom of the display, because the display area provided by the Java VNC client is not as large as that of the default Solaris screen. Using `vncviewer` gets around this problem. Once you have logged in, open a terminal window.

During the first boot after installation, the kernel was unable to find any network devices. The Oracle VM Server presents its virtual networks as instances of the fully virtualized `rtls` network driver to the guest by default. However, Oracle Solaris comes with paravirtualized drivers for network and disk installed instead. To configure the network after Solaris is running, we must cause it to abandon its current network configuration, change the virtual network interface to a paravirtualized interface, and then reboot and rediscover the network.

To do so, the VM must be rebooted and new VM identification information, including the networking parameters, must be discovered. The simplest way to achieve this goal is to issue the `sys-unconfig` command on the VM. The `sys-unconfig` command causes Solaris to "forget" its identity and shut down. Figure 8.11 shows the Solaris 10 user interface and the `sys-unconfig` command.

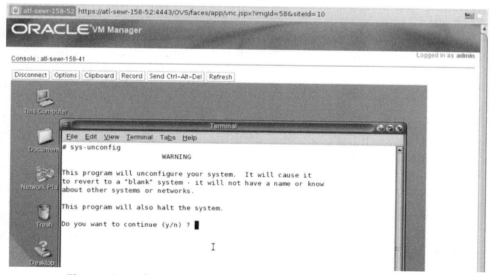

Figure 8.11 Reconfiguring Oracle Solaris After Installation

Once the VM is shut down, it will prompt you for a keystroke to reset the VM. At this point, you can use the Oracle VM Manager console to power off the VM, as shown in Figure 8.12.

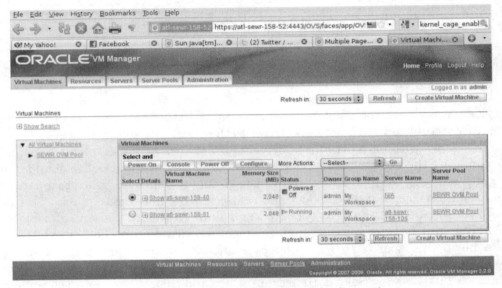

Figure 8.12 Power Off VM for Reconfiguration

When the VM has been powered off, it can be reconfigured. Select the VM from the list and click the Configure button, or just click the name of the VM you want to configure. Either way, you will be taken to the configuration screen.

In the configuration screen shown in Figure 8.13, you can change many of the characteristics of the VM: the number of CPUs, the amount of memory, the network configuration, additional attached disks, and more. We simply want to change the network interface from fully virtualized to paravirtualized. Select the Network tab (between the General and Storage tabs), which takes you to the network configuration panel.

Select Paravirtualized as the Network Type. Notice that when you make this choice, the network type changes from `ioemu` to `netfront`, as shown in Figure 8.14.

Return to the General tab and click Save. Then return to the Virtual Machines panel, select the VM, and click Power On to start the VM. Connect to its console.

Because we used `sys-unconfig` to unconfigure the VM, the VM will prompt for network and naming service identification as it boots. Once it has identified the network, it will reboot a final time. When the VM comes up this time, it will be fully installed and running on the network.

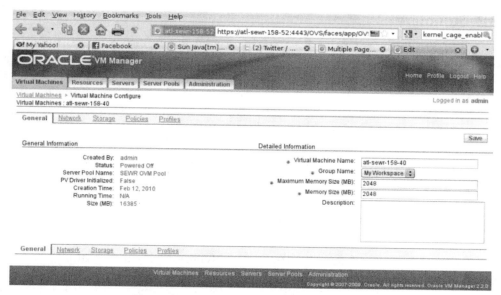

Figure 8.13 VM Configuration Screen

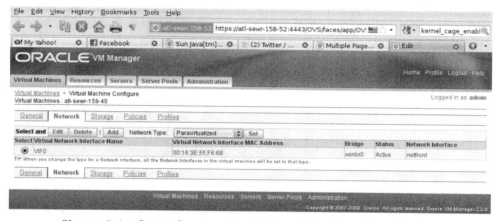

Figure 8.14 Reconfiguring the Network for Paravirtualization

Once the VM has been rebooted, it is ready to be used. At this point, you can also use it as an Oracle VM Manager template from which to instantiate multiple virtual machines. Likewise, before the VM is powered on again, the CPU and memory configuration can be modified as desired. These changes are described in the Oracle VM 2.2 documentation collection at `http://download.oracle.com/docs/cd/E15458_01/index.htm`.

8.3.3 Summary

Oracle VM Server for x86 provides an enterprise-grade hypervisor solution for x86 systems. It does so by combining Oracle VM Server with the Oracle VM Manager provisioning and management interface. Oracle VM supports a number of operating systems as guests, including Oracle Solaris 10. Creation of a Solaris 10 VM is a straightforward process involving installation of the operating system from standard installation media. Small customizations are required when the VM is first booted to enable the network and to ensure that the correct device drivers are used for disk and network access. Once the VM has been created, it can be used to create a template for subsequent Solaris 10 virtual machines or used directly.

8.4 How to Enable xVM Hypervisor Live Migration

An important feature of most virtualization technologies is the ability to move running virtual machines from one physical server to another with no impact to end users. This feature can provide a zero-downtime environment and increase both availability and flexibility. Live migration is useful in the case of a required downtime maintenance window where operating system patching or a hardware swap must be carried out on a target server. Any running virtual machine can be moved to another server and then moved back once the maintenance window has completed, without current users suffering any effects.

Here, using the steps described and the Technical Briefs referenced next, we discuss how to enable the live migration feature within xVM hypervisor and migrate an Oracle Solaris 10 x86 guest from one server to another while it runs. The three Technical Briefs are available as part of the OpenSolaris documentation repository at `http://hub.opensolaris.org/bin/view/Community+Group+xen/docs`.

8.4.1 Technical Briefs

The technical briefs have the following titles:

- How to Install OpenSolaris 2009.06 xVM hypervisor and Use It to Configure Domains
- How to Configure and Use ZFS-hosted iSCSI Guest Storage Within the xVM Hypervisor (Part 1)
- How to Configure and Use ZFS-hosted iSCSI Guest Storage Within the xVM Hypervisor (Part 2)

The Technical Briefs also discuss the use of key Solaris features with xVM hypervisor such as ZFS and iSCSI.

Other useful documentation that describes xVM hypervisor is available at `http://docs.sun.com/app/docs/doc/819-2450/gefwp?a=view`.

8.4.2 Live Migration Prerequisites

The live migration prerequisites include the following:

- Both servers are installed with OpenSolaris 2009.06 x86.
- Both servers are able to access the Internet to enable the downloading of OpenSolaris packages.
- Both the source server and the target server are on the same subnet.
- The source and the target x86 servers have the same CPU model and type.
- Both servers are running the same release of the xVM hypervisor software, which means they must have the same version of OpenSolaris—in our case, 2009.06.
- Sufficient CPU and memory resources exist on the target server to host the migrating guest domain.
- The target dom0 has the same network interface as the source dom0 network interface used by the guest domain. For example, if the guest domain to be migrated has a Virtual Network Interface (VNIC) that is bridged over the e1000g0 interface on the source dom0, then the target dom0 must also have the e1000g0 interface.
- The source and target servers are both able to access a shared NFS resource on a single subnet.

8.4.3 Step 1: Configuring the xVM Hypervisor

The following steps should be performed on both servers.

1. Create and mount a new boot environment.

```
# /usr/sbin/beadm create -a -d 'xVM hypervisor' xvm
# /usr/sbin/beadm mount xvm /mnt/xvm
# /usr/sbin/beadm list
BE          Active Mountpoint Space Policy Created
--          ------ ---------- ----- ------ -------
opensolaris N      /          24.5K static 2010-02-18 11:36
xvm         R      /mnt/xvm   3.14G static 2010-02-18 13:24
```

2. Install the xVM hypervisor packages.

```
# /usr/bin/pkg -R /mnt/xvm install xvm-gui
DOWNLOAD                          PKGS       FILES      XFER (MB)
Completed                          8/8      637/637     8.94/8.94


PHASE                          ACTIONS
Install Phase                   906/906
```

Unmount the new boot environment.

```
# /usr/sbin/beadm umount xvm
```

3. Configure the new boot environment.

Edit the /rpool/boot/grub/menu.lst file so that it contains the following entries:

```
title xVM hypervisor
findroot (pool_rpool,0,a)
bootfs rpool/ROOT/xvm
splashimage /boot/solaris.xpm
foreground d25f00
background 115d93
kernel$ /boot/$ISADIR/xen.gz
module$ /platform/i86xpv/kernel/$ISADIR/unix /platform/i86xpv/kernel/$ISADIR/unix
-B $ZFS-BOOTFS,console=text
module$ /platform/i86pc/$ISADIR/boot_archive
```

Note

The code from `module$` to `console=text` is a single line.

Ideally, dom0 memory should be limited. For example, if there is 4 GB of physical memory, allocate 1 GB for dom0. The setting dom0_mem=1G should be appended to the kernel boot line, as in this example:

```
kernel$ /boot/$ISADIR/xen.gz dom0_mem=1G
```

If this setting is applied, dom0 will see only 1 GB of RAM. The additional 3 GB of RAM is still available for use by guests, but not by dom0.

Limiting the memory of dom0 in this way prevents problems when the system is under memory pressure and minimizes the interaction between the hypervisor and the dom0 balloon process.

A *balloon process* is a thread within the dom0 kernel that works with the hypervisor to dynamically grow and shrink the amount of memory within a domain (dom0 or domU). It is useful in reclaiming unused memory or allocating additional memory within a domain. Reclaiming unused memory is called a *balloon down event*. Not all domain memory is available to be reclaimed, however. For example, the memory may be in use.

When dom0 starts, the kernel allocates many structures related to the size of the available memory. If a large amount of memory is available, then these structures will consume more memory. If a balloon down event occurs for dom0, those structures cannot be freed; thus that memory is wasted. Furthermore, if the hypervisor tries to reclaim domain memory below the level at which memory in use would be affected, then the operation will fail, which will affect system performance.

If the mem setting shown earlier is applied, dom0 will see only 1 GB RAM. The remaining memory can then be used for guests.

4. Verify that the new boot environment is set.

```
# /usr/sbin/bootadm list-menu
The location for the active GRUB menu is:
/rpool/boot/grub/menu.1st
default 1
timeout 30
0 OpenSolaris 2009.06
1 xVM hypervisor
```

The entry number listed as the default menu item should correspond to the menu item for the xVM hypervisor. In this case, the default menu item is number 1, and that menu item is xVM hypervisor. As a consequence, the xVM hypervisor will be booted by default.

If the hypervisor does not boot, change the default menu item by running the following command:

```
# /usr/sbin/bootadm set-menu default=1
```

5. Reboot into the new boot environment.

```
# /usr/sbin/reboot
```

6. Start and check the xVM hypervisor services.

```
# /usr/sbin/svcadm enable -r xvm/virtd ; svcadm enable -r xvm/domains
# /usr/bin/svcs -a|grep -i xvm
disabled        14:28:42 svc:/system/xvm/ipagent:default
online          14:28:40 svc:/system/xvm/vnc-config:default
```

continues

```
online          16:13:14 svc:/system/xvm/store:default
online          16:13:15 svc:/system/xvm/xend:default
online          16:13:16 svc:/system/xvm/console:default
online          16:13:16 svc:/system/xvm/virtd:default
online          16:13:16 svc:/system/xvm/domains:default
```

7. Check the network configuration.

By default, the hypervisor tools will use the first available NIC when creating
guest domains. This link can be determined by examining the output of
`dladm show-link`:

```
# /usr/sbin/dladm show-link
LINK            CLASS       MTU     STATE       OVER
e1000g0         phys        1500    up          --
e1000g1         phys        1500    unknown     --
e1000g2         phys        1500    unknown     --
e1000g3         phys        1500    unknown     --
```

To override the default on a system-wide basis, set the `config/default-nic`
property of the `svc:/system/xctl/xend:default` service instance by
using the `svccfg` command:

```
# /usr/sbin/svccfg -s xend 'setprop config/default-nic = astring: "e1000g0"'
```

Refresh, restart, and check the service:

```
# /usr/sbin/svcadm refresh xvm/xend;
/usr/sbin/svcadm restart xvm/xend
# /usr/sbin/svccfg -s xvm/xend listprop
config/default-nic  config/default-nic  astring  e1000g0
```

8.4.4 Step 2: Configure Access to a Shared NFS Resource

A shared NFS resource is required for migration of xVM hypervisor virtual machines. In this example, an NFS share called `/images/nfs` is available on the
NFS server with IP address 217.30.123.101. To make this resource available on
each server, the following steps should be performed on both servers.

1. Create a mount point `/nfs`.

```
# /usr/bin/mkdir -p /nfs
```

2. Mount the NFS share `217.30.123.101:/images/nfs` on both servers.

```
# /usr/sbin/mount -F nfs -o forcedirectio 217.30.123.101:/images/nfs /nfs
# /usr/bin/mkdir -p /nfs/dumps
```

For performance reasons, the `forcedirectio` option is used to disable any buffering in the client. The NFS share `/nfs` will contain the guest backup data.

8.4.5 Step 3: Create an Oracle Solaris 10 HVM+PVIO Guest

The installation of a Solaris 10 HVM+PVIO guest uses an ISO image file as the install source and the shared NFS resource `/nfs` as the guest image location. The ISO image for this install `s10x86.iso` is located in the directory `/iso`.

1. Configure graphical access to HVM consoles for installs. This configuration is needed for any server that will create HVM guests.

```
# /usr/sbin/svccfg -s xvm/xend setprop config/vncpasswd = astring: newroot
# /usr/sbin/svcadm refresh xvm/xend; /usr/sbin/svcadm restart xvm/xend
# /usr/sbin/svccfg -s xvm/xend setprop config/vnc-listen = astring: 0.0.0.0
# /usr/sbin/svcadm refresh xvm/xend; /usr/sbin/svcadm restart xvm/xend
```

The `newroot` string is used as the password for VNC guest console access.

Now that the VNC session used for the installation has been configured, it is time to create and install the virtual machine. Perform the following steps on only one server.

2. Issue the following commands:

```
# /usr/bin/virt-install -n solaris10HVM --hvm -r 1024 -f \
/nfs/s10hvm.img -os-type=solaris -os-variant=solaris10 -s 10
--vnc -l /iso/s10x86.iso
```

Options for the `virt-install` command include the following choices:

`-n <value>` Name of the guest. This is not the guest operating system host name.

`-l <value>` Installation source for a guest, ISO location, or CD-ROM path.

`-r <value>` Memory to allocate for the guest instance (in megabytes).

`-f <value>` Image file to use as the disk image location.

`-s <value>` The size in gigabytes of the guest disk, in raw image format.

`--vnc` VNC will be used for graphical access to the guest.

`--hvm` The guest is fully virtualized.

The installation will start and a `vncviewer` session will be opened.

3. Log in using the password `newroot` set in the previous step.

4. Install Oracle Solaris 10 by following the procedure for a physical server. Documentation is available at `http://docs.sun.com/app/docs/prod/solaris.10?l=en&a=view`.

8.4.6 Step 4: Configure and Enable Live Migration

To configure and enable live migration, follow these steps:

1. Before configuring live migration, any running guests must be shut down on both servers using the following commands:

```
# /usr/bin/virsh list --all
  Id Name                    State
----------------------------------
  0 Domain-0                running
  4 solaris10HVM            running

# /usr/bin/virsh shutdown solaris10HVM
Domain solaris10HVM is being shutdown

# /usr/bin/virsh list --all
  Id Name                    State
----------------------------------
  0 Domain-0                running
  - solaris10HVM            shut off
```

2. Run the following commands on both servers to enable live migration:

```
# /usr/sbin/svccfg -s xend setprop \
config/xend-relocation-address = \"\"
```

The `xend-relocation-address` field is the address to which `xend` listens for relocation requests. If it is blank or not present, all interfaces are used. In the preceding code, it is set blank, so all interfaces are used. In an enterprise configuration, it would be expected that a separate network would be required to separate live migration traffic from the guest traffic.

```
/usr/sbin/svccfg -s xend setprop \
config/xend-relocation-hosts-allow = \"^server1$ ^localhost$\"
```

The `xend-relocation-hosts-allow` field is a space-separated list of regular expressions. If the host name of a system matches any one of the given regular expressions, it is allowed to connect and interact with the relocation server if the server has been enabled by the `xend-relocation-server` property. The default is `^localhost$`. The host names contained within the preceding command must be known to the host, which means they must be contained within the `/etc/inet/hosts` file or accessible via DNS or LDAP. In this case, `xend` will listen for relocation requests only from `server1` and from the local host. Each server in the pool must be configured to listen for relocation requests from other nodes in the pool.

Here is sample output of the `xend-relocation` fields for `server1`:

```
# /usr/sbin/svccfg -s xend listprop config/xend*
config/xend-relocation-server         boolean   true
config/xend-unix-server               boolean   true
config/xend-relocation-address        astring
config/xend-relocation-hosts-allow    astring   "^server2$ \ ^localhost$"
```

Here is sample output of the `xend-relocation` fields for `server2`:

```
# /usr/sbin/svccfg -s xend listprop config/xend*
config/xend-relocation-server         boolean   true
config/xend-unix-server               boolean   true
config/xend-relocation-address        astring
config/xend-relocation-hosts-allow    astring   "^server1$ \ ^localhost$"
```

If any of the `xend-relocation` fields has been changed, a restart of `xend` is required using the following command:

```
# /usr/sbin/svcadm refresh xend && /usr/sbin/svcadm restart xend
```

3. On all servers, check whether any guests need restarting by entering the following commands:

```
# /usr/bin/virsh list --all
 Id Name                    State
-----------------------------------
  0 Domain-0                running
  - solaris10HVM            shut off

# /usr/bin/virsh start solaris10HVM
Domain solaris10HVM started

# /usr/bin/virsh list --all
 Id Name                    State
-----------------------------------
  0 Domain-0                running
  4 solaris10HVM            running
```

4. Demonstrate live migration of the `solaris10HVM` guest from `server1` to `server2` by entering the following command:

```
# /usr/sbin/xm migrate --live solaris10HVM server2
```

5. On the target server, access the console of the guest, after determining the VNC port number:

```
# /usr/bin/virsh vncdisplay solaris10HVM
:0
# /usr/bin/vncviewer :0 &
```

8.4.7 Summary

Using the steps described here, the referenced Technical Briefs, and other documentation, we are able to achieve the following:

Step 1: Install OpenSolaris 2009.06 and configure the xVM hypervisor.

Step 2: Configure access to a shared NFS resource.

Step 3: Create a Solaris 10 HVM guest on an NFS shared resource.

Step 4: Configure and enable the xVM hypervisor live migration between two x86 servers.

8.5 Running Microsoft Windows in an Oracle Solaris Container

Solaris Containers are a very efficient way to consolidate Oracle Solaris server workloads, and are flexible enough to be used for additional purposes. Oracle VM VirtualBox software can run in a Container when running Solaris on x86 systems, making it possible to apply the benefits of Containers to guest virtual machines running other operating systems. With this approach, Windows and Linux applications can be safely and conveniently run on the same server or desktop system running Solaris applications (see Figure 8.15). The guest applications can take advantage of the isolation and resource controls of Containers as well as other Solaris features such as ZFS and Trusted Extensions.

This type of consolidation need not be limited to server workloads. Notably, the built-in RDP capabilities of VirtualBox make it possible to use this technique for desktop consolidation as well.

In this example we will create a Container configured for just one application: a VirtualBox guest running Windows XP in headless mode. Once the guest is configured, it will be started automatically when the Container boots by placing a script in the directory `/etc/rc.d`.

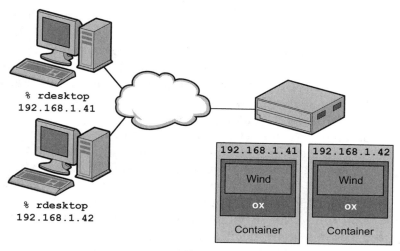

Figure 8.15 Running Remote Windows Desktops or
Applications in Oracle Solaris Containers

This example uses concepts and features described in Chapter 5, "Oracle VM VirtualBox," and Chapter 6, "Oracle Solaris Containers."

The command examples in this section use the prompt `GZ#` to indicate a command that must be entered by the root user in the global zone. The prompt `winxp-desktop1#` shows that a command will be entered as the root user of the Container named `winxp-desktop1`. The prompt `%` precedes a command that is run by a nonprivileged user.

8.5.1 Planning

This example assumes that Solaris 10 10/09 has been installed as the host operating system and that VirtualBox has been installed in the global zone.

In this example, each Container will run a single VirtualBox guest. A remote system will access the desktop using the built-in VirtualBox RDP server. Because only a single guest is present, the network configuration is greatly simplified: Each Container has a single IP address, and the VRDP server listens to the default port number 3389. If we want to run a second desktop session, we can clone the Container and the second user can connect to the same default port number but with the cloned Container's new IP address.

It would also be a good idea to place the Container's `zonepath` inside a ZFS file system. Should a second similar desktop be desired, creating the additional Container will be faster and consume less storage because cloning a ZFS data set takes less time than copying all of the content beneath `zonepath`.

The configuration of the Container itself is straightforward, with the only difference being the addition of the VirtualBox control device /dev/vboxdrv. To reduce the total storage required, we will use a sparse-root zone, as described in Chapter 6. Because running a VirtualBox guest as the root user is discouraged, we must create a regular user account to configure and run the VirtualBox guest. Once the guest is installed, this account would be used only to make changes to the guest configuration, such as adding more storage.

Once the Container is installed and properly configured, we must create the VirtualBox guest and install the operating system, as described in Chapter 5. In our example, an ISO image library with the Microsoft Windows XP installation media is already present on the host system in a directory named /iso. This directory will be made available to the Container using a read-only loopback file system.

Because we will run Microsoft Windows XP in our guest machine, a few of the VirtualBox settings may need modification. The host is a relatively modern x86 system with hardware virtualization features enabled in the BIOS. We will also enable those features in the guest machine. The recommended network device for Windows XP is the AMD PCNet FAST III. Because this is a desktop guest, we recommend using the NAT feature of VirtualBox for the Container's interface. If it were a server, bridged mode would be more appropriate, but would require the Container to be configured as exclusive IP. Finally, for efficiency, we use a SATA boot disk instead of the standard IDE configuration.

8.5.2 Configuring the Oracle Solaris Global Zone

To roughly mimic the performance of a single-CPU PC, we will use a CPU cap for this exercise. Each Container will start off with a cap of 1.00 CPU. This limit can be dynamically adjusted from the global zone later, if required.

Because the Container will include our VirtualBox user's home directory, including all of the guest's disk images, we will place the Container in a ZFS pool that has enough space to hold the data. In this example, a pool named pandora has sufficient free disk space for our needs. We can easily create the ZFS file system for our Container.

```
GZ# zfs create -o mountpoint=/zones pandora/zones
```

Now we are ready to configure and install the VirtualBox Container.

8.5.3 Creating the Container

We begin by creating the Container's configuration. Refer to Chapter 6 for the details of each setting. The Windows Container, named winxp-desktop1, has a single IP address: 192.168.1.41.

```
GZ# zonecfg -z winxp-desktop1
winxp-desktop1: No such zone configured
Use 'create' to begin configuring a new zone.
zonecfg:winxp-desktop1> create
zonecfg:winxp-desktop1> set zonepath=/zones/winxp-desktop1
zonecfg:winxp-desktop1> add fs
zonecfg:winxp-desktop1:fs> set dir=/iso
zonecfg:winxp-desktop1:fs> set special=/iso
zonecfg:winxp-desktop1:fs> set options=[ro,nosuid,nodevices]
zonecfg:winxp-desktop1:fs> set type=lofs
zonecfg:winxp-desktop1:fs> end
zonecfg:winxp-desktop1> add device
zonecfg:winxp-desktop1:device> set match=/dev/vboxdrv
zonecfg:winxp-desktop1:device> end
zonecfg:winxp-desktop1> add net
zonecfg:winxp-desktop1:net> set physical=e1000g0
zonecfg:winxp-desktop1:net> set address=192.168.1.41/24
zonecfg:winxp-desktop1:net> end
zonecfg:winxp-desktop1> add capped-cpus
zonecfg:winxp-desktop1:capped-cpus> set ncpus=1
zonecfg:winxp-desktop1:capped-cpus> end
zonecfg:winxp-desktop1> verify
zonecfg:winxp-desktop1> exit
```

Once the Container configuration is complete, install the Container with the following command:

```
GZ# zoneadm -z winxp-desktop1 install
A ZFS file system has been created for this zone.
Preparing to install zone <winxp-desktop1>.
Creating list of files to copy from the global zone.
Copying <2939> files to the zone.
Initializing zone product registry.
Determining zone package initialization order.
Preparing to initialize <1435> packages on the zone.
Initialized <1435> packages on zone.
Zone <winxp-desktop1> is initialized.
Installation of these packages generated errors: <CSWisaexec SUNWvbox>
The file </zones/winxp-desktop1/root/var/sadm/system/logs/install_log> contains a log of
the zone installation.
```

To simplify the configuration of the Container, we will supply a `sysidcfg` file containing the answers to all of the first boot questions. This file must be placed in the `/etc` directory of the Container before it is booted for the first time. In this example, the Container's root password will be changeme—which would be a very good idea once the Container is running.

```
GZ# cat > /zones/winxp-desktop1/root/etc/sysidcfg <<EOF
system_locale=C
terminal=dtterm
network_interface=NONE { hostname=winxp-desktop1 }
security_policy=NONE
name_service=NONE
nfs4_domain=domain.com
timezone=US/Central
root_password=Yy5CKNb6aROmU
EOF

GZ# zoneadm -z winxp-desktop1 boot
GZ# zlogin -C winxp-desktop1
[Connected to zone 'winxp-desktop1' console]

[NOTICE: Zone booting up]

SunOS Release 5.10 Version Generic_141445-09 64-bit
Copyright 1983-2009 Sun Microsystems, Inc. All rights reserved.
Use is subject to license terms.
Hostname: winxp-desktop1
. . .
winxp-desktop1 console login:
```

8.5.4 Creating the Oracle VM VirtualBox Guest Machine User

The next step is to log into the Container and create the user that will run the VirtualBox guest. In this example, the user and group numbers will be chosen automatically. In contrast, in an enterprise deployment, the group and user numbers should be provided by an identity management system.

```
GZ# zlogin winxp-desktop1
winxp-desktop1# mkdir -p /export/home/vboxuser
winxp-desktop1# groupadd vboxuser
winxp-desktop1# useradd -g vboxuser -m -d /export/home/vboxuser -s \
               /bin/bash -c "VirtualBox Guest User" vboxuser
winxp-desktop1# passwd vboxuser
password: {enter a new password, which will not be echoed}
Re-enter new Password:
{reenter the password}
passwd: password successfully changed for vboxuser
```

8.5.5 Configuring the Windows Guest Machine

Once the Container is running, the next step is to create the guest machine. Log in to the Container as `vboxuser` and perform the guest configuration. This is nearly identical to the process described in Chapter 5.

```
% VBoxManage createvm --name "Windows XP" --ostype WindowsXP_64 --register
Virtual machine 'Windows XP' is created and registered.
UUID: 57c72be5-a466-416b-aea1-03968f84b6a8

Settings file: '/export/home/vboxuser/.VirtualBox/Machines/Windows XP/Windows XP.xml'

% VBoxManage modifyvm "Windows XP" --memory 512 --vram 32 --accelerate3d on \
--audio oss

% VBoxManage storagectl "Windows XP" --name "SATA Controller" \
--add sata --controller AHCI

% VBoxManage createhd --filename "Windows XP.vdi" \
--size 10240 --format VDI --remember

0%...10%...20%...30%...40%...50%...60%...70%...80%...90%...100%

Disk image created. UUID: 388311ed-b303-4405-8689-3dee5abc8f68

% VBoxManage storageattach "Windows XP" --storagectl \
"SATA Controller" --port 0 --device 0 --type hdd --medium \
"Windows XP.vdi"

% VBoxManage storagectl "Windows XP" --name "IDE Controller" \
--add ide --controller ICH6

% VBoxManage openmedium dvd /iso/windows/winxp_sp3_x86.iso

% VBoxManage storageattach "Windows XP" --storagectl "IDE Controller" --port 1
\--device 0 --type dvddrive --medium "/export/iso/windows/winxp_sp3_x86.iso"

% VBoxManage modifyvm "Windows XP" --boot1 dvd --boot2 disk

% VBoxHeadless --startvm "Windows XP"
```

At this point, the guest machine will be booting off the Windows XP installation media. From a remote system, start `rdesktop` and connect to the Container to finish the guest OS installation.

```
% rdesktop 192.168.1.41
WARNING: Remote desktop changed from 800x600 to 640x480.
```

Complete the installation of the Windows XP operating system, including registration and activation as required by your particular licensing arrangements. Once this step is finished, perform the initial customization, such as installing virus protection and firewall software as well as any other applications that will be required for the operation of this desktop.

You should also install the VirtualBox Guest Additions. On the host, these features are found at /opt/VirtualBox/additions/VBoxGuestAdditions. iso. Working as vboxuser in the Container, run the following command to attach them to the guest's DVD device:

```
% VBoxManage storageattach "Windows XP" --storagectl \
"IDE Controller" --port 0 --device 0 --type hdd –medium \
/opt/VirtualBox/additions/VBoxGuestAdditions.iso
```

The Windows XP guest will detect that media has been inserted into the DVD drive and start the guest installation automatically. Once the drivers have been installed, shut down the desktop so that we can complete the last task: making the guest start automatically when the Container is booted.

8.5.6 Creating an Autostart Service for the Guest

The last remaining task is to create a service script that will automatically start the VirtualBox guest when the Container is booted. The script shown here, which is named /etc/init.d/vbox, is a simple method to accomplish this task. To that file, create a hard link named /etc/rc3.d/s99vbox. That will boot the Windows guest at the proper time in the boot sequence of the Container.

```
# cat /etc/init.d/vbox
#!/bin/sh -x

case "$1" in
'restart')
        $0 stop
        $0 start
        ;;

'start')
        su vboxuser -c 'nohup VBoxHeadless --startvm "Windows XP"
>>/var/tmp/vboxguest.log 2>&1 & '
```

```
        ;;

'stop')
        su vboxuser -c 'VBoxManage controlvm  "Windows XP"
acpipowerbutton' >> /var/tmp/vboxguest.log 2>&1
        ;;


*)
        echo "Usage: $0 { start | stop | restart }"
        exit 1
        ;;
esac
```

There are a few things to note about this script. First, it is very basic and could use several improvements, such as checking whether the guest machine is already running before trying to start it. VirtualBox permits only one copy of a machine to run at any time, however, so this change would be more cosmetic than functional. Second, the stop method performs a safe shutdown of the guest using the ACPI power button signal. Another choice of a hard stop might seem like an improvement, but because the Container is running only a single application, this can be accomplished by just shutting down the Container. Third, for monitoring purposes, all command output is logged in /var/tmp/vboxguest.log. Only the guest start and stop commands are logged, so this file should not grow excessively large over time.

8.5.7 Cloning the Windows Container

Now that we have gone through all of the configuration steps to get our Windows XP desktop in a Container, what about adding a second or third desktop? Because all of the configuration data, including the guest disk images, is stored in the Container, all we must do is clone the Container and voila!—we have a second desktop exactly like the first. Because we carefully planned to keep all of the necessary data in ZFS, cloning a desktop in this way is easy and fast.

As described in Chapter 6, a cloned Container starts with a configuration. In this case we will use our existing Container, winxp-desktop1, as a template. We can simply change the location of the zonepath and IP address of the new Container. The following command sequence does just that. The source Container, winxp-desktop1, must be halted before running these commands.

```
GZ# zonecfg -z winxp-desktop2
winxp-desktop2: No such zone configured
Use 'create' to begin configuring a new zone.
zonecfg:winxp-desktop2> create -t winxp-desktop1
zonecfg:winxp-desktop2> set zonepath=/zones/winxp-desktop2
zonecfg:winxp-desktop2> select net physical=e1000g0
zonecfg:winxp-desktop2:net> set address=192.168.1.42/24
zonecfg:winxp-desktop2:net> end
zonecfg:winxp-desktop2> verify
zonecfg:winxp-desktop2> exit
GZ# zoneadm -z winxp-desktop1 halt
GZ# zoneadm -z winxp-desktop2 clone winxp-desktop1
WARNING: device '/dev/vboxdrv' is configured in both zones.
Cloning snapshot pandora/zones/winxp-desktop1@SUNWzone1
Instead of copying, a ZFS clone has been created for this zone.
grep: can't open /a/etc/dumpadm.conf
```

The warning about /dev/vboxdrv is not an error: this device is shareable and will work as expected. The dumpadm.conf error is cosmetic and not a problem either.

The last step is to provide an identity for our new container. We will use the same sysidcfg method that we used earlier.

```
GZ# cat > /zones/winxp-desktop2/root/etc/sysidcfg <<EOF
> system_locale=C
> terminal=dtterm
> network_interface=NONE { hostname=winxp-desktop2 }
> security_policy=NONE
> name_service=NONE
> nfs4_domain=domain.com
> timezone=US/Central
> root_password=Yy5CKNb6aROmU
> EOF
GZ# zoneadm -z winxp-desktop1 boot
GZ# zlogin -C winxp-desktop1
[Connected to zone 'winxp-desktop2' console]
Reading ZFS config: done.
Creating new rsa public/private host key pair
Creating new dsa public/private host key pair
Configuring network interface addresses: e1000g0.

rebooting system due to change(s) in /etc/default/init

SunOS Release 5.10 Version Generic_142901-02 64-bit
Copyright 1983-2009 Sun Microsystems, Inc.  All rights reserved.
Use is subject to license terms.
Hostname: winxp-desktop2
Reading ZFS config: done.

winxp-desktop2 console login:
```

At this point, we have successfully cloned the original desktop. All of the customizations have been preserved and do not need to be performed again. The new guest machine has started automatically, and we can now connect to it from another `rdesktop` session anywhere on the network.

```
# rdesktop 192.168.1.42
```

It is important to consider the effects of cloning a Container. The clone has the same license keys and registration information as the original. If your license agreement requires installation of a new activation key and subsequent registration, these tasks must be performed before the guest can be used.

8.5.8 Summary

This example highlights several facets of Oracle Solaris virtualization. Every virtualization solution has strengths. This example leverages the ability of VirtualBox to run Windows guests on the highly scalable Solaris OS. It also takes advantage of the fine-grained resource controls of Solaris Containers. As you add virtual desktops to this system, you can change the CPU cap of each one, even as they continue running. Finally, this example demonstrates the ability to use two different virtualization solutions to achieve goals that neither can achieve alone.

8.6 Consolidating with Oracle Solaris Containers

Solaris Containers are excellent environments for consolidating many kinds of applications. For example, consolidating multiple Oracle Solaris web servers into Containers on one system is a straightforward process, but you can also consolidate web servers from other operating systems. Consolidating into Containers provides better isolation and manageability than simply collapsing the contents into one web server. Benefits of using Containers in this situation include workload isolation, comprehensive resource controls, delegated administration, and simple mobility, among others.

This section demonstrates the simplicity of migrating Apache web server environments from multiple Red Hat Enterprise Linux systems to one Solaris 10 system. This example is relatively simple because Apache's configuration files use the same syntax, for any one version, on any UNIX or Linux system.

Nevertheless, slight differences in file system layout must be taken into account during this consolidation. On most Linux distributions, the default location for Apache's configuration file is `/etc/httpd/conf/httpd.conf`, while on Solaris it is `/etc/apache2/httpd.conf`. Further, the default home of web pages is `/var/`

`www/html` on most Linux systems, but is `/var/apache2/htdocs` on Solaris 10 systems.

To further simplify this example, we will assume that the web servers are delivering only static web pages. Migrating scripts might require more effort.

The web servers in our example are equally important. We will use resource controls to ensure that each web server has sufficient and equal access to system resources. Each Container will be assigned 100 CPU shares and allowed to use 1 GB of RAM, 2 GB of virtual memory, and 100 MB of locked memory.

The commands shown in this section assume that the original web servers have been stopped. You can check their status and, if necessary, stop Apache on the original servers with the following commands:

```
# /etc/init.d/httpd status
# /etc/init.d/httpd stop
```

If you must minimize the service outage, you can choose different IP addresses for the Containers and change the DNS maps after you have tested the Containers. If the original Apache servers are part of a single load-balanced configuration, you can perform a rolling upgrade from original systems to new Containers.

In the command examples shown here, the prompt `GZ#` indicates that you should enter the command from a shell running in the global zone. The prompt `web01#` indicates that you should enter the command from a shell running in the nonglobal zone named `web01`.

This example assumes that you are familiar with the content covered in Chapter 6.

8.6.1 Planning

The first step is gathering the necessary information. For our example, there are five web servers, each with its home page in `/webpages/index.html`. These servers are named `web01` through `web05`. The new system, running Oracle Solaris 10, will have five Containers named `web01` through `web05`. Each original system had one IP address: 10.1.1.101 through 10.1.1.105. Those IP addresses will move to their respective Containers, as shown in Figure 8.16.

Each web server has its own NFS file system mount at `/webpages`. For example, the server `web01` mounts the NFS file system `nfsserver:/web01`. This directory is used in the Apache configuration file, `/etc/httpd/conf/httpd.conf`, with the directive

`DocumentRoot "/webpages"`

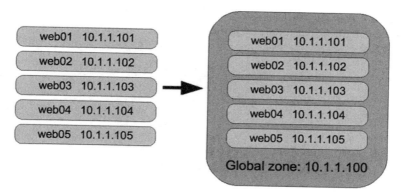

Figure 8.16 Consolidating Web Servers

8.6.2 Configure Oracle Solaris 10

It is possible to enable the Fair Share Scheduler (FSS) as the default scheduler for the system, or for each Container, or any combination of those. However, to effectively assign CPU shares to a Container, you must also make FSS the default scheduler for the system. To make the system boot with FSS as the default scheduler on subsequent reboots, enter this command in the global zone:

GZ# **dispadmin -d FSS**

To change the default scheduler to FSS without rebooting, enter this command:

GZ# **priocntl -s -c FSS -i all**

To immediately make FSS become the default scheduler and be used for all future system boots, you must enter both commands.

8.6.3 Create Containers

After Oracle Solaris 10 is installed on the new system, the process of installing Containers begins with configuring the Containers. Chapter 6 describes the individual commands shown here.

```
GZ# zonecfg -z web01
web01: No such zone configured
Use 'create' to begin configuring a new zone.
zonecfg:web01> create
zonecfg:web01> set zonepath=/zones/web01
zonecfg:web01> add inherit-pkg-dir
```

```
zonecfg:web01:inherit-pkg-dir> set dir=/opt
zonecfg:web01:inherit-pkg-dir> end
zonecfg:web01> set cpu-shares=100
zonecfg:web01> add capped-memory
zonecfg:web01:capped-memory> set physical=1g
zonecfg:web01:capped-memory> set swap=2g
zonecfg:web01:capped-memory> set locked=100m
zonecfg:web01:capped-memory> end
zonecfg:web01> add net
zonecfg:web01:net> set physical=e1000g0
zonecfg:web01:net> set address=10.1.1.101/24
zonecfg:web01:net> end
zonecfg:web01> verify
zonecfg:web01> exit
```

Each of the other four Containers should be configured using the same steps, with appropriate Container names and IP addresses.

You can install the first Container with the following command:

```
GZ# zoneadm -z web01 install
Preparing to install zone <web01>.
Creating list of files to copy from the global zone.
Copying <2898> files to the zone.
Initializing zone product registry.
Determining zone package initialization order.
Preparing to initialize <1098> packages on the zone.
Initialized <1098> packages on zone.
Zone <web01> is initialized.
The file </zones/web01/root/var/sadm/system/logs/install_log> contains a log of the zone
installation.
```

The installation process can take a few minutes. Fortunately, after the first Container is created, you can make copies (clones) of it to speed up the process. Once the Containers have been configured, the cloning process takes just seconds.

```
GZ# zoneadm -z web02 clone web01
Copying /zones/web01...
grep: can't open /a/etc/dumpadm.conf
```

The error message at the end is a cosmetic bug—an error message that should not exist.

The other three Containers can be cloned from web01 with a similar command.

As described in Chapter 6, the first time a Container boots, it assumes that it can ask you for system identification information on the system console. It's usually easier to provide that information via the /etc/sysidcfg file. Recall that if you are working in the global zone, the full path name of that file would be /zones/web01/root/etc/sysidcfg. The following example demonstrates this process, using the correct host name and an encrypted form of the root password you want to use. While copying that file, you can also copy the Apache configuration file from the original web server into the Container's directory structure.

```
GZ# cat /tmp/sysidcfg
system_locale=C
terminal=dtterm
network_interface=NONE { hostname=web01 }
security_policy=NONE
name_service=NONE
nfs4_domain=domain.com
timezone=US/Eastern
root_password=AxtRb9Zd0fNRM
GZ# cp /tmp/sysidcfg /zones/web01/root/etc/sysidcfg
GZ# cd /zones/web01/root/etc/apache2
GZ# scp web01:/etc/httpd/conf/httpd.conf httpd.conf
GZ# cd /
GZ# zoneadm -z web01 boot
GZ# zlogin -C web01
[Connected to zone 'web01' console]

[NOTICE: Zone booting up]

SunOS Release 5.10 Version Generic_141445-09 64-bit
Copyright 1983-2009 Sun Microsystems, Inc. All rights reserved.
Use is subject to license terms.
Hostname: web01
. . .
web01 console login:
```

At this point, you can log in to the Container using zlogin(1M), create a directory /webpages, and add a line to /etc/vfstab that will mount the NFS file system with the web pages. In Container web01, use the following line:

```
nfsserver:/web01    -    /webpages   nfs   -   yes   -
```

This mount will occur automatically the next time the Container boots.

To also mount that NFS file system now, you can use the following command:

```
web01# mount /webpages
```

That form of the mount command will look up the other information in the /etc/ vfstab file.

To enhance security, you may use a read-only mount of the NFS file system. Doing so would prevent a successful intruder from modifying the web page files. If that is an appropriate configuration, you can use this line instead of the one given earlier:

```
nfsserver:/web01    -    /webpages    nfs    -    yes    ro,nosuid
```

The last step for each Container is starting Apache. Additionally, you can modify the IP Filter rules for this Container from the global zone. IP Filter is not discussed in this example.

You can use zlogin to access the Container and start Apache:

```
GZ# zlogin web01
web01# svcadm enable apache2
```

This svcadm command starts Apache immediately, but also tells the Service Management Facility (SMF) to start Apache after the Container boots in the future. The svcadm command is part of SMF. Among other benefits, SMF will restart Apache automatically if it crashes.

8.6.4 Testing

You should now be able to test the Container with a web browser, using its host name or IP address.

8.6.5 Summary

Solaris Containers make it easy to consolidate multiple workloads from separate systems into one system, as there is only one copy of the OS to manage.

8.7 Security Hardening with Oracle Solaris Containers

Server virtualization is commonly used to consolidate multiple workloads onto one computer. But what else is it good for?

Solaris Containers have subtle uses in addition to general-purpose consolidation. These uses rely on a unique combination of features:

- Service Management Facility (SMF) services are configured separately for each Container, allowing you to turn off unneeded services in a Container such as Telnet, FTP, and even SSH, yet still allow secure access from the platform administrator's environment, called the global zone.

- Containers have a strict security boundary that prevents direct inter-Container interaction.

- The immutability of Solaris binaries in a sparse-root Container prevents modification of Oracle Solaris via network-based attacks.

- Privileges granted to a Container are configurable, enabling a platform administrator to further restrict the abilities of a Container, or to selectively enhance the abilities of a Container.

- Resource management controls can be assigned to each Container, allowing the platform administrator to limit the amount of resources that the Container can consume.

How can this combination provide unique functionality?

By default, Containers are more secure than general-purpose operating systems in many ways. For example, even the root user of a Container with a default configuration cannot modify the Container's operating system programs. This limitation prevents Trojan horse attacks that attempt to replace those programs with malicious programs. Also, a process running in a Container cannot directly modify any kernel data, nor can it modify, add, or remove kernel modules such as device drivers. Containers lack the necessary privileges to modify the operating system and its kernel, and there is no mechanism to add privileges to a running Container from within the Container or anywhere else.

By default, a Container cannot modify its own network access. It cannot change either its IP address or its MAC address, and it cannot bring its network interface up or down or change other parameters. It cannot modify or even view its own IP filter rules. Also by default, a Container does not have direct access to devices, nor can it add device access for its processes. All of those limitations thwart tactics used by kernel and user-land rootkits, including ARP and IP spoofing, packet sniffing, and other methods.

Even considering those measures, the ability to selectively remove privileges can be used to further tighten a Container's security boundary. In addition, the ability to disable network services prevents almost all network-based attacks. This feat is very difficult to accomplish in most operating systems without making the system unusable or unmanageable. Without SSH or Telnet service, how would you log in to such a system?

You can combine all of those limitations to achieve *defense in depth*—a strategy conceived by the U.S. National Security Agency to defend computers against unwanted intrusion. Disabling services limits the external attack surface of the Container. An attacker who can take advantage of a weakness in the service being provided, such as web server software, will find that the *internal* attack surface is also very small, because so little of the Container can be modified. If the Container is configured appropriately, an intruder who somehow gains entry cannot access other systems via the network, or can access only a specific list of systems and services provided by those systems.

The combination of the ability to enforce those limitations and the resource controls that are part of the functionality of Containers is very powerful. Collectively, they enable you to configure an application environment that can do little more than fulfill the role you choose for it.

This section describes a method that can be used to slightly expand a Container's abilities, and then tighten the security boundary tightly around the Container's intended application. This section combines individual steps and knowledge from Chapter 6. The example in this section uses the Network Time Protocol (NTP) service. Because this section is intended as a platform for a discussion of security, however, we do not provide a complete description of the configuration of NTP. You can visit http://www.ntp.org to obtain more information about the proper use of NTP. Many other services can be hardened by using this method.

The command examples in this section use the prompt GZ# to indicate a command that must be entered by the root user in the global zone. The prompt timelord# shows that a command will be entered as the root user of the Container named timelord.

8.7.1 Scenario

Imagine that you want to run an application on an Oracle Solaris system but the workload running on this system must not be accessible from the Internet. Further, imagine that the application needs an accurate sense of time, a feat that can be achieved without Containers by using multiple systems and a firewall. With Containers, you can accomplish those goals with one system and offer additional protection as well.

You will need two Containers. One provides a traditional environment for the application, and will not be discussed further in this section. The other one has the ability to change the system's clock, but has been made extremely secure by meeting the following requirements:

- The Container can make outbound network requests and accept responses to those requests.
- The Container does not allow any inbound network requests (even secure ones like SSH).

- The Container can make outbound requests only to a specific set of IP addresses and port numbers associated with trusted NTP servers.
- The Container can set the system's time clock.
- The Container has minimal abilities beside the ones it needs to perform its task.

A Solaris Container can be configured to meet that list of needs.

A Container has its own Service Management Facility (SMF). Most of the services managed by SMF may be disabled if you are limiting the abilities of a Container. The Container that will manage the time clock can be configured so that it does not respond to any inbound network connection requests by disabling all network services. Also, Configurable Privileges enables you to remove unnecessary privileges from the Container, and to add the one nondefault privilege it needs. That privilege is sys_time, which is required to use the stime(2) system call. That system call is the only method that a program can use to modify the system time clock.

Figure 8.17 shows the Container named timelord, the NIC it uses, and the system's time clock, which will be modified by the Container. It also shows a different internal network, plus the Container for the application. The application Container will share the NIC labeled as bge0 with the global zone.

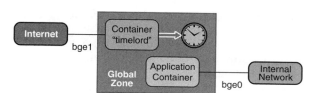

Figure 8.17 A Secure Network Service

8.7.2 Basic Steps

This outline shows the steps to accomplish the goals described earlier in this section. It can be generalized to harden any service, not just an NTP client.

1. Configure a sparse-root Container with a zonepath and zonename, but without any network access yet. This step prevents network attacks while you harden the Container.
2. Install the Container.
3. Add an appropriate /etc/sysidcfg file to the Container.
4. Boot the Container. This automatically configures SMF with default services.

5. Disable unnecessary services.

6. Reboot the Container to verify correct operation without those services.

7. Shut down the Container.

Limit the Container's ability to do undesirable things:

1. Remove unnecessary privileges with the `set  limitpriv` subcommand of `zonecfg`(1M). This step must be performed *after* turning off unnecessary services from within the Container. Some services that we will disable require privileges that will be removed. During the first boot, if a service lacks the privileges it needs, it will fail. Its failure might prevent the Container from booting properly.

2. Identify necessary privileges with `privdebug` (available at `opensolaris. org`). Add nondefault privileges to the Container so that it can fulfill its role.

3. Configure the Container with access to appropriate network interfaces. If possible, this step should be performed *after* services and privileges have been removed to prevent someone from attacking the system while it is in the midst of being hardened.

4. Configure the Solaris IP Filter as necessary to prevent unwanted network access. IP filter settings for a Container using shared-IP access are configured from the global zone. An exclusive-IP Container manages its own IP filter settings. This example uses shared-IP network access.

5. Boot the Container.

6. Configure the Container to run the application.

8.7.3 Implementing Hardened Containers

Chapter 6 discussed the commands that create and boot a Container. The commands in this example assume that the Container already exists and was configured with the following commands:

```
GZ# zonecfg -z timelord
zonecfg:timelord> create
zonecfg:timelord> set zonepath=/zones/roots/timelord
zonecfg:timelord> exit
```

After the Container has been booted and halted once, you can disable unneeded Oracle Solaris services. The `svcadm` command makes that easy, but an even easier method is available: The `netservices`(1M) command enables or disables all

Solaris services that listen to the network except for `sshd`. We will access the Container from the global zone with the `zlogin` command, so we can disable that service as well. The service `rpc/bind` doesn't allow connections, but would show up in a port scan, so we'll disable it, too.

```
GZ# zoneadm -z timelord boot
GZ# zlogin timelord
timelord# netservices limited
timelord# svcadm disable rpc/bind
timelord# svcadm disable ssh
timelord# exit
GZ# zoneadm -z timelord halt
```

The next step is to remove unnecessary privileges. It can be challenging to determine the complete set of privileges needed by a program unless you can exercise all of the code in the program. However, we can make some educated guesses.

We know that this Container will not be using NFS, so we can remove the `sys_nfs` privilege. Also, we choose not to support system accounting or auditing, although we could use those services if we wished. With that choice, we can remove the privileges `sys_audit` and `sys_acct`.

We can use `zonecfg` to remove those three privileges.

```
GZ# zonecfg -z timelord
zonecfg:timelord> set limitpriv=default,!sys_nfs,!sys_audit,!sys_acct
zonecfg:timelord> exit
```

At this point, the Container is configured without unnecessary privileges and without network services. Next, we must discover the privileges needed to run our application. Our first attempt to run the application may succeed. If that happens, there is no need to change the list of privileges that the Container has. If the attempt fails, however, we can determine the missing privileges with `privdebug`, a Perl script.

The `privdebug` script uses the DTrace facility. It watches the kernel verify that processes have the privileges needed to perform privileged operations. When it detects one of these privilege checks, it displays the name of the privilege and the success or failure of the verification. This script will work only within the global zone.

For this example, we will use `ntpdate(1M)` to synchronize the system's time clock with time servers on the Internet. For `ntpdate` to run, it needs network access, which must be enabled with `zonecfg`. As discussed in Chapter 6, the two choices for network configuration are shared-IP and exclusive-IP. For this example, we will use shared-IP to prevent an intruder from successfully modifying the network configuration or launching attacks on other systems.

The following command sequence enables the Container to access the network attached to NIC `bge1`:

```
GZ# zonecfg -z timelord
zonecfg:timelord> add net
zonecfg:timelord:net> set physical=bge1
zonecfg:timelord:net> set address=192.168.0.1
zonecfg:timelord:net> end
zonecfg:timelord> exit
```

This is a good time to configure IP filter rules *for* this Container *from* the global zone. With those rules, you can prevent inbound network access to network ports not used by NTP. You can also prevent outbound network access to systems other than NTP servers if you choose specific NTP servers. Configuring Solaris IP filter rules is outside the scope of this document.

With network access in place, you can discover the list of privileges necessary to run the NTP client. First, boot the Container:

GZ# **zoneadm -z timelord boot**

Wait for the Container to finish booting. Then, in one window, run the `privdebug` script in the global zone:

GZ# **./privdebug.pl -z timelord**

In another window, run the NTP client in the Container:

```
GZ# zlogin timelord
timelord# ntpdate -u 0.pool.ntp.org 1.pool.ntp.org
16 May 13:12:27 ntpdate[24560]: Can't adjust the time of day: Not owner
```

The `privdebug` script displays the following output:

```
STAT PRIV
USED proc_fork
USED proc_exec
USED proc_fork
USED proc_exec
NEED proc_priocntl
NEED sys_time
^C
GZ#
```

The output from `privdebug` shows that the privileges `proc_priocntl` and `sys_time` are requested by `ntpdate`. A quick experiment shows that although `ntpdate` attempts to use `proc_priocntl`, it does not require this privilege to function correctly. The only additional privilege it needs to set the system time clock is `sys_time`.

Use `zonecfg` to modify the Container's privileges:

```
GZ# zonecfg -z timelord
zonecfg:timelord> set limitpriv=default,!sys_nfs,!sys_audit,\
!sys_acct,sys_time
zonecfg:timelord> exit
GZ# zoneadm -z timelord halt
```

While isolating the Container, why not also limit the amount of resources that it can consume? If the Container is operating normally, the use of resource management features is unnecessary, but they are easy to configure and their use in this situation could be valuable. These limits could reduce or eliminate the effects of a hypothetical bug in `ntpdate` that might cause a memory leak or other unnecessary use of resources.

Further, limiting the amount of resources that can be consumed by the Container provides another layer of security in this environment. In particular, resource constraints can reduce or eliminate risks associated with a denial-of-service attack. Note that the use of these features is not strictly necessary. Instead, their use is shown here for completeness, to demonstrate the possibilities.

Chapter 6 described the resource controls available for Containers. Here is a brief explanation of our choices. There are other reasonable choices for this situation.

A few quick tests with `rcapstat(1)` show that the Container needs less than 50 MB of memory to do its job. We could cap the amount of RAM at 50 MB to prevent this Container from consuming an unnecessary amount of RAM, but we also want to prevent it from causing excessive paging. We can prevent a Container from paging by setting the RAM and virtual memory (VM) caps to the same value. However, we don't want to set the VM cap below the amount that is really needed, so we'll be a little generous on both: 100 MB caps for both RAM and VM. A cap on locked memory will further minimize the potential for the Container's processes to disrupt legitimate activities without causing a problem for NTP.

NTP is not a compute-intensive activity, so we will allow it to use one-tenth of the compute capacity of a CPU. Also, capping the number of software threads (lightweight processes [LWPs]) limits the ability to exhaust a fixed resource: process table slots.

```
GZ# zonecfg -z timelord
zonecfg:timelord> add capped-memory
zonecfg:timelord:capped-memory> set physical=100m
zonecfg:timelord:capped-memory> set swap=100m
zonecfg:timelord:capped-memory> set locked=20m
zonecfg:timelord:capped-memory> end
zonecfg:timelord> add capped-cpu
zonecfg:timelord:capped-cpu> set ncpus=0.1
zonecfg:timelord:capped-cpu> end
zonecfg:timelord> set max-lwps=200
zonecfg:timelord> exit
```

Now that we have "shrink-wrapped" the security boundary even more tightly than the default, we're ready to use this Container.

```
GZ# zoneadm -z timelord boot
GZ# zlogin timelord
timelord# ntpdate -u 0.pool.ntp.org 1.pool.ntp.org
16 May 14:40:35 ntpdate[25070]: adjust time server   offset -0.394755 sec
```

The output of ntpdate shows that that it was able to contact an NTP server and adjust this system's time clock by almost 0.4 second.

Experience with privileges can allow you to further tighten the security boundary. For example, if you want to prevent the Container from changing its own host name, you could remove the sys_admin privilege from the Container's limit set. After removing the privilege and rebooting the Container, you can demonstrate the effect:

```
timelord# hostname spacelord
hostname: error in setting name: Not owner
```

We can easily prove that the failure was caused by the missing privilege:

```
timelord# ppriv -e -D hostname spacelord
hostname[4231]: missing privilege "sys_admin" (euid = 0, syscall = 139) needed at
systeminfo+0x139
hostname: error in setting name: Not owner
```

8.7.4 Security Analysis

Many attacks on computers require the ability to take advantage of a security weakness in software that listens to the network. The ability to turn off all such services greatly decreases the security risk. You can also use many of the other features of Oracle Solaris to enhance the security of a Container. Table 8.1 reviews the security features and capabilities used in the example described in this section.

Table 8.1 Security Controls

Security Control	Benefit
IP Filter	Prevents unwanted connection requests from reaching applications; prevents network attacks *from* this Container
Limited network services	Reduces the number of programs listening to network ports
Disabled SSH	Prevents network login
No device access	Prevents ARP and IP spoofing attacks; prevents modification of Physical, Data Link, and Network Layer parameters; prevents access to other networks via other NICs
No device access	Prevents attacks on other types of devices
No kernel access	Prevents attacks on the OS and on other Containers
Sparse-root configuration	Prevents modification of the operating system
Reduced privilege set	Reduces the set of actions that can be performed in the Container
Resource controls	Further limits the ability of processes in this Container to affect other Containers

Before using a security method like the one described in this section, you should validate its ability to handle the types of attacks you want to defend against. The security testing tool Nessus (`http://www.nessus.org/nessus`) was used against the method described in this section and did not find any weaknesses. However, the method described in this section may or may not be suitable for your particular security needs.

8.7.5 Summary

Solaris Containers offer significant security capabilities not available with other virtualization technologies. An understanding of security issues and the features of Containers will help you to balance security and functionality.

8.7.6 Further Reading

You can learn more about the security-related topics discussed in this section at the following web pages:

- The OpenSolaris Immutable Service Containers project can be found at `http://hub.opensolaris.org/bin/view/Project+isc/`. It includes sample configurations and describes methods for autonomic self-assessment, self-cleansing, self-quarantining, self-rollback, and self-destruction.
- The Center for Internet Security describes steps to disable individual Solaris services, including network and non-network services: `www.sun.com/security/docs/CIS_Solaris_10_Benchmark_v4.pdf`
- Glenn Brunette documented the use and hardening of the Solaris NTP service in a three-part BluePrints document:
  - *Part I: Introduction to NTP*:
    `http://www.sun.com/blueprints/0701/NTP.pdf`
  - *Part II: Basic NTP Administration and Architecture*:
    `http://www.sun.com/blueprints/0801/NTPpt2.pdf`
  - *Part III: NTP Monitoring and Troubleshooting*:
    `www.sun.com/blueprints/0901/NTPpt3.pdf`
- "Understanding the Security Capabilities of Solaris Zones Software" by Glenn Brunette and Jeff Victor provides a comprehensive view of security and Solaris Containers:
  `http://wikis.sun.com/display/BluePrints/Understanding+the+Security+Capabilities+of+Solaris+Zones+Software`
- Solaris IP Filter documentation: `http://docs.sun.com/app/docs/doc/816-4554/ipsectm-1?l=en&a=view`
- Privilege Debugging Tool project: `http://hub.opensolaris.org/bin/view/Community+Group+security/privdebug`

8.8 Summary

This chapter provided detailed steps to achieve various goals using Oracle's system virtualization technologies. Many other possible uses exist.

9

Virtualization Management

First there were computers. Data centers soon needed computer management soft-ware, especially as the number of computers grew beyond a handful. As it matured, that software enabled people to manage the entire life cycle of computers and their workloads: asset tracking, operating system (OS) provisioning, OS configuration, OS modification, OS redeployment, application provisioning and configuration, workload assignment and deployment, and resource utilization. Figure 9.1 shows the simplicity of this model.

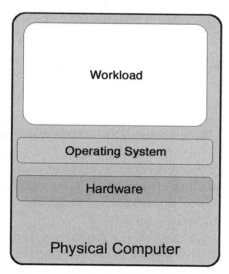

Figure 9.1 Before Virtualization

Then virtualization was created. At first, it was simply a means to consolidate and isolate multiple workloads on one computer. Still, data centers soon needed virtualization management software to cope with the quantity and etherealness of virtual environments (VEs). In many ways, the needs are similar to those of computer management: After all, VEs have life cycles similar to those of computers. To be useful, tools must ease the burden of managing dozens or hundreds of VEs from creation to deletion.

The ease of VE deployment when compared to non-virtualized systems is leading to an explosion of managed entities. It also leads to another level in the hierarchy of those entities, as shown in Figure 9.2.

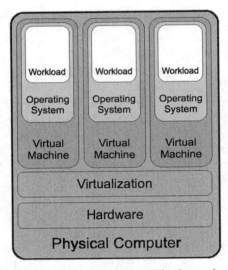

Figure 9.2 Virtualization Adds Complexity

Then an interesting thing happened. People realized that other benefits could be derived from these tools—benefits besides the simple financial efficiencies brought by consolidation. Provisioning VEs became much simpler than provisioning an OS on "bare metal" (directly on the hardware). Taking a snapshot of a VE and moving it across the data center, or to another data center entirely, offered new architectural flexibility, and a new solution to small-scale disaster recovery. All of these abilities, and more, enabled users to focus on the business value that can be derived from virtualization.

This chapter describes the need for virtualization management software in more detail. It begins by discussing life-cycle management for VEs, then explores the newer uses for VE management. Finally, we use Oracle Enterprise Manager Ops Center as an example of such software.

9.1 VE Life-Cycle Management

The economics of "one workload per computer" are, in many cases, difficult to defend—and are the original justification for virtualization. Because of the risk of harmful interaction between two workloads, in certain environments it was necessary for these workloads to be isolated. The deployment of "one workload per VE" has led to an explosion of entities in need of management. Fortunately, software developers have responded with increasingly sophisticated tools for managing these large populations of VEs.

In addition to consolidation and isolation, virtualization increases the separation between workloads and the computer. Virtualization makes it easier to think of a workload and its surrounding software as an object that may be transferred from one bucket to another. This approach, which is called VE migration, was discussed in detail earlier in this book.

9.1.1 Life Cycle of a VE

Like a computer, a VE has a life cycle. It is created, used, monitored and managed, and, ultimately, destroyed. Unlike the life cycle of a workload running on a single physical computer, however, the various stages of the VE life cycle might take place on different computers. Each stage of the life cycle is described in this section.

9.1.1.1 Discover

Existing data centers have many servers, and may already have many VEs. Tracking all of these resources manually is difficult. An automated tool that uses the network to discover computer equipment obviously has value in these circumstances. These systems, and the VEs running on them, are sometimes called "assets" in this context. Understanding the population of existing systems, virtualization platforms, and VEs on the data center floor makes the choice of a home for a new VE much easier.

Data center management (DCM) tools can discover assets via standard protocols such as SNMP and IPMI. Once they have been found, DCM tools aggregate the information so you can view the information and manage those assets.

9.1.1.2 Provision

Once the asset population is understood, you can choose appropriate hardware for future "bare metal" installation of hypervisors or operating systems. Virtualization management tools should also allow you to customize individual platforms or, even better, groups of similar platforms. Such customizations include infrastructure services such as directory services. Existing assets, including virtual ones, should be imported into the DCM framework. The DCM tools should be able to manage the assets after they have been imported.

After the virtualization layer has been deployed on a system, you can provision VEs and customize them to run specific workloads. Resource controls should be applied at this point.

Many workloads run the same software but with different data, or as different phases in the software life cycle. Although maintaining consistency between application instances is important, human error is difficult to avoid in doing so. VE profiles, or templates, can be used to enforce similarities automatically and expedite the provisioning process. A profile can include a choice of OS, configuration of network services such as DNS, and other aspects.

Capacity planning must also be performed before provisioning. If the workload cannot meet the required response time, the deployment can be considered a failure. Fortunately, principles of operational flexibility, discussed later in this chapter, can be used to solve this problem.

9.1.1.3 Update and Report Compliance

All hypervisors, operating systems, and applications are eventually updated with both enhancements and fixes to bugs. Manually tracking the status of dozens of updates to hundreds or even thousands of individual entities can be an impossible task. Data center software is able to reduce this burden significantly by automating many of the processes and verifying the status of updates.

Virtualization complicates the situation by adding another layer of entities on a physical computer. A non-virtualized computer has only one status for an entire OS package. A computer with 16 VEs, however, may have as many as 16 different levels of updates for that one package.

You can use DCM tools to group similar assets and easily perform actions that they all need. For example, three OS updates can be applied to 50 Apache web servers running in 50 VEs spread over 6 computers, all in one operation run from a centralized console. If the DCM tool supports a browser user interface (BUI), it may even be possible to perform this action remotely.

You cannot achieve compliance with data center policies without knowing what is installed on your computers and how they are configured. To this end, DCM tools should provide charts that reveal at a glance which systems and VEs are out of compliance, along with an explanation of the problem. They should also generate compliance reports for archival and for regular audits.

9.1.1.4 Monitor and Audit Usage

Proactive support of computer systems and their workloads requires understanding their current health. A VE's health can be evaluated using current performance characteristics and trends as well as activity patterns and access attempts.

Who is using the VE? Which applications are they running? What is the processing load caused by those applications? Are all of those loads expected and normal, and can the system continue to provide sufficient resources if current trends continue and expected changes occur?

Individual workloads inevitably grow and shrink over time; likewise, the set of workloads on a system changes over time. If you don't monitor the performance characteristics of your systems, you cannot make plans to avert a performance crisis or system failure.

Although most data centers monitor CPU and memory utilization, other measurements are important as well. Current resource utilization provides little insight into the health of the system or VE. A system running at 85% CPU utilization may be providing the response times needed, but one running at 10% may include a workload providing unacceptable performance for reasons unrelated to CPU performance. Further, the bottleneck in the latter case may be either a physical limitation, such as I/O bus rate, or a configured limitation, such as a memory cap.

Consolidated systems, including those with multiple VEs, complicate this situation. Is a VE not meeting the desired response time because system resources are insufficient, or because a resource control is overly aggressive, or because another VE does not have a sufficiently tight resource control? If VEs are owned by different business groups, the initial complaint may come from one group that does not have any visibility into another group's VE, and may simply report that "the system is slow."

Complete monitoring and tracking of resource utilization and transaction times is necessary to diagnose performance problems. DCM tools should gather and store the necessary data so that trends can easily be detected. After all, you can avoid a problem only if you can predict it.

In addition to performance monitoring, tools are needed to detect inappropriate access and take appropriate action. An audit trail is used as a record of accesses, and can aid in the analysis of access patterns as well as intrusions and intrusion attempts.

Some virtualization tools can audit only low-level I/O transactions such as network connections. All other auditing occurs in the VEs, using the existing auditing method of the OS. Other methods, such as operating system virtualization (OSV), can perform auditing of VEs in the OS kernel, not in the VE. An intruder who gains access to the VE would not know that there is an audit trail and, therefore, might be less careful about the evidence being generated.

Recent changes in the computer industry have yielded a heightened awareness of computer systems and their configurations. Conversations about compliance enforcement are now common. One factor contributing to the increased attention being paid to this area has been the lack of automation, which leads to human error in security configuration, system standardization, and auditing.

The industry has responded to these concerns by facilitating automation of system and VE provisioning and updating. The newly introduced tools ease the tasks of standardization, security checks, and detailed compliance reporting. Further, automated workflow tools reduce opportunities for error, reduce the administrative burden, and reduce the elapsed time to provision or update systems.

9.1.1.5 Manage

Ready availability of up-to-date data about VE configurations and health reduces the burden of managing systems. Although consistent, holistic monitoring certainly reinforces proactive management, exceptions are still bound to occur. Having baseline data about activities and performance can simplify and drastically shorten the time needed to diagnose and resolve a problem.

Newer DCM tools support new methods of optimization in the data center. In the past, people avoided activities such as load-balancing workloads across servers because of the difficulty and risk involved. Virtualization provides a layer of separation between the hardware and the VE. This structure makes redeploying a VE (moving it to a different computer) easier because the VE is mapped to a hardware abstraction that is commonly supported on many computers.

Armed with performance data, target performance criteria, and the current assignment of VEs to computers, it is possible to consider regularly balancing the load of VEs across the data center. A detectable service outage may not be necessary.

This process is simplified by consistency of hardware across the data center. With most virtualization technologies, a VE can run on only one CPU architecture, and is usually limited to specific instances of an architecture. In most cases, a pool of computers of similar architecture is grouped so that they are managed as one entity. VEs can be moved within the pool to balance the workload. Guidelines for determining which systems are similar enough to be pooled together and for making assignments of VEs to pools are given in Chapter 7, "Choosing a Virtualization Technology."

Despite the promise inherent in this technology, caution should be exercised when implementing VE migration. This functionality is relatively new to the computer industry, and many people do not have experience with it. Also, few software developers have considered the impact of migrations. Many do not support their applications if VE migration is used.

The business value of VE migration is discussed further in the next section.

9.2 Opportunities for Business Agility and Operational Flexibility

As mentioned earlier, virtualization has led to a new way of viewing a data center and its systems and workloads. Ideally, quick and easy deployment of workloads combined with greater workload mobility will lead to a more flexible compute environment. Let's take a look at the problems and solutions in more detail.

9.2.1 Problems

Data centers have suffered with limitations of computer technology for decades. This section discusses some of those limitations and the problems they cause.

9.2.1.1 Limitations of Physical Computers

Physical computers have several limitations, all tied to the fact that they are physical objects containing components with fixed capabilities. The physical frame has a volume into which a limited quantity of components can be installed. A motherboard or system board is assigned a maximum data rate and minimum latency for transfers between CPU and memory. It also has a maximum quantity of I/O slots for communication with the outside world.

Physical computers do not grow or shrink easily. Ultimately, the ability to change is related to the original cost of the computer: The least expensive computers cannot change at all. Today's netbooks have a single CPU, which is soldered to the motherboard, and I/O is limited to one network port. In contrast, more expensive computers have multiple CPU and/or memory sockets, some of which can be left empty when the system is originally purchased. Even larger systems have multiple motherboards, usually called system boards or CPU boards, that hold CPUs and memory.

Adding a CPU, memory, or I/O controller requires an outage on most systems. Users don't like service outages, so proper planning is strongly recommended if systems administrators decide to take this course.

Even though larger systems can be expanded, at some point every physical computer reaches its maximum performance with a particular workload. Maximum overall system performance is usually limited by one subsystem: compute capacity, memory transfer rate, or storage or network bandwidth. At a certain point, that computer's workload or set of workloads cannot perform better, and it cannot handle additional work. Also, new workloads cannot be added to that system, whether they are in VEs or not.

9.2.1.2 Dynamic Resource Consumption

The resource needs of most workloads are dynamic, growing and/or shrinking over time. Some of these changes are periodic—with the period perhaps being as short as the 9 A.M. to 5 P.M. workday or as long as the quarterly business cycle. Other workloads change in the same direction over time. A primary workload for a growing business will probably grow along with it. Other workloads, especially smaller ones, may change unpredictably as unforeseen events occur.

Single-workload systems can be sized to accommodate the peak processing needs of that one workload. By comparison, capacity planning for consolidated systems is complicated by the need to understand the timing of each workload's processing peaks and troughs. Insufficient planning risks experiencing simultaneous peaks of two workloads, with the possibility of insufficient processing capacity to handle both peaks.

The processing needs of two workloads are either related or unrelated. One example of related workloads comprises the application server and database server of a two-tier or three-tier architecture. Whenever users submit transactions to the application server, that workload then executes database queries. Unrelated workloads tend to peak at different times if their peaks are short.

Some workloads are related, but in subtle ways. For example, two file servers may not interact with each other, yet both may peak at 9:15 A.M. because most workers begin to use their computers at that time.

This knowledge about the relationship between workloads can be used to maximize consolidation density. An example is shown in Figure 1.8. If a computer already has three workloads that peak in the morning, a fourth workload that peaks in the evening may be a good choice for further consolidation and offers the best financial savings.

Nevertheless, some concerns exist with such an approach. Namely, maximizing virtualization density restricts workload mobility. If every computer is configured with a set of workloads that utilize 85% of the system's capacity, migrating one VE to another system may cause unacceptable system behavior. In other words, there isn't a potential destination with enough room for the VE being moved. If a computer is a likely migration target, you should ensure that there is sufficient excess capacity for workloads that might potentially move there.

9.2.1.3 Problems Caused by Dynamic Workloads

Multiple dynamic workloads are more likely to expose the limitations of physical computers described in the previous subsection.

Often a workload grows to consume all of a resource of its physical computer. Its needs continue to grow until the pain is unbearable: Perhaps the impact on sales is noticed, or a sufficiently large number of customers complain, or the platform fails, causing unplanned service outages. Although some computers may originally be purchased with spare capacity, eventually every computer with a growing workload runs out of empty slots for CPUs, memory, and I/O controllers.

When the pain becomes unbearable, employees are assigned the task of identifying a replacement system. This effort may involve middle or executive management, have a significant impact on budgets, and last weeks to months. During that time, the business's revenue may be severely (and negatively) affected by the current system's shortcomings. Customers may begin using a competitor. The loss of these customers—and the associated revenue—may be permanent.

The opposite problem is also possible, although it is typically viewed as an opportunity for improved efficiency: An existing workload does not use all of a physical computer's resources, or its demand on the system has shrunk over time. This situation offers an opportunity to host another workload on the same system (consolidation), requiring workload isolation via virtualization.

The ideal solution is an elastic computer—one that can automatically and immediately grow or shrink to meet the workload's needs. No computer exists that can be scaled infinitely up or down. A growing workload needs a larger computer; a shrinking workload leaves room for another workload. Sometimes a growing workload can be partitioned into smaller workloads, but partitioning requires a service outage. Even when that is possible, at least one portion of the original workload must be moved to a different system.

A critical facet of consolidation, and therefore of virtualization, is resource management. Resource controls must be available to prevent one workload from using so much system capacity—compute capacity, RAM, or I/O capacity—that other workloads suffer. Virtualization can popularize and extend existing methods of resource control and can also enable a new solution: workload mobility.

9.2.2 Virtualization Offers New Opportunities

Today's virtualization technologies go beyond the traditional consolidated system to offer new, exciting opportunities. They can be categorized based on their focus. Some technologies provide business benefits by enhancing business agility and operational flexibility, which are related in some ways. Others achieve business continuity, which is largely a different topic. The next sections explore each of these possibilities.

9.2.2.1 Operational Flexibility

Operational flexibility is the ability to change one or more properties of the environment in which the workload is running. It is the domain of data center teams, and accommodates smaller changes in resource demands. Nevertheless, these changes, if ignored, can affect the response times of that workload or of others.

Resource controls are often used to limit the ability of one workload to consume system resources. They are needed for consolidated systems, to ensure that all workloads have access to appropriate resource capacity.

Imagine a workload that normally requires two CPUs to achieve its desired response time; during the last week of each fiscal quarter, however, it needs four CPUs to complete its tasks. If it is the sole workload on the system, the system must have four CPUs, but two of them will be idle for most of the quarter, wasting the investment in them. In contrast, if this workload is found in one of a few VEs on a larger, eight-CPU system, a resource control can limit the workload to two

CPUs for most of the quarter. When the end of the quarter nears, two more CPUs can be assigned to the VE.

This flexible assignment of resources becomes even more valuable when the unexpected occurs. Continuing with the previous example, a surprisingly successful fiscal quarter might put even more demand on that VE. Upon noticing that four CPUs are not sufficient to handle the workload, a fifth CPU can quickly be assigned to the VE, thereby enabling the VE to complete its task on time. Business-critical workloads will benefit the most from this ability to quickly respond to changes in resource consumption.

Configurable resource controls are necessary to achieve operational flexibility. In many virtualization implementations, these controls may be modified while the VE and its application are running. The resource controls commonly available today were described in Chapter 1, "Introduction to Virtualization," and include exclusive CPU assignment or CPU capacity limits, RAM and virtual memory assignment or limits, process schedulers, and others.

Some virtualization technologies have had resource controls added to them over time. Others have inherited existing, proven technologies. For example, Oracle Solaris Containers take advantage of the resource controls that have been part of Solaris for many years, but also use new controls implemented more recently.

Some of these tools can use other existing features, such as time-based command execution, to make scheduled changes to resource controls. Still other tools can be used to make changes if certain conditions exist. For example, a CPU might be added to a VE's set of CPUs if CPU utilization exceeds a certain threshold. An example of this approach was described in Chapter 6, "Oracle Solaris Containers." Alternatively, if the utilization of all CPUs becomes too high, the virtualization management system might move a VE to a different, under-utilized system. The latter scenario is described later in this chapter, and is part of the topic of workload mobility, which was described in general terms in Chapter 1. Workload mobility relies on virtualization because it takes advantage of the weaker bond between a VE and the hardware on which it runs.

Conversely, data center flexibility can be improved if tools can be used to free up resources that are no longer needed. Those resources can then be used to handle new or growing workloads. In some cases, a workload in a VE might become *less* utilized over time. If it no longer needs all of the RAM assigned to it, the virtualization tools should make it possible to dynamically change the memory assignment or memory cap for that VE without a service outage. This tactic might make room for a new workload, which may be deployed as another VE on the same computer. In contrast, without the flexibility achieved by virtualization, the purchase of a new computer might be necessary to handle the new workload.

Resource controls can certainly improve operational flexibility, but other workload properties can help, too. Physical location can be considered a property of a VE, and many of today's virtualization tools allow this property to be modified. A workload that outgrows the physical constraints of a computer needs a larger computer. Although you could re-implement that workload and its software infrastructure on a different system, that choice would require considerable investment of effort, would probably include many manual steps that provide opportunities for human error, and would require a service outage. New virtualization tools enable you to move the VE to the larger computer with a small service outage—perhaps one short enough that no one would notice. In addition, a very small number of steps are used in this migration process, thereby minimizing the chances for human error.

The economics of the computer industry limit the RAS (reliability, availability, and serviceability) characteristics available on smaller systems. Such low-end systems tend to run small, less important workloads, which do not justify the expense of redundant, hot-swappable components that are not necessary for computation. For example, a server that is sold for $1000 will not include a second redundant $100 power supply.

By comparison, larger, more expensive systems are needed for large business-critical workloads. The business value of these workloads justifies the additional component cost of redundant power supplies. These enhanced RAS features improve the computer's ability to run after suffering a hardware failure—for example, a failed power supply. The value of this type of workload often justifies the additional cost. Multiple CPUs, memory DIMMs, and I/O controllers can also be redundant in this setting. In addition to the value that enhanced RAS offers a single critical workload, these features are more important for a server that will house multiple workloads because more people and business processes are affected by a hardware outage.

Every physical computer has its own properties, so moving a VE from one computer to another can modify many properties at once. Besides increasing physical resources such as CPUs and memory, the VE's new home might also have better RAS characteristics. A workload that was originally unimportant might have been implemented on a small computer with minimal RAS. Over time, that workload might have evolved to become very important, justifying its placement on a more expensive computer with multiple redundant components.

Virtualization, when properly managed, can improve the operational flexibility of a business, providing tools to deal with both expected and unexpected changes in business needs.

9.2.2.2 Business Agility

Business agility is the ability of a business to adapt to changing conditions. In the context of a data center, this concept focuses on the ability to nondisruptively match changing business needs with workloads and changing workload capacity.

The latter topic was discussed previously in terms of "operational flexibility"; in this subsection, we will discuss other facets of business agility.

Consider two businesses vying for a competitive opportunity. In this scenario, the business that can first deploy a service will win the opportunity.

One business plans to purchase a new computer for this service, install an operating system on it, and then deploy the application needed to provide the service. This process will take two to three weeks. The other business has previously prepared for rapid deployment of this application for customers such as this one. It constantly tracks its spare processing capacity, and has a provisioning management system configured to deploy a VE and that application. Service deployment will take two to three *hours*, including customer-specific customizations and data download. Which business will win this opportunity?

In this example, the second business has achieved superior business agility in the data center. Its processes that facilitate accelerated workload provisioning may include one or both of the following:

- Predefined workload templates, sometimes called *profiles*
- Optional "golden master" images of the application and OS, waiting to be copied and used as a VE

Predefined workload templates specify the application needed for a particular type of workload, an appropriate OS for the application, and, potentially, other properties such as configuration information for the application and OS, initial resource controls, and security rules. A template provides all of the initial parameters needed to install a VE, including the application.

A *golden master* is an entire disk image of an installed OS and application. It is a snapshot of a VE, including its applications and customizations. Deploying the image is usually as simple as copying a file (the image) and then deploying the copy.

The concepts of workload templates and golden masters can be combined. For example, a template might specify a master image along with resource controls and steps to be performed immediately before booting the new VE.

9.2.2.3 Business Continuity

In the data center context, business continuity provides an organization with the ability to perform its critical computing and communications functions after a disaster disrupts normal computing functions. Disaster recovery is closely related to business continuity, and includes the method to restore those functions, usually on equipment that does not normally support those functions. Such equipment might have another use, or might be sitting idle in another data center.

Sometimes bad things happen—intruders intrude, software crashes, hardware breaks, electric service fails. For some problems, the simplest solution is restarting the application, either manually or automatically. When that step is not enough, restarting the computer usually is, assuming it runs at all. But how do you know that a restart is the best solution? Did the intruder change data, or even modify the application? Did a software bug cause data corruption? Is all of the data recoverable?

In some situations, the only safe alternative is to restore data, or the whole system, from backup tape. This effort can cause lengthy service outages and abandons any legitimate transactions executed between the time of the most recent backup and the time of disaster. Organizations with multiple data centers may use storage replication to minimize the amount of lost data.

Some of these problems can be solved more easily if virtualization is in use. We will explore some of those methods in the next section.

9.2.2.4 Disaster Recovery

As we discussed earlier, virtualization reduces the attachment between a workload and the hardware it is using. This looser connection makes it easier to think of VEs as not being tied to a particular computer, which in turn simplifies the planning for recovery and increases flexibility. Virtualization management software can assist in the recovery of services and tracking of the physical location of those services. The large number of VEs that a data center might include makes virtualization management software a necessity.

Some virtualization solutions manage each VE as a single storage entity, perhaps even storing it as a single file. Combine that capability with a file system that can quickly take a snapshot, or with storage replication, and you have a new method of restoring a service after a problem occurs. Not only is application data replicated, but the application and OS, and their respective configuration information, are also stored in a convenient package.

For example, the management platform (or storage subsystem) for a VE can periodically take a snapshot of the file system in which the VE is stored. If the application or VE fails, the workload's service can by restored by booting the VE from the snapshot. The original copy of the VE remains, waiting to be analyzed. A thorough forensic analysis should allow you to determine whether the problem was caused by a person, accidentally or maliciously, or by a software or hardware error.

Copies of VEs should be kept on shared storage. This strategy allows you to quickly restore service on another, sufficiently similar computer, even if the original computer will not start at all. It also gives you the flexibility to restart the VE elsewhere even if the computer can start, and to avoid using a faulty component such as a bad memory module. If you start the VE elsewhere, you can replace broken components, perhaps moving the VE back to its original home after component replacement is complete.

Storage replication tools enable you to keep an identical copy of any data, including data that represent VEs, synchronized across large distances. Using this model, you can start VEs at a remote disaster recovery site, restoring critical services hours or even minutes after a large-scale disaster occurs.

For some workloads, such as web servers with static contents, you can take snapshots at infrequent intervals. Restoration is simple and quick in such circumstances, and the damaged environment can be retained for analysis of the bug or attack.

For dynamic workloads that temporarily store state-related data, such as application servers, you can regularly quiesce the workload, if necessary, and take a snapshot of it. Any transactions being processed when the problem occurred may be lost, but service can be restored very quickly. A transaction processing monitor will minimize or prevent lost transactions. As with web servers, the damaged VE will be retained on persistent storage, waiting for analysis.

Database servers can also be managed using this method. It is more likely that the database must be quiesced, or in some cases even stopped, before taking the snapshot. This practice ensures that the database on disk is self-consistent and can be restored by simply booting the copy of the VE in the snapshot.

With virtual machines, you must restart the VE on an identical alternate computer, or you must track the compatibility between computers very closely. The organization that created the hypervisor will determine how similar the two must be to safely restart a VE on a different system.

This kind of matching is rarely an issue for operating system virtualization (OSV) because CPU architecture details matter much less, if they matter at all. However, I/O device configuration must still be taken into consideration.

When it comes to migration, workloads running on hardware partitions can be restored on a similar system with partitions or on separate systems. The separate systems need not support partitioning at all. Although use of separate systems will retain the isolation characteristics of individual partitions, it loses the flexibility inherent in a partitioned system.

Another general caution concerns network identity. VEs typically have one or more IP addresses and network names by which they are known. After a disaster, the IP address must be accessible at the new location of the VE. Other computers, including personal computers, may then use this address to regain access to services they require. Whenever the VE is running properly on the original system, however, any testing of the alternate system must not advertise the IP address of that service.

VE migration is further complicated by the need for, and limitations of, shared storage. The most common choices are network attached storage (NAS) and storage area networks (SANs). NAS is typically simpler to configure and manage than SANs, and this simplicity makes it easier to perform a migration. During the migration process, along with ensuring some coordination between the two systems, the original system unmounts the file system, if necessary, and the destination system mounts it. Compared to NAS solutions, SANs typically offer better quality of service (QoS) features and provide more predictable performance. When designing mobile VEs, you should try both methods to determine which is a better fit for your computing environment.

Virtualization management software can be used to manually restart alternate VEs, either on the same system, on a different system in the same site, or on a different system at a different site. Disaster recovery planning should identify alternate equipment on which to run the virtualization management software itself in case of total site failure.

There is some overlap between virtualization management software and high-availability clustering. Some clustering tools understand virtualization and can automatically restart a VE on a different node in the cluster—a tactic that can also apply to geographically separated nodes. There is still room for integration of clustering tools and other virtualization management tools.

9.3 Oracle Enterprise Manager Ops Center

The Oracle Enterprise Manager Ops Center software product is a full-service data center management package, whose features provide a good example of a comprehensive virtualization management tool. This section describes the features of Ops Center and explains how they fulfill the needs described earlier in this chapter.

Ops Center manages the life cycle of Sun computer systems and VEs. Its feature set greatly simplifies life-cycle management of physical systems as well as VEs.

9.3.1 Basic Structure

Ops Center has a three-tier architecture to enhance scalability. The three tiers include a centralized Enterprise Controller (EC), one or more Proxy Controllers (Proxies), and software agents that run on the assets being managed.

The EC provides a console that can be accessed from standard web browsers. This browser user interface (BUI) makes it possible to configure remote access to the EC, though that step is not required. The EC also has a command-line interface (CLI) so that you can script multiple actions into one command.

The EC maintains a central database and data cache, and tracks all management activities. It is important to note that the EC does not *perform* these tasks, but merely manages them and tracks them. When a Proxy needs contents from the cache, such as an OS image or a software package, it downloads the contents. If a Proxy will provision the same software onto multiple systems, it needs to perform only one download, reusing the downloaded copy as needed. This reuse reduces network traffic.

The EC and Proxies can run on Oracle Solaris 10, on x86 or SPARC hardware, and in a Logical Domain. Also, the EC can run in a Solaris Container or on an Oracle Enterprise Linux 5 system (OEL) or on a Red Hat Enterprise Linux 5 system (RHEL5). Supported BUIs include Firefox 3.*x* and Internet Explorer 7.

Ops Center must be able to determine the existence of OS packages and patches. Oracle maintains a knowledge base (KB) of this information, specifically for this purpose. For most configurations, the EC needs Internet access to use the KB. With that access, it periodically downloads KB updates, including patches, new package versions, and information about the dependencies between them. It uses this information, including dependencies, to coordinate provisioning and updates.

The first instance of a Proxy Controller will be co-located on the same system as the EC, but the EC also configures and installs remote Proxy Controllers as scale and geography demand. The Proxies perform provisioning, updates, and management and monitoring of assets. In a small localized environment with just a few managed assets, only a single Proxy is needed; it can be cohosted with the EC. Larger environments with many assets, and multiple-site environments, will benefit greatly from one or more Proxies per site. This removes the need to perform provisioning over WAN links, which would consume too much of the WAN bandwidth. Proxies are the key to the scalability of Ops Center.

Figure 9.3 shows the relationship between the two types of the controllers and the agents. You should have at least one Proxy Controller per site. A computer that will be provisioned by Ops Center must have a Proxy on its subnet.

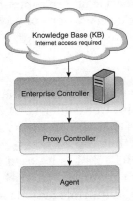

Figure 9.3 Architecture of Enterprise Controller, Proxy Controller, and Agents

Ops Center agents are software modules that run on the managed assets. They perform operations within an operating system, such as installing packages and patches. They also perform monitoring tasks, sending the gathered information to the Proxy Controller. This information is aggregated by the EC and presented in user-friendly formats. Agents automatically discover CPU type and quantity, memory quantity, and information about the OS, including the packages installed.

One special type of agent is the Virtualization Controller (VC), which runs on an asset to manage the life cycle of VEs on that computer. Currently, Ops Center manages Containers and Logical Domains, the VEs of Oracle VM Server for SPARC. To manage Containers, the VC runs on Solaris 10 in the global zone. To manage Logical Domains, the VC runs in each control domain. If a domain has Containers, a VC runs in the system's control domain and another VC runs in the domain's global zone to manage its Containers.

9.3.2 Concepts

This section describes two concepts that are specific to Ops Center.

9.3.2.1 Library

Ops Center uses NAS and SAN storage for collections of disk images (that is, an operating system installation disk) and virtual machine images. The latter can be booted or can be used as a golden master image from which other virtual machine images are created. Libraries are sometimes called storage libraries.

9.3.2.2 Virtual Pool

Although a primary goal of Ops Center is the simplification of a repeated operation performed on many systems in a data center, it provides other functionality as well. One example is virtual pools.

A virtual pool is a set of VEs configured to run on a specific set of systems. With this feature, you can enable Ops Center to manually or automatically rebalance the VEs across the systems. The workloads deployed in a pool can be related or unrelated. In Ops Center 2.5, a virtual pool must consist of SPARC CMT systems. Logical Domains can be members of a virtual pool.

Creating a VE in a pool adds it to a library of shared VEs. Its disk content will reside on shared storage, where it is available to all physical members of the pool. NAS is typically used as the shared storage method in such a case.

You can configure a VE to be a member of a pool. When such a VE boots, Ops Center automatically boots it on the least-loaded or least-allocated VP node. You choose which of those placement policies will be used to determine the new home for the VE. "Least-loaded" means "having the lowest CPU, memory, and network utilization." The configuration with the smallest assignment of CPU and memory resources is "least-allocated."

Ops Center also provides a feature that manually rebalances running VEs in a pool. To achieve this outcome, Ops Center determines the best new configuration based on the placement policy you select and the recent usage patterns of CPU, memory, and network usage.

The third load-balancing method is very similar to the manual rebalancing just described. However, instead of requiring user interaction, Ops Center automatically rebalances the VEs on a regular basis. You choose the interval between the rebalancing actions.

Whenever a Logical Domain in the virtual pool boots, it will boot on the most lightly loaded system in the pool. You can also configure a Logical Domain to restart automatically on a running system in the pool if the system it was running on suddenly halts. Because all of the domains in one VP use shared storage, they can be moved from one CMT system to another in an effort to balance the load on the computers.

9.3.3 Secure or Isolated Data Centers

Ops Center can operate in one of two modes: connected and disconnected. Connected mode is appropriate for most data centers. In connected mode, the EC downloads new information from the KB so that it can understand the patch (or package update) deficiencies in the data center. As part of its analysis, it creates reports for its own use and for your records. The EC then downloads updates (patches or new package versions) from the Internet as needed. The EC uses the reports, patches, and packages to bring the managed systems into compliance with your policies. The KB is maintained by Oracle.

The security policies of some data centers forbid these centers from having a direct connection to the Internet. For these operations, Ops Center offers a stand-alone tool called the "harvester," which downloads information from the KB. You can run this tool on a computer that is attached to the Internet, and then manually move the information to the EC. The EC can then generate the deficiency reports.

Armed with the information in the deficiency reports, you can gather the patches and packages needed to fill the gaps. For example, Oracle provides Solaris patches on the Enterprise Installation Standards (EIS) DVD. You must manually copy the patches and packages to the EC system, where the EC can use them and the deficiency reports to bring the managed systems into compliance.

9.3.4 Discovering Assets

Ops Center automatically discovers systems and chassis via Sun Service Tags and Open Service Tags. You can also use a wizard to discover the various assets by IP address, subnet address, host names, or other criteria. Under control of the EC, Proxies use the following network protocols to discover systems, their service processors (SPs), and operating systems[1]: IPMI, WMI, JMX, SNMP, SSH, Telnet, Sun Service Tags, and Open Service Tags.

---

1. For an updated list of support operating systems, see http://wikis.sun.com/display/OC2dot5/Supported+Operating+Systems.

Ops Center can discover and manage the following types of service processors: ALOM, ELOM, ILOM, IPMI, RSC, and XSCF. The type of SP used by each type of Sun system is preconfigured in Ops Center.

Figure 9.4 shows a discovered asset.

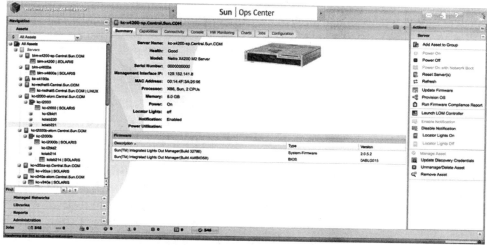

Figure 9.4 Discovered Asset

Table 9.1 lists the operating systems that Ops Center can discover, monitor, and update.

Table 9.1 Ops Center Compatibility Matrix

Feature	Solaris 10	Solaris 9	Solaris 8	OEL	RHEL	SLES	Windows
Enterprise Controller	Solaris 10 11/06 and newer	–	–	OEL 5.3	RHEL 5.0, 5.3	–	–
Proxy Controller	Solaris 10 11/06 and newer	–	–	OEL 5.3	RHEL 5.0, 5.3	–	–
Discovery	✓	✓	✓	✓	✓	✓	✓
Provisioning	✓	✓	–	✓	✓	✓	–
Monitoring	✓	✓	✓	✓	✓	✓	✓
Updating	✓	✓	✓	✓	✓	✓	✓
Live Upgrade	SPARC: P and V x86: P only	SPARC	SPARC	–	–	–	–
Solaris Containers	Solaris 10 8/07 and newer	–	–	–	–	–	–
Branded Zones	–	✓	✓	–	–	–	–

The result of discovery is a list of assets—chassis, systems, service processors, and operating systems—which can then be managed. If you have more than a few systems, you will benefit from grouping them by hardware type, or by OS or OS version, or by other criteria. Ops Center provides the ability to place an asset into multiple groups. Once you establish groups of assets, you can apply changes to several systems at once based on criteria you choose. You can also report on the status of several systems with a single operation. For example, you can update the firmware on all of your T5120 systems, using a group you have created for them, and then apply a patch to all of your Solaris 10 5/09 systems, using a different group.

9.3.5 Provisioning Assets

Once Ops Center knows about your hardware assets, it can provision firmware, an operating system, or VEs to a single system or to groups of systems at once. It uses a combination of standard tools to perform provisioning.

You can use the Ops Center BUI to initiate a provisioning action, which may include one or more computers. This action is registered with the EC. The EC begins the process by sending appropriate binary images to one or more Proxy Controllers, unless they already have those images. The Proxies then use those images to provision systems on their subnets.

9.3.5.1 Provisioning Firmware

As the first step in provisioning assets, you define firmware images, which consist of a file containing the firmware and associated metadata. Metadata includes system types, firmware version, and a list of other firmware on which this firmware depends. The last piece of information helps Ops Center to prevent incompatible combinations of firmware—for example, firmware on a blade chassis and firmware on the blades.

Firmware images are then used to define firmware profiles. A *profile* is a set of one or more firmware images and provisioning policies. These policies define the process that Ops Center will use to update the firmware images. You can use profiles to update firmware, and to generate compliance reports showing the firmware version installed on a set of systems.

Ops Center also generates compliance reports to verify that a firmware update to multiple systems—perhaps hundreds of them—has completed successfully.

9.3.5.2 Provisioning Operating Systems

Ops Center provisions several UNIX-like operating systems and can provision Logical Domains and Containers as well. Operating systems that can be provisioned are listed in Table 9.1. Ops Center uses the JumpStart Enterprise Toolkit (JET) to provision Oracle Solaris, Kickstart for RHEL and OEL, and AutoYAST for SLES.

Wizards greatly simplify Ops Center tasks, especially OS provisioning. These wizards hide the implementation details of those different installation tools. Provisioning quality is strengthened by the use of a software dependency engine to avoid errors and omission of OS components.

Provisioning is also simplified by the use of a library of OS profiles and images. An image is a copy of an installable OS distribution. In addition to vendor-supplied images (which are often distributed as ISO files on DVDs), you can create your own images—for example, a Solaris Flash Archive (FLAR). Profiles specify particular configurations of an OS, starting with an OS image. For instance, you might define a web server profile using an image of a particular Solaris 10 update and specifying a list of OS packages to be installed.

An OS profile library includes multiple profiles. In addition to using images that include all of the OS packages, your library might include an image preconfigured to be a database server. With that profile in your OS library, provisioning a new DB server is as simple as identifying the target system and the profile, and letting Ops Center do all of the work. Ops Center delivers the image and updates its repository of system information—and a new system is soon waiting for SQL commands.

9.3.5.3 Provisioning Logical Domains

Ops Center has special features for SPARC CMT systems and Logical Domains. Every CMT system has the ability to host Logical Domains. If a CMT system will include guest domains, it must first have a special-purpose domain called the *control domain*. You use the control domain to create and otherwise manage other domains, including service domains and I/O domains. See Chapter 3, "Oracle VM Server for SPARC," for more information about SPARC CMT systems and Logical Domains.

You can use Ops Center to install a control domain on a CMT system, an action that also installs a VC on the control domain to create and manage other domains. Ops Center also automatically uses the control domain as the service and I/O domains. After the control domain has been installed, Ops Center can install guest domains.

Although a primary goal of Ops Center is the simplification of one operation being performed on many systems in a data center, it provides additional functionality. For example, a virtual pool is a set of domains configured to run on a set of SPARC CMT systems. Using this feature, you can enable Ops Center to automatically load-balance the domains across the systems.

Whenever a domain in the virtual pool boots, it will boot on the most lightly loaded system in the pool. You can also configure a domain to automatically restart on a running system in the pool if the system it was running on suddenly halts. Because all of the domains in one VP use shared storage, they can easily be moved from one CMT system to another to balance the load on the computers.

9.3.5.4 Provisioning Oracle Solaris Containers

You can also provision, update, manage, and monitor Containers with Ops Center on both x86 and SPARC systems. A BUI wizard guides you through the process of configuring the Container, include choosing a computer for it, assigning network connections and file system access, and setting resource controls. Ops Center installs a VC in that computer's global zone.

Figure 9.5 shows the wizard that simplifies the process of creating a Container.

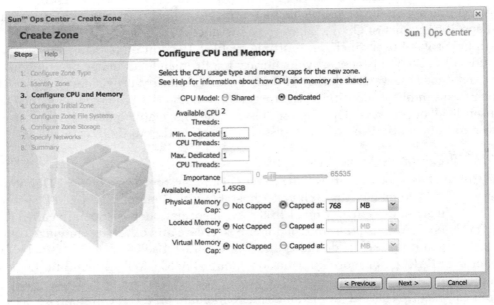

Figure 9.5 Oracle Solaris Container Configuration Wizard

9.3.6 Updating Assets

Ops Center 2.5 can update firmware for Sun systems, whether they are based on x86 or on SPARC CPUs. Updating the firmware on a CMT system also updates the Logical Domains hypervisor firmware.

Ops Center also updates Oracle Solaris, popular Linux distributions, and Microsoft Windows. Table 9.1 lists the specific versions that are supported. A software agent deployed on each OS instance performs these updates.

In addition to replacing or patching live OS packages, the agent for Solaris 10 can discover and update the Alternate Boot Environment (ABE), which is the basis of the Live Upgrade feature. The use of Live Upgrade significantly reduces the service outage, if any, needed when patching the OS.

Ops Center uses the Microsoft Windows System Center Configuration Manager (SCCM) to update Windows systems. Ops Center does not use an agent for this task.

For other operating systems, normally updates and patches are automatically downloaded from the vendor via the Internet, and deployed to systems as you choose. Ops Center is preconfigured to connect to major vendor package and patch repositories, including those operated by Oracle, Microsoft, Red Hat, and Novell. Systems not directly connected to the Internet can be updated with an offline option. An analysis engine determines which packages and patches are needed for each system. Related features include the ability to roll back an update and the ability to simulate an update to learn whether it will succeed and how long it will take.

Systems can also be collected into "smart groups" using the BUI. A smart group can be updated with one operator action, which simplifies the process of keeping a set of computers at a consistent update level.

A key feature of Op Centers is its comprehensive auditing facility. The auditing process starts by generating a baseline configuration for each system. As updates are applied, they are recorded in the audit trail so that you can view the history of changes. Later, if necessary, you can generate compliance reports to determine whether a particular system or set of systems complies with corporate update policies.

Updating Containers and Logical Domains is as easy as updating non-virtualized systems. Ops Center understands any special requirements or methods needed.

9.3.7 Monitoring Assets

Another important feature set of Ops Center is the ability to monitor status and performance characteristics of the entities (systems and VEs) being managed. The Proxy Controller gathers the necessary data from the system's service processor and the operating systems running on the computer.

Using the Ops Center dashboard, you can tell at a glance whether a computer has power, is turned on or off, or requires servicing. SPARC Enterprise M-series systems also provide information from fan and temperature sensors. Information regarding the state of each Dynamic Domain is available as well, and you can power each domain on or off as needed.

Systems with an ILOM processor also report power utilization data to Ops Center, enabling it to create graphs of power consumption over different intervals, such as a five-day period or a six-month period. This data can also be exported in CSV or XML formats for use with other software. You can also view data on electric current, disk, fan and power supply states, and temperature and voltage.

The Proxy Controller also collects data from operating systems, including VEs. Table 9.1 lists the operating systems and VEs that can be monitored in this way. If an agent is installed on the system, the Proxy Controller queries the agent for parameters being monitored. Otherwise, the Proxy uses SSH to access UNIX-like systems and VEs, and then uses their native tools to collect current performance data. The Proxy communicates directly with Microsoft's Windows Management Instrumentation (WMI) to retrieve data from those systems. The EC gathers data from the Proxies and stores it for later retrieval.

Figure 9.6 shows a few graphs of resource utilization for a VE.

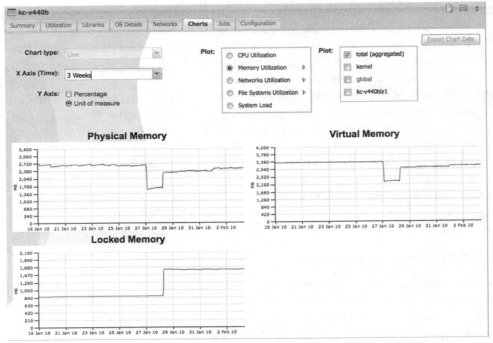

Figure 9.6 Ops Center Usage Graphs

If keeping usage within a certain range is important, you can set thresholds on variables being monitored. You can also configure Ops Center to send a notification if a threshold has been exceeded on any of the data being monitored. A notification can be sent to the BUI, to an e-mail address, or to a pager. The data can also be exported in CSV format.

Ops Center collects and displays the following data, in either tabular and graphical formats:

- CPU utilization, in percentage
- RAM use

- Network bandwidth consumed
- Power consumed

For Logical Domains, Ops Center collects and displays the following data regarding the host, in addition to the data mentioned above:

- Virtual pool assignment
- Total and available CPU threads
- Total and available cryptographic units
- Total and available memory

This information will help you configure domains. Data is also collected about each domain—the same data collected about a non-virtualized system.

9.3.8 Managing Assets

Once you know how well your systems and VEs are performing, you can make educated decisions about their futures. Is there a problem that needs to be addressed? Does the system have sufficient spare capacity to support another VE?

As mentioned earlier in this chapter, Ops Center can provision systems and their VEs. For example, you might create a group called "Unused and Underutilized Systems" and search it to find an appropriate home for a new workload. The BUI can also start and stop systems and their VEs.

Eventually you will discover a system with VEs that is overloaded—perhaps CPU utilization is too high, or maybe the system has been paging regularly. Ops Center provides two types of solutions to this problem, each of which improves operational flexibility.

The first solution is to dynamically modify resource controls of VEs. Perhaps you have reserved 16 of the 256 CPUs in a T5440 for unplanned demand by one VE. You can use Ops Center to assign some of those CPUs to a VE that needs them, while that VE continues to run. Or perhaps one of the 24 Containers on a system is unexpectedly busy. You can use Ops Center to increase the number of FSS shares assigned to that Container without rebooting it. By doing so, you enable the system to continue to meet its response time goals while you investigate the cause of the new demand.

If there simply aren't enough resources on a system to meet the needs of its VEs, it's time to use the second solution provided by Ops Center: VE migration. Under your direction, Ops Center can move a VE from one system to another using the migration features of the VE technology. By moving the VE to a system with sufficient available resources, you allow that workload to perform well, while also freeing up resources on the original system.

For both types of VEs, shared storage is required. In the case of Containers, the list of supported shared storage includes NFS, which is normally not a supported configuration. By using shared storage, Ops Center can move the VE without copying its files from the original system to the new one. Instead, it simply performs any necessary reconfiguration of the systems so that the VE boots or continues operation on its new system. Shared storage minimizes the service disruption associated with the migration operation.

If you plan to manage Containers with Ops Center, you should create them within Ops Center. Although Ops Center will discover existing Containers, it cannot reconfigure all of the parameters of Containers it discovers.

9.3.9 Oracle EM Ops Center Summary

Ops Center provides many of the features needed in a virtualization management environment as well as the ability to manage non-virtualized systems. You can use Ops Center to streamline the process of provisioning and managing systems, thereby improving business agility and operational flexibility.

9.4 Summary

Only a small percentage of data center computers have been virtualized. But the trend is clear: More and more workloads are running in VEs each year. Virtualization offers so many benefits—reduced total cost of ownership (TCO), reduced power consumption, improved business agility and operational flexibility—that the trend toward virtualization will undoubtedly be with us for many years. Virtualization management tools are a critical component of the present and future of virtualization.

Appendix: History of Virtualization and Architectural Evolution

A Brief History of System Virtualization

This appendix describes the origin and evolution of server virtualization, and describes design issues, problems, and solutions that still affect and influence today's systems.

Then and Now, Why and How

A 40-year-old overnight success in commercial use since the 1960s, server virtualization is now experiencing renewed interest. Available in different forms on every modern computer family, server virtualization permits multiple computing environments to coexist on a single computer, with each environment behaving as if it has its own dedicated computer. IT organizations use this approach to run multiple computing environments—even different operating systems—on the same server at the same time. Server virtualization is perhaps a misnomer, because the virtualized environments can also be desktop or embedded systems, but virtualizing server systems is its most prominent use.

In today's data centers, server virtualization is primarily used to consolidate multiple low-utilization physical servers, reducing costs for power, cooling, rack space, software licensing, and administrative effort. This usage contrasts with the original economic driver for virtualization: to avoid the high acquisition costs associated with the then-expensive computer systems. Despite the different reasons driving virtualization trends in the past and in the present, the effects are similar: multiple virtual computing environments on the same physical machine.

While server virtualization is now available on almost every computer product line and in multiple architectural forms, the original and most widely used form of server virtualization is the *virtual machine*, pioneered by early hypervisors that ran on IBM mainframes in the 1960s and 1970s. This development inspired and influenced many technologies that emerged in the following decades—obviously the current mainframe hypervisor, z/VM, but also hypervisors for other system families such as Xen, VMware, and Oracle VM VirtualBox. The early hypervisors also influenced hardware/firmware solutions like Amdahl's Multiple Domain Facility, IBM's PR/SM and LPARs, and Sun Microsystems' Dynamic Domains, from the Enterprise 10000 in the late 1990s to the current SPARC Enterprise M-Series Dynamic Domains, and finally to SPARC-based Logical Domains (now called Oracle VM Server for SPARC), as well as operating system virtualization solutions, such as BSD Jails and Oracle Solaris Containers.

Challenges and issues faced in the early days still confront modern virtualization technologies, making an understanding of early systems valuable and relevant.

CTSS and the Early Hypervisors

Virtualization has its roots in the Compatible Time-Sharing System (CTSS), written at Massachusetts Institute of Technology (MIT) in the mid-1960s. CTSS was among the first operating systems to share a single computer among multiple interactive users. Previously, computers ran in batch mode, and programmers often had to wait for dedicated time periods to use the one-and-only computer. The CTSS project, under the direction of Professor Fernando Corbató, was the first to time-slice a single computer between interactive users at terminals. CTSS introduced architectural features that would be central to subsequent virtualization environments—namely, address relocation to permit separate address spaces for each user, preemptive multitasking of user processes, and isolation of physical traps, devices, and interrupts from user processes. In addition, it provided a virtualized form of the FORTRAN batch environment typically run on that processor. CTSS also introduced early forms of shell scripts, text formatting, and inter-user messaging.

CTSS influenced all interactive systems created since then: Many CTSS designers went on to MIT's Project MAC to create MULTICS, which in turn inspired the development of UNIX. Project MAC was responsible for some of the most influential research in artificial intelligence, theory of computation, and operating systems. The Association for Computing Machinery (ACM), the preeminent computing science organization, presented Professor Corbató with the 1990 Turing Award in recognition of his contribution to computing systems.

Another major event of that decade was IBM's introduction of System/360, a family of architecturally identical computer systems with models at different price and performance points. IBM wanted System/360 sites to run a single batch-oriented operating system called OS/360, without provision for time sharing. System/360 lacked address relocation hardware to support virtual memory—at the time, a new and controversial feature. While this batch-oriented system became very successful in the commercial space, its lack of support for address relocation and time sharing were among the reasons it was not selected for Project MAC. The loss of this highly visible project spurred IBM to create a system that could be used to understand time sharing and virtual memory systems.

IBM studied virtual memory with an experimental system called CP-40. This system ran on a customized System/360 model 40 and used an associative memory to translate virtual memory addresses to real memory addresses. CP-40 introduced a concept its developers named a "virtual machine," and was the parent of all subsequent hypervisor-based virtualization. CP-40 proved that a physical computer could concurrently run multiple virtual computers, each of which could run a different operating system. The hypervisor was also referred to as a "virtual machine monitor" or "host," while the virtual machines running under it were commonly called "guests."

CP-40 was based on technical prerequisites for virtualization that have remained consistent over the subsequent decades. These requirements were described by Popek and Goldberg (*Communications of the ACM*, Volume 12, Number 7, July 1974) as follows:

- *Equivalence*: Execution in a guest environment is "essentially identical" to execution running on bare metal.
- *Resource control*: Guest environments only have access to a physical machine's resources that are explicitly granted to it by the hypervisor.
- *Efficiency*: A dominant fraction of the instructions executed by the guest are executed directly by hardware at native speed, without intervention by the virtual machine monitor.

These properties are provided by hardware architectures that support a system mode of execution in which all instructions can be executed, and a user mode in which privileged instructions are suppressed and generate a program trap. In non-virtualized environments, this architecture protects system integrity by preventing malicious or buggy applications from issuing instructions that change machine state (such as enabling or disabling interrupts, or changing memory mapping) and potentially crashing the system or creating security exposures.

This mechanism works differently in virtual machine environments, as guest operating systems are expected to execute privileged instructions and have them function in the same way as they would on the real machine. An attempt by a guest operating system to execute a privileged instruction generates a program trap to the hypervisor, which then emulates the instruction (in software) solely in the context of the virtual machine. This behavior has performance implications that will be discussed later in this appendix.

This paradigm supports the Popek and Goldberg properties and is still used by hypervisors. Note that the x86 architecture does not satisfy the "trap and execute" virtualization described by Popek and Goldberg. Instead, x86 virtual machines can tell that they have been "deprivileged," and some privileged instructions (such as popf) are suppressed but do not cause a trap. The x86 hypervisors handle this situation in different ways: VMware performs binary translation to replace these instructions with code that manipulates guest state without privileged instructions, or with a call to the hypervisor, whereas Xen uses paravirtualization to eliminate use of privileged instructions.

Virtual Machines Emerge from the Laboratory

CP-40 was ported to the System/360 model 67, IBM's first production virtual memory computer, and renamed CP/67. The 360/67 was intended to be IBM's official time-sharing system, as IBM began to adopt this style of computing as an addition to OS/360's batch workloads. A new and ambitious operating system, TSS/360, was written for it. While TSS/360 introduced novel concepts, it was burdened by delays and had reliability and performance problems. CP/67, which had a simpler design and was based on virtual machines, began to be used for time sharing and program development using a simple interactive single-user OS called the Cambridge Monitor System (CMS).

Instead of a single OS instance shared by multiple users, as in CTSS, Multics, and UNIX, CMS provided a lightweight single-user OS instance for each user, and exploited a separation of functions with the hypervisor for resource management and access control. This strategy permitted use of a very simple design: a single flat per-user address space, a non-multitasking program model (multitasking was provided by overlapped execution of multiple CMS users), a minimal permission model (all security was implemented in the virtual machine monitor), and a basic non-hierarchical file system (each user had virtual disks called "minidisks," implemented by cylinder extents on physical disks).

This design—a simple OS leveraging services from the hypervisor—permitted the system to have a small memory footprint and a short instruction-path length well suited for providing short response times on the computers of the day. The idea of a lightweight virtualization environment can be seen in unrelated later systems such as Solaris Containers that shift "heavy lifting" to the hosting environment. This design pattern was also deployed for non-interactive users: CMS guests running disconnected from a terminal were used to implement "service virtual machines"—a precursor to UNIX daemons—for scheduled or event-driven work. Soon, a significant client base used CP/67 virtual machines and interactive computing.

It also became clear that the extremely complex (for the times) OS/360 would be shipped too late to satisfy many customers' needs, and would require more memory than was available on many 360 models. As a result, the 360 used several incompatible operating systems (DOS/360, OS/360) with different programming conventions. Several institutions began to use CP/67 to run multiple-guest OS instances on the same physical machine, so the same machine could be shared by different workloads.

Even though deployment of virtual machines remained limited, technology and business drivers for virtual machines had clearly arrived by the early 1970s. At this point, the virtual machines concept had already taken on its defining role—running multiple OS instances on the same physical server.

Virtual Machines Become More Widely Adopted

Virtual memory in the IBM 360 line was available only on the 360/67, which was considered a special-purpose system. When IBM's System/370 was announced, it notably lacked virtual memory (typically called "virtual storage" in IBM documentation, distinguishing it from "real storage"—that is, RAM), but that capability was introduced in 1972. CP/67 was ported to the new hardware architecture and renamed VM/370 (and CMS was retitled "Conversational Monitor System").

Many customers found virtual machines essential for operating multiple workloads or converting to new operating systems. There was no alternative, short of dedicated test systems, to run a new operating system in parallel with the existing production environment. VM reduced the risk of converting to a new operating system by permitting more comprehensive testing. Customers could ensure that a new operating system environment was reliable before installing it on bare metal.

Because VM permitted OS testing to occur during normal daytime hours instead of on weekends or during the third shift at three in the morning, it was not surprising that system programmers were among VM's biggest advocates. System programmers discovered that VM could be used for a lot more than just converting operating systems, and they began to promote its use for CMS-based time sharing for application developers and end users.

While it may seem odd from today's perspective, in the 1970s very few people directly interacted with a computer. Those who did generally used time-shared multiuser computer systems in the style pioneered on CTSS. VM extended this concept, and anticipated the emergence of the personal computer by giving each user a virtual personal computer with a private, lightweight CMS instance. Although the PC eventually made the time-sharing style of computing largely disappear, interactive computing in the 1970s and 1980s was dominated by time sharing on VM, UNIX, and VAX VMS. In fact, time sharing never completely disappeared: It eventually re-emerged in conjunction with thin-client computing, such as Sun Ray thin clients and Virtual Desktop Integration (VDI), which provides the economic advantages of shared infrastructure using modern user interfaces and application interfaces.

The division of function between the VM hypervisor and the simple CMS guest was extended in non-time-sharing contexts by inter-user messaging APIs that presaged TCP/IP sockets. These APIs, which were implemented by a protocol that let a guest virtual machine request services from the hypervisor, permitted creation of interacting collections of daemon-style "service virtual machines." These applications were often implemented in scripts, which reduced the difficulty associated with their creation and let a wider population of developers create services. Many applications were soon implemented by communicating virtual machines, a forerunner of later client/server systems with applications implemented by physical machines.

Service virtual machines also implemented functions typically implemented in the OS kernel in conventional operating systems: Access control for login and data access, communications virtual machines for file transmission, and even the SNA and TCP/IP network stacks were implemented in virtual machines rather than in the VM hypervisor. While this strategy had some negative performance implications, the simpler programming model working in "user land" offered several advantages over adding code to the kernel. In particular, it made it much easier to develop services, provided kernel insulation from programming errors and security attacks, and kept the hypervisor from growing in complexity.

VM systems were sometimes used exclusively for running many time-sharing users, or for running a limited number of heavy virtual machines that ran a full multiprogramming OS, such as OS/360 and its descendants. This arrangement was often called a "guest workload," even though technically all virtual machines were guests. VM was also used for mixed workloads that combined both, which placed additional demands on its resource management.

Performance and Manageability Challenges and Responses

VM systems pushed the limits of contemporary systems in hosting multiple workloads. Early implementations were particularly prone to delivering disappointing performance due to poorly understood causes. Some workloads took several times longer to run in a virtual machine than natively, even when no other users were competing for resources. Solutions were slow to evolve, and a few problems remain for which there are still no complete answers. Some issues discovered in early virtual machine systems continue to affect today's systems, and current solutions to these issues are influenced by the early experiences. This section describes some of the most notable issues, the early attempts to resolve them, and solutions for handling them on current systems.

Performance Effects of Instruction Emulation

The most obvious form of overhead in virtual machine environments is the cost of emulating privileged operations executed by a guest's OS, as described previously. Guest operating systems need to execute these instructions correctly—for example, disabling or enabling interrupt masks to enter or exit a critical section, issuing I/O, marking memory pages as referenced, or changing memory maps when dispatching different processes. These instructions must not be allowed to run directly on the real machine because they would break the integrity of the hypervisor and its guests. Therefore, guests run in a mode where executing these instructions results in a hardware trap. The general (and greatly simplified) flow of execution is as follows:

1. The guest OS in the virtual machine executes a privileged instruction that generates a hardware trap.
2. Context-switch to the hypervisor saves the machine state and determines the trap's cause.
3. The hypervisor emulates the instruction in software, in the context of the guest.
4. The hypervisor does a context switch back to the guest, if it is still runnable.

A similar effect occurred with the SVC ("supervisor call") instruction that applications used to request OS services. This instruction is similar in purpose and implications for virtual machines to instructions used to request system calls on other platforms. The latter include the `ta` software trap instruction on SPARC and the `int $0x80` and `sysenter` instructions on Intel. When executed in a real machine, these instructions causes a context switch to a location pointed to by an interrupt vector in real memory, and thus a context switch into the OS. When executed in a virtual machine, they do exactly the same thing, but the vector in physical memory is owned by the hypervisor (which uses it for its own purposes) and, therefore, points to a location in the hypervisor instead of the guest OS. The hypervisor's interrupt service routine determines whether the trapped system call was from a virtual machine. If so, it reflects the system call instruction to the guest OS by using the equivalent guest's virtual memory address—a process that inflates CPU path lengths and adds overhead.

A similar process occurs when reflecting a physical interrupt (timer or I/O event completion) to a guest. The program running at that moment is interrupted with a context switch to the hypervisor. The hypervisor then determines which virtual machine the physical interrupt is associated with and maps the interrupt into the virtual machine's state. Several context switches take place between hypervisor and guest.

Instruction simulation and interrupt reflection require thousands of instructions and may occur thousands of times per second. As such, these operations constitute a substantial source of overhead, especially for I/O intensive workloads generating many system calls and many privileged operations, and pose a challenge on most hypervisor-based systems.

Sometimes the emulated hardware capability is trivial in nature and can be implemented with a few instructions. For example, simulating an instruction to mask interrupt classes might take just a few instructions. In such cases, most of the added CPU time is spent context switching—purely overhead—and very little time emulating the instruction causing the trap. In other cases, the instruction to be simulated requires substantial processing. This is typical for I/O instructions, which may have complex semantics on real hardware, and can require substantial CPU time when emulated via software.

Early VM systems were seen to spend a majority of their CPU time emulating instructions rather than running user applications. One obvious answer was to instrument and tune high-frequency code paths. An alternative approach was to move this privileged instruction simulation into "virtual machine" assist firmware.

Because IBM controlled the guest operating systems and hypervisor, and the hardware they ran on, they could coordinate their designs and move heavily used hypervisor software code paths into microcode. With these assists, privileged instructions caused a branch to a microcode routine in firmware rather than the original trap. The microcode determined whether the interrupting instruction was one it could handle, as many privileged instructions were too complex to emulate in firmware, or involved guest state changes that required intervention by the hypervisor. If microcode could handle the instruction, it would emulate the instruction entirely in firmware. This process was faster than the original trap and software emulation approach, and reduced instruction simulation overhead. These assists made it possible to run guest operating systems with near-native performance (exclusive of slowdown caused by competition for resources with other virtual machines running at the same time, of course).

Integrated design of software and hardware was not as straightforward in the x86 marketplace, where hardware designers (Intel, AMD) do not create hypervisors (VMware ESX, VirtualBox, Hyper-V, Xen), or operating systems (Microsoft Windows, Oracle Solaris, Linux distributions). Nevertheless, the increased importance of virtualization in the x86 marketplace has led AMD and Intel to create architectural enhancements to their products that reduce "trap and emulate" context switches and make virtualization more efficient. Paravirtualization is now used by all the hypervisors to reduce or eliminate guest execution of privileged instructions.

Oracle's Chip Multithreading (CMT) servers with Solaris guests under the Oracle VM for SPARC (Logical Domains) hypervisor benefit from coordinated designs to solve this problem. The Logical Domains hypervisor dedicates CPU strands (virtual CPUs) to each domain rather than sharing them among all guests, so a guest does not have to be restricted from changing processor state. This strategy was made possible by defining a new `sun4v` CPU architecture (other contemporary SPARC servers use the `sun4u` architecture) and porting Solaris to it to the extent needed to exploit CMT's paravirtualization. Context switching has been moved into the processor architecture, where it can be performed much more quickly than in software, requiring only a single clock cycle. Solaris Containers solve this problem even more directly: Only one kernel exists, no matter how many virtual environments are present in Containers, and application system calls invoke the kernel in the same way whether they reside in a Container or not. These architectures eliminate instruction emulation's complexity and overhead.

The Question of Time (Does Anybody Really Know What Time It Is?)

A problem first faced by early hypervisors is "clock skew," a situation in which time proceeds in a virtual machine at a different rate than on the real hardware. A guest operating system has no way of knowing that between two sequential instructions it may have been interrupted by the hypervisor and delayed for an arbitrary amount of time. Perhaps the hypervisor decided to run a different guest for a few milliseconds, or the guest suffered a page fault and stalled until a page was brought in from disk. In either case, real "wall clock time" advanced, while virtual clock time stayed the same.

Clock skew between virtual and actual time has significant consequences. The time and date reported by a virtual machine might be wrong, or interval-based time slicing within a guest may fail to work correctly.

On the original CP/67 hypervisor, the only timer mechanism was an interval timer based on a location in memory that was decremented on a periodic basis and caused a timer interrupt when it underflowed. Clearly, this practice could not scale, as it would have required the hypervisor to accurately update a location in each guest's memory many times per second. The next hardware architecture added hardware timers that were accessed by privileged instructions and maintained both the current time of day and the accumulated CPU time. The guest OS referred to these clocks via intercepted instructions, giving the hypervisor a chance to provide correctly adjusted time-of-day clock values, and updated CPU-usage timers that reflected the time that the virtual machine was dispatched and executing instructions.

This problem persists among current hypervisors. x86 has several hardware time facilities, and hypervisors such as VirtualBox, VMware, and Xen have provisions for dealing with clock skew. For example, VMware emulates the x86 CMOS Real Time Clock (RTC) and Programmable Interval Timer (PIT) and provides "apparent time" that can lag real time but catch up to it. Clock skew may also occur when several operating systems (Windows, Linux) keep time by recording timer interrupts (ticks, or "jiffies") whose duration may be longer than the specified timer interval. VMware provides add-on tools for different hypervisors to compensate for clock skew. Modern operating systems can also use the Network Time Protocol (NTP) for coordinating time against an external standard.

Solaris Containers completely bypasses this problem, as each container runs off the same clock and timer environment provided by the kernel. Clock skew is also avoided with Logical Domains, as clock resolution is provided by the firmware and per-CPU hardware. The hypervisor additionally maintains a TOD offset for each domain.

Synthetic Instructions for Guest–Hypervisor Service Protocols

VM/370 introduced a private interface using a synthetic instruction for guest communication with the hypervisor and access to the APIs it exports. The DIAGNOSE instruction is one of the few instructions on the 370 defined to have model-dependent behavior; it is used only by operating systems in the supervisor state, so it could be borrowed for this new purpose when in a virtual machine. The trap and emulate operation still occurred, but DIAGNOSE-based services permitted shorter path lengths than the real-machine instructions they replaced. This advance was especially significant for I/O, where a simple synchronous, interrupt-free protocol provided a lower-cost I/O interface than emulation of native instructions.

Synthetic instructions also made it possible to add services to make a virtual machine more functional than a real one. Different APIs provided a command interface to the hypervisor, inter-user message passing, input/output services, timer management, loading of shared memory segments, and other useful functions. Most of these features were exclusively used by CMS, the only IBM OS designed to run under the hypervisor.

Over time, this design pattern influenced other virtual machine systems. For example, similar cooperation between guest OS and virtual machine monitor is a hallmark of the Xen hypervisor, in which a guest can use hypercalls to efficiently request services such as I/O and memory management. Other hypervisors also now use hypercalls. A variant method is provided with VMware, which supplies device drivers for virtual network devices for some guest operating systems, which can be emulated more efficiently than the highly specific aspects of different physical network cards.

Nested CPU Resource Manager Problem

One largely unsolved problem is that of the nested CPU resource manager. VM/370 provided a "fair share scheduler" that permitted delivery of preferential CPU service to important guests, later refined into a share-based scheduler similar to ticket, share, or proportional weight schedulers like the Solaris Fair Share Scheduler (FSS) and VMware scheduler. In these schedulers, users or virtual machines are given access to CPU time based on relative proportions or weights assigned to them.

This approach works well when a guest has only one purpose and one level of importance, but it can be problematic when a virtual machine is itself a multi-programming environment with work of different priorities, or when the guest OS does background tasks that are not performance critical. Consider a modern virtual machine in a VDI implementation: It should be given good response time for mouse and keyboard events and interactive applications, but may also have low-priority housekeeping work such as running a virus scanner or indexing a file system. In the original mainframe context, this problem occurred with guests that required good service for consoles, network devices, and interactive users, yet also had low-priority number-crunching workloads.

Two types of problems can result from this situation in a resource-constrained environment. First, if the guest is given a share value high enough to provide preferential CPU access for both critical and unimportant work, it will have better-than-needed CPU access and may run its unimportant work with better service than other guests. Second, if the preferred guest's CPU share is large enough for its important work but not for all of its tasks, a low-priority process may potentially absorb the preferred CPU shares, causing the high-performance work to be starved when it runs later. Both cases can produce CPU starvation at unpredictable times, causing inconsistent response times. The root cause is that the hypervisor does not generally recognize the relative importance of the work the virtual machine is executing, and it cannot differentiate between the important guest's important work and its unimportant work.

An approach to addressing this problem was invented in the mid-1970s by Robert Cowles, then at Cornell University and now at the SLAC National Accelerator Laboratory. Cowles created an API to let his primary guest OS provide hints to VM about the importance of the work it was about to run. Reacting to this information, VM would not waste high-priority CPU access on the preferred guest's low-importance work, and the priority for the entire guest could be reduced to cover only its high-importance work. With this scheme, it was possible to run work with different priorities on the same guest and give each application its due level of service. The result was reduced CPU starvation for other guests and for the high-priority work of the preferred guest, with measurable improvements in response time and throughput for both.

Unfortunately, this approach has not been generally adopted, and the problem still remains in modern-day systems. Most guest operating systems today are complex operating environments that sometimes do background tasks that could tolerate being delayed. The approach with contemporary systems is to separate the work of different priority classes into different single-purpose virtual machines. This increases the number of virtual machines needed, which increases overhead (as each guest has its own CPU and memory footprint) and can make it harder for them to share data. Another approach is made possible by partitioning environments such as Logical Domains, which avoid the entire issue because CPUs are dedicated rather than time-sliced subject to scheduler decisions. Finally, it is now more economically feasible to "throw" hardware at the problem by not consolidating as aggressively as was necessary when hardware was so much more expensive.

Memory Management: Controlling Thrashing

An even more challenging performance problem facing virtualization was learning how to efficiently provide virtual memories. This problem persists in current systems to some degree, but was especially problematic when computer memory was limited by price and architectural restrictions.

The implications of hosting virtual memories whose aggregate sizes exceeded physical memory was not well understood in the early days of virtual machines. The concept of a "working set" was still extremely new, and the separate research efforts by Lazslo Belady and Peter Denning on virtual memory had just been published when CP/67 was written. One of the few operational virtual memory systems of the time was the Atlas Ferranti, which was known to suffer performance problems under high loads.

The main problem was "thrashing," a state in which applications struggle to establish a working set of pages (the set of memory they will access in a small window of time) in real memory so they can operate without spending most of their time waiting for pages to be swapped to and from disk. When virtualization was first introduced, the replacement algorithms and multiprogramming controls needed to prevent thrashing had yet to be developed.

In a thrashing system, an application runs briefly, and then experiences a page fault by referring to a virtual address that is not currently in memory. It stalls and waits for that page to be fetched from disk, which may take millions of instruction times. Most elapsed time is spent waiting for disk rather than running applications. In a thrashing system, an application spends its time slice page-faulting its working set from disk into memory, and in so doing evicts the pages of other applications from memory to disk. At the end of the application's time slice, the next application runs and does the same thing to pages loaded by its predecessor. Applications continually evict one another's pages and try to reestablish their own working sets, rather than accomplishing actual work.

Thrashing can happen on any virtual memory system, but was especially intense with virtual machines because guest operating systems have larger memory footprints than a single application, and because they exhibit poor locality of reference. An application program running in a virtual memory OS such as Oracle Solaris or a Linux distribution has a working set size based on its application needs. In contrast, most operating systems refer to as much RAM as is installed on the computer, typically for buffering file contents. If such an OS runs on a machine with 8 GB of RAM, it will use 8 GB of RAM, regardless of application needs. When an OS runs in a real machine, this practice makes perfect sense, as unused RAM is wasted and could have been used to reduce I/O delays. In a virtual machine, however, memory seen by the guest is virtual memory, backed by physical RAM shared by all guests. Using extra virtual memory in one guest reduces the physical memory available for other guests. It is typical for the physical memory footprint of a guest to approach the virtual memory size of the guest. For example, a Solaris or Linux guest running in a virtual machine sized as 1 GB would tend to occupy 1 GB of RAM because it will touch all of the pages it thinks it owns. A "best practice" for virtual machines is to reduce the virtual memory size as much as is feasible to reduce this effect.

A pathological situation called "double paging" can occur when the guest operating system itself provides virtual memory. Consider a guest's application that suffers a page fault, causing the guest OS to write a least recently used (LRU) page to its swap disk to provide a real-memory page frame to page-in the faulted location; this operation requires a disk write and a disk read. Recall that what the guest considers "real memory" is actually "virtual memory" from the hypervisor's view. If that guest's page has already been swapped out by the hypervisor, there will be an additional disk read (from the hypervisor's external swap/page space) to bring in the page, which the guest will immediately write to its swap/page space and then discard.

The algorithms used to implement virtual memory can work paradoxically in a virtual machine environment. Approximations of the LRU replacement algorithm are used in most virtual memory systems. LRU is based on the expectation that a page that has not been used recently is likely not to be used in the near future; hence it is the best one to "replace" by writing its contents to disk so its RAM can be used for an active working set page. Most operating systems proactively write LRU pages to disk so that pages will be available when an application has a page fault and needs to have data paged in. However, when a guest selects its oldest untouched page for replacement, the act of doing so references the page from the point of the hypervisor, making it the most recently used (MRU) page. That has the effect of making the guest's actively used pages *older* in terms of actual memory access than pages that the guest hasn't used in a long time! Depending on the relative page pressure within the guest OS and among the hypervisor's various guests, a nested LRU system could wind up evicting the very pages it should retain. This behavior has, in fact, been observed under pathological circumstances.

VM/370 ran in extremely memory-constrained environments; thus its developers designed a scheduler that ran only those virtual machines whose working sets fit in memory. With this approach, other guests were held in an "eligible" queue and occupied no RAM at all. As delayed applications aged, they eventually reached a priority high enough to evict one of the running applications. Essentially, applications in a memory-constrained system took their turns running, but when they did run they had enough RAM for their working sets, and so ran efficiently.

A "handshaking" mechanism let the guest and host environments communicate with each other. The VM hypervisor could tell the guest that it had incurred a page fault, so the guest could dispatch a different user process rather than being placed into page wait. This approach proved useful for guests running multiple processes, though it could have the undesired effect of inflating working sets, and it was unproductive if there was no other runnable process for the guest to run. Also, a hypercall API let a guest tell the hypervisor that it no longer needed a block of memory, and that pages in real memory and the swap area backing it could be released. When these resources were freed, it reduced guest working-set size and prevented double paging. If the guest subsequently referred to those pages, the hypervisor gave it new page frames with zeroed contents rather than retrieving the discarded contents from a swap file.

These methods anticipated cooperative memory management and ballooning techniques available with VMware and Xen, in which the hypervisor can cause the guest OS to use a smaller working set during times of high load on real memory. Typically, a guest daemon allocates a memory buffer and maps it into the guest's RAM. When memory pressure in the hypervisor is low, the memory buffer shrinks, so the guest has more pages it can allocate to its applications. When memory pressure in the hypervisor is high, the daemon is told to increase the size of the buffer ("inflate the balloon"). This action reduces the number of pages the guest OS can allocate to applications, which reduces the size of its working set and its contribution to memory pressure on the hypervisor.

Another approach is exemplified by Solaris Containers, which use a single resource manager for a Solaris instance with many virtual environments. Because only one memory manager is present, the problem is neatly and elegantly side-stepped.

Finally, the economics of memory prices now make it feasible to simply not oversubscribe memory as was necessary in the VM/370's day. This practice is used with Logical Domains, which allocate to each guest an amount of real memory that matches the guest's virtual memory size. While this tactic constrains the number of domains that can run at any moment in time, it eliminates this entire complex category of problem. Instead, Logical Domains keep all MMU logic in the hypervisor.

Memory Management: Multiple Address Spaces

Another expensive situation arose in trying to efficiently provide virtual memories to guest operating systems that themselves provide virtual memories. The difficulty in this case is not the ability to provide enough RAM to support memory requirements for each guest, but rather the task of efficiently translating their virtual addresses to the real RAM addresses in which they reside.

This problem can be explained by describing how most processors translate virtual addresses into real ones. One common scheme divides virtual memory addresses used by processes into segment, page, and offset components. The segment number is used as an index into an array (the segment table) of virtual address segments owned by the process, to point to the pages belonging to that segment. The page number is used as an index into this table, and points to an entry containing the address of the physical page in RAM containing the virtual address page. Finally, the offset part of the virtual address is added to the page address, producing the real memory address corresponding to the virtual address.

If this scheme was implemented literally as described above, every application reference to memory would require at least two more memory references. Requiring three memory references for every user memory reference would impose an intolerable overhead. Instead, most processors cache recently translated virtual page addresses in a translation look-aside buffer (TLB), a fast associative memory that can be probed for a page table entry (PTE) with a matching segment and page address in a single cycle. (The SPARC name for this associative table is the Page Descriptor Cache [PDC], but this appendix uses the generic term.)

If a segment and page address has been recently used, it will appear in the TLB and the matching real-memory address will be used. If the entry is not present, the slow table lookup is used, but the resulting address is stored in a PTE in the TLB for later reuse. If the TLB is full, the least recently used PTE is replaced. If the page is not resident in memory, a page exception trap is generated.

Normally this approach works very well. In fact, contemporary processors have separate TLBs for instructions and data, just as they typically have separate on-chip instruction and data caches. SPARC processors keep statistics that Oracle Solaris can probe to determine the hit rate being achieved, and large page sizes (up to 256 MB) can be used to reduce the number of TLB entries needed for a large memory application. This SPARC feature helps reduce TLB thrashing for vertically scaling applications like Oracle.

Unfortunately, a serious complication arises in a virtual machine environment. The TLB translates from a virtual address to a real one—that is, it uses two levels of address. In contrast, a virtual machine environment typically uses three address levels:

1. The address of the machine's RAM—sometimes called the physical address, or "host real"—which is visible only to the hypervisor.

2. The virtual address for each virtual machine's virtual memory, which appears to the guest OS as if it was a physical memory address. This is called a "guest real" or simply "real" address, or "host virtual," indicating that what the guest thinks is an address in RAM is actual a virtual memory address. The hypervisor maintains segment and page tables to map a guest's level 2 address to a level 1 address.

3. The virtual address spaces created by the guest OS for each guest application process, called "guest virtual." Each guest OS maintains segment and page tables to map every process virtual address (level 3) to what it thinks is a level 1 address.

Non-virtualized systems perform one translation from the virtual address to a real one, but two translations are needed in a virtual machine environment.

VM/370 bypassed this problem for its CMS time-sharing users by having CMS run only one program at a time and use only a single address space. For guest operating systems that themselves provided virtual memory (MVS, or VM/370 itself), the solution was to create per-guest shadow page tables that are indexed by the guest-virtual segment and page numbers, and contain the host-real addresses corresponding to those guest pages. While implementation details vary, this is conceptually the same method used today in virtual machine monitors such as VMware.

Maintaining these tables can be a resource-intensive endeavor. When the guest OS context switches between different processes, the hypervisor must intercept the change in guest address spaces and switch to a different shadow page table. When the hypervisor context switches from one guest to another, it must purge the contents of the hardware-provided TLBs (so that address references from the now-running guest don't point to memory in the recently running guest) and switch to the set of shadow page tables associated with the new guest. This operation requires a substantial bookkeeping effort, adding to the CPU overhead of virtualization. It also adds to the memory cost of virtualization: Shadow page tables are sizable, and there must be enough of them to efficiently represent all the active processes of each virtual machine.

Modern systems from AMD and Intel use several methods to reduce the overhead of maintaining shadow page tables, using nested page tables and tagged page tables with hardware support for changing address mappings. Intel's VT-i provides tagged page tables that are marked with the virtual-processor identifiers (VPIDs) of the guest's virtual CPU, which are operational when the VPID is running. That removes the need to purge TLB entries on VM entry and exit. AMD's Nested Page Tables (NPT) provides a hardware managed per-guest translation table, which contains each guest's address spaces and provides a hardware page table walk. Although the AMD and Intel implementations differ, both provide a hardware capability that dramatically reduces this virtualization overhead. To provide better performance, hypervisors such as VirtualBox and VMware leverage these technology enhancements on systems implementing them.

Oracle's virtualization technologies bypass the issue entirely. Solaris Containers do not run a virtual memory environment nested under another virtual memory environment, so there are only virtual and physical memory addresses: It is just as efficient as running Solaris without Containers. The Logical Domains technology addresses this issue by binding guest-real memories to physical ones on a one-to-one basis. Address mappings between host-real and host-physical addresses can be cached externally to the OS-visible TLB. Because each CPU strand on an Oracle CMT server running Logical Domains runs no more than one domain, and because each has its own memory mapping unit (MMU) and TLB, there is no need to purge and replace TLBs when context switching, because CPU strands aren't context switched at all. The hypervisor manages TLBs that translate virtual addresses directly to physical memory addresses, bypassing the need to perform a double translation. These architectural innovations avoid the overhead of maintaining guest virtual address spaces.

Summary and Lessons Learned

This appendix described the early hypervisors, their evolution, and the problems and design choices that they addressed. While today's computers have become far more powerful than in the early days, the experiences from the early virtual machine systems continue to influence today's systems. Current virtualization technologies draw heavily on the concepts, architecture, and even the language invented in relation to the early hypervisors.

The economic incentives for virtualization have evolved since server virtualization was invented. Originally, it helped avoid mainframe acquisition costs by sharing a single computer among many virtual machines (or conversely, amortizing its expense over their combined workloads) in circumstances where an individual computer was extremely expensive. Today, server virtualization is used to reduce environmental and license costs resulting from server sprawl, and to consolidate the load from under-utilized computers whose individual costs are low. While they seem to be very different, these issues are actually opposite sides of the same coin. Both yesterday and today, substantial benefits can be obtained by reducing the number of physical servers, and virtualization is a powerful tool for turning that goal into a reality.

Index

345

FREE Online Edition

Your purchase of **Oracle® Solaris 10 System Virtualization Essentials** includes access to a free online edition for 45 days through the Safari Books Online subscription service. Nearly every Addison-Wesley Professional book is available online through Safari Books Online, along with more than 5,000 other technical books and videos from publishers such as Cisco Press, Exam Cram, IBM Press, O'Reilly, Prentice Hall, Que, and Sams.

SAFARI BOOKS ONLINE allows you to search for a specific answer, cut and paste code, download chapters, and stay current with emerging technologies.

Activate your FREE Online Edition at www.informit.com/safarifree

> **STEP 1:** Enter the coupon code: YMWTREH.

> **STEP 2:** New Safari users, complete the brief registration form.
> Safari subscribers, just log in.

If you have difficulty registering on Safari or accessing the online edition, please e-mail customer-service@safaribooksonline.com